AMERICAN CONSPIRACIES AND COVER-UPS

AMERICAN CONSPIRACIES AND COVER-UPS

JFK, 9/11, THE FED, RIGGED ELECTIONS,
SUPPRESSED CANCER CURES, AND THE GREATEST
CONSPIRACIES OF OUR TIME

DOUGLAS CIRIGNANO

Skyhorse Publishing

Skyhorse Publishing books may be purchased in bulk at special discounts for sales promotion, corporate gifts, fund-raising, or educational purposes. Special editions can also be created to specifications. For details, contact the Special Sales Department, Skyhorse Publishing, 307 West 36th Street, 11th Floor, New York, NY 10018 or info@skyhorsepublishing.com.

Skyhorse® and Skyhorse Publishing® are registered trademarks of Skyhorse Publishing, Inc.®, a Delaware corporation.

Visit our website at www.skyhorsepublishing.com.

10 9 8 7 6 5 4 3 2 1

Library of Congress Cataloging-in-Publication Data is available on file.

Cover design by Qualcom

ISBN: 978-1-5107-4297-0
Ebook ISBN: 978-1-5107-4298-7

Printed in the United States of America

CONTENTS

INTRODUCTION

In today's world, the phrase "conspiracy theory" is pejorative and has a negative connotation.

To many people, a conspiracy theory is an irrational, over-imaginative idea endorsed by people looking for attention and not supported by the mainstream media or government. History shows, though, that there have been many times when governments or individuals have participated in conspiracies. It would be naïve to think that intelligence agencies, militaries, government officials, and politicians don't sometimes cooperate in covert, secretive ways.

Following are five instances when it's been proven that the government engaged in a conspiracy.

THE GULF OF TONKIN RESOLUTION

On August 4, 1964, Captain John J. Herrick, the commander of the USS *Maddox*, a US Navy vessel that was on an intelligence-gathering mission in the Gulf of Tonkin, reported to the White House and Pentagon that North Vietnamese patrol boats had fired torpedoes at his ship, and, so, the *Maddox* had fired back. Two days later, Secretary of Defense Robert McNamara testified to the Congress that he was certain that the *Maddox* had been attacked. On August 7, the Gulf of Tonkin Resolution was passed, the Congressional act that allowed President Johnson free reign to commence war; Johnson immediately ordered air strikes on North Vietnam and the Vietnam War—which would eventually kill fifty-eight thousand Americans and two million Asians—was underway.

Since then, it has been shown and proven that no North Vietnamese boats ever fired on the *Maddox*, and that McNamara had been untruthful when he testified before Congress. According to the official publication of the Naval Institute, ". . . once-classified documents and tapes released in the past several years, combined with previously uncovered facts, make clear that high government officials distorted facts and deceived the American public about events that led to full US involvement in the Vietnam War."

In the weeks prior to the Gulf of Tonkin incident, South Vietnamese ships had been attacking posts in North Vietnam in conjunction with the CIA's Operation 34A. According to many inside sources, the Johnson administration wanted a full scale war in Vietnam and through Operation 34A was trying to provoke North Vietnam into an attack that would give Johnson an excuse to go to war. But when McNamara was asked by the Congress on August 7 if these South Vietnam attacks had anything to do with the US military and CIA, McNamara lied and said no.

Within hours after reporting that the *Maddox* had been attacked, Captain Herrick was retracting his statements and reporting to the White House and Pentagon that "in all likelihood" an over-eager sonar man had been mistaken and that the sonar sounds and images that he originally thought were enemy torpedoes were actually just the beat of the *Maddox's* own propellers. Herrick reported that there was a good probability that there had been no attack on the *Maddox*, and suggested "complete reevaluation before any action is taken." McNamara saw these new, updated reports and discussed them with President Johnson early in the afternoon of August 4. Even though this was so, on the evening of August 4, President Johnson went on national television and announced to the American public that North Vietnam had engaged in "unprovoked aggression" and, so, the US military was retaliating. A few days after the Gulf of Tonkin Resolution, Johnson remarked, "Hell, those damn stupid sailors were just shooting at flying fish."[1]

Recently, new documents related to the Gulf of Tonkin incident have been declassified and according to Robert Hanyok, a historian for the National Security Agency, these documents show that the NSA deliberately "distorted intelligence" and "altered documents" to make it appear that an attack had occurred on August 4.

When President Lyndon Johnson misrepresented to the American public and said he knew that North Vietnam had attacked a US ship, and when Defense Secretary Robert McNamara lied to the Congress and said he was sure that the *Maddox* had been attacked and that the CIA had nothing to do with South Vietnam aggression, and when NSA officials falsified information to make it appear that there had been an attack on the *Maddox*, that was a government conspiracy.

OPERATION NORTHWOODS

In 1962, the most powerful and highest ranking military officials of the US government, the Joint Chiefs of Staff, felt strongly that the communist leader Fidel Castro had to be removed from power and, so, came up with a plan to justify an American invasion of Cuba.

The plan, entitled Operations Northwoods, was presented to Secretary of Defense Robert McNamara on March 13, 1962, and was signed by the chairman of the Joint Chiefs of Staff, Lyman L. Lemnitzer.

Operations Northwoods was a proposal for a false flag operation, a plan in which a military organizes an attack against its own country and then frames and blames the attack on another country for the purpose of initiating hostilities and declaring war on that country.

The proposal was originally labeled *Top Secret* but was made public on November 18, 1997, by the John F. Kennedy Assassination Records Review

Board. The complete Operation Northwoods paper was published online by the National Security Archive on April 30, 2001, and this once-secret government document can now be read by anyone.

The actions that General Lemnitzer and the other chiefs wanted to take under Operations Northwoods are shocking. According to the plan, CIA and military personnel and hired provocateurs would commit various violent acts and these acts would be blamed on Castro to "create the necessary impression of Cuban rashness and irresponsibility" and "put the United States in the apparent position of suffering defensible grievances."

One of the most ambitious plans of Operation Northwoods was to blow up a plane in midflight. The strategy was to fill a civilian airplane with CIA and military personnel who were registered under fake ID's; an exact duplicate plane—an empty military drone aircraft—would take off at the same exact time. The plane of fake passengers would land at a military base but the empty drone plane would fly over Cuba and crash in the ocean, supposedly a victim of Cuban missiles. "Casualty lists in US newspapers" and conducting "fake funerals for mock-victims" would cause "a helpful wave of national indignation" in America.

The Operation Northwoods proposal also states: "We could blow up a US ship and blame Cuba." Whether the ship was to be empty or full of US soldiers is unclear. The document also says: "Hijacking attempts against US civil air and surface craft should be encouraged."

Some of the recommendations of Operation Northwoods would have surely led to serious injuries and even deaths of Cuban and American civilians. The plan suggests: "We could sink a boatload of Cubans on route to Florida (real or simulated)." And, "We could foster attempts on lives of anti-Castro Cubans in the United States even to the extent of wounding in instances to be widely publicized. . . . We could explode a few bombs in carefully chosen spots."

Lemnitzer and the chiefs wanted many of these staged terrorist attacks to be directed at the Guantanamo Bay United States Naval Base in Cuba. The plans were: "Start riots near the entrance to the base"; "lob mortar shells from outside the base to inside the base"; "blow up ammunition inside the base; start fires"; "burn aircraft on airbase (sabotage)"; "sabotage ship in harbor; large fires—napalm."

When Secretary of Defense McNamara was presented with the Operation Northwoods plan, he either stopped and rejected the plan himself or passed it on to President Kennedy and JFK then rejected it. But if Kennedy and McNamara had agreed with the plan, then the Joint Chiefs of Staff wanted to begin enacting Operation Northwoods "right away, within a few months."

Even though Operation Northwoods was never initiated, when the chairman of the Joint Chiefs of Staff and the other highest ranking military officials of the United States Government planned to organize violent attacks on Americans and anti-Castro Cuban citizens, knowing those attacks could severely injure and kill those citizens, and when they planned to blame those attacks on Cuba and then use that as an excuse to invade Cuba, that was a government conspiracy.

FBI AND THE MAFIA

In March 1965, the FBI had the house of New England organized crime boss Raymond Patriarca wiretapped and overheard two mobsters, Joseph Barboza and Vincent Flemmi, asking Patriarca for permission to kill another gangster, Edward Deegan.

Two days later, Deegan's blood-soaked body was found dead in a Boston alley. Within days, an official FBI report confirmed that Joseph Barboza and three other mobsters were the murderers.

Instead of those men going to prison for murder, though, three years later a man named Joseph Salvati was brought to trial for the murder of Edward Deegan. At that trial Joseph Barboza testified and lied that Salvati was one of the murderers. On the basis of Barboza's testimony, Joseph Salvati was convicted of murder and sentenced to life in prison.

At that time, in the mid 1960s, the FBI was being pressured more and more to do something to stop organized crime. The bureau began using members of the mafia—criminals and murderers—to inform against fellow mafia members. Joseph Barboza was one of these FBI-protected, paid informants. The FBI didn't want Barboza to go to prison for the murder of Deegan because they wanted him to continue infiltrating the mafia and testifying against other mafia members. The bureau, apparently, did want a conviction in the Deegan murder case, though, and, so, let Barboza lie under oath and let a man they knew to be innocent, Joseph Salvati, go to prison.

The Witness Protection Program was first created for Joseph Barboza, and Barboza was the first mafia informant to be protected under the program. After helping to convict a number of mobsters, Barboza was sent off to live in California. While under the Witness Protection Program, Barboza committed at least one more murder, and probably more. On trial for a murder in California, FBI officials showed up for Joseph Barboza's trial and testified on his behalf, helping Barboza to get a light sentence.

Joseph Salvati ended up serving thirty years in prison for a murder that he was innocent of. During that thirty-year period, lawyers for Salvati requested documents from the FBI that would have proved Salvati's innocence, but the bureau refused to release them. Finally, in 1997, other evidence came forth suggesting Salvati's innocence and the governor of Massachusetts, William Weld, granted Salvati's release. A few years later, the FBI was ordered to release all its reports on the case; hundreds of documents showed the FBI knew that Barboza was a murderer, that he had murdered Edward Deegan, and that Joseph Salvati had had nothing to do with the crime. Salvati was exonerated in a court of law, and was eventually awarded millions of dollars in a civil lawsuit against the government. (Three other defendants were also exonerated. At the 1968 trial,

Joseph Barboza had testified that three other men—men who were also not guilty—had participated in Deegan's murder. These three innocent men were, with Salvati, also sent to prison.)

Perhaps the most shocking thing that the FBI documents showed, though, was that FBI Director J. Edgar Hoover himself knew Salvati was innocent and that Barboza had killed Deegan. Hoover was working closely, almost daily, with the agents handling Joseph Barboza, and it was probably Hoover directing the operation. The congressional committee that investigated the case was the House Committee on Government Reform and Congressman Dan Burton was the chairman. When asked by CBS's *60 Minutes* journalist Mike Wallace "Did J. Edgar Hoover know all this?" Burton replied, "Yes . . . It's one of the greatest failures in the history of American justice . . . J. Edgar Hoover knew Salvati was innocent. He knew it and his name should not be emblazoned on the FBI headquarters. We should change the name of that building."

Congressman Burton claimed there was evidence that there were more cases when the FBI did the same sorts of things they did in the Joseph Salvati case; when Burton and his committee requested the files on these cases, the Attorney General and the White House refused to release them.

When FBI Director J. Edgar Hoover and top FBI officials let a known murderer lie and perjure himself in a courtroom, when they let four men they knew to be innocent suffer in the hell of a prison cell for thirty years, and when they deliberately covered that up for decades, that was a government conspiracy.

THE MANHATTAN PROJECT

In 1939, Albert Einstein and two other European physicists sent a letter to President Franklin Roosevelt informing Roosevelt that the German government was working on developing the science that could lead to the creation of a nuclear bomb. FDR immediately formed a committee to look into the idea of the US government making an atomic bomb. In 1942, the Manhattan Project, the United States program to build a nuclear bomb, headed by General Leslie R. Groves of the US Army Corps of Engineers, was formed.

The program existed from 1942–1946, spent two billion dollars, had plants and factories in thirty cities, and employed 130,000 workers.

But virtually no one knew about it.

The Manhattan Project is considered the "Greatest Secret Ever Kept." The US government wanted to keep the Project a secret lest Germany or one of America's other enemies found out about it and built—more quickly—a larger, better bomb. In the early 1940s, when American scientists began working on splitting atoms and nuclear fission, US government officials asked the scientists to not publish any reports on the work in scientific journals. The work was kept quiet. In 1943, when newspapers began reporting on the large Manhattan Project construction going on in a few states, the newly formed United States Government Office of Censorship asked newspapers and broadcasters to avoid discussing "atom smashing, atomic energy, atomic fission . . . the use for military purposes of radium or radioactive materials" or anything else that could expose the project. The press kept mum.

The government didn't talk about the Manhattan Project, the press didn't report on it, and the public knew nothing about it.

Not even the 130,000 Manhattan Project laborers knew they were building an atom bomb. In 1945, a *Life* magazine article wrote that before Japan was attacked with a-bombs, "probably no more than a few dozen men in the entire country knew the full meaning of the Manhattan Project, and perhaps only a thousand others even were aware that work on atoms was involved." The workers were told they were doing an important job for the government, but weren't told what the job was, and didn't understand the full import of the mysterious, daily tasks they were doing. The laborers were warned that disclosing the Project's secrets was punishable by ten years in prison, and a hefty financial fine. Whole towns and cities were built where thousands of Manhattan Project workers lived and worked but these thousands didn't know they were helping to build nuclear bombs.

The Manhattan Project finally became known to the public on August 6, 1945, when President Harry Truman announced that America had dropped a nuclear bomb on Hiroshima, Japan.

Truman, himself, had not been informed of the Manhattan Project until late April 1945.

When the government kept the purpose of the Manhattan Project a secret from the press, from the public, from America's enemies, from Harry Truman, and even from the 130,000 laborers who worked for the Manhattan Project, that was a government conspiracy.

THE CHURCH COMMITTEE INVESTIGATION

In the early 1970s, after the Watergate affair and investigative reports by the *New York Times*, it became apparent that the CIA and other US intelligence agencies might be engaging in inappropriate and illegal activities. In 1975, the Church Committee, named after the Committee's chairman Senator Frank Church, was formed to investigate abuses by the CIA, NSA, FBI, and IRS.

The Church Committee reports are said to constitute the most extensive investigations of intelligence activities ever made available to the public.

Many disturbing facts were revealed. According to the final report of the Committee, US intelligence agencies had been engaging in "unlawful or improper conduct" and "intelligence excesses, at home and abroad" since the administration of President Franklin Roosevelt. The report added that "intelligence agencies have undermined the Constitutional rights of citizens" and "checks and balances designed by the framers of the Constitution to assure accountability have not been applied."

One of the most well-known revelations of the Committee was the CIA's so-called "Family Jewels," a report that detailed the CIA's misdeeds dating back to Dwight Eisenhower's presidency. The committee also reported on the NSA's SHAMROCK and MINARET programs; under these programs the NSA had been intercepting, opening, and reading the telegrams and mail of thousands of private citizens. The Church Committee also discovered and exposed the FBI's COINTELPRO program, the bureau's program to covertly destroy and disrupt any groups or individuals that J. Edgar Hoover felt were bad for America. Some of the movements and groups that the FBI tried to discredit and destroy were the Civil Rights movement, the anti-Vietnam War movement, the Southern Christian Leadership Conference, and individuals such as Martin Luther King Jr.

The most alarming thing that the Church Committee found, though, was that the CIA had an assassination program. It was revealed that the CIA assassinated or had tried to assassinate Dinh Diem of Vietnam, Raphael Trujillo of the Dominican Republic, General Rene Schneider of Chile, Fidel Castro, Patrice Lumumba of the Congo, and other political leaders throughout the world. The Committee learned about the different ways the CIA had developed to kill and assassinate people: inflicting cancer, inflicting heart attacks, making murders look like suicides, car accidents, boating accidents, and shootings. At one point, CIA Director William Colby presented to the Committee a special "heart attack gun" that the CIA had created. The gun was able to shoot a small poison-laden dart into its victim. The dart was so small as to be undetectable; the victim's death from the poison would appear to be a heart attack, so no foul play would be suspected.

In response to the Church Committee report, in 1976 President Gerald Ford signed Executive Order 11,905, which forbade employees of the US government from engaging in or conspiring to engage in political assassinations. In that same year, the Senate approved Senate Resolution 400, which established the Senate Select Committee on Intelligence, the committee responsible for providing vigilant oversight over the intelligence agencies.

Many former CIA employee-whistleblowers and other people, though, claim that US intelligence agencies are still acting in improper ways. In 2008, it was revealed that the CIA had hired Blackwater, a private company made up of ex-Navy Seals, to track down and assassinate suspected terrorists. Later in the 2000s, when the Congress formed a committee to investigate if CIA waterboarding and other methods of interrogation constituted torture, congressmen complained that they couldn't get to the bottom of the matter because CIA officials and the CIA director were lying to the congressional committee.

Forty-five years after the revelations of the Church Committee, it seems US intelligence agencies are still engaging in covert and improper conduct.

When US intelligence agencies and the CIA plot to influence the affairs of foreign nations, when the CIA plots assassinations and assassinates foreign leaders and political dissidents, when the CIA develops new ways to kill and assassinate and interrogate and torture, and when the CIA keeps all that from Congress, the press, and the public, that's a government conspiracy.

If these five instances of government engaging in conspiracies have been proven to be true—and they have been—isn't it logical to assume that government agencies may have engaged in other conspiracies? It is the very nature of intelligence agencies and militaries to act in secretive, conspiratorial ways. The phrase "conspiracy theory" shouldn't have a negative connotation. Politics always plays out with backroom handshakes. It is the suggestion of *American Conspiracies and Cover-Ups* that government agencies and officials and the special interests that influence them are often engaging in conspiratorial actions, and that conspiracies have been behind some of the most iconic and important events of American history.

A conspiracy theorist was regaling a friend with one conspiracy theory after another. Finally, the friend interrupted and said, "I bet I know what would happen if God Himself appeared out of the sky right now, looked down at us, and said, 'There is no conspiracy.' I bet you would look up and say, 'So the conspiracy goes higher than we thought.'"

Perhaps if the Almighty appeared to inform us that politicians and governments and government officials don't act in secretive, covert, conspiratorial ways, then we could accept that.

But when the evidence indicates otherwise....

Theories questioning if multiple people might have shot at JFK, or if interior bombs brought down the World Trade Center, or if somebody was able to rig the 2000 and 2004 presidential elections can make for dramatic, sensational storytelling. But it is not the purpose of *American Conspiracies and Cover-Ups* to be sensational; the purpose of this book is to talk about "conspiracy realities" that can hopefully give us a deeper and more meaningful understanding of politics. If elements in the intelligence agencies participated in assassinating President Kennedy, then how can the intelligence agencies be better controlled? If elements in the government allowed or caused 9/11 to happen to give us an excuse to go to war in the Middle East, then how much of the War on Terror is disinformation and propaganda? If presidential elections can be rigged, then how can we have fairer, uncorrupted elections? If secretive influences behind the scenes, a Deep State, are controlling our social, political, and financial systems for their own selfish purposes, then it would benefit us to expose who and what these secretive influences are.

American Conspiracies and Cover-Ups may give us a glimpse into the way that government and politics work.

Or don't work.

journalist, and William Donovan, the founder of the Office of Strategic Services. Later, Donovan told an assistant that he believed FDR welcomed the attack and didn't seem surprised. The only thing Roosevelt seemed to care about, Donovan felt, was if the public would now support a declaration of war. According to *Day of Deceit*, in October 1940 FDR adopted a specific strategy to incite Japan to commit an overt act of war. Part of the strategy was to move America's Pacific fleet out of California and anchor it in Pearl Harbor. Admiral James Richardson, the commander of the Pacific fleet, strongly opposed keeping the ships in harm's way in Hawaii. He expressed this to Roosevelt, and so the President relieved him of his command. Later, Richardson quoted Roosevelt as saying: "Sooner or later the Japanese will commit an overt act against the United States and the nation will be willing to enter the war."

To those who believe that government conspiracies can't possibly happen, *Day of Deceit* could prove to them otherwise. Stinnett's well-documented book makes a convincing case that the highest officials of the government—including the highest official—fooled and deceived millions of Americans about one of the most important days in the history of the country. It now has to be considered one of the most definitive—if not *the* definitive—book on the subject. Gore Vidal has said, ". . . Robert Stinnett has come up with most of the smoking guns. *Day of Deceit* shows that the famous 'surprise' attack was no surprise to our war-minded rulers . . ." And John Toland, the Pulitzer Prize-winning author of the Pearl Harbor book *Infamy*, said, "Step by step, Stinnett goes through the prelude to war, using new documents to reveal the terrible secrets that have never been disclosed to the public. It is disturbing that eleven presidents, including those I admired, kept the truth from the public until Stinnett's Freedom of Information Act requests finally persuaded the Navy to release the evidence."

The following is my interview with Robert B. Stinnett.

Cirignano: What led you to write a book about Pearl Harbor?
Stinnett: Well, I was in the Navy in World War II. I was on an aircraft carrier. With George Bush, believe it or not.

You wrote a book about that.
Yes, that's right. So, we were always told that the Japanese targets, the warships, were sighted by United States submarines. We were never told about breaking the Japanese codes. Okay. So, in 1982 I read a book by a Professor Prange called *At Dawn We Slept.* And in that book it said that there was a secret US Navy monitoring station at Pearl Harbor intercepting Japanese naval codes prior to December 7. Well, that was a bombshell to me. That was the first time I had heard about that. I worked at the *Oakland Tribune* at that time. . . . So I went over to Hawaii to see the station to confirm it. And then, to make a long story short, I met the cryptographers involved, and they steered me to other sources, documents that would support all of their information. And so that started me going. My primary purpose was to learn about the intercept procedures. And so I filed Freedom of Information Act requests with the Navy because communications intelligence is very difficult. It's a no-no. They don't want to discuss it. But the Navy did let me, gave me permission to go to Hawaii and they showed me the station. . . . So that started me on it. And then I would ask for certain information, this is, now, we're talking about in the 1980s, the late 1980s. And they're very reluctant to give me more information. I'm getting a little bit.

Historians and government officials who claim that Washington didn't have a foreknowledge of the Pearl Harbor attack have always contended that America wasn't intercepting and hadn't cracked Japan's important military codes in the months and days preceding the attack. The crux of your book is that your research proves that is absolutely untrue. We were reading most all of Japan's radio messages. Correct?

That is correct. And I believed that, too. You know, because, *Life* magazine in September 1945, right after Japan surrendered, suggested that this was the case, that Roosevelt engineered Pearl Harbor. But that was discarded as an anti-Roosevelt tract, and I believed it, also.

Another claim at the heart of the Pearl Harbor surprise-attack lore is that Japan's ships kept radio silence as they approached Hawaii. That's absolutely untrue, also.

That is correct. And this was all withheld from Congress, so nobody knew about all this.

Until the Freedom of Information Act?

Yes.

Is this statement true?—If America was intercepting and decoding Japan's military messages then Washington and FDR knew that Japan was going to bomb Pearl Harbor.

Oh, absolutely.

You feel it's as simple as that?

That is right. And that was their plan. It was their "overt act of war" plan that I talk about in my book that President Roosevelt adopted on October 7, 1940.

You write that in late November 1941 an order was sent out to all US military commanders that stated: "The United States desires that Japan commit the first overt act." According to Secretary of War Stimson, the order came directly from President Roosevelt. Was FDR's cabinet on record for supporting this policy of provoking Japan to commit the first overt act of war?

I don't know that he revealed it to the cabinet. He may have revealed it to

Harry Hopkins, his close confidant, but there's no evidence that anybody in the cabinet knew about this.

I thought you wrote in your book that they did . . . that some of them were on record for . . .

Well, some did. Secretary of War Stimson knew, based on his diary, and also probably Frank Knox, the Secretary of Navy knew. But Frank Knox died before the investigation started. So all we have really is Stimson, his diary. And he reveals a lot in there, and I do cite in my book . . . You must mean his war cabinet. Yes. Stimson's diary reveals that nine people in the war cabinet—the military people—knew about the provocation policy.

Even though Roosevelt made contrary statements to the public, didn't he and his advisors feel that America was eventually going to have to get into the war?

That is right. Well, his statement was, "I won't send your boys to war unless we are attacked." So then he engineered this attack—to get us into war really against Germany. But I think that was his only option. I express that in the book.

Who was Lieutenant Commander Arthur McCollum and what was his connection to the Pearl Harbor attack?

He worked for Naval intelligence in Washington. He was also the communications routing officer for President Roosevelt. So all these intercepts would go to Commander McCollum and then he would route them to the president. There's no question about that. He also was the author of this plan to provoke Japan into attacking us at Pearl Harbor. And he was born and raised in Japan.

McCollum wrote this plan, this memorandum, in October 1940. It was addressed to two of Roosevelt's closest advisors. In the memo, McCollum is expressing that it's inevitable that Japan and America are going to go to war, and that Nazi Germany's going to become a threat to America's security. McCollum is saying that America's going to have to get into the war. But he also says that public opinion is against that. So, McCollum then suggests eight specific things that America should do to provoke Japan to become more hostile, to attack us, so that the public would be behind a war effort. And because he was born and raised in Japan, he understood the Japanese mentality and how the Japanese would react.

Yes. Exactly.

Has the existence of this memo from Commander McCollum ever been revealed to the public before your book came out?

No, no. I received that as pursuant to my FOIA request on January 1995 from the National Archives. I had no idea it existed.

FDR and his military advisors knew that if McCollum's eight actions were implemented—things like keeping the Pacific fleet in Pearl Harbor, and crippling Japan's economy with an embargo—there was no question in their minds that this would cause Japan—whose government was very militant—to attack the United States. Correct?

That is correct, and that is what Commander McCollum said. He said, "If you adopt these policies, then Japan will commit an overt act of war."

Is there any proof that FDR saw McCollum's memorandum?

There's no proof that he actually saw the memorandum, but he adopted all eight of the provocations—including where he signed executive orders . . . And other information in Navy files offers conclusive evidence that he did see it.

The memo is addressed to two of Roosevelt's top advisors, and you include the document where one of them is agreeing with McCollum's suggested course of action.

Yes, Dudley Knox, who was Roosevelt's very close associate.

The "splendid arrangement" was a phrase that FDR's military leaders used to describe America's situation in the Pacific. Can you explain what the "splendid arrangement" was?
The "splendid arrangement" was the system of twenty-two monitoring systems in the Pacific that were operated by the United States, Britain, and the Dutch. These extended along the west coast of the United States, up to Alaska, then down to southeast Asia, and into the Central Pacific.

These radio monitoring stations allowed us to intercept and read all of Japan's messages, right?
Absolutely. We had Japan wired for sound.

You claim that the "splendid arrangement" was so adept that ever since the 1920s, Washington always knew what Japan's government was doing. So to assert that we didn't know the Japanese were going to bomb Pearl Harbor would be illogical?
That is correct.

Your book claims that in 1941 Japan had a spy residing in the Japanese consulate in Honolulu.
Japan secreted this spy—he was a Japanese naval officer—in Honolulu. He arrived there in March 1941 under an assumed name, and he was attached to the Japanese consulate there. But when the FBI checked on him they found out he was not listed in the Japanese foreign registry, so they were suspicious immediately. They put a tail on him. And then the spy started filing messages to Japan that we were intercepting. This was in a diplomatic code now. And so the FBI continued to tail him, and so did Naval intelligence.

Naval intelligence, the FBI, and Roosevelt knew this man was spying on the fleet in Pearl Harbor and they let the espionage go on. The policy of FDR's government then was to look the other way and let Japan prepare itself for attacking us?
That's right. That is correct. He was providing a timetable for the attack.

The spy was even sending bomb plots of Pearl Harbor?
Yes. From March to August he was giving a census of the US Pacific fleet. Then starting in August he starting preparing bomb plots of Pearl Harbor, where our ships were anchored and so forth.

And Roosevelt even saw those bomb plots, right?
Yes, that is correct.

You claim that twice during the week of December 1 to 6 the spy indicated that Pearl Harbor would be attacked. According to a Japanese commander, the message on December 2 was: "No changes observed by afternoon of 2 December. So far they do not seem to have been alerted." And on the morning of December 6 the message was: "There are no barrage balloons up and there is an opportunity left for a surprise attack against these places." These messages were intercepted by the Navy, right? Did Roosevelt know about these messages?
They were intercepted. That is correct. They were sent by RCA communications. And Roosevelt had sent David Sarnoff, who was head of RCA, to Honolulu so that this would facilitate getting these messages even faster. Though we were intercepting them off the airways anyway. And on December 2 and on December 6 the spy indicated that Pearl was going to be the target. And the December 2 message was intercepted, decoded, and translated prior to December 5. The December 6 message . . . there's really no proof that it was . . . it was intercepted, but there's all sorts of cover stories on whether or not that reached the president. But

he received other information that it was going to happen the next day anyway.

You saw the records of those intercepts yourself?
Yes, I have those.

And all these other messages that the Navy was constantly intercepting showed exactly where the Japanese ships were, that they were preparing for war, and that they were heading straight for Hawaii. Right?
That's right. Our radio direction finders located the Japanese warships.

You say Roosevelt regularly received copies of these intercepts. How were they delivered to him?
By Commander McCollum routing the information to him. They called it monograph . . . it was sent to the President through Commander McCollum who dispatched it through the naval aide to the President.

On page 203 of the hardcover edition of your book it reads, "Seven Japanese naval broadcasts intercepted between November 28 and December 6 confirmed that Japan intended to start the war and that it would begin in Pearl Harbor." Did you see the records of those intercepts yourself?
Yes. And also we have new information about other intercepts in the current edition that came out in May 2001 . . . There's no question about it.

According to Day of Deceit, on November 25, Admiral Yamamoto sent a radio message to the Japanese fleet. Part of the message read: "The task force, keeping its movements strictly secret and maintaining close guard against submarines and aircraft, shall advance into Hawaiian waters, and upon the very opening of hostilities shall attack the main force of the United States fleet in Hawaii and deal it a mortal blow . . ." What's the proof that the record of that intercept exists? Did you see it yourself? Again, did Roosevelt know about it?

The English version of that message has been released by the United States, in a government book. The Japanese version—the raw message—has not been released by the US. I have copies of the Station H radio logs—a monitoring station in Hawaii. They prove that the Navy intercepted eighty-three messages that Yamamoto sent between November 17 and 25. I have those records, but not the raw intercepts, eighty-six percent of which have not been released by the government . . . As far as Roosevelt, early in November 1941 Roosevelt ordered that Japanese raw intercepts be delivered directly delivered to him by his naval aide, Captain Beardall. Sometimes if McCollum felt a message was particularly hot he would deliver it himself to FDR.

Late on December 6 and in the very early morning hours of December 7, the United States intercepted messages sent to the Japanese ambassador in Washington. These messages were basically a declaration of war—Japan was saying it was breaking off negotiations with America. At those times, General Marshall and President Roosevelt were shown the intercepts. When FDR read them, he said, "This means war." When the last intercept was shown to Roosevelt, it was still hours before the Pearl Harbor attack. In that last intercept, Japan gave the deadline for when it was breaking off relations with the US . . . The deadline was the exact hour when Pearl Harbor was attacked. FDR and Marshall should have then sent an emergency warning to Admiral Kimmel in Pearl Harbor. But they acted nonchalantly and didn't get a warning to Kimmel.

Yes. This is a message sent from the Japanese foreign office to the Japanese ambassador in Washington, DC. And in it he directed . . . it broke off relations with the United States, and set a timetable of 1:00 p.m. on Sunday, December 7, eastern time.

Which was the exact time when Pearl Harbor was bombed.

That's right. So they realized, with all their information, this is it. And then General Marshall, though, sat on the message for about fifteen hours because he didn't want to send . . . he didn't want to warn the Hawaiian commanders in time . . . he didn't want them to interfere with the overt act. Eventually, they did sent it but it didn't arrive until way after the attack.

Roosevelt saw it, too. They should have sent an emergency warning to Admiral Kimmel in Hawaii, right?

That's right. But, you see, they wanted the successful overt act by Japan. It unified the American people.

This seems like a classic case of higher-ups doing something question-able, and then getting the people below them to take the blame for it. Admiral Husband Kimmel was in charge of the fleet in Pearl Harbor, and he was demoted and took the blame for the attack. Was that justified?

No, it was not. And Congress, you know, in October of 2000 voted to exon-erate him because the information was withheld from them. That's very important. But it was subject to implementation by President Clinton who did not sign it. But at least Congress filed it, made the finding.

You claim that Admiral Kimmel and General Short—who headed up the Army in Hawaii—were denied by Washington the information that would have let them know the attack was coming. In what ways were Kimmel and Short denied intelligence?

Well, they were just cut off. . . . They were not told that the spy was there, and they were not given these crucial documents, the radio direction finder information. All this information was going to everybody but Kimmel and Short. That's very clear. . . . At one point Kimmel specifically requested that Washington let him know immediately about any important develop-ments, but they did not do that.

Kimmel was given some information, because two weeks before the attack he sent the Pacific fleet north of Hawaii on a reconnaissance exercise to look for Japanese carriers. When White House military officials learned of this, what was their reaction?

Admiral Kimmel tried on a number of occasions to do something to defend Pearl Harbor. And, right, two weeks before the attack, on November 23, Kimmel sent nearly one hundred warships of the Pacific fleet to the exact site where Japan planned to launch the attack. Kimmel meant business. He was looking for the Japanese. His actions indicated that he wanted to be thoroughly prepared for action if he encountered a Japanese carrier force. When White House officials learned this, they directed to Kimmel that he was "complicating the situation." . . . You see, the White House wanted a clean cut overt act of war by Japan. Isolationists would have charged FDR was precipitating Japanese action by allowing the Pacific fleet in the North Pacific. . . . So, minutes after Kimmel got the White House directive he canceled the exercise and returned the fleet to its anchorage in Pearl Harbor. . . . That's where the Japanese found it on December 7, 1941.

The White House was handcuffing Kimmel? They wanted him to be completely passive?

That is right.

FDR did send a war warning to Kimmel on November 28. Was that enough of a warning?

Well, that was a warning, but also in there they directed Admiral Kimmel and all the Pacific commanders to stand aside, don't go on the offensive, remain in a defensive position, and let Japan commit the first overt act. That's right in the message, and it's in my book. And Admiral Kimmel, the message he received, it was repeated twice . . . stand aside and let Japan commit the first overt act, the exact wording is in my book.

Your book makes it abundantly clear that FDR and his advisors knew Japan was preparing for war, and knew that Japan was eventually going to attack. But can it be said that FDR knew that the attack was going to take place specifically on the morning of December 7 at Pearl Harbor?
Yes. . . . Absolutely.

Through the radio intercepts.
Through the radio intercepts. Right. Both military and diplomatic.

Did America's ambassador in Japan, Ambassador Joseph Grew, have any indications that Japan was planning a surprise attack on Pearl Harbor?
The information is that he did. I do quote him in the book, and he warned Washington to be on the alert because he couldn't give them the last minute information.

Well, according to your book, Ambassador Grew had a reliable source in the Japanese embassy tell him that Japan was planning the attack, and then Grew sent dire warnings to the White House that an attack on Hawaii was a very real possibility.
Yes, well, he was the first one to—after President Roosevelt adopted this eight action memo—Ambassador Grew learned about the Pearl Harbor attack in January 1941. And then Commander McCollum was asked to evaluate this, and he said, "Oh, there's nothing to it"—even though it was his plan!

He was being disingenuous, McCollum.
Yeah, exactly.

On December 5, the Navy intercepted a message telling Japanese embassies around the world to burn their code books. What does it mean when a government is telling its embassies to burn their code books?
That means war is coming within a day or two.

That's common knowledge in the military. And the military officials in Washington saw this intercept and the meaning of it wasn't lost on them.

Yes. That's right.

FDR and Washington also knew that Japan had recalled from sea all its merchant ships. What does that mean?

It's known in government and the military that if a nation recalls its merchant ships then those ships are needed to transport soldiers and supplies for war.

So, in your opinion, if there had been no Pearl Harbor, then would America have ever have ended up dropping nuclear bombs on Hiroshima and Nagasaki?

Well, that's what the survivors, the families of those who were killed at Pearl, and other people say. They claim that if there hadn't been Pearl Harbor there would have been no Hiroshima. But, of course, that's a "what if" question. And I don't know how to answer it.

One could only speculate on that. But it seems in a way Hiroshima and Nagasaki were maybe retribution for Pearl Harbor.

I think it was more really to bring a close to the war. You know, I was out there at the time, and, frankly, I . . . we were subject to kamikaze attacks, they were attacking our carriers, and about half of our carriers were knocked out as of July 1945, so, personally, I was very pleased with the atom bombing because that ended the war. It probably saved my life.

If what you're saying is true, then Pearl Harbor is a prime example of government treating human beings like guinea pigs. Yet, you, yourself, don't disparage and don't have a negative view of FDR.

No, I don't have a negative view. I think it was his only option to do this.

And I quote the chief cryptographer for the Pacific fleet, who said, "It was a pretty cheap price to pay for unifying the country."

That cryptographer, Commander Joseph Rochefort, was a confidant of McCollum's. He worked closely with Kimmel in Pearl Harbor. It could be argued that Rochefort was the closest one to Kimmel who was most responsible for denying Kimmel the vital intelligence. And he did make that statement. But do you agree with that? A lot of people would be offended and angered by that statement. A lot of people wouldn't agree with it.

A lot of people would not, but I think under the circumstances this was FDR's only option. And, of course, this was sort of used in the Vietnam War, you know. The Gulf of Tonkin Resolution was based on a provocation aimed at the North Vietnamese gunboats—something like that. That's how President Johnson got the Gulf of Tonkin Resolution passed through the Congress. There was a provocation.

Apparently, it's a military strategy, but the families—obviously—of the people who get killed when a military uses this strategy wouldn't agree with it.

Oh, right, I know. Oh, when I speak about this with the families they just start crying about it, you know. They're terribly upset . . . But, you know, it was used by President Polk in the Mexican War in 1846. And also by President Lincoln at Fort Sumter. And then also, as I say, another example is Vietnam, this Gulf of Tonkin business.

It could be a traditional military philosophy, the idea that a military has to sometimes provoke the enemy to attack, sacrifice its own soldiers, so as to unify a country for war.

I think so. I think you could probably trace it back to Caesar's time.

How much in your book has never been revealed to the public before?
The breaking of radio silence. The fact that the Japanese ships did not keep silent as they approached Hawaii . . . The breaking of Japanese codes—I mean the full proof of it. Military codes, I want to emphasize that . . . And, also, McCollum's eight action memo—that's the whole heart of my book. If I didn't have that it wouldn't be as important. That is the smoking gun of Pearl Harbor. It really is.

Your research seems to prove that government conspiracies can exist. In your view, how many people would you say ultimately knew that Japan was going to attack Pearl Harbor, and kept quiet about it and covered it up before and after the event?
I cite about thirty-five people there in the book that most certainly knew about it. And it's probably more than that.

It also seems like a classic Washington cover-up. In your book, you use the phrase "Pearl Harbor deceits." Ever since the attack, there have been missing documents, altered documents, people being disingenuous, and people outright perjuring themselves before the Pearl Harbor investigation committees. Correct?
That is right. Absolutely. And, you know, the Department of Defense has labeled some of my Pearl Harbor requests as B1 National Defense Secrets, and they will not release them. I say that in the book. Janet Reno would not release them to me.

And all the official congressional Pearl Harbor committees were denied and weren't privy to all this revealing information?
That's right. They were cut out, also.

A lot of people probably don't want to believe that a president would let something like Pearl Harbor happen. Have you gotten any criticism for contending that FDR had a foreknowledge of the attack?

Yes. I get about a seventy percent approval rating. From, you know, comments, news media, radio, and all that. And there's about thirty percent just don't accept this . . . But the nitty gritty questions are fine to me. You know, the people who are attacking me, what they are really quoting from is 1950 information. They don't have the 1999 or 2000 information . . .

The information you put out in your book. You're talking about new things here.

That's right. And this thirty percent, I feel they just don't want to accept it, or they regard FDR as an icon who brought Social security, and all that. But he also unified this country, and we were able to stop Hitler, you know, and the holocaust, and everything else that was going on. So, you could also say that this was a victory for President Roosevelt.

But it seems under our system of government if President Roosevelt felt it was an emergency to go to war with Germany then he should have come before the American people and the Congress and explained it and convinced us that we had to go defeat Hitler.

Well, you see that was the problem. The strong isolation movement. Eighty percent of the people wanted nothing to do with Europe's war. And, you know, German submarines were sinking our ships in the North Atlantic. That did not rouse the American public. Nobody gave a damn. The USS *Reuben James* was a destroyer that was sunk, and lost a hundred lives about a month before Pearl Harbor. And there were other ships, merchant ships, and other ships in the North Atlantic that were sunk or damaged. But no one cared about it. I think the American people thought that Roosevelt was trying to provoke us into the German war, or Europe's war. They didn't want anything to do with that. But, you see, Commander McCollum was brilliant. He fashioned this—it was a real PR job—he got Japan to attack us in a most outrageous manner that really did unite the country.

A lot of people would probably be of the opinion that it wasn't so brilliant. The families of the three thousand people who were killed and injured at Pearl Harbor probably wouldn't think it was brilliant.
I know, I know. You see, that's the argument today.

But if this is true, then you agree with what FDR did?
I do. I don't see what other option he had.

Because a lot of the tone in your book seems to be questioning and disagreeing with Roosevelt's actions.
Well, I disagree with the way he treated Admiral Kimmel and General Short, letting them hang out to dry.

Kimmel and Short were cut off from the intelligence loop.
They were cut off. And Congress, you know, last October, the Senate and the House, found that they were cut off. They made the finding. That would have never happened five years ago. Or ten, twenty years ago.

It happened because of the Freedom of Information Act?
I think so. And the Short and Kimmel families have credited my book with getting that through Congress.

Did you ever read Clausen's book? Colonel Henry Clausen was part of a Pearl Harbor investigation of November 1944. He wrote a book that was published in 1992 that claimed FDR didn't have a foreknowledge of the attack.
Well, you know, I read that. But I fault Colonel Clausen because he had access to all of these military intercepts and he did not bring them out.

And I think that was a crime for him to have done that. He should have been court-martialed for that.

You imply in your book that at one point Clausen was probably trying to cover up for General Marshall's actions of December 6 and 7.
I think so. You know, he was acting on the behalf of the Secretary of War. He had carte blanche with these intercepts.

When was he acting on behalf of the Secretary of War?
Well, Clausen was authorized by Secretary of War Stimson to conduct the Pearl Harbor investigation in November 1944. He traveled to the Hawaiian monitoring stations and interviewed cryptographers but failed to obtain any evidence or testimony concerning the intercepts the Navy was making prior to December 7. So when Congress opened its Pearl Harbor investigation in November 1945 there were no pre-Pearl Harbor Japanese naval intercepts available. Clausen was told by Stimson to get the intercepts, but he didn't do it.

Did you ever talk with Clausen? Did he criticize you?
He died. I had tried to contact him. He was an attorney in San Francisco, and I did write him but he would never answer me. I wanted to ask him why he didn't obtain the intercepts. His book doesn't address that major issue. He didn't return my calls, and he never answered my letters. I guess he just didn't want to be exposed to this. Clausen was obviously a part of the conspiracy that kept the pre-Pearl Harbor intercepts from Congress and the American public.

Why do you think the information in your book is important?
It's important because it reveals the lengths that some people in the American government will go to deceive the American public, and to keep this vital information—in our land of the First Amendment—from the people. And that's against everything I believe in.

CHAPTER 2

One of Lyndon Johnson's Lawyers Claims Johnson Participated in a Conspiracy to Assassinate President Kennedy

An interview with LBJ attorney Barr McClellan

C urrent Gallup polls show that many Americans believe that President John F. Kennedy's assassination was the result of a conspiracy, and that Vice President Lyndon Johnson participated in some way, either knowing in advance or at least assisting in the cover-up.

In November 2003, *The History Channel*, to commemorate the fortieth anniversary of the assassination, finished its *The Men Who Killed Kennedy* series by doing a show that supported the theory that Lyndon Johnson was behind the assassination of JFK. The principal source of information for the segment was Barr McClellan, an attorney who from 1966 to 1971 worked for the Austin, Texas, law firm of Edward Clark. Edward Clark was perhaps Lyndon Johnson's closest confidant, and it was Clark's law firm that handled all of Johnson's legal affairs. According to a 1950 *Reader's Digest* article, Clark was also the "secret boss" of Texas. From the late '30s until the late '60s, through his many and close relations with Texas judges and legislators, and through his control of the secretive "round table" that ran the state, Clark was the de facto head of the Lone Star State. Barr McClellan claims that Edward Clark was also Lyndon Johnson's kingmaker and mastermind, that Clark's power and influence were essential in forging Johnson's political career. Barr McClellan also claims that in the wake of Lyndon Johnson's rise to political stardom lie many suspicious deaths that can be theoretically and evidentially linked to Edward Clark.

One of the first of these suspicious deaths was connected to the infamous 1948 Texas Senate race. On the evening of the election, when the results were announced, it was clear that Johnson had lost his bid to be the Democratic nominee for Texas senator. Three days later, after Edward Clark had sent one of his lawyers to pay a visit to George Parr, a corrupt political boss in south Texas, the precinct chair for the town of Alice, Texas, called into election central and announced that a mistake had been made in Box 13 and that Lyndon Johnson had more votes than originally reported. The new tally gave Johnson a victory by eighty-seven votes. Everyone in Texas knew the fix was in. Paying precinct chairs to rig votes was, after all, a common practice in Texas state politics. After Clark used an associate's relationship to a Supreme Court judge to get the Supreme Court to give the now-contested election to Johnson, Lyndon Johnson became known as "Lyin' Lyndon." Johnson was a joke to the officials and politicians in Texas, who felt that there was no way that "Lyin' Lyndon" would ever get to serve more than one term as a senator. Later, in 1952, a man named Sam Smithwick, one of Parr's sheriff deputies, announced that he could produce the missing ballots from Box 13 and prove what everyone around Texas knew—that Johnson had stolen the election. At the time, Smithwick was in prison for shooting one of Parr's political enemies, and thought coming clean about the election could help him with his sentence. Shortly before Smithwick was to meet with Coke Stevenson, Johnson's defeated opponent, he was found dead in his cell. The prison coroner quickly ruled it a suicide. After the 1948 election, Edward Clark had arranged for a friend, Pete Coffield, to serve on the State Board of Prisons, and Barr McClellan feels Clark could have easily arranged a murder through Coffield. Having convicts or guards eliminate "problem" prisoners was another Texas tradition.

Newspapers reported that the death "stunk to high heaven" and "reeked of corruption." Texans openly suspected that Lyndon Johnson was connected to Smithwick's death.

A year prior to that, a man named Mac Wallace was arrested and convicted for killing a man named Doug Kinser. On the night he was apprehended, when the arresting officer asked Wallace what he did for a living, Wallace replied, "I work for Senator Johnson."

Wallace, in all likelihood, wasn't consciously attempting to hint that he had done the murder for Johnson. He was, rather, simply stating a fact. Wallace had been the student body president at the University of Texas in Austin and in the 1940s he had become acquainted with Clark and Johnson. In 1950, Johnson—for the purpose of making him a political operative— had personally arranged for Wallace to take a job in the Department of Agriculture. Doug Kinser was one of the leaders of the community theatre in Austin, and had become friends with Lyndon Johnson's sister, Josefa Johnson. At that time, Kinser, Josefa Johnson, and others in the theatre community were engaging in heterosexual and lesbian threesomes and orgies.[2] After the 1948 election controversy, Clark and Johnson knew that not even a hint of a scandal could ever attach itself to Johnson's name again. If "Lyin' Lyndon" wanted to fulfill his desire for higher political office, then his reputation had to remain pure. A sexual scandal connected to Johnson, or even to one of his family members, could have quickly spelled the end of his political career, especially in the staid 1950s. Doug Kinser had opened a small business, and there are indications that Kinser was pressuring Josefa Johnson to influence her famous brother, who was in charge of the precursor to the Small Business Administration in Texas, to get Kinser government money. Kinser may also have been blackmailing her, threatening to go public with stories of Josefa's wild, libidinous life. Barr McClellan and other writers believe that Edward Clark directed Mac Wallace to kill Doug Kinser. After Wallace was convicted, eleven jurors were for the death penalty, while one held out for life in prison. The judge handling the case, apparently, though, was one of the many judges that Clark "owned." The judge intervened and gave Wallace a mere five-year sentence. Then he suspended the sentence. Shortly after being convicted of the crime of murder, Mac Wallace walked out of the courthouse a free man.

Barr McClellan contends that with that murder, Mac Wallace had become Clark's and Johnson's hit man. In 1998, a fingerprint expert identified one of the Warren Commission fingerprints taken from the sniper's lair in The Texas School Book Depository from where Lee Harvey Oswald supposedly shot JFK to be a match for Mac Wallace. To McClellan, this implicates Mac Wallace—and, so, Clark and Johnson—in President Kennedy's assassination.

Barr McClellan isn't the only person who claims that Lyndon Johnson behaved more like a Mafia chieftain than the fairly elected, upstanding leader of a democracy. In April 1962, a federal grand jury indicted a Texas cotton farmer named Billy Sol Estes. In the early '60s, cotton farmers required a cotton allotment—the government-controlled amount of cotton a farmer was allowed to grow—to produce their crop, and Estes had been obtaining more cotton allotments than were legally allowed. Lyndon Johnson knew Estes, and there were suspicions that Johnson was using his influence in the Department of Agriculture to allow Estes to acquire the illegal cotton allotments and then pay Johnson off. Soon after Estes was indicted, the Senate began investigating Estes and the death of Henry Marshall, a United States Department of Agriculture investigator who had been pushing for a deeper investigation into Estes that could have revealed that inappropriate and illegal arrangement. On June 3, 1961, Marshall was found dead on his Robertson County, Texas, ranch, a victim of five gunshots, a rifle lying next to his corpse. A Texas sheriff quickly ruled the death a suicide. The sheriff's ruling was suspect; it would have been virtually impossible for Marshall to commit suicide by shooting himself five times with the rifle. Billy Sol Estes was eventually convicted of fraud, and sent to prison. While he was incarcerated, Estes vowed to a Texas Ranger that when he got out he would come clean about his cotton allotment dealings and about the death of Henry Marshall.

Estes was released from prison in December 1983, and agreed to tell his story to a Robertson County grand jury in March 1984. Estes informed the grand jury that he had made millions acquiring illegal cotton allotments, that Vice President Lyndon Johnson had helped him to obtain the allotments, and that a portion of Estes's wealth was being transferred to Johnson. According to Estes, Johnson had been concerned that Henry Marshall's intended investigation would reveal Johnson's illegal activities, and on a few occasions Estes had met with Johnson and one of Johnson's aides, Clifton Carter, to discuss what could be done about Marshall. Estes testified that at one of these meetings Mac Wallace was with Johnson and Carter, and after the four men concluded that they weren't going to be able to stop Marshall's investigation by getting him a promotion in the Department of Agriculture, Johnson said, "It looks like we'll just have to get rid of him." Later, Mac Wallace, Estes claimed, was directed by Lyndon Johnson—through Clifton Carter—to kill Henry Marshall. According to Billy Sol Estes, it was Mac Wallace who shot Marshall. Estes also told the grand jury that Wallace had committed other murders to save the political career of Lyndon Johnson, including the murders of two of Estes's accountants, and the murder of President John F. Kennedy. Regarding Henry Marshall's death, the grand jury believed Estes and changed the official cause of death from a suicide to a homicide. In the written statement released by the jury it was declared that the parties—meaning Johnson, Carter, and Wallace—named as the participants in the homicide were deceased and so no indictments could be made. If Lyndon Johnson had been alive in 1984, then, in all likelihood, the Robertson County grand jury would have indicted him for conspiracy to murder.

Barr McClellan has received much criticism from the many people who feel that it's outrageous and un-American blasphemy to claim that a former president was a murderer. McClellan asks only that people take the time to look at the facts, and then decide for themselves what they think. McClellan traveled in the same Texas and Washington social and political circles as Johnson, knew some of the people who worked for and against Johnson, and was privy to the inside whisperings about the true nature and deeds of the man. To McClellan, it was perfectly clear what was meant when two senior partners in Edward Clark's law firm said to him: "Clark handled all of that in Dallas."

These facts, the identification of Mac Wallace's fingerprint on the sixth floor of The Texas School Book Depository, and the testimony of people like Billy Sol Estes led attorney McClellan to his unwavering conviction: The vice president did it.

Cirignano: Did you know Lyndon Johnson personally?
McClellan: As personally, I guess, as a lawyer could, one step removed. I'd shaken his hand several times, yes, and had talked with him briefly. I wasn't ever to his home. I was to his penthouse in Austin for lunch at a time when Johnson wasn't there. The last time I saw him was at the LBJ library when it was dedicated. He was standing out front with Ed Clark and I walked over and we visited for a minute.

From the time he left the White House in January 1969 until his death in January 1973, it's been written that Johnson suffered from a deep, life-threatening depression. Beginning in 1971, Johnson began consulting with a psychiatrist. The lawyers in your law firm became concerned that whatever Johnson told the psychiatrist had to be kept secret. At that time, your senior partners gave you the job of preparing a memo on how to legally keep the psychiatrist from disclosing what Johnson had told him. As outrageous as this question might sound to some people: Do you believe that Johnson confessed to the psychiatrist that he had engaged in conspiracies to murder?

I would really like to know. I can't say, but I know that he had some pretty in-depth sessions with the psychiatrist. I don't know what came out of it, though, but I'm sure the notes are there. I would love to be able to get them.

Where are the records of what Johnson said to the psychiatrist?
Clark would have kept a very close control over that. They are most likely with what I call the penthouse records. On the penthouse floor of the building where Clark's law offices were there were a lot of papers and records that were kept under a very strict lock and key. These were all the things that Clark wanted to remain hidden behind the attorney-client privilege.

In your book, you make it clear that you believe that Johnson did confess to conspiracies to murder.
Well, to me, that was why he was there. When Don Thomas later told me Johnson had an act of redemption, it all seemed to fit together.

You also believe that your law firm set up a trust fund for the psychiatrist? A trust fund to keep him quiet?
That was the way we did business. We set one up involving Johnson's child with his mistress, Madeline Brown. That was just the way we did business.

You believe one was set up for the psychiatrist?
There had to be.

Texas has had a history and culture that's unique to the rest of the United States, hasn't it? Texas's history has been especially violent and lawless.
Texas was born of an especially violent war with Mexico. After that, for years, violent roving militia bands and vigilantes ruled over the counties of Texas. There was an inbred contempt for the law that was uniquely Texan. A devotion to the culture of the gun and the idea that might makes

right. Even into the 1950s, Texas legislators would show up on the floor of the Texas legislature with holsters and pistols. And into the 1950s and even the early '60s there were still corrupt political bosses running Texas and the gun still ruled.

East Texas had an especially rough culture and frontier—a place for fugitives, outlaws, vigilantism, and rough justice. When America's largest oil field was discovered in East Texas in 1931, that brought even more crime and lawlessness. Large tracts of oil land were available for anyone who had the muscles and guns to take them. Edward Clark, Lyndon Johnson, and Mac Wallace all grew up in East Texas, right?

Clark and Johnson grew up in a subculture and at a time when the idea that violence is okay could have readily been accepted by them.

Clark, Johnson, and Wallace also grew up in Texas at a time when the KKK had a lot of political power, and frequent lynchings were an accepted part of a Texan's culture.

At a time in the 1920s, the majority of Texas legislators were members of the Ku Klux Klan. Johnson and the other citizens in the area where he lived would have sanctioned the practice of lynching. Edward Clark's grandfather was a sheriff and in 1908 he presided over a particularly grisly lynching of eight young black men. A photo of that lynching was printed on a handbill and was widely circulated throughout Texas. Clark kept a copy of that handbill throughout his life.

It's pretty much accepted as historical fact that Johnson stole the 1948 Texas Senate race, isn't it?

I think it's just admitted by everybody now. He virtually admitted it, yes. So the people who have attacked me and criticized me for claiming that Johnson was a scoundrel who committed high crimes can look at that election. Johnson stole that election and that was a crime.

You claim you have an insider's knowledge about that election that's never been revealed before. You wrote that your senior partner and mentor, Don Thomas, told you that he was the one who traveled to Alice, Texas, in Jim Wells County, paid off George Parr, the political boss there, and then falsified the votes for Lyndon Johnson in Box 13.

He told me that he was the only one that knew what really happened there. He laid it out for me. Thomas met with Parr and then Parr got him in touch with the precinct chair in Alice, Texas. Thomas himself went there and wrote in the votes for Johnson. It got late, he was tired, so he just started putting the votes in alphabetical order. Citizens don't show up in alphabetical order to vote. Then he started adding the names of the dead. Thomas told me all this because he wanted me to understand how it worked and show me that he and I could do it again for our political friends. He said sometimes you just had to call up a precinct chair, tell him how many votes you needed, send the money, and the precinct chair would just call election central and report your count. He said sometimes the precinct chairs didn't come through. Sometimes you paid them off, but they didn't give you the votes you wanted.

This George Parr was an infamous Texas state political boss. Eventually the IRS convicted Parr of income tax fraud, and Parr committed suicide. Before his death, though, some returning WWII vets had founded a group that tried to challenge Parr's political power in one of his counties. Three of those men met violent, suspicious deaths?

In all likelihood, those men were taken care of by Parr's *pistoleros*, the armed men who roamed his counties, and who stood guard over the polling places on Election Day.

Is there any hard, direct evidence that Clark had Mac Wallace murder Doug Kinser? Or is it just suspicion and circumstantial evidence?

This is where we just have to go with a lot of circumstantial evidence. I mean, it's just overwhelming circumstantial evidence.

Other writers and investigators have suspected that Clark had Kinser killed?

There are a number that have looked into it and they pretty well concluded that. There's some research going on now, an investigation effort that's underway of Clark and Mac Wallace and that Kinser murder. . . . One suspicious thing is that shortly after Wallace was convicted of murder, he got a job with LTV, a military-industrial conglomerate that was well financed from Big Oil in Dallas. Murchison and D. H. Byrd, two oilmen friends of Clark's and Johnson's, were big supporters, and for a while Byrd ran the company. Generally, a convicted murderer doesn't get a good corporate job in the military industrial complex, but Wallace got top security clearance with LTV. Johnson and Clark got Wallace that job.

Did you ever meet Billy Sol Estes?

Yes. Billy Sol is still alive. We still talk.

What was going on between Estes and Johnson? Johnson was using his influence in the Department of Agriculture to allow Estes to get illegal cotton allotments and Estes was paying Johnson off?

I would say there's no doubt in my mind that that is true. Those things were always arranged so that they couldn't be traced. But Estes said it, and that's direct evidence as far as I'm concerned.

In a press conference held on May 17, 1962, the first question asked to President Kennedy was about the investigation into Billy Sol Estes. The Kennedys were very concerned that Johnson's relationship with Estes was going to be a real problem for JFK's administration, weren't they?

Yes, they were. And Bobby Kennedy and Lyndon Johnson had a real enmity for each other. Bobby was pushing hard for an investigation into Johnson. Bobby wanted to nail Johnson.

When the Senate was investigating Billy Sol Estes's dealings and Henry Marshall's death in 1962, witnesses were testifying that Johnson had a direct relationship with Estes and that they had heard Johnson talking to Estes about cotton allotments. It didn't look good for Johnson, did it?

No, it didn't. Estes was going down. And Johnson was going with him. . . . Those hearings got postponed, though, because Estes had been indicted by the feds and he had to attend that trial. By the time Estes was available to appear before the Senate again, President Kennedy had been assassinated. So, then, of course, Johnson was able to use the power of the presidency to block any investigation into his relationship with Estes. That's what the assassination did.

If President Kennedy hadn't been assassinated, was there a real chance that Johnson would have gone to prison?

Oh, yeah. Yes, there was. The politics could be overwhelming in a situation like that. Here's where you get up into high levels of politics. I don't want to say, necessarily, that the Kennedys would have buried it, but at that level, you know, I think Kennedy would have been thinking, "It's my running mate. The vice president."

Was Kennedy going to drop Johnson as his vice presidential running mate for 1964?

I don't have any doubt that Kennedy would have cut him loose if he needed to. There are mixed reports on whether he was going to drop Johnson, or not. The last I saw was his personal secretary wrote that John Kennedy did say that he was going to, in effect, "throw Johnson to the wolves."

You believe that the possibility of Johnson going to prison and the possibility of Kennedy dropping Johnson from the Kennedy-Johnson ticket could have been real motivations for Johnson wanting Kennedy eliminated?

Yes. I put those two down and about three other good motivations that you can trace back to Johnson.

When Estes testified before a grand jury in Robertson County in 1984 that Lyndon Johnson, Clifton Carter, and Mac Wallace were behind Henry Marshall's death, the grand jury believed him, correct? Johnson would have been indicted then if he had been alive?

Yes. The grand jury said that. They returned an indictment that, you know, there were three people involved and they're deceased so we can't indict them but we would if we could. And it wasn't just Billy Sol Estes testifying. A lot of people say, you know, well, Estes is a born liar. He's a Texas con man. Clint Peoples was one of the great Texas rangers, and he worked with Estes very closely. Peoples coordinated the evidence and there were several things immediately available. Like the mugshot.

A mugshot?

Well, on the day Marshall was killed, a man drove up to a local gas station and asked for directions to Marshall's farm. Later, the police had a drawing made up of that man based on the description of the gas attendant and the drawing looks almost exactly like Wallace. Ranger Peoples felt certain that it was Mac Wallace who killed Henry Marshall.

In your book, you include a copy of an actual memo that Edward Clark wrote to Lyndon Johnson in 1949. In the memo, Clark is apparently talking about paying back somebody who had probably made some illegal donations to Johnson. In the memo, Clark also writes that another man has to be "taken care of for good." Do you think that it's obvious that Clark is talking about murdering somebody there?

I think it is. I came close to finding out who the guy was. But I couldn't quite get it. The records are just vague. It happened too far back.

Could there be any other explanation for Clark using the phrase "taken care of for good"? Could he be talking about paying him off financially or something else?
I think the "for good," to me, is all I needed to know that it was permanent. . . . It was somewhat of a small miracle that I discovered that note. Lawyers will destroy incriminating correspondence. Certainly, Clark would have. There are other letters that show that Clark and Johnson had a close relationship, but nothing like that note that shows what was really going on between them.

You've written that it was rumored around Clark's law office that Clark had arranged JFK's assassination. Six months after you started working for Edward Clark, senior partner John Coates specifically told you, "If the truth be told, Clark arranged the assassination of Kennedy." Then a few years later, Don Thomas, Clark's closest partner, also was being specific when he said to you, "Clark handled all of that in Dallas." Is it possible that Coates and Thomas were just expressing to you their theories on the Kennedy assassination? Or do you think they had a direct, intimate knowledge of what had happened?
I couldn't say how much direct knowledge they had. I'm sure they heard it in the law firm. Among partners, that's really privileged information that is only passed along between lawyers.

But when they said that to you, was it clear to you that they meant that Clark had taken care of the JFK assassination?
Well, that's what Coates convinced me of. We were discussing another client's case. We left that, the subject came up—it was a confidential conversation going on—and he just went ahead and said it. But, you know, he said it and I really didn't want to believe it at the time. But then more things developed, circumstantial evidence started falling into place for me. Then Thomas said that to me when we driving back from Dallas that afternoon.

Not only that, but, later, after the assassination when Clark gets his bonus from Big Oil, I go up to see him and he says, "You know, these people in Dallas owe me a lot of money and that's what this is for." It was clear to me he was talking about the assassination. All these things, you have to understand, these things come out in these privileged conversations that lawyers have.

In 1998, fingerprint expert A. Nathan Darby identified one of the Warren Commission fingerprints taken from the boxes from which Lee Harvey Oswald supposedly shot Kennedy to be a match of Mac Wallace's fingerprint. Darby was a highly qualified fingerprint expert, wasn't he?
His record was impeccable. Every identification he made in court was affirmed on appeal. He'd helped the Philippines set up their fingerprint system. He ran the Austin Police Department's fingerprint identification unit. He studied the prints for two weeks, and came back and said he had a match for Wallace, and he was willing to put it in an affidavit. So I had all the FBI required, and that is that a qualified expert says there's a match.

Did other fingerprint experts agree with Darby's conclusions?
Predictably, the fingerprint experts connected to the government said Darby was wrong. The politics involved in the assassination cannot be escaped. Two other experts also disagreed with Darby but they weren't as qualified as him and their assessments wouldn't have held up in a trial. Another expert in Texas agreed with Darby and so did examiners for Interpol in Paris, France. There can always be some questions because some of these print identifications can be difficult, but Darby went over the print a few times and he was always satisfied and comfortable with his conclusion.

You believe that at the time of the assassination Mac Wallace was with Lee Harvey Oswald on the sixth floor of the School Book Depository, and that Wallace positioned another shooter behind the grassy knoll. Many assassination researchers believe that Lee Harvey Oswald was a passive patsy. That he never took a shot. You believe that Oswald was a part of the conspiracy and that he did fire at Kennedy?

I think he fired at Kennedy, and, again, this is drawing on the best evidence I can put together considering the conspiracy I know was there. And I know a lot of people don't even want Oswald there. They don't believe Oswald took a shot. But I do think he was a patsy, and that's what I've tried to develop in my book. It's circumstantial evidence, but I'm very comfortable as a lawyer that you can make that kind of argument to a jury, and that's what I did.

Oswald failed a paraffin test on the day of the assassination. A paraffin test is a test that police give to determine whether or not someone has recently shot a rifle. Oswald's test indicated he hadn't shot a rifle that day.

He barely failed it, and it was contested. But he had gone back to his room in the boarding house and he apparently did clean up there and that can compromise the test some.

Do you believe that Oswald worked for US intelligence? A lot of assassination researchers believe Oswald was connected to US intelligence.

I haven't seen anything convincing on that. There are a couple of agencies—CIA—that researchers are really digging into but I just don't know how it has come out.

The evidence has come out. On the History Channel program that you were interviewed on, an ex-girlfriend of Oswald's said that she and Oswald were low-level operatives of US intelligence. Various writers have interviewed ex-CIA men and ex-military intelligence men who say they knew Oswald was connected to US intelligence. You claim Oswald was serious about being a communist. But after Oswald defected to Russia, the US government just let him right back into America. Wasn't Oswald pretending to be a communist for the probable purpose of infiltrating communists groups for the government, or for whatever other purpose US intelligence wanted to use him for? And if Oswald worked for US intelligence, doesn't that indicate the possibility that US intelligence set him up to be the patsy?

I don't know if . . . as far as I know, Oswald didn't work for US intelligence. You could show me more. You could show me more evidence.

You believe that Mac Wallace fired a shot from the Texas School Book Depository that hit Kennedy in the back, deflected upward, and then exited through his throat. But the doctors in the Dallas hospital who saw Kennedy's throat wound all felt certain that that was an entrance wound—not an exit wound. They felt sure that Kennedy was shot in the throat from the front.

I do believe that the throat wound was an exit wound, that that's the best explanation of the forensics there. The doctors did make a slit there in the throat, and it may have looked like an entry wound, but—

When they made a slit it would have made it look more like an exit wound.

The doctors didn't have any of the forensics. And the forensics, I think, indicate pretty good that Kennedy was hit in the back and the shot went out through his throat.

Even on the afternoon of the assassination, it was being broadcast that Kennedy was shot from the front because the doctors were certain that that was an entrance wound. . . . You believe that the JFK assassination conspiracy was small, and compact. You believe the conspiracy began and ended with Edward Clark, Mac Wallace, Oswald, and the shooter behind the grassy knoll. You don't believe any agencies of the US government had anything to do with the conspiracy? Or that anyone else had anything to do with it?

No. And the reason is, I know how Clark operated. He was very much a conspirator in a number of other things and he kept it very close. And the beauty of it is, as a lawyer you can always claim the attorney-client privilege and really protect your client, if it ever comes to that.

The autopsy pictures of JFK from the military-government hospital had to have been faked. When Kennedy was taken into the civilian hospital in Dallas, all the doctors said that Kennedy had a large gaping exit wound in the back of his head. The civilian doctors said that the President was shot from the front and the exiting bullet blew out the back of his skull. But the official autopsy photos from the military-government hospital showed the back of Kennedy's head was intact except for a small entrance wound. The autopsy photos were apparently faked to make it appear that Kennedy was shot from the back. Doesn't that indicate a military-government conspiracy? Edward Clark wouldn't have had the influence to get the military hospital to fake autopsy photos, would he have?

No, he wouldn't have. But in the trauma that hit everybody when the assassination happened, they could have easily been told by Johnson, who was on the plane that was carrying the body, that, "Look, we got to have this as a one-man assassination." I don't know what happened on the plane. I have just had a little information about it. But it could have happened that way.

You think it's possible that Johnson could have gotten the military hospital to fake the autopsy photos?

Yes. And he would have told them, "Look at it, but we need this result. We can't have any suspicions, or tensions, or an international war, or anything else. Make sure you keep it a one-man assassination."

Many assassination researchers believe that a synthesis of elements in the CIA, the FBI, and military intelligence was behind the assassination. Do you think it's possible that Clark and Johnson knew that a conspiracy was in the works, and when Clark found out Kennedy was coming to Texas he got in touch with somebody connected to the assassination, and said, "Okay. Kennedy is going to be in my backyard now. I'll take care of the assassination." And then Clark, with Wallace, became a part of the larger conspiracy?
I don't think so. And the main reason I don't is I knew Clark's modus operandi, and that would just be extending it way too far. There'd be too many people that could leak information like that. He really kept this close to his vest.

The identification of Wallace's fingerprint on the sixth floor is strong evidence that Wallace was there. But it seems the US government has been covering up the facts of the Kennedy assassination all these years. There are retired government operatives who have said they have information on the assassination and there is evidence of a wider conspiracy.
You see, Wallace has no connection that I've been able to find with the federal government. With the CIA, with the intelligence. Now, after the Kinser murder he was watched closely by the Office of Naval Intelligence for a while and he was given clearance to work at LTV. But I have not seen anything that connects him to the government, and there have been some pretty good Freedom of Information Act disclosures.

But maybe Clark and/or Johnson got in touch with someone connected to the conspiracy and Wallace was dropped down into this wider conspiracy.
See, I can't say, but I can just bring you, from a very privileged position of a lawyer on the inside, that it just wouldn't have been that way. I couldn't see that. I mean, again, you could show me more evidence. But, no, I just don't see that.

You claim Edward Clark received a payoff from Big Oil after the assassination. You believe Clark made it clear to the wealthy oilmen in Texas that something big was going to happen and, so, after the assassination Big Oil paid Clark off because the assassination meant that JFK wouldn't be taking away the oil depletion allowance? The oil depletion allowance was a tax break that the oil industry received and JFK was planning to abolish it.

That was one thing he could easily sell to the oil billionaires, you know.

You were the lawyer that Clark used for the legal work needed to get that payoff?

He had me making some legal maneuvers in the courts. It was a power play. Clark was attempting to get control of a hundred oil wells in east Texas. Clark never said to me, "Big Oil is paying me off because I arranged the Kennedy assassination." But at one point he did say, "This is a payment for a very great service done for my friends in Dallas." He said, "They owe me. They owe me!" After he said that, it was clear to me that the only possible connection was the assassination.

You say this payoff came from Exxon? It's understandable if Clark got a payoff from the corrupt independent Texas oilmen whom he and Johnson had known for years. But how did the payoff from Exxon work? Are you saying that executives at Exxon knew that Clark had handled the Kennedy assassination and they knew that the oil industry owed him a payoff?

No. They would have known, though, that there was a power play going on and would have responded. Clark set it up. The big east Texas field was huge and there was a huge amount of oil and Murchison and his allies—and there were several—would have controlled a great deal of it and Exxon was the producer of the east Texas field. They wouldn't have called up Exxon and said, "Look, we have to pay off this guy Clark because he took care of

Kennedy for us." They would have said, "We are going to allocate some of our production and you're going to make adjustments for it for Clark and he's going to get his way." They couldn't sell that. Exxon would not buy that at first. But Exxon had this huge field, and Johnson had represented that area for years. So Clark could have used that to really put another source of pressure on Exxon and Exxon would have said, "Okay. Instead of you guys getting an oil well in the middle of the east Texas field and producing more oil than we want, we'll make an arrangement and get him some cash." Clark got cash. It's Texas politics. It's the way things were done.

When you were working to get this payoff for Clark, you were dealing with two lawyers from Texas's L&G Oil. One day, you went to meet with these two lawyers and Mac Wallace was with them? You met Mac Wallace?
He had to be there. I cannot say with certainty what his name was, because he was very quiet, but he did resemble Wallace. If I could have had my old records back—and again they're in the penthouse records—you would probably see his name there.

You feel that Wallace knew that Clark was getting the payoff from Big Oil and Wallace was pressuring Clark for more money for the "work" that he had done for him?
Wallace had gotten a divorce, and he'd come back to Dallas. He needed work, and he needed money and he wanted more. He probably became a party to the expected money. . . . But then Clark was having trouble getting the bonus.

So, later, an attorney told you that the manager of L&G had taken care of Wallace "for good"? Wallace ended up being murdered?
Yeah. The exhaust from his car was probably rigged to flow into his car. He drifted off the road and crashed. . . . My best suspicion is that Clark was having trouble getting the bonus, and he said, you know, this guy's gotta

go. And Harry Lewis, the manager of L&G, would have been a perfect guy to do it.

Wallace died of massive head injuries. Was it officially ruled an accident or a murder?
It was ruled an accident. But it was one of these things where they found an empty bottle of drugs with him and they weren't sure. His injuries didn't seem like they could have come just from the accident. As I understand it, the death certificate has been amended several times. That doesn't tell you that much, but when you know who Wallace was it looks suspicious.

Did you know or ever meet LBJ's mistress, Madeline Brown?
No.

Madeline Brown said that before JFK was killed LBJ made it clear to her that he knew President Kennedy was going to be assassinated. Would you say Madeline Brown was credible and reliable?
Well, that's the biggest question with Madeline. Some researchers feel strongly that Madeline couldn't be trusted. She wasn't reliable. I have a good friend, though, and a fellow researcher who was very demanding and he was convinced that she was reliable. But she's really kind of irrelevant to the heart of the story. It doesn't matter. The facts are strong as they are . . . Madeline could have been a witness, you know. The things I've brought out could make a strong case. You could open up Clark's penthouse records. You could open up the psychiatrist's records. The records of the grand jury in Henry Marshall's death. I've laid out things that it would be so easy for the government to go get. They won't do it. The closest they ever came was when Billy Sol Estes was going to talk to the feds. Tell them what he knew about Johnson. See, the US attorney can give you immunity in a federal case, but not in a state case. And then the D.A. out in El Paso said, "Estes starts talking and I'll put him in the lock out here." So Estes said no.

After Jack Ruby shot Oswald, his lawyer was a man who used to be Edward Clark's brother-in-law?
Oswald was supposed to have been killed right after the assassination. When Oswald wasn't killed, that became a problem for the conspirators. Clark could have used Murchison to recruit Ruby. Clark was still good friends with his ex-brother in law, Joe Tonahill, and when Clark got Tonahill to be Ruby's lawyer, Clark then had Ruby under control.

Didn't Ruby write a letter from jail saying that Lyndon Johnson was behind the killings of JFK and Lee Harvey Oswald?
Yes. Shortly after writing that, Ruby died from—what some people believe to be—strange circumstances. People who believe that there was no conspiracy say that that letter of Ruby's was nonsense and gibberish. But Ruby could have known things.

E. Howard Hunt was a Watergate figure, and worked for the CIA for twenty-five years. In the early '60s, Hunt was working with the CIA's brigade of Cuban exiles, and since 1963 many people have had strong suspicions that Hunt had something to do with the Kennedy assassination. Hunt died in 2002, but before he did he left a taped and written statement with his son detailing what he said he knew about the assassination. Hunt told his son very matter-of-factly that the Kennedy assassination was the "Big Event" of the CIA, and that three CIA agents, Cord Meyer, David Atlee Phillips, and Frank Sturgis, organized the assassination. Hunt also said that Lyndon Johnson had the most to gain from the assassination and that Johnson had a foreknowledge of the plan and participated in the conspiracy. Rolling Stone magazine took this story to be credible and ran a story on it.
Well, Hunt's charges would require substantiation and corroboration—some kind of hard evidence from the scene or something that could be corroborated or stand the test of cross-examination. Hunt is interesting,

though, because he points directly to Johnson and his allegations may dove-tail with my own research. The men Hunt names warrant further investigation because they could have been working with Johnson's allies. Maybe. For now, though, my case is still the one with the most solid evidence.

You don't believe that Lyndon Johnson wanted to become a politician to be a public servant, do you?
No. All indications are is that Johnson wanted political power for a purpose that was traditional and very common in Texas: to use the government and politics to get rich.

Billy Sol Estes said that he made millions with the cotton allotment scheme. One could only speculate how much of that might have ended up in Johnson's pocket.
It wasn't only Estes. Bobby Baker was one of the most corrupt figures ever associated with Washington. Baker was the secretary to the majority leader and used his insider's status to gain wealth in a number of industries. Lyndon Johnson was Baker's crony and mentor. Baker eventually went to prison for theft and conspiracy, and if President Kennedy hadn't been assassinated, then Johnson—because of his relationship with Baker—might have gone with him . . . Johnson lived through a childhood of extreme poverty. By the time he left the White House in January, 1969, he had about ten million in cash and ten million in assets. Most of that was being handled by Brazos-Tenth St. Co., an illegal money-laundering corporation run by our firm.

Don Thomas ran Brazos-Tenth St.?
Yes.

How did Brazos-Tenth St. Co. work? Clark and Johnson would take "campaign donations"—legal and illegal—from people and businesses around Texas and Washington, put the money into Brazos-Tenth, and then Johnson would use that money for his own personal life and investments?

The company was set up in the 1950s when income to LBJ was outrageous—he was in the senate and a powerful leader, commanding whatever he wanted. The money went through the corporation and out again, nothing to report. Money laundering at its worst.

Brazos-Tenth was known only to the lawyers in your law firm, right? Has the existence of Brazos-Tenth ever been revealed or written about before your book came out?

Some Austin newspapers might have dug up some information back in the '60s but, as I recall, nothing ever came of it.

Could you estimate how much money went in and out of Brazos-Tenth over the years?

I could not even to begin to estimate the total funds paid in and out. The totals would have gone up and down with Johnson's power. There would be records available—possibly—at the Johnson library or in Clark's penthouse files.

Do you think it's likely that any of today's politicians could be accumulating wealth through a money laundering enterprise like Brazos-Tenth?

The use of Brazos-Tenth as a cover with the protection of the attorney-client privilege was relatively easy in the fifties and sixties. The cover would not be nearly so successful these days. Today, the main vehicle seems to be offshore corporations. I cannot say how such illegal funds are accumulated now, but I suspect that "ill-gotten" gains are going full force. I had the benefit of insider information regarding Johnson. I'm not on the inside with current politicos and that insider information is required for saying how the funds are handled.

Clark and Johnson were first seen pounding the pavement together in Austin, Texas, in the late 1930s when Johnson was trying to become a congressman for the first time. You believe that ever since that time Clark and Johnson were in a conspiracy together to get political power and then use political power to become wealthy?
Exactly.

What would you say to people who say it's outrageous, irresponsible, unpatriotic, and un-American blasphemy to claim that a former president was a murderer?
I'd say deal with the facts. All I'm going with are the facts, as I know them. And I've laid them out for you. You can say what you want to about them, but I think the facts are very strong.

So just because a person becomes president of the United States doesn't necessarily mean that he's a good human being?
No. It does not make him immune to anything.

It seems a lot of people get the idea that if you claim that there was a conspiracy in the government then that means that you hate America, or you're criticizing America. But if you believe there's been a devious conspiracy in the government, you're not hating America, and you're not criticizing the American ideal, or the Constitution, or the American system of democracy. What you're criticizing is the things that some of the human beings and politicians are doing or have done with America.
Presidents are human like everyone else. A president puts his pants on—what's the old saying—one leg at a time just like the rest of us.

Johnson did get Medicare and Medicaid passed during his administration, didn't he?
Oh, he did some wonderful things. I think it was the sense of guilt he had

that he had to do something to redeem himself. I don't think he really believed in that legislation, because he could have passed a lot of legislation back when he was the majority leader. He was really running the country back in '59, '58. Eisenhower wasn't really a politician and Eisenhower would say, "You go on and do what you want to do." He could have passed that legislation, and he didn't.

Does that go for the Civil Rights bills, too?
Oh, the civil rights is just, to me, one of the most clear indications of the character of the man. Johnson didn't give a damn about civil rights when he was a congressman and a senator. I mean, there were lynchings going on, more lynchings, I think, in the county next to his than in many a county in Texas, and he knew about it and nothing was done. Looking back on it was outrageous. It was outrageous.

You think, as president, he got the Civil Rights bills passed out of a sense of guilt, too?
Yeah. His heart wasn't really there. I mean it was where he grew up, he got habituated to the prejudice and the violence, the mores of the time. That's the way he was.

So was Kennedy the light and Johnson the darkness?
Like many, I was inspired to public service after hearing Kennedy's inaugural speech. Kennedy was basically a good man with good ideas who could bring highly qualified assistants to the demanding task of running the nation in very difficult times. I believe he was motivated by solid ideals and was not corrupted in the sense of political graft. Johnson was corrupt to the core but could take the political issues and—like no one else—power through solutions that kept his party together. But his corruption was the worst example of absolute power corrupting absolutely. Johnson had a streak in him that could make him one of the meanest men on the earth.

He had his achievements such as the Civil Rights Act but his methods were far too often criminal—and evil.

One of your sons, Mark McClellan, was commissioner of the Food & Drug Administration under President Bush, and your other son, Scott McClellan, was President Bush's White House Press Secretary from 2003 until 2006. What do your sons think of your contention that LBJ killed JFK?
They go with that. They've read the book. If they're asked, they'll just say, as Scott did, "I have no comment on that." And I've just left it with that. I think it's best to leave it there.

Recently, renowned Los Angeles prosecutor Vincent Bugliosi, the man who prosecuted Charles Manson, has written a 1600-page book claiming Oswald acted alone and that there was no conspiracy in the Kennedy assassination. Now HBO is planning to do a miniseries based on Bugliosi's book. Seventy-five percent of the American population believes there was a conspiracy in the Kennedy assassination, and Bugliosi says that it's time to "straighten them out."
I've read the book. All I can say is if he's trying to be a lawyer then he needs to start over. He's gotten awfully rusty. Bugliosi attacked me personally. I'm going to answer him in my new book, *JFK vs LBJ*. The sequel to my first book. I've written a chapter on Bugliosi.

Assassination researchers have said that Bugliosi has made some clear and obvious mistakes in his book.
Bugliosi made awful mistakes. He starts out saying, "But Johnson wasn't a criminal." Well, he was a criminal. He stole the '48 election. That was a crime. And then he says, "Well, they didn't really indict Johnson." Bugliosi, can you read English? The Robertson County jury said we would have indicted these three guys, and we know they were talking about Johnson.

So you say they didn't do that? In his book, he never discredited the finger-print. So the fingerprint evidence stands. I got Mac Wallace on the sixth floor of the School Book Depository. There's several other mistakes, and it's going to be in my book. But what I love is Bugliosi says, "There was no conspiracy." Unfortunately, Bugliosi, your own client, Lyndon Johnson, said there was. You're saying, "No conspiracy. No conspiracy." Your client's sitting at the defendant's table, stands up, and, says, "Yes there was."

Lyndon Johnson said that.

Yes. Johnson himself said he believed there was a conspiracy. He didn't say it once, or twice, but several times. And he would have been the best one to know, right? So, Bugliosi, you lose. You have just put on an awful case.

Regarding the 1948 Texas Senate race, you wrote that Edward Clark used an associate's relationship with a democratic Supreme Court judge to get the Supreme Court to give Johnson the election. Isn't that how George Bush stole the 2000 presidential election from Al Gore? Before Gore could get an official recount in Florida, didn't Bush use his connections to a conservative Supreme Court to get the Supreme Court to give him the election?

I can't say. And I hate to back off on it. It could have been. But the only way you can really know, in my view, is you have to have an insider who is protected by the privilege. Like a lawyer. If any lawyer who knows and wants to say something about the Bush thing, that would help. But I can't say. . . . The election system is at the heart of our democracy. It should be protected.

Around the turn of the century, many people were concerned that the influence and power of Rockefeller's Standard Oil was taking over the government. Activist Ralph Nader once stated that "The oil industry is the State Department." Lyndon Johnson's closest political ties were to conniving Texas oilmen, and you believe that Edward Clark received a payoff from Big Oil for his participation in the Kennedy assassination.

In the 2000s, did a corrupt oil industry influence a Texas oilman presi-dent, George Bush, to lie about weapons of mass destruction so that a Texas oil company, Halliburton, could get a seven billion dollar con-tract in the Middle East and other American oil corporations could get control of one of the largest oil reserves in the world? Did we go to war in Iraq "for the oil"?

See, I can't answer that. The only way I can feel comfortable saying it about Johnson in the '60s is because I was on the inside. But regarding the Iraq war, I don't know. Again, if someone on the inside would come forward who was similarly situated to me that would make the case. There are probably more than one who could come forward now.

It seems that the same corrupt Texas oil industry that was influencing and controlling Johnson and Clark back in their day is probably influ-encing things in Iraq today.

If you want a connection from the guys I dealt with back then to the pres-ent day you can look at Oscar Wyatt. Wyatt is a Houston oilman. Just now, in September 2007, Wyatt pleaded guilty to stealing all that money for the Food for Oil program the UN had for Iraq. Apparently, he's going to prison and has to refund eleven million dollars. Back in the '70s, Clark and Thomas wanted me to represent Wyatt. I refused, because, among other reasons, I'd been representing a lot of other people against him. It wasn't right. Leon Jaworski, you see, was also representing Wyatt and he wanted us to represent him. Jaworski was the prosecutor during Watergate, but back in '64 Johnson had made Jaworski one of the Warren Commission investigators. Johnson put Jaworski with the Warren Commission to help cover up the assassination. They wanted me to represent Oscar Wyatt and I just flat said no. And for Clark, it was, "Hey, baby, you don't work with us as a partner if you can't take care of what Jaworski wants. If Jaworski wants something, he gets it." Clark owed Jaworski because Jaworski—knowingly, or unknowingly—helped cover up the assassination. And that's when I parted company with Clark. I left his firm soon after that. . . . When I wouldn't represent Wyatt, that was at least one time when I was on the side of the angels. After I left Clark's firm I eventually got religion, you know. I'd been representing the big corporations, and I went out and started representing the little guy. I say I got on the side of the angels because back then I was working with guys who weren't the best people.

You worked as a lobbyist for oil companies in Washington, and have done a lot of legal work for gas and oil companies. How much of a corrupting influence does the oil industry have over our government today? Is there anything that can be done to control the influence of this most powerful of special interests, the oil industry?

My whole thing on it is we have to do something with the lobbyists and we have to do something with the lawyers. They get away with murder. We really have to do something, and I don't know what that's going to be. I mean, I suggested more disclosure. The lobbyists should be regulated. . . . I think we can look at President Kennedy's assassination and come away with at least two things. Two changes that could limit corruption. The first thing is to require full disclosure. What our public officials are doing must be disclosed to us, in detail and completely. Knowing their records could be disclosed at any time may just prompt our representatives to be honest and trustworthy. And the second thing is we have to get rid of the attorney-client privilege. You cannot privilege crimes. And yet they do. I mean, some of the examples are just awful. The privilege needs to go. It wasn't even invented to protect the confidence of the client. It was invented to protect the lawyer's reputation. So he can keep doing it? We have to get rid of the privilege. Get rid of it. A lawyer shouldn't be able to hide a crime behind the attorney-client privilege.

CHAPTER 3

Civil Trial Jury Concludes That the United States Government Participated in the Assassination of Martin Luther King Jr.

An interview with author, attorney, and
Martin Luther King Jr. associate Dr. William F. Pepper

In November 1999, the family of Martin Luther King Jr. brought a lawsuit against a man named Lloyd Jowers. For years, Jowers had been confessing that he had been a part of a conspiracy that had assassinated the Civil Rights leader. During the trial, a Memphis resident named Betty Spates testified that on the evening Dr. King was assassinated, she had walked into Jim's Grill, a restaurant that Jowers owned, which was directly behind the Lorraine Motel where Dr. King was slain. Spates, who was having an affair with the married Jowers, walked to the back of the restaurant and into an empty kitchen. According to Spates's testimony, at approximately 6:00 p.m., the time when Dr. King was assassinated, Spates heard a loud gunshot. Moments later, Jowers, ashen-faced, came rushing into the back of the kitchen, holding a rifle. Jowers looked up at Spates, and, shocked, said, "You wouldn't do anything to hurt me, would you?" Then he disassembled the rifle, covered it with a cloth, and concealed it under a counter.

The testimony of Spates was one of the many reasons why the jury quickly concluded that there had been a conspiracy to kill Martin Luther King Jr., and that Lloyd Jowers had been a part of it.

The attorney for the King family was Dr. William F. Pepper, an English barrister and part-time Oxford University professor. William Pepper had also been a close associate of Martin Luther King's. It was a magazine article that Pepper wrote in 1967 claiming that the US military was committing atrocities in Southeast Asia that inspired Dr. King to begin speaking out against the Vietnam War. After King read the article, he asked for a meeting with Pepper. During the meeting, Pepper brought out photos that showed the effects that the US bombings were having on Vietnamese children. Dr. King openly wept. A short time later, at the Riverside Church, on the west side of Manhattan, Martin Luther King Jr. issued one of his most well-known quotes: "I believe the United States government to be the worst purveyor of violence on the face of the earth." The last time Pepper saw King was in late February 1968, during an informal meeting between Pepper, King, civil rights activist Dr. Benjamin Spock, and future ambassador Andrew Young. During the meeting, the discussion, which was dominated by Pepper and King, revolved around trying to keep the Civil Rights movement away from the radical direction that Malcolm X had advocated. A month and a half later, Martin Luther King Jr. was assassinated.

According to William Pepper, it was elements in the United States government that orchestrated the assassination. Due to racial tensions and unrest, in 1968 riots and fires were breaking out in cities across America. Although Dr. King had always strongly advocated nothing but non-violence, when blacks were asked who was inspiring the uprisings, many of them answered: Martin Luther King. According to William Pepper, the government considered Dr. King a threat to the stability of America. Dr. King was planning a march on Washington in May 1968, the Poor People's Campaign, that would have brought hundreds of thousands of poor people into the nation's capital. King's plan was to have these thousands camp out in Washington until the Congress enacted legislation to aid the poor.

At the time, more troops were needed in Vietnam, and there may not have been enough military manpower to deal with the uprisings that may have ensued from the Poor People's Campaign. According to Pepper, the government considered Dr. King a dissident, a danger, and a revolutionary whose leadership may even have led his followers to physically take over the government buildings in Washington. In Pepper's view, it was the government's perverse logic that it was justified to eliminate one person—Dr. King—rather than to have dozens more be hurt and killed in the civil unrest, riots, and fires that his presence was provoking.

The evidence that Pepper presented during the trial to support his contention that the government assassinated King startled the jury. Beginning in 1993, Pepper had been communicating with Steve Thompkins, a journalist who had been in touch with retired US military men who had claimed that they had been a part of an official Pentagon mission that has assassinated Dr. King. The claims of these retired military personnel were read into the court record. One of the ex-military men, "Warren," testified that on the morning of April 4, 1968, he and seven other Army intelligence covert operatives were sent to Memphis, Tennessee, with specific orders to assassinate Martin Luther King. Warren claimed that when Dr. King was shot, he and another sniper were on a roof across from the Lorraine Motel, aiming their rifles at the balcony where Dr. King stood, waiting for the orders—via walkie-talkie—to fire. When Warren heard a gunshot emanate from the area of the bushes behind Jim's Grill, he and his cohort were ordered to pack up and leave Memphis. Another retired military operative who testified was an Army photographer. For years the military and the government—through the FBI's COINTELPRO program—had had Dr. King under surveillance, trying to come up with information to discredit him and stop his movement. The photographer testified that he was in a building across from the Lorraine Motel and took a photo as Dr. King was shot and fell to the balcony. The photographer claimed that he then swung his camera around towards the area of Jim's Grill and took a photo of a kneeling man lowering a rifle from his shoulder. According to the photographer, the man was not James Earl Ray. Yet another retired military man who testified wasn't a contact of Steve Thompkins's, but was someone who came forward to William Pepper. Jack Terrell worked as a covert operative for US military intelligence during the '60s and '70s, testified at the Iran-Contra hearings, and was a trusted source to top journalists at CBS and ABC news. Terrell didn't claim to participate in a government conspiracy to assassinate Dr. King, but testified that another covert operative—a close friend—had told Terrell that this operative and other black, or covert, operatives were in Memphis, Tennessee, on April 4, 1968, for the purpose of assassination.

At the end of the trial, the jury was asked to deliberate on two questions: one, Did Lloyd Jowers participate in a conspiracy to do harm to Martin Luther King? and, two, Did agencies of the US government engage in a conspiracy to do harm to Martin Luther King?

It took the jury approximately sixty minutes to come back with the same answer to both questions: Yes.

Beginning in 1988, William Pepper had also been the lawyer for James Earl Ray. When James Earl Ray plea bargained a guilty plea to assassinating Martin Luther King in 1968, he was being guided by Percy Foreman, a well-known mob attorney. (William Pepper claims there is evidence that the government utilized the Mafia to assassinate Dr. King.) In 1968, Foreman told Ray that he didn't have time to take his case. He then told Ray that if he didn't make a fuss and pleaded guilty, then Foreman would give Ray—who was broke—five hundred dollars, and within a week Ray could get a new lawyer and change his plea. But Ray was never able to change his plea. For thirty years, Ray had been claiming his innocence and trying to get a new trial. When Ray died in 1998, William Pepper informed the King family that the only way the truth would ever come out in a courtroom now was if they filed a civil suit. It was Coretta Scott King, Dr. King's widow, who gave Pepper the go-ahead to file the civil suit. Coretta Scott King was the first of seventy witnesses during the four week trial. One of Dr. King's sons, Dexter Scott King, also testified. Before the trial, Lloyd Jowers had made his confession in a private meeting with Dexter Scott King and Andrew Young. Both King and Young found Jowers to be believable, "an old man who wanted to clear his conscience." Pepper's current book about the case is entitled *An Act of State*. His first book, published in 1995, was called *Orders to Kill*, and in that book Dexter Scott King was quoted:

> Dr. Pepper has shown quite conclusively, in my view, that my father was assassinated not because of the racism of one man, but because of his leadership of the growing popular movement to end the war in Vietnam, his decision to organize a massive, interracial coalition to end poverty, and his possible role in the 1968 presidential election.
>
> The assassins ended Martin Luther King Jr.'s mortal life. But they have not and never will still his voice, which can be heard wherever people of good will gather for the causes of justice, peace, and brotherhood.
>
> Dr. Pepper's book, in my view, brings us a step closer to the day when the truth about Martin Luther King's assassination is revealed, and justice will prevail, and I wholeheartedly recommend it to everyone who would follow my father's legacy into the future.

Cirignano: How well did you know Dr. King?
Pepper: I knew him pretty well. I knew him only, though, in the last year of his life. And I knew him during the period of time when he was under a great deal of stress. I had come back from Vietnam and he had read my stuff and was interested in it, and he had met with me and that had started the relationship. And then he decided finally to formally, explicitly oppose the war and he did that. And then the Coalition Group decided—and Dr.

King became convinced that this was the thing to do—to forge an independent political party in '68.

The National Conference for New Politics. You introduced Dr. King at that party's convention, didn't you?
He asked me to do that, yes. There were five thousand delegates, the largest people's convention in the history of the country. I introduced him, and he delivered the keynote address.

Where were you and what was your reaction when you heard Dr. King had been assassinated?
I was back in New York. And I was shocked. Just shocked. Broke down. In those days, I have to say, it wasn't expected. He had a premonition about it. But we were naïve enough to think that that wasn't going to happen.

You started believing that James Earl Ray was innocent when you first met Ray in 1978 with Dr. King's associate, the Reverend Ralph Abernathy. What kind of person was James Earl Ray?
He was very quiet. Passive. Even docile. I never saw James lose his temper. I spent hundreds of hours with him. And I never saw him get upset. For ten years before I decided to represent him I met with him regularly to get information from him because I was actively investigating the case. He kept asking me to represent him. I kept refusing until I was certain that he had no knowing role.

So he really didn't look and seem like an assassin to you?
Oh, no, no. I interrogated him for five hours the first time and we were all convinced—Abernathy, myself, I had a body language expert from Harvard there—we were all convinced that this guy was not the shooter. It was totally inconceivable. But we didn't know what knowing role he had played, and that's what took me ten years to sort out.

*Isn't there evidence that back in the '60s and early '70s the govern-
ment—the FBI—was involved with the assassinations of a number of
Black Panther leaders?*

There is strong evidence that there was a hit squad, and that the bureau
was involved in—from what I understand—some of these hits. In my
books I didn't go in depth into, for instance, the Fred Hampton killing. You
see, the FBI would use local police or even Mob guys when they could. In
'67-'68 there were military snipers who were placed across the country and
they were involved in a number of selective take-outs.

*But Dr. King was a reverend, a follower of Mahatma Gandhi, and the
winner of the Nobel Peace Prize. You don't think the government would
have seen Dr. King as a different sort of leader—one that wasn't militant or dangerous?*

No. They saw him exactly the opposite. When they arrested people following the riots in Detroit, military intelligence questioned them and they
were amazed that the most militant radical leaders of that group all named
Dr. King as their idol. This was a real surprise to these guys, to the military
. . . but that's not the *main* reason they killed him. In my view, there were
two real reasons they killed him. Number one, he was a visible threat to
the multi-industrial war machine in America and all of the energy corporations that were profiting from that war in Vietnam. So he was a major
threat to their bottom lines when he came out against the war. That's number one. Number two, the second reason they killed him was because he
was going to lead this massive march which was not going to be a march,
but an actual tent-in in Washington. And that was going to attract upwards
of half a million people. Poor people. From all across the country. And they
were going to go visit their congressmen and senators, and they were not
going to get what they wanted. And military intelligence was *convinced*
that King would lose control of that group. He, himself, was non-violent.
Nevertheless, they felt that this force of protesters would see that this

tent-in was not working, and that force would have turned into a revolution that the military couldn't control.

You first started concluding that the government was behind the assassination when you began talking to journalist Steve Thompkins.
Yes, that started it. He was the first source. There were other sources after that. But he was the main one.

Doesn't Thompkins now say that he believes his sources weren't saying that they were given orders to assassinate Dr. King?
Well, you know, I don't know what Steve has said recently. But I know that they put enormous pressure on him. He lost one job after another. I haven't talked to Steve in years. But I will tell you that Steve gave me a signed, sworn affidavit that everything I wrote about what he said was true. He went under oath to swear it. I did that and that shows what government can do to people.

Do you think Steve Thompkins may have become scared and frightened because he was implicating the government and trained killers?
Well, you know, how it started, Thompkins did an eighteen-month study on the activities of military intelligence going back to the 1920s. And he found military intelligence had the King family and other black leaders back in those days—right after the Russian Revolution—under surveillance. The government believed that blacks in America were ripe candidates for the Communist party. So they started watching blacks way back then. So Thompkins started that research and carried it all the way through up to the present time. Now his article, his story, was to have been eight installments. And his editor got killed. His editor was hit by a car, or something. And the new editor who came in was very friendly to the FBI. And they cut down that work of Steve's to one installment. That front page article came out on—I believe it was March 28, 1993. In that article he mentioned that

there was an eight-man sniper team in Memphis on the day of the assassination. And no one has ever explained what they were doing there.

What publication was that?
It was the *Memphis Commercial Appeal* newspaper. You can pick that up on their website. He wrote that, and I saw that, and I said, "I have to go talk to this guy." I badgered him to help me. And he refused. He said, "I don't want to deal with these covert military types anymore." He said, "They're the scum of the earth. They'll kill you, and they'll kill your wife and your kids." Finally I said, "Look. I got this guy in jail. I'm trying to get him out. I don't believe he's guilty. Will you help me?" Then, finally, he said, "Okay, I'll do it." He became the intermediary. I would give him questions and he would take them off to these guys. And during that process these guys made it clear that they were in Memphis on the day of the assassination with orders to kill Dr. King. There was never any question. Never any question. Everything, word for word, in both books, that I attribute to Steve Thompkins was sworn to under oath by him.

Over the years Lloyd Jowers hinted and confessed to a number of people that he had been part of the conspiracy. He didn't start claiming that just in the early '90s, right?
When Lloyd would drink, he would tell people. And as I gained the confidence of some of those people they would tell me. So we managed to put together about four people we could put before a grand jury and Jowers was afraid he was going to be indicted and that's when he tried to make a deal.

In 1993, Jowers started confessing his story to—seemingly—everyone. Why did he do that? He wanted to confess so that he might be able to plea bargain?
He was trying desperately to get the story out because he knew that we had the evidence and he knew that I was determined to get an indictment.

So, yes, he wanted to make a deal with the King family, and with me so that we would not force a prosecution.

Jowers claimed and you believe that Memphis policemen and a Mafia figure were a part of the assassination conspiracy.

There is ample evidence to suggest that Memphis police were a part of the assassination. Jowers testified that there were meetings in Jim's Grill to organize the assassination, and that these meetings were attended by Memphis policemen. Also, there was a special group of black detectives who always protected Dr. King when he came to Memphis. That group was told by the police hierarchy that they weren't needed on April 4. Another tactical unit, the TACT 10 unit, that was supposed to be guarding Dr. King was also pulled out from the Lorraine Motel on the afternoon of April 4. Right after the assassination, at the scene of the crime, a witness testified that he saw a man jump from the wall behind Jim's Grill, run down the street, and then get into a Memphis police car which then drove away. And there are other reasons. Jowers also always said that Frank Liberto, a local Mafioso, was the one who brought Jowers in and organized the assassination. Liberto was a part of the Carlos Marcello crime organization. He had relations with the Memphis police for years.

Do you believe it was the government's modus operandi here to use the Mafia to set up a plausible denial? That some people in the government wanted Dr. King killed, and so it used the Mafia to do it, and so that way if there were ever any suspicions later that there was a conspiracy the government could say: "Yes, there was a conspiracy. The Mafia did it?"

If the shooter behind the bushes had missed, the military snipers on the roof wouldn't have let King leave alive.

Is there any other evidence that Frank Liberto organized the assassination in Memphis?

Liberto owned a produce company in Memphis. On the afternoon of the assassination a man named John McFerren went into Liberto's store. Liberto was talking on the phone and, apparently, didn't know that McFerren was standing nearby. McFerren heard Liberto say into the phone, "Shoot the son of a bitch when he comes on the balcony." About an hour later, McFerren heard that Dr. King had been killed.

Is there any reason this man, John McFerren, would have lied about that?
No. On the contrary, McFerren had every reason to keep quiet. McFerren knew that Liberto was a violent Mafioso. A number of times, over the years, McFerren was attacked violently, even shot at. He stuck to his story.

Is there any other evidence that points to Liberto?
In the years after the assassination, Liberto use to frequent a restaurant owned by a woman named LaVada Whitlock. Liberto would go to the restaurant everyday. He became friendly with Whitlock, and he used to drink and bare his soul to her. One afternoon, right around the time the Congress was investigating King's assassination, Liberto told Whitlock that he had arranged the killing of Martin Luther King. Whitlock later told this to her son, Nathan Whitlock. Later, when Nathan Whitlock had Liberto alone, he asked him if he had killed Dr. King. Among other things, Liberto said, "I didn't kill the nigger, but I had it done." Liberto also said that James Earl Ray was "just a front man," "a set-up man." Both LaVada Whitlock and Nathan Whitlock testified at our trial that Frank Liberto had told them that he had arranged Dr. King's assassination.

Lloyd Jowers never claimed, and you don't believe, that Jowers shot and killed Dr. King from the bushes behind Jim's Grill. Jowers said Liberto gave him the job of taking the rifle from the assassin and then hiding it in Jim's Grill until it was picked up the next day.
Yes.

At the time of the assassination, did any witnesses claim to see anyone behind those bushes?
A lot of witnesses claimed to see somebody back there. The government claimed that Ray shot Dr. King from a window in a boarding house, but there was no credible evidence that a shot came from anywhere *but* from behind the bushes. Earl Caldwell, the reporter and columnist for *The New York Times*, said he saw someone back there. So did Solomon Jones, Dr. King's chauffeur. There were others.

So do you know who fired the fatal shot from the bushes?
I believe I do.

Do you want to say?
That will come out in the epilogue of the paperback edition of *An Act of State*. In many ways the paperback is going to be almost another book because so much more new evidence has come out since the hardcover *An Act of State* was written. It all substantiates and supports and makes the case stronger.

Didn't the police have those bushes cut down the morning after the assassination?
Yes.

Wasn't that a criminal act? They were altering the crime scene.
They actually destroyed the crime scene. They were obviously trying to make it appear that no one could have taken a shot from that area because there would have been no bushes there to conceal a shooter.

And the police tried to deny that the bushes were cut down?
Initially, they did try to deny it. But, they can't deny it now because I put the guy on the stand who ordered it. The head of the public works department,

Maynard Stiles, testified under oath that he got a call from Sam Evans the morning after. Evans was a police inspector who was in charge of the tactical units that were supposedly in charge of protecting Dr. King in Memphis. Stiles said he got a call and Evans said to get a team over there as early as possible and work with the police and clean that area up and cut down the bushes. The bushes were cut down early in the morning the day after the assassination.

Most Americans might not know, but one of the main pieces of evidence the government had against James Earl Ray is that it claims that after Ray shot Dr. King he walked outside, laid the rifle and his belongings on the sidewalk, and then drove away. If it was 1968 and you had just assassinated Martin Luther King, is it likely you would immediately walk outside, lay the rifle and your belongings on the sidewalk right next to the boarding house you were registered at, and then leave? That seems like planted evidence.

Yes. The government claims that James left the rifle and his bundle in front of Canipe's, a store that was right next to the boarding house. But the owner of Canipe's testified that the rifle and bundle were there ten minutes before the assassination. Ten minutes *before.*

Who was Charles Stephens?

Charles Stephens was the state's chief witness against James Earl Ray. He was a boarder in the same boarding house that James had a room in. Stephens was an alcoholic. A bad drunk. The FBI forced Stephens to say that he saw James leaving the boarding house moments after the assassination. On the basis of that statement, the government was able to extradite James from England. Detective Tommy Smith, though, interviewed Stephens very shortly after the assassination, and Smith said Stephens was so drunk he couldn't stand up and wouldn't have been able to identify anyone. Even author Gerald Posner wrote that a detective took Stephens's written statement a few hours after the assassination and the detective remembers Stephens saying that he couldn't identify James leaving the boarding house.

The infamous Raul. James Earl Ray always contended that some mysterious figure named Raul had been manipulating him, and set him up to be the patsy. The government adamantly insisted that Raul never existed. Did Raul exist? Did you find Raul?
Yes. We found Raul. I know who he is and where he lives.

You feel that whenever James talked about Raul he gave so many details about Raul and about his activities with Raul that it was highly unlikely that he could have been lying.
Yes . . . in 1994, I became acquainted with a woman named Glenda Grabow. In the early '60s and then starting again in the late '60s Glenda was friends with a group of South American immigrants in Houston where Glenda lived. These guys were engaged in a number of illegal activities—gunrunning, forging passports, pornography, and other things. They were a part of the Carlos Marcello criminal organization. At that time, the Army's 20th Special Forces Group operating out of Camp Shelby, Mississippi, was using Marcello's organization—these guys—to help with gunrunning activities. One of the immigrants was named Raul Pereira. On a couple of occasions these guys told Glenda that Raul had killed Martin Luther King. They gave accurate details about the assassination. Later, Raul himself made it clear to Glenda that he had participated in the assassination of Dr. King.

And you were able to get photographs of Raul Pereira?
A British producer, Jack Saltman—he produced *The Trial of James Earl Ray*—he had some photographs of these guys in Houston who worked for the Marcello organization. Glenda Grabow immediately recognized one of the photos to be of Raul Pereira. We put this photo together with five photos of

men who looked like Raul Pereira. We showed these six photos to James, and asked him if any of these men was the Raul he knew. James instantly pointed to the picture of Raul Pereira.

Lloyd Jowers was shown these photographs too, wasn't he?
Jowers claimed that when the assassination was being planned he had met—through Liberto—a man named "Raoul" or a "Raul." Jowers said that this "Rauol" or "Raul" delivered the payoff money from Liberto, and brought the rifle to Jim's Grill on the day of the assassination. Dexter Scott King and Andrew Young were there when I spread out the six photos for Lloyd. Jowers identified the picture of Raul Pereira as the Raul he had dealt with.

You found this Raul and even talked to him on the telephone. Who did Raul claim to be?
Raul said that he had worked for GM for thirty years, and was a retired auto worker. But we checked Raul's work history at GM, and there were long periods of time when he wasn't working. You see, if you're a covert operative for US intelligence you are often given a fake job with some big corporation that has ties to the government. A job that you don't have to show up to. That's your fake identity. And around that time I was working on filing a lawsuit against Lloyd Jowers on behalf of James Earl Ray. I decided that I had enough evidence against Raul, so we were going to sue him, too. Raul then hired two expensive prestigious law firms to help him with the case. How could a retired auto worker afford to pay two expensive prestigious law firms? We also got Raul's daughter to mention that government agents were visiting him at his house, helping him with the lawsuit. If a lawsuit is brought against a retired auto worker, then why would the government reach out to help him? Raul had been an operative of US intelligence. Apparently, US intelligence was intent on covering up the identity of its own covert operative.

Didn't an FBI agent also have some information on Raul?

Minutes after the assassination, when James heard that Dr. King had been shot, he drove away out of Memphis. James eventually abandoned his Mustang in Atlanta. One of the two FBI agents who found James's Mustang was Donald Wilson. When Wilson opened the back door of the Mustang, some papers fell out. Thinking they were meaningless, Wilson put the papers in his pocket. Later, when Wilson looked at the papers, he saw they had the name Raul on them and a list of phone numbers. Thinking he would be reprimanded for taking the papers from the car, Wilson never reported this to his superiors. Wilson also thought that the Atlanta FBI office might bury the information. Wilson kept those papers for almost thirty years until he decided to bring them and his story to myself and the King family.

Wasn't one of the phone numbers on those papers the number of a club in Dallas that was owned by Jack Ruby, the man who killed Lee Harvey Oswald?

Yes. So out of curiosity I brought some photos of Raul down to Dallas and I showed them to some of Jack Ruby's strippers. I also showed the photos to Madeline Brown, an acquaintance of Ruby's who was also Lyndon Johnson's mistress. All those women were certain that Raul was someone who knew and who spent time with Jack Ruby. One of the women distinctly remembered one occasion when Raul gave Ruby a bagful of money. . . . Glenda Grabow also said that on a number of occasions back in the early '60s she saw Jack Ruby with Raul.

There's evidence and you believe that the Army's 20th SFG out of Camp Shelby, Mississippi, was using the mafia—Carlos Marcello's organization—to help with gunrunning operations. You believe that this Army Intelligence-Mafia connection was behind the assassination of Martin Luther King. Do you also believe that this connection assassinated John F. Kennedy?

I would have to answer that in the affirmative. Yes.

You had a lot of strong witnesses during the civil trial. Judge Joe Brown was an interesting witness.

Judge Brown was a ballistics expert. At the trial, he made it clear that the scope on the rifle supposedly belonging to Ray hadn't even been sighted, which meant that the rifle couldn't be fired accurately. On the day after the assassination, even the FBI reported the same thing. Brown also made it clear that the metallurgical composition of the slug taken from Dr. King was different from the composition of the bullets found in the bundle in front of Canipe's. The composition of all the bullets found in the bundle matched each other—but not the death slug. Judge Brown had no doubt that the rifle in evidence was not the murder weapon.

If Memphis policemen were a part of the assassination, then does that mean that the majority of or the entire Memphis police department was in on the conspiracy?

No, it does not. Absolutely not. They are some very good cops there and some of them I've known for over twenty years now. Those cops were frustrated as hell. Detectives like Tommy Smith, who since has died. Tommy desperately wanted to solve that crime. He told me, "A crime like this we could solve in a week. No problem." He was taken off the case. Black detectives who were Dr. King's guards whenever he came to Memphis, of course, were not put on duty to guard him that day.

So it was just a few bad seeds at the top of the department?

Yes, it was mainly at the top of the ladder.

If this was a government operation, then how does the government cover up something like this for decades? If this is true, then since 1968 how many people in the government do you think knew or know that this was a government act?

I think there are significant number of people in intelligence and in the military and in the FBI at senior levels who knew this. And it's obviously filtered down to some others—not the details but just the idea that this was afoot. But there was only one person who knew all of the details, and there's only one person who coordinated every aspect of that operation.

It would seem that if the government wants to engage in a covert operation then it is probably good at keeping things quiet.

They're really very good in a lot of ways. Carthel Weeden was in charge of Memphis's fire station no. 2 which overlooked the Lorraine Motel. Weeden testified that on the afternoon of the assassination two men who had identification showing that they worked for Army intelligence—two army officers—asked Weeden to let them up on the roof of the firehouse. They had photography equipment. So there were two photographers on the roof of the fire station. They were there for the purpose of taking photographs of everybody in and around the crime scene just to see if there was anybody there who might have seen something he or she shouldn't have seen. And there were a number of people killed after the assassination.

You believe that the mainstream media has never made a genuine, legitimate investigation into Dr. King's murder. And in 1999 when your jury concluded that agencies of the US government participated in the assassination, you felt that the mainstream media didn't cover that enough. At the trial you had a media expert testify that the CIA has influence over media outlets and has connections to and can manipulate the media. Do you believe that the government and CIA can control the mainstream media?

I believe that the mainstream media is controlled through a very complicated network of filters and influences. It's not a question of government, so much as it is corporate control. Anybody in government, particularly in intelligence, is a foot soldier for the real powers in this country, the people who run this nation. . . . Rob Townsend was president of American Express, right? When he resigned from American Express—he was fired—he decided to speak his mind at one point and he said, "This country is run by five thousand people." They control, basically, the fourteen major corporations and there are overlapping directorships. And these are the people who decide who runs for office, who gets control in the key constituencies, and what decisions are made in government. And Townsend was a guy who was in a senior corporate position who had to deal with this.

Do you have a special pride that you were the one who inspired Martin Luther King to protest against the Vietnam War?
No, I don't. I really don't. Because it was one of the reasons he got killed. He broke down in tears, you know, I had him in tears when I showed him the photographs of the Vietnamese kids. I don't have any special pride. You know, look, what happened? Martin came out against the war in April '67. That war didn't end until, what, another six or seven years after that. And, you know, we lost *him*. I'm not happy at all. I felt guilty, very sad that I contributed to pushing him further, closer to his death. They were going to struggle on with that war and bleed it for every dollar they could. Lyndon Johnson's advisors would plead with him, would give him a million reasons why America should have pulled out. But Lyndon Johnson had friends and acquaintances who were making a lot of money off the Vietnam War.

What was it like to work with Martin Luther King?
Kind of awesome. He was really a very regular person, you know, when you got him off of the pulpit and you worked with him. He was always consistent in terms of values, in terms of tactics. He was always gentle. He was soft spoken . . . except when he got angry at people like Jesse Jackson.

I've had some major disagreements with Jesse myself . . . but Martin was a magnificent human being.

You wrote in your book that acquaintances told you that they had solid information that if Bobby Kennedy had been the Democratic Party's presidential nominee in 1968 that he would have chosen Dr. King to be his vice presidential running mate.
Yes, that's true. That very well could have happened.

That would have been some ticket.
Yes. But I knew Bobby, you know, and I didn't like Bobby. I was Bobby's citizen's chairman in Westchester County in '64 and I thought he was an opportunistic son of a bitch. I didn't like it. But the Bobby they killed was not the Bobby I knew. I didn't know him after '64, and I regret that.

What do you think Dr. King would have done with his life if he hadn't been killed?
I think he would have continued to press and push for the rights of poor people, in particular, and for a world where there's peaceful negotiation and diplomatic settlements of dispute. I think he would have been that kind of force. I don't think after '68 that he would have necessarily engaged in politics. He was not really interested in political power. He was interested in being on the outside. He was interested in running in '68 only in order to call attention to the war . . . So he was intent on a different path than, say, a Hugo Chavez. I'm friends with Chavez, and I'm writing a book about him now . . . whereas Chavez decided to go the political route and take power, King would have stayed on the outside. . . . King's and Chavez's goals were and are very similar, though. They both focused on the wretched of the earth, and how to cure the problems of poverty and how to empower the powerless.

CHAPTER 4

Was the Income Tax Created to Bail Out the Banks? Is the Income Tax Unconstitutional and Should It Be Abolished?

An interview with former IRS agent and
Tax Honesty movement leader Joe Banister

In 1984, President Ronald Reagan impaneled a private sector committee, the Grace Commission, to look into ways to cut government spending. In the final report of the Grace Commission, it was written: "Resistance to additional income taxes would be even more widespread if people were aware that . . . one hundred percent of what is collected is absorbed solely by interest on the federal debt. . . . In other words, all individual income tax revenues are gone before one nickel is spent on the services which taxpayers expect from their government."

Much of the federal debt refers to the interest that American taxpayers pay to the Federal Reserve Bank to use the Fed's money. When the Congress needs money to run America, it borrows the money from the Federal Reserve; the Congress has to pay interest to the Fed for this money and does so from the taxes the IRS takes from the American worker.

The current American income tax and the Federal Reserve Bank were both created by Congress in 1913. In 1921, William P. G. Harding, then chairman of the Federal Reserve Bank, said: "From a legal standpoint, these banks (the Federal Reserve Banks) are private corporations." In 1982, the Ninth Circuit Court ruled: ". . . the Federal Reserve Banks are not federal instrumentalities . . . but are independent, privately owned and locally controlled corporations." The money that the Federal Reserve—a private corporation—lends to America is fiat money, paper money—money that is off the gold standard, and not backed up by gold or silver. Federal Reserve notes are, essentially, green paper with pictures of presidents on it that can't be traded in for gold or silver and are intrinsically worthless. The Federal Reserve simply turns on printing presses and prints up green paper, and, according to the Grace Commission report, much of the American worker's income tax goes to pay for this intrinsically worthless fiat money. Because the income tax and the Federal Reserve Bank were created in the same year, the suspicion of the Tax Honesty movement—a political action group made up of many people that feel that the income tax is unjust and should be abolished—is that the private bankers who gained a controlling interest in the Federal Reserve and who were manipulating the Congress got the income tax created so that America would have a way to start paying millions and then billions of dollars of interest to the Fed for borrowing the Fed's money. This, along with many other reasons, is what has led the Tax Honesty community to believe that the income tax should be abolished, or is already unconstitutional.

Critics of the Federal Reserve conspiracy theory say that the notion that the income tax was created to pay the Federal Reserve interest is wrong because the Fed eventually repays that money to the US Treasury. Those who believe that Americans shouldn't have to pay for fiat money wherever their money ends up would also point out that through the income tax the American worker bails out the commercial banks of the Federal Reserve system, and also funds the International Monetary Fund and the World Bank, and that all of these banks are owned by the same banking interests that own the Federal Reserve Banks. To those who are suspicious of the motivations of special interest-influenced government, the coincidence of the income tax and Federal Reserve being created in the same year indicates a collusion between politicians and bankers, whether the money ends up in vaults with the bankers or in Washington with the politicians.

The Founding Fathers never wanted an income tax in the American system, and this is another reason that the Tax Honesty community believes that the income tax should be abolished, or is already unconstitutional. The Founding Fathers were the Tax Honesty movement of their day. The main reason we separated from England is because King George III was over-taxing the American colonies. The Founding Fathers recognized that the historical and inevitable trend of governments and kings was to unfairly tax the people. To not have an income tax in America was perhaps the most important aspect of the Founders' vision for America because they saw taxation as the basic and essential way that governments oppressed the citizenry and ruined societies. As one 20th century Tax Honesty community member put it: "Invariably, government—in one way or another—tries to get the people's money." The Founders were acutely aware of this, and so were intent on making America a unique nation, a nation like no other, in which a man would be free to labor and keep the fruits of his labor without having to hand a large part of it or any part of it to government. This was an essence of liberty and freedom. To keep an income tax forever out of the American system was, to the Founding Fathers, a sacred conviction.

It is, of course, the position of the Tax Honesty movement that when the Congress passed the Sixteenth Amendment that created the income tax in 1913, this vision of financially free Americans was poisoned and annihilated. To the Tax Honesty movement, the Internal Revenue Service is the King George III of the present day. From 1789 to 1913 the US government was financed without a problem in the way that the Constitution mandated: through taxes imposed on imported foreign goods. Around the turn of the century, the biggest problem in Washington was a surplus: the government had too much money. But since 1913, the national debt has been steadily rising and now is at an unthinkable eighteen trillion dollars. It is the contention of the Tax Honesty movement that the national debt is a direct result of the debt-producing Federal Reserve System and the financing of that system through the income tax. With more and more Americans finding it difficult to make ends meet, with it becoming increasingly rare for only one spouse to have to work to support a household, the very thing the Founding Fathers would have feared is a menacing government bureaucracy like the Internal Revenue Service breathing down the necks of people with liens and levies, threatening to destroy the fortunes and lives of too many Americans. As awarding-winning former IRS agent and current Tax Honesty movement leader Shirley Peel Jackson has said: "I've seen the actions of the IRS ruin many families, marriages, and businesses."

The Founding Fathers felt so adamantly that there shouldn't be an income tax that they drafted the Constitution in a way that makes it virtually impossible for the government to oppress Americans with a tax. The original Constitution allows for two types of taxes: direct and indirect. Indirect taxes are import duties on foreign goods, or excise or sales taxes on certain domestic products. Indirect taxes were designed to be the principal way that the US government was financed. A direct tax—a tax like the current income tax, a tax citizens have to pay directly to the government—was to be levied only very rarely, in times of an emergency such as a war. The Founders wanted a direct tax to be levied only very rarely because they knew a direct tax is what makes governments corrupt, and the people abject. The current state of taxation in America, a direct income tax levied every year against millions of Americans, was never intended by the original Constitution. The Constitution also mandated that a direct tax had to be apportioned. Apportionment meant that when the government had to raise money in a state of emergency such as war, Washington would send a bill to the states and the states would pay a percentage of the tax bill according to that state's population. More populated states would pay more of the bill, less populated states would pay less. In 1894, the Congress created a new income tax, but in 1895 the Supreme Court outlawed and declared this new income tax unconstitutional because it wasn't being levied by the law of apportionment. The Tax Honesty movement genuinely contends that nowhere in the current tax code does the IRS specifically and clearly say that Americans are *required* to pay an income tax, because the IRS fears that if it did, the Supreme Court could again declare that unconstitutional due to the lack of apportionment. In 1989, the office of Hawaii Senator Daniel Inouye sent a letter to tax protester Fred Ortiz that stated: "There is no provision of the Internal Revenue Code that specifically and unequivocally requires an individual to pay an income tax. . . ." What is happening, according to the Tax Honesty movement, is that the tax code is intimating, insinuating, and making it appear that Americans are required to pay an income tax, and then IRS agents are using persuasion, coercion, intimidation, and guns to force—and essentially trick—Americans into paying a tax that is, in reality, unconstitutional.

There are other aspects of the income tax that the Tax Honesty movement deems suspect. In the past, the government has used information citizens give on their income tax returns as evidence to convict citizens in criminal cases. Regarding this, some highly regarded Constitutional lawyers have claimed that therefore having to file an income tax return violates a citizen's Fifth Amendment Right against self-incrimination. In 1953, Dwight Davis, a high-ranking IRS official, told the Congress: "Let me point this out now. Your income tax is one hundred percent voluntary . . . ." Throughout the tax code, the IRS continually refers to the income tax as "voluntary." The Tax Honesty movement believes this is done because the IRS knows if it refers to the income tax as mandatory, the tax could be declared unconstitutional on the grounds that being required to file a return violates the Fifth Amendment. In 1913, the people and the Congress wanted a new income tax to "soak the rich." Men like Rockefeller and Carnegie were monopolizing American business, and the Congress wanted to start taxing the "profits" and "gains" of big corporations. In the first half of the twentieth century, the Supreme Court ruled many times that the word "income" as used in the Sixteenth Amendment refers to the net "gains" and "profits" of businesses, and doesn't mean and isn't synonymous with the "salaries" of workers. The income tax didn't fully kick in until after World War II when millions of Americans began paying a tax on their salaries, but nowhere is there any evidence from 1913 that the people or the Congress wanted this new tax to eventually be levied against the salaries of the American worker. According to the Tax Honesty movement, there is a reek coming from Washington, there is a corruption or conspiracy in government to force Americans to pay an income tax that the Founding Fathers never wanted, that the Constitution doesn't mandate, that was declared unconstitutional in 1895, and that wasn't even intended in 1913 with the Sixteenth Amendment.

From 1993 to 1999, Joseph R. Banister worked as a gun-toting special agent in the Criminal Investigation Division of the Internal Revenue Service, where his job was to investigate and arrest money launderers, drug dealers, and other criminal violators of the tax code. In December 1996, Mr. Banister was driving to work one morning, listening to a radio show, when tax protester Devvy Kidd came on and began explaining the various tax protester arguments: that having to file an income tax return violates the Fifth Amendment; that there is an absence of a specific law that requires citizens to pay an income tax; that the states never legally ratified the Sixteenth Amendment; etc. "It was my job to enforce the income tax, so I felt I had an obligation to investigate these claims," Mr. Banister has said. In 1997, Mr. Banister began a long and exhaustive reading and research project to investigate the claims of the Tax Honesty movement. "Either the Tax Honesty movement people were lying, or the IRS was lying. I was determined to find out who it was," Banister said.

By early 1999, Mr. Banister had concluded that the tax protester arguments were valid, and that it was the IRS that was being deceptive. In February 1999, Banister had prepared a report and approached his superiors, top IRS officials, asking them to answer the various tax protester claims. Instead of answering Mr. Banister's questions, the IRS informed him that they would accept his resignation. "I had a strong family background and I was always taught that you were supposed to work hard and do the right thing in life. And at that point I saw that the only right thing to do was to resign from the IRS."

Although he was in line for a long, lucrative career, in February 1999, Mr. Banister resigned from his $80,000 -a-year job as an IRS agent. Today, he is considered the most recognizable face in the Tax Honesty movement. In 2001, Banister was interviewed by CBS's *60 Minutes*, but feels that the editing of the show caused his views to be misrepresented. Mr. Banister, who is also a CPA, believes that the Tax Honesty arguments make perfect logical and legal sense, but whenever you approach IRS officials to talk about them, "the IRS won't pull out a chair and discuss them . . . but they will pull out a club."

Cirignano: When you heard tax protester Devvy Kidd talking that morning on the radio, what impressed you about her? Why did you decide to investigate her claims?

Banister: The show that Devvy Kidd was on was hosted by a man named Geoff Metcalf. Geoff Metcalf is a respected, reputable journalist, and, as far as I knew, he never had any illegitimate people on his show. Devvy Kidd sounded, to me, like a down-to-earth, sensible person.

You had the reputation of being a hardworking, outstanding IRS employee and asset. When you approached IRS officials with these questions—with the tax protester arguments—did they give you any answer at all? Did they talk to you at all?

The IRS wouldn't talk to me for one second. They "encouraged" me to resign. To this day, the IRS won't talk and has never given me any answers.

Some people claim that people in the Tax Honesty movement are being irresponsible and trying to get out of "paying their fair share." Is that why the Tax Honesty movement believes the income tax should be abolished, or is it already unconstitutional? Or is it something else?

The Tax Honesty movement believes that the income tax is unfair. We believe that the government should be primarily financed in the way that the Constitution mandates: through indirect taxes. The Tax Honesty movement defines fair as what the law requires and what it doesn't. The lawyers, CPAs, and other tax honesty people that I "hang with" pay very close attention to what the law does require.

And you believe that, in fact, there is no law that specifically requires Americans to pay an income tax.

In most cases. Certainly not for the average American. There are some provisions that apply to some people. But the vast majority of Americans who are working here, and living here—that's where you come up short when you look for statutes and regulations.

The senator who wrote the Sixteenth Amendment—the income tax amendment—and who was most influential in getting the income tax and Federal Reserve created was Senator Nelson Aldrich. Senator Aldrich's daughter was married to John Rockefeller Jr., and it was no secret that Aldrich represented the interests of the Rockefellers and the banking industry. It was Rockefeller and these other bankers who developed a controlling interest in and whose descendants now have a controlling interest in the various Federal Reserve Banks.

Yes. The twelve banks of the Federal Reserve are owned by other banks and these banks are owned by private investors. The Rockefellers and others.

Do you believe Senator Aldrich and the other senators aligned with him started the income tax so that his son-in-law and his son-in-law's

banker associates could start receiving millions and then billions of dollars of interest for lending America fiat money?
I definitely believe that the income tax system and the Federal Reserve are joined at the hip. That they both serve a common purpose, shall we say.

Which is what? To pay interest to the Federal Reserve? To supply the banks with money?
Basically, yes. To have a mechanism in place where people's labor, their blood, sweat, and tears can be harvested through the monetary system.

Critics of the Federal Reserve conspiracy theory claim that the notion that the income tax was created to start paying the Federal Reserve interest is wrong because—the critics say—the Fed ultimately rebates this money back to the US Treasury.
Claims made about the legitimacy of the Federal Reserve are very difficult to prove because the Federal Reserve—I think all sides would have to agree—has never been audited and it's not subjected to the kind of scrutiny that every American certainly is, and even a lot of government agencies are. The Federal Reserve is removed from any scrutiny so it would be hard to really tell, I think, exactly what's done with the money.

The confluence of the income tax and Federal Reserve being created in the same year by the same senator who was in bed with the banking interests seems too convenient for the Federal Reserve System to be a coincidence. The Federal Reserve Bank is modeled on the Bank of England and other privately owned central banks of eighteenth and nineteenth century Europe that had a monopoly on providing their countries money. With all those systems, the way that the governments paid the interest to borrow the money from the central banks was by taxing the public.
So Aldrich and the bankers needed a way to pay the Fed interest, yes. That might not have been the most important thing, though. They also wanted

a way to cover the inevitable losses of the system—a way to bail out the banks of the Federal Reserve System when they were having financial difficulties. So, now, whenever one of the Fed's banks is having serious financial difficulties who gets the bill to bail those banks out? Who has to give millions to the banks? The American taxpayer.

Yes, a lot of people would say that—more than having a way to pay interest to the Fed—the main reason the income tax was created was to have a way to bail out the banks when they're having trouble.
Yes, that could have been the main reason. Now, the banks can make risky loans but it doesn't matter. The public—the income tax—is there to bail them out.

Is it also possible that Senator Aldrich spread the word around that this new tax would only apply to the wealthy, when the plan all along was to eventually twist it around and levy the income tax against the general public?
I think that's entirely possible. Yes.

Did Aldrich also intentionally make the wording of the Sixteenth Amendment confusing and complex so that it could be eventually directed away from the corporations and onto the American worker? The Congress and the people wanted a new tax in 1913 to "soak the rich"—to start taxing the net gains and profits of corporations. The wording of the Sixteenth Amendment is complex, and the tax code is known to be extremely confusing, and now millions of Americans are paying a tax that was never meant to be levied against their salaries.
I think so, yes. The tax code is *extremely* confusing. Even one of the IRS commissioners himself said that the tax code is so confusing that nobody—not IRS agents, not judges—nobody understands the tax code. I believe the IRS intentionally and deliberately makes the tax code confusing because

it knows that if it was clear it could easily get caught stating something that could be declared illegal and unconstitutional. If the IRS clearly stated that the government is levying a direct tax against people's salaries then the Supreme Court could immediately declare that unconstitutional due to the lack of apportionment. Through this web of complexity and confusion the IRS is trying to jam a square peg—the income tax—through a round hole—the Constitution.

The Supreme Court has ruled in many cases that the legal meaning of the word "income" as used in the Sixteenth Amendment does not refer to the salaries of American workers. The word "income" in legalese means the "profits" and "gains" of business transactions, right?

That's correct. That's what numerous cases said in the early nineteen hundreds and to my knowledge those cases have never been overturned. And in legalese, a "salary" isn't a net gain or profit. A salary is an even exchange of your labor for your compensation.

In the early 1900s, the Supreme Court also ruled a number of times that the Sixteenth Amendment didn't create any new type of tax. The Supreme Court ruled that any direct tax still has to be ruled by the law of apportionment.

Yes. A direct tax is a tax that has to paid directly to the government, as opposed to going through a middleman like a retailer or an importer. How could this income tax that the IRS forces millions of people to pay every year—which is not being apportioned—be considered anything but a direct tax?

Phil Hart is a representative in the Iowa state legislature who has written a book claiming that the income tax as it is administered now is illegal and unconstitutional. Hart researched extensively all the records and archives from around the time of 1913 to see what congressmen, newspaper editors, and citizens were then saying about the new income tax. Representative Hart has written that is clear that in 1913 everyone took the word "income" to mean the profits and gains of businesses and corporations and that there is absolutely no evidence that any congressmen, newspapers, or citizens wanted an income tax that would eventually be levied against the wages and salaries of the American worker.

The people approved the passing of the Sixteenth Amendment in 1913 because everyone thought that they were never going to have to pay this new tax. Because the tax code then specified that you had to have an income—a net gain or profit—of, what was in 1913, a very large amount of money. The tax was meant to be levied against those who owned corporations and very profitable businesses. In 1914 less than one percent of Americans were paying this income tax, and by 1939 only about three percent were paying it. But during and after World War II, IRS officials started claiming that it was the patriotic thing to do to pay a tax to help pay for the war. IRS bureaucrats were altering the tax code, and leaving out that the Supreme Court had ruled that this income tax doesn't apply to the salaries of workers. So, then, millions of American workers began being duped into paying a tax that they were never intended to pay. Apparently, none of these taxpayers ever did the research to see if this tax was legal and Constitutional, and today millions of Americans are paying this income tax simply because millions of people before them paid it. . . . The income tax is like a herd of cattle led to the cliff by a few confused bulls in the front of the herd. Those in the back have no idea where they are going—they are simply following the herd.

In 1989, Hawaii Senator Daniel Inouye sent a letter to Tax Honesty movement member Fred Ortiz that said, ". . . there is no provision of the Internal Revenue Code that specifically and unequivocally requires an individual to pay an income tax . . . " So, again, you believe there is no statute or law anywhere that specifically says that Americans are required to pay an income tax? It's not the law?

As I said earlier, I think there are provisions—for instance, for an American who goes and works abroad, and yet retains their US citizenship, there are provisions that would tax that kind of income. And there are other provisions. But when you look at the provisions that would tax the average Americans' labor, they are just not there. There are certainly laws, but the question is who do they apply to.

And you feel they don't apply to the vast majority of Americans.
Correct.

The IRS has claimed that the requirement to file an income tax form is clearly set forth in Internal Revenue Code 6011(a), 6012(a), and 6072(a).
Those codes—and all the codes that the IRS always cites—they just insinuate that an American worker is liable to pay. They don't make it *clear* who's liable. It doesn't come right out and say it. But a law has to be clear otherwise, it's not a law. The tax code is hundreds and hundreds of pages. There's plenty of room there for the IRS to be clear. They could say, you know: "If you're an American and you work and you have a pulse then you are liable to pay a tax on your salary." But as a CPA and a former IRS agent, I know the tax code extensively and I don't see anywhere where it states anything like that.

Does filing an income tax form violate your Fifth Amendment rights, and should the income tax be declared unconstitutional on those grounds?
I think it does. But the way the IRS has created this system is that they're allowing people to voluntarily waive their rights.

Because the IRS constantly refers to the income tax as voluntary.
Exactly. The way the government and the IRS gets around it is to treat it as a voluntary waiver. It's semantics. But in practice they do actually compel people under threat of jail, or destroying them economically. The basic

fact is the people can waive their rights and the government can certainly even invite them to waive their rights but the government isn't supposed to require you to waive your rights.

Through the Freedom of Information Act, the Tax Honesty movement was able to acquire something called the Handbook of Tax Audit Guidelines. This was the actual guidebook that the IRS gives out to IRS agents. In this guidebook, the IRS tells agents to deal with citizens carefully because "An individual taxpayer may refuse to exhibit his books and records on the grounds that it might violate his right against self-incrimination under the Fifth Amendment. . . ." In the guidebook it's also written that "this information is confidential, and shouldn't be viewed by the public." The IRS is admitting there and even telling their agents that forcing a person to comply with the IRS violates an American's Fifth Amendment right.

Yes. The IRS knows all this. I think somewhere in that guidebook it was also written that if a judge ever ruled that the IRS violated an American's Fifth Amendment rights then "the whole tax system could come down." The IRS is lying to the people.

So is the income tax voluntary or mandatory?
I looked at all the IRS literature, and the IRS literature that came right out and said that the tax was voluntary was quite voluminous. In fact some of the regulations, the actual laws that were promulgated by the secretary of the treasury, come right out and use the word voluntary. So I would have to say that according to the government's own published literature, in many cases, much of what we do is voluntary.

When somebody is being prosecuted in an American court and the court is using information the person has given on his income tax form as evidence, and the person claims to the court that that violates his

*Fifth Amendment rights, the judge will say, "No, it doesn't. The gov-
ernment didn't force you to pay an income tax. You volunteered to file
an income tax return." But then, when a tax protester makes the case
that he doesn't have to file an income tax because it violates his Fifth
Amendment rights, the judge will say, "No. The tax is compelled. You
have to pay the income tax."*

Yes. This is more of the unfairness and hypocrisy of the courts and of the
tax system. . . . Federal judges themselves, in open court, have stated that
the income tax is voluntary.

*Even the government is confused as to what the income tax is. Some
judges and courts have said that the income tax is a direct tax. Other
judges and courts have said that the income tax is an indirect tax.*

That's true. And that can be verified by court records.

*We have to know if the income tax is direct or indirect, because that
determines if it's being levied legally, or not. . . . The government might
not care if the income tax is direct or indirect, or legal or illegal, or violates the Constitution, but the people have a right to know because it's
the people's money, fortunes, and lives that the government is messing
with, right?*

Yes. And this is why the Tax Honesty movement exists. You know, the Tax
Honesty movement has a reputation that it's full of charlatans and nuts.
But nobody I know in the Tax Honesty movement is an irrational person.
Everybody I know is a hardworking, sincere, intelligent person. But we
see too many contradictions within the tax system. We believe that the IRS
is too abusive, and that we'd be better off keeping our own money, and
better off financing the government through indirect taxes. We also genuinely believe that, as it is now, the government doesn't have a legal right to
impose this tax on us.

Devvy Kidd has run for Congress and her book, **Why a Bankrupt America?,** *has sold two million copies. One year Kidd decided she was going to challenge the IRS. Instead of filing a tax return, she sent letters to the IRS asking a number of questions: Where is the statute that specifically requires an American to pay a federal income tax? How can she file a tax return without waiving her Fifth Amendment right? If the income tax is a direct tax, then how can it be levied without apportionment?, etc. The IRS just kept avoiding her questions, weren't answering her questions, and just kept insisting that she file a 1040.*

The reason for that is the IRS doesn't want to get caught saying anything contradictory or something that a judge could declare illegal and unconstitutional. And they know they very well could say something contradictory because the system is full of contradictions. So IRS agents just strap on their guns and point to their badges and say that's the reason we have to pay the income tax. The IRS is just using fear and intimidation to force us to pay.

Finally, the IRS sent Kidd a form that declared the income tax is an excise tax and if she didn't pay it they would put a lien on her property and then send her to prison. But an excise tax is a tax put on the sales of alcohol, tobacco, and other products. Kidd's not in the business of selling alcohol, tobacco, or anything else. She's a writer.

Yes. And the IRS tells that to many Americans. People who are late in filing their tax return—they get this form saying that the income tax is an excise tax. But if the income tax is an excise tax, then very few people are liable to pay it. Only a small percentage of Americans are in the business of selling the things that excise taxes are put on. After her experience, Devvy Kidd said "the whole system is a fraud." And she's right. It is a fraud.

The Tax Honesty movement believes the Sixteenth Amendment was never legally ratified. To get an amendment passed into law, the Congress has to send the proposed amendment to all the state legislatures and then three-quarters of the states have to pass the amendment. Bill Benson is a tax protester who traveled to all the continental forty-eight states and looked at the archives and the records of when the state legislatures were asked to ratify the Sixteenth Amendment in 1913. According to Benson's book The Law That Never Was, *not one state sent back to Washington the proper forms required to ratify the Sixteenth Amendment. Yet, Secretary of State Philander Knox reported that the states had ratified the amendment, and passed the Sixteenth Amendment–the income tax—into law?*

Bill Benson has gathered overwhelming evidence that the Sixteenth Amendment was never legally ratified. To get an amendment passed, the secretary of state has to send the resolution for the amendment to the states and then three-quarters of the states have to send the resolution back to Washington confirming that the state legislature ratified the proposed amendment. But the law is clear that the resolution for the proposed amendment has to be sent back to Washington with the same exact wording. Language is everything in law, and if one or two words are changed that can change the entire meaning of an amendment. Benson examined the certified copies of the actual documents used in 1913 and it was undeniable that not one state sent the resolution back to Washington in proper form—in the same exact wording. That could indicate that the state legislatures didn't want the amendment passed as it was being proposed. In two states—Michigan and Kentucky—it's clear that the legislatures didn't ratify the amendment even in a differently worded form— but Philander Knox said they did. Knox didn't investigate any of this—he didn't look into the true intentions of any of the states. Even though not one state properly ratified the amendment, Knox reported that they all had, and Knox declared the Sixteenth Amendment ratified.

Do you believe Knox committed fraud?

Many people who have looked into it believe Knox committed fraud. Prior to 1913, other amendments proposed to the states had been declared unratified because the states didn't send the resolution back to Washington with the same exact wording. Knox even stated that a legislature is not authorized to alter in any way the amendment proposed by Congress. How this high government official could quote the law verbatim and then ignore a multitude of changes is certainly suspicious.

Is there any evidence that Knox was connected to Senator Aldrich or the other senators who were being influenced by the banking interests that could have been slyly pushing the income tax into existence?
I don't know if anyone's ever looked into that. But it's certainly easy to suspect that some political shenanigans could have been going on.

It's clear to you that the income tax was never properly ratified?
If you go by the exact word of the law—that legislatures are not authorized to alter in any way the amendment—then the Sixteenth Amendment was never legally ratified.

Many lawyers and accountants claim that the tax protester arguments are valid and accurate points. Yet whenever a tax protester tries to make these arguments in a court, the judge doesn't allow evidence that would prove the argument, and then sends the tax protester to prison. Do you believe these judges are ignorant, or corrupted?
I think it's more corrupt than ignorant. Or probably a little of both. But maybe biased might be a better word. Because the bias is that there are plenty of law school professors, and other judges and legal professionals, who are of the opinion that so-called "tax protesters" like myself or attorney Larry Becraft or Tom Cryer are just charlatans out to make a buck off of people's misfortune, as opposed to sincere, well researched people who are pointing to facts that back up our arguments.

People in the Tax Honesty movement believe that there is a "judicial conspiracy" to force Americans to pay this unconstitutional income tax. In other words, the judges in America won't acknowledge that the income tax is unconstitutional and don't allow evidence permitted in their courts to show that the Supreme Court itself has said that the income tax doesn't apply to a worker's salaries, and that there can't be this income tax without apportionment. If there is this conspiracy amongst American judges, then where does it come from and how does it operate?

The only thing I'm aware of is that judges do have associations and conventions where they share information. And it's my understanding that over the years there have been seminars or get-togethers where they specifically talk about the so-called "tax protesters." And the information that's fed to them is that they're all a bunch of cheats and lawbreakers and charlatans. . . . It's hard for the average citizen to get five minutes with a judge outside of court, to let them actually meet you or listen to you. Judges tend to be surrounded by prosecutors, and government officials. I'd probably stop short of saying that there's this grand conspiracy where they all meet and say, "Now how are we going to hammer these people?" I think it's more that if a bunch of prosecutors and government officials tell them that this is a bad group of people they just go along with it. They're out to keep their salaries and jobs.

But you feel strongly that the tax protester arguments are valid and sensible arguments.

Well, certainly. Like the legal definition of the word "income." What is illogical, or unfair, or unfounded about pointing to Supreme Court cases that have never been overturned as part of your thesis for a belief? It certainly confounds me why judges don't recognize that.

After the Sixteenth Amendment was passed, didn't Senator Aldrich use his influence to get the laws passed that created tax-free foundations?

These foundations allow super-wealthy families like the Rockefellers to operate their money out of these foundations and avoid paying income and inheritance taxes?

Yes. And Aldrich did that immediately after the income tax was created. So it would seem obvious that he was creating a way for his son-in-law—and probably his son-in-law's associates—to avoid paying this new tax.

Many people contend that super-wealthy people like the Rockefellers can use tax-free foundations and other loopholes to hide their wealth or avoid paying income taxes or the same percentage of taxes that the average working man pays. When Nelson Rockefeller was being considered for vice president in 1974, it was revealed that his accountants had set up his finances in a way that Rockefeller wasn't paying any income tax, right?

Yes. That's true.

A multibillionaire like Nelson Rockefeller can use his political influence to alter the tax code so he doesn't have to pay any income taxes, but armed IRS agents will barge into the home of a waitress, or auto mechanic, or teacher and seize their possessions and demand that they empty their pockets because the IRS claims they might owe the federal government a few thousand dollars? It's not just, is it?

I don't think it is. Not at all.

Former Texas Congressman Ron Paul, who ran for president in 2008 and 2012, agrees with all the tenets and beliefs of the Tax Honesty movement. Congressman Paul, who has a libertarian bent, made a respectable run to be the 2008 and 2012 Republican Party presidential nominee, and sparred with the major candidates—McCain, Guiliani, and Romney—during the television debates. Congressman Paul has said that the tax code only insinuates and intimates that Americans are required to pay an income tax. He has said that nowhere is there a statute or a law that requires Americans to pay an income tax, "but the government believes there is, and they have the guns."

Yes, and Ron Paul is someone that the Tax Honesty movement people really look up to. We feel that he is one of the only politicians in Washington who is telling the truth about the income tax and Federal Reserve. People can sense that he is a knowledgeable, down-to-earth, genuine person, and I believe that's why he's becoming more and more well known.

Could the federal government be financed without an income tax?
I personally believe it could. Absolutely. It was financed that way from the beginning of the country until the early 1900's. And then even beyond that, because the income tax really didn't come into full fling until after World War II. So you're talking about a long period of time. Certainly over a hundred and fifty years.

Author G. Edward Griffin has pointed out—as many people probably have—that if the federal government didn't spend money unnecessarily, then we could easily abolish the income tax. He said if we cut out the waste—if we cut out, for instance, certain subsidies, foreign giveaways, interest on the national debt, transfers into the International Monetary Fund, support of the World Bank, and the cost of running the IRS itself, then the government could operate as it was intended to on the indirect taxes that it now collects.
I'd agree with that. Especially about the cost of running the IRS. There are a hundred thousand IRS bureaucrats that are administering this system, so if got rid of that we'd be getting rid of a lot of dead weight right there.

And Tax Honesty movement leader Bob Schulz claims that the building of roads and bridges is financed through a gasoline tax. The revenue for schools and education is provided for by state and local taxes. The weapons and arms needed to have the military is paid for by a corporate tax which is legal and Constitutional. So what do we need an income tax for?

That's right. The income tax doesn't even pay for what people expect it pays for. It doesn't pay for government services. That's what that President Reagan commission said. The Grace Commission.

Was the Grace Commission accurate? It said that after the money's wasted or lost that one hundred percent of the income tax goes to pay the national debt. Other researchers have said that thirty to forty percent of the income tax goes to pay the debt. Do you think the Grace Commission was accurate?

Yes, because I saw the report. I have a copy of it. Peter Grace was a wealthy man, a successful businessman, and supposedly all the people on the commission were likewise, and, so, if they do a study that's funded and sponsored by the federal government and come to the conclusion that the money's either wasted or transferred from one pocket to another, I'd put some stock in that.

Some people contend that the income tax actually leads to less revenue, and more debt. The theory is that with a large amount of revenue coming in from the income tax, the congressmen become spoiled and greedy, and so they create more government programs, and then they have to raise taxes for more spending money. So instead of an income tax paying for our needs it leads to a perpetual raising of taxes and more debt.

That sounds logical to me. There wasn't a problem with debt in Washington before 1913. It's only since we implemented the income tax that the debt has been rising.

Yes, right around the turn of the century, the big problem in Washington was a surplus. The government had too much money. But since the

92

income tax and Federal Reserve were created in 1913, the debt has been steadily rising and now we have an eighteen trillion dollar debt that threatens to destroy America and the American economy. You believe that the rise of the national debt is directly related to the creation of the income tax and the Federal Reserve?

Absolutely. Under the Federal Reserve System—a system in which we borrow and pay interest on the money we use—it is inevitable that a national debt will incur.

It's not just a matter of the Federal Reserve system leading America into debt, is it? The Congress has to spend less. The government spends money in so many unnecessary, wasteful, and even unconstitutional ways.

Sure. We have to cut out the waste. But the way I view it—the reason the Congress can get away with unconstitutional spending is because of the Federal Reserve System. The monetary system allows them to have the funds to waste because they can just inflate and print and spend money they don't have. They can just have the Federal Reserve print billions of dollars of fiat money. And, of course, ultimately, the people that hurts the most is people like us, working people, because when the government and Federal Reserve floods the economy with fiat money—cheap money that's off the gold standard—that's what causes inflation. Prices will have to rise. It affects us if our money is worth ninety percent of what it was worth last year. Inflation is a sort of hidden tax, but it could be the most injurious, hideous tax of all.

So, ultimately, why should the income tax be abolished and why would America be better off without it?

It's unfair. The officials that administer it are unaccountable. People's rights are violated by the millions. It doesn't go to pay for what people think it goes to pay for. And most of all, it's used as a method of controlling the public, much more so than just raising revenue.

How so?

The income tax is used to manipulate society and redistribute the money. It's not needed for revenue. But, also, through fear. The average person in the public doesn't have the knowledge of tax law, administrative law, and they're having to deal with this agency that can run circles around them even before they even know what hit them. And the IRS can devastate someone with levies and liens before they even know what to do about it. Anyone who's ever been hammered by the IRS knows that within a span of a week you have to learn what these tax laws are all about and that's not enough time.

If people got to keep the money that they usually give to the IRS, it could really better their lives, couldn't it? They'd have some significant extra money at the end of the year. And wouldn't America be better off if the trillion or so dollars taken every year by the IRS was circulating in and stimulating the economy instead?

Absolutely. I think, ultimately, the marketplace and the economy would adjust to people having more money. Prices might go up somewhat to compensate for that.

Catherine Fitts is the former Assistant Secretary of Housing who is now a tax protester. Fitts feels it's not right that Americans have to account to the IRS for every nickel they make and spend, but the government doesn't give an equal accounting. Fitts has pointed out that in 1999 the Department of Defense reported $1.1 trillion dollars of "undocumentable adjustments." "Undocumentable adjustments" means the money is missing. Then, in 2000 the Department of Defense—Defense Secretary Donald Rumsfeld himself—reported $2.3 trillion dollars in "undocumentable adjustments." Is that possible? Could the Department of Defense really have lost a trillion dollars one year and then two trillion another year?

I'm not sure about the numbers. But I think it's entirely possible. I've read enough government audit documents, and even just reports about what the IRS does with the money it gets from the budget. Government officials are notorious for not being able to document what they did with the money. If you go to the Government Accountabilty Office's website you can get hundreds of reports of IRS mismanagement of funds. I'm sure that the military inspector generals' offices have websites and Fitts's statements are probably provable there.

If the American taxpayer is going to give the government about a trillion dollars a year and then the government is going to tell us that it doesn't know where the money went, then that's probably another reason why we should eliminate the income tax, isn't it?
Right. If you keep giving your brother money that he spends on gambling and drinking, you have to stop giving him the money.

Do you believe that the IRS acts in improper, illegal, unconstitutional ways?
I absolutely believe that. Yes.

The IRS has a reputation for harassing and abusing citizens. In what ways does the IRS harass and abuse American citizens?
Well, one way is that they send people notices that are not accurate, claiming that they owe money that they don't owe. And if the amount is small enough, many people would just pay it rather than have to deal with it. Of course, there's the audit process—the hell they put someone through trying to defend themselves against an audit, where you're basically guilty until proven innocent.

You saw this with your own eyes when you used to work for the IRS?
I did. I was in the criminal investigation division so we were investigating criminal violations of the federal tax laws, but I certainly saw the civil auditors and how they would go about doing what they did.

There had been such a long tradition of complaints of IRS agents abusing and harassing people that in 1998 the Congress and President Clinton passed the IRS Restructuring and Reform Act. What was the purpose of that act?
The purpose was to hold IRS agents accountable for improper conduct. It was designed to prevent them from doing things like falsifying documents, or lying under oath, or assaulting taxpayers. Or threatening to audit a taxpayer for the purpose of personal gain or benefit. Things like that.

Do you think that worked? Or is the IRS as bad as ever?
I don't' think it worked. No. That was signed into law when I was still at the IRS. Interestingly, we went to a seminar when I was still there to learn about this new law and it was funny to hear all these IRS agents complaining that it would violate their own Constitutional rights. But the act was passed because the IRS had been violating the Constitution. It's been ten years since that was passed and I've never heard of a single IRS employee being terminated—that's the penalty if they violate these various aspects, they're supposed to be terminated from employment—and I've yet to hear of a single agent actually being terminated.

Do you believe that when the IRS seizes a person's possessions that it has a legal, Constitutional right to do that?
In most cases, no. There are some legitimate functions that the IRS actually has. For example, gasoline excise tax. Or even wagering, and betting. There are excise taxes there that the IRS collects and they have absolute authority in that area.

But with the income tax it's a whole different deal?
Right. If the IRS is seizing some kind of equipment related to a diesel excise tax fraud, then they have perfect authority to do that. If they're taking money out of a bank account of somebody who didn't file a tax return, that's another matter.

There has been evidence and allegations in the past that the IRS has used the Post Office to intercept somebody's mail. And if the IRS claims that the person is behind in his income taxes then the IRS takes any checks that person's written and cashes them.

Yes. And, of course, that's clearly an abuse of power.

Does the IRS have a legal, Constitutional right to barge into someone's home and put a gun to their head just because that person is suspected of something but hasn't even been charged yet?

Well, when that occurs the IRS special agents—the kind of guy I used to be—they will get a search warrant signed by a judge. But the question I would have is was the probable cause that was articulated in the search warrant affidavit true? If they claim in the affidavit that this person made so much money and they were required to file is that, you know, actually true? The judges will sign a warrant and with a warrant the IRS agents have the right to—

But the IRS might not be telling the truth to the judges.

Exactly.

Producer Aaron Russo's film From Freedom to Facism *told the story of how the IRS ruined the business and lives of a family who owned a restaurant in Virginia. The owners of the restaurant were accused of being tax cheats—it was later proven they weren't—and fifteen armed IRS agents barged into their restaurant, told the patrons they couldn't finish the food they had paid for, and started seizing the records, money, and possessions of the family that ran the restaurant. This was all before the family had even been charged with anything. The family was prevented from continuing to run their business; their cars were seized, and they were unable to send their child to college. The man who owned the restaurant has testified before Congress and has said the IRS is treating many people in the*

same way until the people surrender, give up, and say, "Okay. I'll pay the money." Even though it's likely that they don't owe any money.
The movie showed a good example of how the IRS can operate in horrendous and—I believe—illegal ways to devastate citizens' lives. People need to be aware of this. Since the IRS behaves in such ways this is obviously a very good reason to do away with it and the income tax.

Do you think, ultimately, that the income tax and Federal Reserve could be a conspiracy by bankers and the banking industry—the Rockefellers and others—to take the wealth of society? . . . It's historical fact that a very influential group called the Bavarian Illuminati was founded in the late 1700s. The Illuminati was made up of some of the wealthiest, most powerful men of Europe and their goal was to manipulate society from behind the scenes and destroy national governments and set up and control a world government.
The Illuminati. Yes.

There's evidence and it's believed that wealthy international bankers— the Rothschilds, the Rockefellers, and others—eventually adopted this idea of a powerful elite controlling society and setting up and controlling a world government. Back in the 1700s, the leader of the Illuminati—a man named Adam Weishaupt—wrote the Illuminati Manifesto. The Illuminati Manifesto included ten ways to form the perfect totalitarian world government. One of the ways was to have an income tax, and another was to have a privately owned central bank lending and charging interest on society's money. . . . The Illuminati saw that an income tax and a private bank that charged interest to a society was a way for all the wealth of that society to end up with the banks and the government. And that's what a fascist, totalitarian government is—the banks and corporations behind the government having all the power. . . . The income tax—and the Federal Reserve—could be a specific covert plan to intentionally weaken

*the American economy, so that eventually 99 percent of the wealth will be
owned by the banks, and, so, then maybe America will have to merge into
a new type of government: a world government?*

It's possible. The Federal Reserve System or the income tax system—I've
never seen that it's had a beneficial effect on the average person. But I certainly can understand the benefits it would have to a banker. Or to a lawyer. But I've never seen evidence that the average American benefits from
these systems and that does make me question who is benefiting. And you
know the people that brought the system into place back in the early 1900's
were the bankers who were behind Senator Aldrich. And the banks continue to appear to benefit from the system.

*The Federal Reserve System could lead America deeper and deeper into
debt; the American dollar could eventually become completely devalued, until one day there's an unfixable financial breakdown, and then
some bought-off politicians could sign laws that force America to use
a new currency from the International Monetary Fund and that hand
America over to a United Nations world government. . . . Are you a person that believes that there is this agenda or conspiracy to have a one-
world government, a New World Order?*

I've seen enough evidence. I mean, it came right out of the first President
Bush's mouth—he used the term New World Order. Government officials
have used the term. And I certainly see a progression—all of Europe now
has the European Union, this European super-state that is destroying the
sovereignties of the individual European nations. Most people might not
know, but there's a move afoot to do the same in North America—to have
Canada, America, and Mexico merge into a North American Union. There's
an agenda in the US government to do that. I have yet to see that a bunch
of grassroots Americans are getting out there and pushing for a North
American Union. It doesn't seem to be from the ground up. It's coming from
the top—from the banks and corporations that control the governments.

When Karl Marx and others founded the Communist movement in 1848, they seemed to be just following the agenda of the Illuminati to create a totalitarian world government. Marx wrote the Communist Manifesto, and the ten planks of the Communist Manifesto—the ten ways to get to the perfect Communist world government—were just about exactly the same as the Illuminati Manifesto. One plank was to have an income tax, and another plank was to have a privately owned central bank.

Yes. The communists loved the income tax.

In 1956, T. Coleman Andrews, a commissioner of the IRS said: "We're confiscating property now." That's socialism. It's written into the **Communist Manifesto.** *There's evidence and it's in all likelihood true that the Rothschilds, Rockefellers, and other international bankers financed Russia's Communist Revolution and that Communism was an attempt by the super wealthy international bankers to get to world government. Is it possible that the Rockefellers and the banking industry have used their influence over the US government to go by the Illuminati Manifesto and the Communist Manifesto here—to establish an income tax that destroys the middle class, seizes the possessions and the wealth of the public, and transfers the wealth of the country into the hands of a wealthy elite—the banks?*

I think it's very possible. When I was first doing my research while I was still working for the IRS, I didn't know what the planks of the Communist Manifesto were, let alone what was in them. But what I thought was odd was in America we have the Constitution, the Declaration of Independence, and the writings of the Founders, and you compare what they advocated to what was advocated in the planks of the Communist Manifesto, and I thought it was very ironic that the income tax was something advocated and supported by the communists. And yet the founders of this country, and the founding documents, were completely the opposite. The Founding Fathers abhorred the income tax.

The Founders wrote the Constitution in an airtight, ironclad way that prevents the government from oppressing us with a tax, and in a way that allows us to keep our liberties and freedoms, and now the government is going against the Constitution.

Right. And to the Communists, the income tax was their darling.

On May 30, 1985, President Ronald Reagan said, "Thirty and forty years ago, you didn't hear people brag at social get-togethers about how they got their tax bill down by exploiting a loophole. But now you do. And it's not considered bad behavior. After all, goes this thinking, what's immoral about cheating a system that is itself a cheat? That isn't a sin, it's a duty. . . . Our federal tax system is, in short, utterly impossible, utterly unjust, and completely counterproductive. It's earned a rebellion, and it's time we rebelled." This seems like a cause that wouldn't be hard to get a lot of people to support. This isn't some eccentric notion. Many people would probably agree that the IRS is too abusive, and the great majority of people would probably agree that we'd be better off without the IRS and an income tax.

Right, but as soon as people begin to speak up about it, then they come and get hammered. The government comes after them. It's happened to me, it's happened to Tom Cryer, to Sherry Jackson. People who have tried to speak up—especially people with extra credibility like people who used to work for the IRS—there's a mechanism in place to hunt those people down and to either destroy them economically, or discredit them, or imprison them. Whatever it takes to silence the message.

Bob Dole once suggested that we should eliminate the IRS. One of the Republican House majority leaders said that the income tax should be done away with. Many mainstream politicians would probably have no problem with the idea that we should eliminate the IRS and income tax.

True, but it's easy to say something like that, but when you actually look at what they do to further that, you can see that they do nothing. It sounds good, and that's a typical politician telling you what you want to hear, but then he goes right back to business as usual.

Maybe they feel the established tax system is too entrenched for them to change. Or maybe these politicians are just talking out of their hind end. Pretty much. That's pretty much the case. Somebody like Ron Paul will actually say something like that and actually work towards implementing it.

Some politicians have talked against the income tax, but a lot of them probably like it. It probably puts the politicians on a big power trip because they get to handle billions and billions of dollars. Plus, a lot of them probably get elected by promising their constituents some multibillion dollar aid program. So with these politicians, there's probably no hope of stopping the income tax. Yes. Certainly. And that has to be a big part of the problem.

Many people in the Tax Honesty movement believe that the best way to fight the government is to be willing to go to prison for the cause. They believe that tax protesters should not file an income tax form, then try to make the IRS and government admit in the courts that the income tax is illegal, and if the tax protesters lose in the courts then they should be willing to fill up the prisons to show that the Tax Honesty movement is serious and means business. I'm not real fervent in pushing people to do something other than to educate themselves. I certainly don't push people to file, or not to file, to pay, or not to pay. I just try to push people to learn what the truth is, and then hope that once they learn the truth then their own conscience will tell them what to do next. Yes, there are people that are saying, you know, "Rah, rah. Stop paying them. Stop feeding the beast." Everybody kind of has their own way of looking at it. But, to me, I used to investigate people to put them in jail and if they were truly breaking laws I'd still be doing that. But the fact that these people are not breaking laws and the IRS is just prosecuting them to scare the rest of the public—I'm trying to expose that. But, ultimately, if I don't have enough Americans around me who are concerned about that, then we probably never will get a change.

Instead of tax protesters going to prison "for the cause," might it not be a better idea to get a few million, or five million, or ten million people to join a tax protester group and then lobby the Congress, or march on Washington? It shouldn't be difficult to get a lot of people to join up for this cause. One lawyer who is also a CPA once said that all the tax protester arguments make perfect legal sense, and the only reason the government can force us to pay the income tax is because "the government has a bigger stick." If a few million tax protesters marched on Washington then the people's stick would start to look as big as the government's stick and then maybe something would be done about stopping this unfair tax that the people and the Founding Fathers never wanted.

It'd be nice. But I've encountered in my life, both as a CPA and as a special agent and now as a citizen, that the fear level is just monstrous. And I think that that's been put there over sixty or seventy years of publicity—of the IRS just devastating people. So there's just such a huge fear that it's difficult to get people to listen to the truth. They're just so fearful about the consequences.

Maybe we should have gotten Ron Paul elected president.
He's great because people really listen to what he has to say. He's very articulate. And he always has very sturdy, solid reasons for his beliefs and his statements. And I think that appeals to people. Unlike a Bob Dole, when Ron Paul says something is true, he'll actually work to implement it.

It'd be great if more politicians like Ron Paul came forward. Paul did respectably with his 2008 and 2012 presidential campaign. He developed a loyal following. Maybe that's a good sign there.

I hope so. At least, he's certainly opened up the eyes of more and more people.

CHAPTER 5

Is the Federal Reserve Bank Bad for America's Economy? Is the Federal Reserve Unconstitutional and Should It Be Abolished?

An interview with The Creature from Jekyll Island
author G. Edward Griffin

Thomas Jefferson once said, "I sincerely believe that banking institutions are more dangerous to our liberties than standing armies, and that the principle of spending money to be paid by posterity, under the name of funding, is but swindling futurity on a large scale. The issuing power should be taken from the banks and be restored to the people to whom it properly belongs."

Most Americans might not realize it, but the Federal Reserve Bank is precisely the kind of banking institution that Thomas Jefferson didn't want. Over the years, many judges and courts have ruled that the Federal Reserve Banks are private corporations. In 1982, the Ninth Circuit Court decreed: ". . . the Federal Reserve Banks . . . are independent, privately owned and locally controlled corporations." The Federal Reserve Banks are owned by the commercial banks of the Federal Reserve System and these commercial banks are owned by private individuals. When Congress needs money to run America, it borrows the money and pays interest to the Federal Reserve. Because America doesn't issue its own money—as Thomas Jefferson wanted—whenever we borrow money from the Federal Reserve, America goes further into debt. We now have an eighteen trillion dollar debt that threatens to destroy the country. Because of the financial system and the banking institution—the Federal Reserve Bank—that has a monopoly on supplying America's money, America has swindled its "futurity on a large scale."

The way that the Federal Reserve Bank was created causes many people to believe that the entire matter is a conspiracy. Or more of an open secret. In 1910, seven men—some of the most powerful banking officials in the world who represented the biggest banks on Wall Street—took a trip to attend a meeting at a resort in Jekyll Island, Georgia. Senator Nelson Aldrich, the head of the Senate Finance Committee, and Abram Andrew, the assistant secretary of the Treasury, were also part of this group. The banking officials represented banks that were owned and controlled by the wealthiest banking dynasties in the world: the Rothschilds, the Rockefellers, the Morgans, the Warburgs. No reporters were allowed near the group, the meeting was held in secret, and the men were told not to speak to anyone after the meeting concluded. The purpose of the meeting was to form the Federal Reserve Bank. The bankers knew that if it was known that representatives of the big Wall Street banks were meeting to form a central bank that that would be unacceptable to the American public. At that time, more and more of the nation's banking business was being taken over by rural, local banks and taken away from the Wall Street Banks. The Federal Reserve Banks are owned by the big New York banks and one of the things that the Federal Reserve did was give a monopoly and a firmer control of the nation's banking business to Wall Street. Also, at that time, more and more businessmen and businesses were financing their own business ventures without having to borrow money from banks. Another thing that the Federal Reserve did was to make money more elastic—to make it easier for the banks to have plenty of money to lend to businesses and borrowers so that the banks are receiving endless streams of interest payments. The Federal Reserve Banks are allowed to print money—they are allowed to, in effect, create money out of nothing. This allows the banks to have endless amounts of money and lure borrowers into loans so that millions of businesses and homeowners are paying the banks billions of dollars of interest.

The very name "Federal Reserve" was meant to be misleading. The bankers wanted the public to believe that the new central bank was a government agency created to guard and protect the economic health of the country. The real purpose behind the Federal Reserve, though, was to give the Wall Street banks a monopoly over the banking industry and to give the banks the right to create money out of nothing so they could lure the public into interest-bearing loans. The "Federal" Reserve isn't federal; the Federal Reserve banks are privately owned. Neither does the Federal "Reserve" have any reserves. It creates money out of nothing. Under the Federal Reserve System, if a commercial bank of the Federal Reserve System has $1 billion dollars, it is allowed to lend out $10 billion dollars. The bank just types numbers into a computer and that becomes money that it lends out and charges interest on. Money becomes numbers typed into a computer; the banks create money out of thin air. They have no real reserves. "Federal Reserve" is a misnomer.

On December 23, 1913, when most senators and congressmen were away for the Christmas holiday, Senator Nelson Aldrich used his influence over the politicians who were present to surreptitiously get the Federal Reserve Act passed, and the Federal Reserve Bank was born. The Federal Reserve Banks and Federal Reserve Board act independently of the government, and the interest rates that they set and the banking policies that they adopt have more power than the Congress or the president to control the lives—the economic well-being or economic problems, the employment or unemployment—of the American people. So, since 1913 America and the lives of millions of Americans have been controlled by a private corporation. Right before the Federal Reserve Act was passed, Congressman Charles

A. Lindbergh, the father of the famous aviator, said, "This Federal Reserve Act establishes the most gigantic trust on earth. When President Wilson signs this bill, the invisible government of the monetary power will be unleashed. . . . The worst legislative crime of the ages is perpetrated by this banking and currency bill." And in 1932, Congressman Louis T. McFadden, the chairman of the United States House Committee on Banking and Currency, said, "We have, in this country, one of the most corrupt institutions the world has ever known. I refer to the Federal Reserve Board. This evil institution has impoverished the people of the United States and has practically bankrupted our government. It has done this through the corrupt practices of the moneyed vultures who control it."

Critics of the system say that that the nature of the Federal Reserve will inevitably destroy the American economy with debt and inflation. If the government isn't issuing its own money—if the government is existing on borrowed money—then the debt and the interest on the debt will continually and inevitably rise. The money that the Federal Reserve lends to America isn't on the gold standard. When the commercial banks of the Federal Reserve System create money out of nothing—when the banks type numbers into a computer and lend out more money than they actually have—this money isn't, of course, on the gold standard either and will cause billions of more checkbook money to circulate in the American economy. When too much paper money off the gold standard is circulating in a society, that will cause prices to rise and destroy an economy through inflation. The antidote to all this debt and inflation is simple: abolish the Federal Reserve and get back to the Constitution. Thomas Jefferson and the Founding Fathers understood clearly that America being dependent on a central bank and borrowing money from a central bank would destroy America with debt and swindle America's "futurity on a large scale," so, the Founders put into the Constitution that "only Congress shall coin and regulate the currency." According to the Constitution, the government is supposed to raise money through excise and import taxes and that's to be the money that finances America. If the government raised its own money and stopped borrowing money, then there wouldn't have to be a debt.

The Founders also understood that too much of a paper currency will lead to crippling inflation. During the Revolutionary War the Americans colonies printed millions of dollars of paper money to finance the war and this caused severe hyper-inflation in the 1770s; the term "coin" in the Constitution refers to gold and silver, and, so, according to the Constitution only gold and silver is to be used as money. There's only so much gold in the world, so if money is gold—if a nation's currency stays on the gold standard—then there can't be too much money causing inflation. If America raised its own money and if that money remained on the gold standard, then there would be no debt, no inflation, and America could have a healthy economy. But because Wall Street controls our politicians and government, the banking industry has been able to foist a scamming, economy-destroying financial system on America: the Federal Reserve Bank.

Many of the thousands or millions of people who believe that the Federal Reserve Bank is bad for America believe it because of author G. Edward Griffin's book *The Creature from Jekyll Island*. *The Creature from Jekyll Island* and the tape of the book have sold more than a million copies worldwide. Former Texas Congressman Ron Paul recommends *The Creature from Jekyll Island* in his *New York Times* number one bestseller *The Revolution: A Manifesto*. Congressman Paul has called the book, "A superb analysis." In the bibliography to his tome, Mr. Griffin lists 250 books on economics, banking, politics, and history as sources for his work. To the many people who believe that the Federal Reserve doesn't have the right to charge America interest for printing up green pieces of paper with pictures of presidents on it, that the Federal Reserve is good for the banks and bad for everybody else, and that the Federal Reserve is leading America into economic disaster they are citing facts and data "because G. Edward Griffin has done the research."

Cirignano: The commercial banks of the Federal Reserve System own the Federal Reserve Banks, so the Federal Reserve is always going to operate in a way that profits the banks regardless of how that effects the welfare of the American people, isn't it?. . . . Officials who work for the banking industry are running the Federal Reserve. . . . In other words, if the Fed wants to raise interest rates so the banks profit more, then the Fed will do that even if it means many Americans won't be able to pay their bills and the American money supply will be contracted—there will be less money circulating in the American economy—which will lead to an unhealthy economy?

Griffin: Well, absolutely, yes. When there is a conflict between the advantages of the Federal Reserve System or the purpose of the nation at large there has to be no choice. The Fed always goes for the purposes of the banks.

The interest rates that the Fed sets is perhaps the most important factor effecting our economy, correct? And even a tiny raising of interest rates can cause real problems for the economy and the public. If the Fed raises interest rates a little, that causes more money to flow into the banks, less money will be circulating amongst the public, and that small act can cause recessions, depressions, and unemployment.

Oh, absolutely. Our system of credit determines how much money is circulating in America. The actions of the Federal Reserve can devastate the economy.

Some people would say, though, that the Federal Reserve chairman runs the Federal Reserve and he's appointed by the president and has to be approved by the Senate. So isn't there democratic input and control there from elected officials?

Since the Federal Reserve was created in 1913, every Federal Reserve chairman has been someone who has come from the banking industry, and is a friend and agent of the banks. Some years, when it's time for the president to pick a new Federal Reserve chairman, Federal Reserve banking officials will actually give the president a list of names of men who come from banking and the president picks somebody from that list. The Federal Reserve chairman is always someone who is, basically, working for the banks. There have been no exceptions.

In your opinion, is the Federal Reserve Bank unconstitutional?
Many people would claim that the Federal Reserve Bank is unconstitutional because the Constitution states that "only Congress shall coin and regulate the money." I also think the Federal Reserve System as it is constituted today is unconstitutional because we are forced to be part of the Federal Reserve System. If it was voluntary, then it would be Constitutional.

In America, we don't use a debt-free currency. When the Congress needs money to run America, it gets the money—in most cases—from the Federal Reserve. The Congress, in reality, is borrowing this money from the Fed, and when it's paid back the American taxpayers have to pay interest on it. So whenever we get money from the Federal Reserve, America goes into debt. One of the main claims of people who believe in the Federal Reserve conspiracy theory is that the Federal Reserve System is the cause of America's national debt. Is that true? Is America's eighteen trillion dollar debt a direct result of the Federal Reserve System— of the fact that we have to pay interest on the money we use?
That's not entirely true. It is true that as long as the Federal Reserve System exists America will have to be in debt. But first let me address this notion that the Federal Reserve is a conspiracy. There's no conspiracy here. Everything is out in the open. The Federal Reserve and the government don't want people to know too much about it, but anybody's who's a student and really wants to understand this can go to any well-stocked library. Books about the Federal Reserve are certainly not hidden from view. There's no conspiracy.

It's not so much a conspiracy, as it is a corrupt banking system.
It's a very corrupt banking system that survives, to a large extent, because of ignorance on the part of the people.

So, the many people who believe the Federal Reserve is a corrupt banking system believe this system is the cause of America's enormous national debt.
As long as the Federal Reserve System exists America will be in perpetual debt.

But most of the national debt isn't owed to the Federal Reserve, right?
The Fed *facilitates* the debt. The government has to borrow money. But many people don't realize that most of the national debt is borrowed from the public. It's borrowed from people, or from corporations, from investment funds and other governments and all kinds of institutions. Only a relatively small portion of the national debt is borrowed from the Federal Reserve.

So all these people who say, "The Fed causes the national debt"—that's not exactly right.
Not exactly right. The Federal Reserve makes it possible, because the Fed allows the interest rates to be artificially low. On that basis, the government can borrow more money because the interest rate is low.

Would it be more accurate to say that because we're locked into this Federal Reserve System, because we're locked into a system in which the government doesn't issue its own money, then the government has to borrow money to operate and that's the cause of the national debt?
That might be a better way of putting it.

The Congress could and should just issue America's currency, right? We don't need the Federal Reserve, a private bank—or any other institution—charging us interest to use its money. The government could raise

money through excise and import taxes and simply issue a debt-free currency, right? That would go a long way in solving the problem of debt.
The government should issue a currency based on gold or silver. That's the way the Founders designed it according to the Constitution. We don't need the Federal Reserve, at all.

The debt can't be paid off, can it? The debt is eighteen trillion dollars, but there probably isn't even eighteen trillion dollars circulating in the American economy. Tax revenue isn't going to satisfy the debt, so to pay off the debt we'll have to borrow more money and go further into debt. So it's impossible to pay off the debt, isn't it?
But, also, you see, because of the Federal Reserve System every dollar circulating in America has been borrowed into existence. And has to be paid back. When the government gets money from the Federal Reserve—or from anywhere else—every one of those dollars, of course, has to be paid back. Our money supply is tied to debt. Our money supply *is* debt. As long as the Federal Reserve System exists America *must* be in debt. And, so, if every dollar was paid back then all money would go back to from where it came and there wouldn't be one penny circulating in America. The debt can't possibly be paid off. The debt is a farce.

The way the Federal Reserve operates seems like an utter scam. The way our money system works is like this: say the Congress needs some money—say the government needs a billion dollars. The government will give the Federal Reserve a billion dollars worth of government bonds—a promise to pay back the money—and the Federal Reserve just prints up a billion dollars worth of Federal Reserve notes for the government. The Federal Reserve's money isn't backed up by gold, of course, and, so, the Federal Reserve just has to pay for the paper and ink to print up those notes—something like two cents a bill, whether the bill is one dollar or one hundred dollars—and then gets a billion dollars worth of government bonds. So through those bonds, the Federal Reserve Banks—privately owned corporations—become a billion dollars richer. But to get that billion dollars the Federal Reserve just had to spend a few thousand dollars printing up green paper, right?

Yes. But most of the time they don't even print up currency. Most of the time it's checkbook money. The Federal Reserve just has to turn on a computer and type in a one with a lot of zeros after it. Then the government has a billion dollars worth of credit and the Federal Reserve banks have received those billion dollars worth of government bonds.

The Federal Reserve is, of course, paid back that billion dollars and then also charges interest on all that credit?

Yes.

So the Federal Reserve gets a billion dollars worth of government bonds, is paid back its billion dollars—which it created out of nothing—and charges interest on that for, essentially, doing nothing?

Well, basically, that's it. Yeah.

That's some deal, isn't it? That's some racket. How does the Federal Reserve get away with that? How does the Federal Reserve just spend a few thousand dollars on ink and paper or just type some zeros into a computer and get billions and trillions of dollars worth of government bonds in return, and get to charge interest on billions and trillions of dollars that it creates out of nothing?

Well, they get away with it because nobody's watching. Nobody seems to care. And most people don't really understand what's going on. . . . Also, of course, once the government has borrowed money from the Fed and it's distributed out, that money is eventually going to be deposited in the commercial banks of the Federal Reserve System. Those Federal Reserve member banks will then start lending that money out with interest. And through fractional reserve banking those banks can lend out ten times as much money as they have and charge interest on that. So this system allows the banks to create billions and trillions of dollars out of nothing and charge interest on it all.

These old banking families of Europe had been setting up privately owned central banks like the Federal Reserve since the Bank of England was chartered in 1694. William Paterson, the first director of the Bank of England, once remarked, "The bank hath benefit of interest on all moneys which it creates out of nothing."

This has been and is really a scam and a racket between politicians and bankers. Politicians always promise the public favors. Governments always need money to operate. But politicians don't like to raise taxes because the public doesn't like higher taxes and if they raise taxes then the politicians will be voted or run out of office. So a system like the Federal Reserve gives politicians access to virtually unlimited amounts of money without having to raise taxes. It's good for the politicians because they get to stay in power—they get their money without raising taxes—and it's good for the banks because they get paid for creating money out of nothing and charging interest on it all. But it's bad for the public because all that fiat money—all that cheap money—going into an economy will inevitably cause massive inflation and destroy the middle and lower classes through the hidden tax of inflation.

All this is why you wrote in your book that the Federal Reserve is "the biggest scam in the world."
Absolutely.

To make the point again: the United States government doesn't have to and shouldn't pay interest, borrow money, or go into debt to anyone

for America's money. The Government should issue a debt-free, gold-backed currency directly into the economy.
Yes. And it's a point worth making again.

Many statesman and other well-known people have made statements criticizing the Federal Reserve. The inventor Thomas Edison said: "If the nation can issue a dollar bond it can issue a dollar bill. The element that makes the bond good makes the bill good, also. The difference between the bond and the bill is that the bond lets the money broker collect twice the amount of the bond and an additional twenty percent. Whereas, the currency, the honest sort provided by the Constitution, pays nobody but those who contribute in some useful way. It is absurd to say our country can issue bonds and cannot issue currency. Both are promises to pay, but one fattens the usurer and the other helps the People."
Right there, Edison was expressing clearly exactly what we're talking about.

And in 1941, Congressman Wright Patman said: "The Federal Reserve Banks buy government bonds without one penny." And Henry Ford, the founder of Ford Motor Company, said: "It is well that the people of the nation do not understand our banking and monetary system, for if they did, I believe there would be a revolution before tomorrow morning."
Ford put that very succinctly, didn't he?

Apparently, the Federal Reserve gets the privilege of receiving government bonds and is paid interest for printing fiat money or typing numbers into a computer because the Federal Reserve is supposedly this big beneficent financial institution that is looking out for America's welfare. The Federal Reserve was created to supposedly keep the economy steady, curb inflation, and to be "the lender of last resort." These banks banded together because they're supposed to have so much money and reserves that they will always save America's banks from ruin and the American economy from ruin. But the Federal Reserve doesn't keep America's economy steady. There's been terrible recessions and depressions and economic problems. The Federal Reserve is an utter failure, isn't it?

Well, just look at the record since 1913. We had the crashes of 1921 and 1929. The Great Depression of the 1930s. Recessions in the '50s, '60s, '70s, and '80s. Black Monday in 1987. We've had a thousand percent inflation which has destroyed ninety percent of the dollar's purchasing power. The debt has risen to eighteen trillion dollars. Bankruptcies and bank failures are at an all time high. Interest on the national debt is consuming half of our tax dollars. We have a wrecked economy heading for a cliff. And now the mortgage crisis. There can be no argument that the System has failed.

You've written that the reason the Federal Reserve hasn't achieved its supposed goals of keeping the economy steady and healthy and controlling inflation is because that wasn't the real reason the government—which was being controlled by the banking interests—created the Federal Reserve in 1913.

The Federal Reserve was created so that banks of the System could make money. At the time that the Federal Reserve Act was passed, new banks outside of New York were gaining more and more of the nation's banking business. That was unacceptable to the big banks on Wall Street. The Federal Reserve was created and certain banks—especially the big Wall Street banks—were given the controlling ownership of the Federal Reserve Banks. The Federal Reserve Banking System is a banking monopoly. A cartel. It gives the banks that own the Federal Reserve a monopoly on providing the nation its money, and a monopoly over the banking industry. It was also created so the banks can create money out of nothing for the purpose of lending. The Federal Reserve was not created for the benefit of the public to keep the economy steady and healthy. It was created so the member banks of the Federal Reserve could have a monopoly over banking and could profit and make money.

Regarding this eighteen trillion dollar debt America has, and that America goes deeper into debt each day, what is America's fate? Can America survive this? Or will the effects of the debt eventually destroy America and the American economy and we'll have a depression much worse than the great Depression of the 1930s?

I believe America can survive, but the real question is will it survive all this debt in freedom? Or will the government take over all our industries? I think the country can survive but I'm afraid that out of the other end of that process will be our loss of personal freedom. Because what's happening right now is that all this free money, this money created out of nothing, is being pushed into the economy and particularly at the top into the segments of society that are politically connected. Into the financial institutions, the heads of the giant corporations, and the big banks. They're getting billions of dollars being created out of nothing. So they're doing very well. But meanwhile that money is just beginning now to filter into the economy and that influx of that huge amount of money is going to cause massive inflation. So it will be paid for by the common man through higher prices for bread and butter, and everything else. So what's happening is there's a wealth transfer that will go from the middle class up to the politically favored class. In the process, when the government gives this money—let's say they bail out the banks, they give the money to the banks. Now, what happens at the end of that process, the government owns the banks. You see that happening all around the world now. And politicians are now clamoring, "Oh, let's nationalize the banks. We funded them. We bought them. Why don't we own them?" That's where that will go. So, the government will own the banks. Then the government is giving money to the mortgage industry. So, now the government will own the houses. And the government will give money to the corporations. So that the government will own and run the corporations.

Piece by piece, the whole economy and the whole fabric of American life is rapidly going into this total government control and ownership. The definition is Communism, or Fascism. You can call it what you will—you can look at it from the left or the right—it's totalitarianism. So, America will survive but it will come out the other side as a totalitarian system.

Perhaps the most damaging aspect of the Federal Reserve Banking System is fractional reserve banking. Through fractional reserve banking, the commercial banks of the Federal Reserve System are allowed to lend out and charge interest on a lot more money than they have in their vaults, right? . . . If a bank has, say, $10 billion dollars, it's allowed to lend out ten times as much—$100 billion dollars. The bank is allowed to create $90 billion dollars out of thin air and lend that out and charge interest on it . . . the bank just types a number into a computer or writes a number on a check and that becomes money.

That's right. Through fractional reserve banking the banks are allowed to lend out and charge interest on ten times as much money as they have.

How is fractional reserve banking bad for America?

Fractional reserve banking is bad for America because it allows the banks to create this money out of nothing. If it weren't for fractional reserve banking, the banks would have to issue money based only on gold or silver reserves. But the way the laws are set up through the Federal Reserve System it makes it legal for the banks to loan—or to create out of nothing I should say—considerably more money than what they have in reserve.

So fractional reserve banking is going to cause more, severe inflation?

History shows that wherever fractional reserve banking has been practiced the economy can't be healthy and is destroyed because too much money created out of nothing—too much money off the gold standard—will cause prices to rise and destroy a society through inflation. And the banks are collecting interest on nothing.

Do you think most people don't know about fractional reserve banking? Most people don't even understand that banks can lend out and charge interest on about ten times as much money as they actually have?
My experience is that until very, very recently that not one in five hundred people knew that.

But there have been many times in history when depositors have made a run on the banks to withdraw their deposits and the banks don't have the money because they've lent it out through fractional reserve banking, right?
Oh, yes. That's happened dozens of times in history.

This is another real racket and scam, isn't it? Through fractional reserve banking, the banks are making billions and trillions lending out and charging interest on money they don't have. That's good for the banks and causes nothing but debt and inflation for the public. If you or I or anybody else tried to lend out and charge interest on money we don't have we'd be put in prison, wouldn't we?
Of course.

But the banks can do it?
Yes, because the banks went into partnership with the federal government back in 1913 and drafted the Federal Reserve Act which makes it legal.

As strongly as you feel that the Federal Reserve Bank should be abolished, do you feel just as strongly that fractional reserve banking should be abolished?
Well, fractional reserve banking is the bane of any society where it exists.

An economy can't be healthy where there's fractional reserve lending. But as offensive as the practice is itself, it's equally offensive that people are dealing with a system where it's all mysterious and they think the government's protecting them, and all that. Nothing is transparent. People don't realize they're paying interest on money that the banks don't actually have. What I object to is the fact that all of this is done in secrecy.

Fractional reserve banking causes more inflation because more fiat money—ten times as much as the Federal Reserve released—floods the economy. This seems to be the main point of your book, that the Federal Reserve System causes inflation because this system allows our government to borrow endless supplies of fiat money and then pour all that money into the American economy. When there's too much money circulating in a society that will cause prices to rise—inflation.
The Federal Reserve is a perpetual, non-stop, inflation-creating machine. Inflation *is* the main, crippling and potentially fatal disease that the Federal Reserve has inflicted on America. As I mentioned before, the Federal Reserve is a system that prevents politicians and governments from becoming unpopular by having to raise taxes. But whenever politicians pump up the money supply by borrowing fiat money from the Fed, they are destroying the public through the hidden tax of inflation.

You're saying that we have inflation because the Fed's money is off the gold standard. For anyone who doesn't know what the gold standard is, the gold standard is when every paper dollar circulating has to be backed up by a certain amount of gold being held either in the treasury or a bank. But America didn't get off the gold standard until President Nixon took us off in 1971. So has inflation been rising since the creation of the Fed in 1913, or since we went off the gold standard in the early '70s?
Technically speaking, we have never been one hundred percent on the gold standard.

Since 1913, we haven't been?
Yes, and even before that.

But to get on the gold standard would be the magic bullet to cure America's economic problems?
Yes. We were on the gold standard before Nixon, but we didn't have one hundred percent backing. I've forgotten the exact ratio now, but I think by the time 1971 came along, I think all we had was about twenty-five percent total money supply backed by gold.

That's not very much right there.
That's not much. But it's better than zero, which we have now. The twenty-five percent ratio did serve as a break on the amount of money that could be created out of nothing. And prior to that I think it was fifty percent. And prior to that it was sixty percent. But our money should be backed by gold or silver one hundred percent. I don't think we've ever had that in our history.

The rates of inflation since 1913 have been steadily rising and are astro-nomical, aren't they? As you said, inflation has risen one thousand per-cent and the dollar has lost ninety percent of its purchasing power since the Federal Reserve was created in 1913. That's what the Fed has done?
There's been a constant, steady rise of inflation since 1913. Then when President Nixon took us completely off the gold standard, inflation sky-rocketed even more.

At times, though, there isn't bad inflation, is there? At the present time, there doesn't seem to be bad inflation. But do you believe that it's inevi-table that there will be bad, hyper-inflation?
It is inevitable. The economy can't survive all this cheap money—this fiat money—coming into circulation. The dollar will have to collapse—maybe sooner, maybe later. Hyper-inflation will come.

You claim—and economists agree—that what inflation does is destroy the middle class. How is that?
It's undoubted that what inflation does is destroy the middle class. The best example in the twentieth century was in Germany—run-away inflation came, and the middle class got wiped out. When prices rise who, in general, is going to suffer the most? The people who can afford it the least. People on fixed incomes. Low or middle income people, poor people. So our monetary system is wreaking havoc and destroying the financial well-being of the majority of our public.

The middle class is dwindling, disappearing in America. This is what economists and politicians are saying now, right?
That's right. Now we know why.

What's going to become the ultimate result of all this inflation? The American dollar will become totally devalued, the economy will collapse, and we'll have a depression worse than the 1930s? Then the government will take all control?
I'm afraid that's where it's headed. The best analogy is that we're dealing with an alcoholic here. The economy is the equivalent of an alcoholic. The nation and the economy have been on an alcoholic binge—of fiat money—for decades. They've needed more and more and more to keep the effect up. And now the patient has had so much alcohol, he's going to die—of inflation and economic disaster. He's sick, very, very sick. And so what do you do? Well, you have to get him off of it. The solution is not, as they're doing now, "Oh, give this guy another drink—give him another trillion dollars of fiat money. No, give him five more drinks—five more trillion." And that's what they're doing. So is the patient going to live or die? It depends—if they keep forcing drinks down his gullet he's going to die. So what do you advocate? You advocate that they stop doing that. What most people probably don't understand is that more money put into an

economy isn't necessarily going to improve the economy. The only thing that matters is that the amount of money put into an economy is in proper proportion with the expanding goods and services that can be purchased with the money. If you have too much fiat money, then that's going to be out of proportion with goods and services and cause prices to rise. But if you don't have too much money, if the money put into the economy is in proportion with expanding goods and services, then prices won't rise and the people won't need more money because the paycheck you received last year will be just as good as the one you receive this year because prices didn't go up. History shows that whenever gold is used for money—whenever a society stays on the gold standard—the amount of gold added to the money supply will always be closely proportional to the expanding services and goods. Automatically and impartially, long-term stability of prices will ensue. To cure the alcoholic, we have to stop feeding him fiat money and get him on gold.

And that's the other main point of your book. The American economy is being destroyed by the Federal Reserve through inflation, but there's a simple solution to the problem. And that solution is to get on the gold standard. Because, as you say, history shows that whenever gold is used as money then there can never be this mass injection of too much money, causing prices to rise. The amount of gold added to the money supply will naturally be closely proportional to the expanding services and goods that can be purchased. Prices will stabilize. There will be no inflation.

Yes. And the Founding Fathers were keenly aware of this. That's why the Constitution decrees that only gold and silver is to be used as money. The Founders had firsthand experience with the disastrous effects of fiat money because during the 1770s the American colonies printed up millions of dollars of paper money to pay for the Revolutionary War. All that fiat money destroyed the economy and led to a depression and severe inflation. So, if you read the writings of the Founders, they all expressed how America should never again use fiat money. In fact, never in history were there so many men in a legislative body who understood the disastrous effects of fiat money and the hidden-taxation nature of inflation. So, when the Founders decreed that only gold and silver were to be used as money they gave us a *treasure map* to set us on a safe course to economic security and national prosperity.

The reality is that there's only so much gold in the world, right? And the time it takes for miners to dig new gold from the earth and for governments to attain new gold has traditionally always been closely proportional to the expansion of goods and services in societies.
That is right. That is what a study of history will show you.

So it's as simple as that? Get on the gold standard, there will be no inflation, the economy will be healthy, and we'll have prosperity, no unemployment, and a happy citizenry?
Abolishing the Federal Reserve would be the first and most important step to fixing the economy and getting back our economic and personal freedom. But it's not the only step needed. We also have to do something about government over-spending, get rid of an income tax that's destroying the middle class, and do some other things. But to abolish the Fed and get on the gold standard would immediately be a magic bullet. It wouldn't be easy at first. There would be withdrawal symptoms. But it can be done. It could iron out all our difficulties. Recently, when Argentina quit expanding their paper money supply, their inflation immediately went down from hundreds of percent a year to just two or three percent. So the effects would be seen very quickly. We'd see an immediate benefit. It would iron out the severe swings in the boom-bust cycle. So, it would be a tremendous boost to the American people, to the economy. It would be great. For the middle class person, the low income person, jobs would become available. It would not take a long time.

Some people say that it's not necessary to be on the gold standard to have a stable economy and no inflation. These people say that the government could issue a paper currency and as long as that currency was issued in proper proportion with the expansion of goods and services and population growth, then there wouldn't be too much money devaluating the currency and causing inflation.

I couldn't disagree with that more. If the government's going to issue a paper currency, then who's going to be responsible for determining how much money is issued? Politicians and government officials who will be influenced and corrupted by bankers and special interests? Gold is meant to be money. Make the dollar a fixed weight of gold and keep it there.

But if a paper currency were issued in proper proportion, then that wouldn't destroy the economy and lead to inflation, would it?

The Constitution states that "only Congress shall coin and regulate the currency." "Coin" means gold and silver. . . . Gold has always been a good money. Gold is money.

You've written that historically whenever a society stays on the gold standard then that society's economy remains healthy. You've said that the Byzantine Empire is the best example of what staying on the gold standard will do for an economy.

For eight hundred years, beginning with the emperor Constantine at around A.D. 330, the monetary unit of the Byzantine Empire stayed at a fixed weight of gold. During that time, Byzantium never fell into bankruptcy, or even into any debt. It's been written that Constantinople was said to be a perfection of human civilization. There was economic, social, and political stability. Due to this honest, sound monetary policy, the Byzantine Empire flourished as the center of world commerce for eight hundred years.

You mentioned the boom-bust cycle. Economic booms and busts are a major issue and problem for the American economy. Some people claim that this economic trend known as the "boom and bust" cycle is a direct result of the Federal Reserve System, and that booms and busts are not haphazard occurrences but are deliberately and intentionally caused by the Federal Reserve, and are beneficial to and profit the Federal Reserve banks. When the Fed sets interest rates low, then the banks are lending a lot of money, and more people will borrow and buy houses and have more money for their businesses, and the economy booms. But when the Federal Reserve raises interest rates and calls in loans, and the banks don't lend out as much money, then eventually there will be mass foreclosures and bankruptcies and recessions and depressions. The bust period. How does this boom and bust cycle benefit and profit the Federal Reserve and the banks of the Federal Reserve System?

There's a big debate over that. Some people believe that the Federal Reserve and the banks of the Federal Reserve System deliberately cause expansion and contraction of the money supply—by raising and lowering interest rates. The theory is this accordion effect is useful to the banks because during the busts they can pick up foreclosed properties at low prices and so forth. I don't particularly see it that way. I think that the banks and the Fed are more interested in manipulating the money supply so they can collect this fantastic stream of interest on money created out of nothing. And as a result of that process, the money supply does expand and contract. And when it contracts and they wind up with all of the houses—for example—they have to get rid of those houses. The banks don't want those houses. They want the interest from the loans on those houses. So I've never quite believed that the expansion and contraction—the boom-bust cycle—was the goal of the system. I think it was just one of the results of it.

But in your book you wrote that this method of lowering interest rates and then raising them and calling in loans has been used many times by central bankers so the banks can take over properties. In your book, you cite the Agricultural Depression of 1920–1921. In the early 1920s, American farms were doing very well financially, but they were using rural banks which weren't a part of the Federal Reserve System. So, in the early 1920s, the Federal Reserve Board met in secret and raised interest rates and this caused a depression, and the farmers went bankrupt, and the rural banks had to fold. Those rural banks then came under the financial control of the banks of the Federal Reserve. According to your book—and other researchers—it was a clear case of the Federal Reserve operating in a way to take over properties and destroy smaller banks.

Well, yes that was a case in which the Fed wanted those farms because they weren't taking loans from banks which were part of the Federal Reserve System. In general, though, in my opinion, the banks want the interest from the loans and not to have to deal with foreclosed properties.

If we abolished the Federal Reserve and the United States government were issuing its own money on the gold standard then there wouldn't be these boom-bust cycles, correct?

There would not be, no. If the Federal Reserve wasn't drastically expanding and contracting the money supply, if we were on the gold standard, and if the government weren't interfering with the economy, then what you're talking about is a free market. The booms and busts would be so small, almost undetectable. I mean there always has to be some interplay. If you're dealing with a free market there always are changes in supply and demand, but they're so small, and they're so quickly absorbed that you can almost not see them.

So if we eliminated the Federal Reserve and got on the gold standard then there wouldn't be any booms and busts, there would be little or no inflation because there wouldn't be too much money causing prices to rise, and there wouldn't have to be any debt because the government would be issuing its own money. It seems like we should eliminate the Fed and get on the gold standard.

My point exactly.

The banking cartel, of course, doesn't want us to get on the gold standard because then the Federal Reserve wouldn't be receiving billions of dollars worth of government bonds for typing numbers into a computer and the banks couldn't charge interest on billions of dollars created out of nothing through fractional reserve banking.

Precisely.

Has it ever been revealed who owns—who are the stockholders—of the Federal Reserve Bank?

That's another debatable thing here. I don't know who the stockholders are. Technically, the Federal Reserve System is owned by all of the member banks in the system and technically all of the banks have stock. So the easy answer would be "All the banks own the Federal Reserve System." But the stock that they hold does not carry the usual prerogative of ownership. For example, you cannot sell the stock. Also, the stock doesn't give the holders of the stock the right to vote for the directors of the Federal Reserve System.

The Federal Reserve Banks are privately owned, but they're owned in a strange way? The structure of the Federal Reserve is unique and unusual, isn't it?

In a strange way, yeah. Unique. The Federal Reserve is structured like no other institution in the world.

Don't Americans have a right to know who owns the Federal Reserve Bank?

Of course, we do.

If it's so obvious—and it does seem obvious—that the Federal Reserve Bank is bad for the people of America, then why doesn't the media ever bring this up? In 1922, President Theodore Roosevelt was posthumously quoted saying the Rockefeller interests and the international banking interests control the media. Is that why? Is the media controlled by corporate-banking conglomerates?

The financial conglomerates that dominate the Federal Reserve are parallel or synonymous with the same ones that dominate the major media. We're talking about members of the Council on Foreign Relations. The Council on Foreign Relations is a think tank that the Rockefellers and their associates created in 1921. People from the CFR dominate the media and the banking system, both. And the educational system. Everywhere you look, these guys are kind of running the show. That's what they do, that's their policy, you know, to get behind the scenes. And it's not in their best interests to have people criticize the Fed. In the media, you're allowed to criticize the Fed in a certain way, but not in another way. For example, you're allowed to say, "Oh, yeah, the Federal Reserve System needs reform." Or "It needs an audit." But you're not allowed to say "The Federal Reserve System needs to be abolished." The beat is severely controlled.

The theory that since 1913 the banking industry controls corporate conglomerates that control the media and that's why there's no questioning of the Federal Reserve System could be true, because throughout America's history one of the most open and important political issues debated in Washington and in the media was whether America's money should be issued by the government or a privately owned central bank. In the past, this has been a publicized issue. But since 1913, we don't hear anything about it, do we?

Who controls and issues the currency was probably the influencing factor in the some of the most important events of American history. In his autobiography, Benjamin Franklin wrote that the real reason for the Revolutionary War was that England wouldn't let the American colonies print their own money and forced the colonies to use and pay interest on Bank of England currency . . . and in the late 1700s and early 1800s, Thomas Jefferson and Alexander Hamilton debated this matter openly and vigorously. . . . Then this issue may have also been the real cause of the War of 1812.

Maybe.

In 1791 the First Bank of the United States—a privately owned central bank that operated like the Federal Reserve—was created. The principle stockholders of the Bank were the Rothschilds and other private bankers. When it looked like the Congress was going to vote to abolish the First Bank of the United States in 1811, Nathan Rothschild made a statement to the effect of "If the bank is abolished then there will be hell to pay."

It'd be easy to believe that the Rothschilds didn't want the bank abolished.

The Congress did abolish the First Bank of the United States in 1811, and, so, then in 1812 England invaded America. The War of 1812.

Yes, it could be that Rothschild—who was very powerful and influential in England—used his influence to get England to attack America in 1812. Punishment for abolishing the Bank, and an attempt by England to reclaim America so America would come under the control of the Bank of England.

That might have been the real cause of the War of 1812.

It might have been.

Then in 1816 the Second Bank of the United States—another privately owned central bank that operated like the Federal Reserve—was chartered. It could be argued that the entire presidency of Andrew Jackson from 1828 to 1836 was characterized by a debate on whether the government or a privately owned central bank should issue America's money. Jackson wanted the Second Bank eliminated.

Andrew Jackson may have been our most populist president. Jackson wanted the Second Bank abolished. Thanks to Andrew Jackson, the Second Bank of the United States lost its charter in 1836.

Jackson wrote that his main contention with the Second Bank is that it was privately owned, and that private bankers were profiting from providing America with its currency. President Andrew Jackson wrote: "If Congress has the right under the Constitution to issue money, it was given them to use themselves, not to be delegated to individuals or corporations."

To tell an anecdote from Jackson's life: When Jackson was president, some banking officials from the Second Bank came to meet with him to try to convince him to let the Second Bank exist. When they did, Jackson yelled at the bankers, "You are a den of vipers!" and kicked them out of the White House.

About twenty-five years after Jackson's time, the Civil War broke out and President Abraham Lincoln needed money to finance the Union's war against the South. Instead of borrowing money and paying interest to private bankers, Lincoln did something that politicians rarely do: he had the government print its own money. Greenbacks. After Lincoln did that, there was a major debate over whether the government should continue issuing its own money—the greenbacks—or borrow money from private banks. President Abraham Lincoln said: "The Government should create, issue, and circulate all the currency and credits needed to satisfy the spending power of the Government and the buying power of the consumers. By the adoption of these principles, the taxpayers will be saved immense sums of interest. Money will cease to be the master and become the servant of humanity."

Many people who believe in monetary reform believe that Lincoln's printing of greenbacks was a great act of statesmanship. They believe Lincoln was being a revolutionary, a maverick—that he was going against this central banking system of having to pay interest to private bankers. But the greenbacks were paper money—fiat money—that weren't backed up by gold or silver. Yes, it was very good that Lincoln realized that the government should issue its own money and not have to pay interest to bankers. But, Lincoln, apparently, didn't realize that government issued money should be gold or silver, and, in my opinion, that was not good.

The banking cabal wanted a privately owned central bank in America ever since President Andrew Jackson got the Second Bank of the United States abolished in 1836. The bankers finally succeeded with Woodrow Wilson. Before the 1912 presidential election, Woodrow Wilson visited the Democratic headquarters in New York City where he was influenced and recruited by members of the Democratic Party who were controlled by Wall Street. These influences made Wilson president in 1912 and Wilson approved the passing of the Federal Reserve Act in 1913.

That's right. There's no question that Wilson was a representative of the big banks on Wall Street, which are the dominant banks of the Federal Reserve.

Later, a few years after Wilson approved the creation of the Federal Reserve, he apparently regretted it. Many people claim that Woodrow Wilson said this: "A great industrial nation is controlled by its system of credit. Our system of credit is concentrated. The growth of the nation, therefore, and all our activities are in the hands of a few men. We have come to be one of the worst ruled, one of the most completely controlled and dominated governments . . . no longer a government by free opinion and the vote of the majority, but a government by the opinion and duress of a small group of dominant men."

Well, it wouldn't be surprising if Wilson wrote that. What's said there is certainly true. A few dominant men—the men who run the Federal Reserve—control the country.

So, throughout the history of America the issue of if a privately owned bank or the government is going to issue America's money has always been openly and vigorously debated talked about in the media and amongst politicians. But since 1913, according to President Theodore Roosevelt, the banking industry has the media and the politicians muted?

I would agree with Roosevelt.

Regarding Franklin Roosevelt's presidency, many economists agree that the Great Depression was caused by the Federal Reserve. In 1996, Nobel Prize winning economist Milton Friedman said: "The Federal Reserve definitely caused the Great Depression by contracting the amount of currency in circulation by one-third from 1929 to 1933." So the Fed caused the Depression?

I believe that's a correct statement, yes. From my reading of history I believe that when it came to that point in 1929 when the Fed did contract the money supply it was only after they knew that there was going to be a bursting of the bubble anyway. I think they were trying to keep the economy going and they finally came to the realization that "This thing is going to implode." So rather than just sit around and wonder what day it is going to be or when, they decided "Okay. We will insert the pin into the bubble, so that we will know exactly the day and the hour so we can try to control it and benefit from it."

It's been said that when central bankers cause a depression that means they want something from the government. The Republican presidents of the 1920s were critical of the Federal Reserve, and didn't seem to be giving the Fed all the power that it wanted. Then, according to Milton Friedman, in 1929 the Fed began contracting the money supply and that began the Great Depression. Soon after FDR became president in 1933, though, he passed some laws that gave the Federal Reserve more power and influence and right after that the Federal Reserve stopped the contraction of the American money supply and let more money flow into America. Do you think the Federal Reserve caused the Depression until it got what it wanted from the government?

Well, anything is possible. It could be. I'd have to think about that and go back over some of that history. I do know that all of the presidents from Woodrow Wilson on have been friends of the Federal Reserve System. Even though they may say critical things now and then for political purposes, when it comes to push to shove, they have always been friends of the Federal Reserve. The Depression wasn't completely alleviated, of course, until World War II broke out.

This is what can happen when a privately owned central bank has a monopoly on providing a country with its currency, right? The private bankers or banking officials who own or run the central bank—or in this case, who are pulling the Federal Reserve Board's strings—can raise interest rates, or control loans in a way that contracts the money supply, causes a depression, and puts millions of people into poverty, unemployment, and misery.

Of course. And this also happened, you know, during Andrew Jackson's time. When Jackson was reelected president in 1832, he immediately ordered all new government deposits to be put into state banks and not in the Second Bank of the United States. Jackson wanted the Second Bank destroyed. Nicholas Biddle, the head of the bank, then made statements to the effect that he "was going to show Jackson who's boss." Biddle tightened credit, called in loans, and this caused the contraction of the money supply. A full-scale national depression ensued. Men were out of work, and companies went bankrupt. Biddle then tried to blame the depression on Jackson's actions, and said that the country couldn't survive without the Second Bank of the United States. Ultimately, the people and the Congress saw through Biddle's deceit, and they sided with President Jackson and the Second Bank of the United States was abolished in 1836. And the Congress eventually investigated Biddle for intentionally causing the depression.

So, really, doesn't the Federal Reserve have more power than the president and the Congress to control America? It's really the actions of the Federal Reserve that determines how much unemployment there will be, if people will have enough money for food and shelter, and the overall state of the economy, right?
The Fed has the dominant control over our economy. I believe that the people and the institutions that control the Federal Reserve System control—have the political control—over America. And that does not include Congress and the president.

And the Federal Reserve acts absolutely independently, doesn't it? The president and the Congress never meet with the Federal Reserve Board and talk about how to control interest rates and improve the economy. Congress may question the Fed after it does what it does, but the System is independent of the government? We're at the mercy of the Fed?
To a very large degree, yes. That's certainly true. Also, there is *never* a *complete* and *true* audit of the Fed. Congress, if it ever got the courage to do so, could abolish the Fed. But it doesn't have the courage to do so because all of those little congressmen and women are all up to the trough. They're benefiting from the system, and they wouldn't dare speak out against it because they would lose their political clout—they would be smeared in the media, they'd be turned into demons, and they're all afraid of it. The power centers do not really include the congressmen and the president because they're captives.

So much of the debate between Democrats and Republicans, then, is just rhetoric and political hogwash, isn't it?
It's a joke.

No matter what the Republicans and Democrats are saying and doing, if we don't abolish the Fed then there's going to be more inflation and debt and the economy's going to be destroyed. The real problem with America is we have to get rid of the Federal Reserve.
Get rid of the Fed and get rid of the control that these people have that represent the Fed. Again, the Council on Foreign Relations. The CFR is, I believe, the focus point for this group of people who want to convert the United States and the rest of the world into a collectivist system. A world government. And they're well on the road.

What do most economists, Ivy League economists, and "establishment" economists, say about the Federal Reserve?
Oh, they think it's wonderful. They think it's necessary. They think that, "Well, we may have some problems there but if we just keep working on it and fine tuning it and find smarter people to run it everything will be fine. Don't mess with it."

Haven't many of America's most respected colleges been financed by Wall Street and big moneyed interests?
To a large extent. I wouldn't say totally, of course. The educational institutions, long ago, were pretty much taken over by moneyed interests through tax exempt foundations of the Carnegie Fund, the Guggenheim Foundation, the Rockefeller Foundation, and so forth. They put a lot of money into supposedly raising the educational standards of America. And, you know, where the money goes, control follows.

Right after the Federal Reserve System was devised, J. P. Morgan and John Rockefeller implemented a specific plan to fund the most influential universities and to influence economics professors to support and agree with the Federal Reserve plan.

That's true. Woodrow Wilson, the president who approved the Federal Reserve Act, had been the president of Princeton University.

William Greider would be considered an "establishment" writer because he is the former managing editor of the **Washington Post.** *In 1987, Greider wrote an award-winning, eight hundred page book about the Fed that was entitled* **The Secrets of the Temple: How the Federal Reserve Runs the Country.** *Was Greider's book any good?*

Greider's book was supposed to be a scathing expose of the Federal Reserve System. His history was excellent, but his conclusion was flawed. Greider's research proved that the Fed was conceived as a weapon of the banking elite against the common man and showed that this is exactly the function the Fed has always served. But after proving that, Greider didn't call for the abolishing of the Fed or for even making any serious changes. He said we should stop worrying about it. The Fed has made mistakes, but all we need are better men to run it. It was a powder puff criticism. *Secrets of the Temple* was published by Simon & Schuster, and is a case in which the corporate elite let a book be released to the public that criticized the Fed because the criticism wasn't too severe, and didn't recommend the Fed being abolished.

So is a person like Alan Greenspan a bad, dishonest person?

Back in the 1960's, Alan Greenspan was an eloquent spokesman advocating for America to keep on the gold standard. Greenspan was also critical of how the Federal Reserve System serves the banking interests. But then Greenspan became a director of J. P. Morgan & Company and then was appointed chairman of the Federal Reserve in the late '80's. After that, Greenspan became silent on the issue of the gold standard and no longer criticized the System he came to serve. History shows that even the best of men can be corrupted by the rewards of politics, by being given a position of power.

Many people contend that "the banks own the Congress." Though it's apparent that the banking industry lobbies and controls the congress and the government, over the years there have been some maverick congressmen and senators who have spoken out against the Federal Reserve, correct?

There have been. There have been those who have passionately tried to make their colleagues understand that the Federal Reserve banks are privately owned and that the system exists to make a profit for the banks. Representative Charles Lindbergh Sr. ranted and raved against the system. So did Senator Robert LaFollette and Congressman Louis McFadden, who was chairman of the House Banking and Currency Committee. Barry Goldwater said that most Americans don't understand the operations of the international moneylenders and the Fed. Today, there's Dennis Kucinich, and of course, Ron Paul.

Texas Congressman Ron Paul, who made a respectable run to be the Republican presidential nominee in 2008 and 2012, believes that the Federal Reserve is at the root of our economic problems, is unconstitutional, and should be abolished. Did Ron Paul learn about that from reading your book?

Oh, I don't think so, no. Ron Paul has been a stalwart in this field and very knowledgeable for as long as I can remember.

Do you know Congressman Paul?

Yes, I know him. I remember talking with Dr. Paul before I wrote my book. We were in total agreement on everything and I would say he was one of the very first to call for abolishing the Federal Reserve.

A lot of people did learn about the Fed from your book, though.
Perhaps many people have. But prior to that there were other books out there—they were other people and writers—criticizing the Fed, but they just didn't have much exposure.

Texans have always been independent thinkers. Down in Texas now, there's a political action movement to have the Federal Reserve abolished because the Texans say that the Federal Reserve is privately owned and, so, unconstitutional. Did that come about because Ron Paul is from Texas?
Well, I don't know about that. But if they're trying to get the Federal Reserve abolished they would certainly have my support.

You still believe, though, that there should be banks, don't you? What is the fair, legitimate way that banks should operate?
I think that banks have a very important role to play in the economy if the banks are not favored. The trouble is that the banks have so much influence that they get laws passed that give them great advantages over any other business. They're protected, they're bailed out, they're allowed to renege on their contracts without going to prison. Basically, the banks are involved in counterfeiting.

Because of the Federal Reserve System?
Yes. It institutionalizes the practice of counterfeiting. They print money. They create checkbook money out of nothing—there's nothing behind it. But they're the only ones who are allowed to do it.

Thomas Jefferson felt strongly that a privately owned central bank shouldn't have a monopoly on providing America with its currency. Jefferson said: "If the American people ever allow private banks to control the issue of their currency, first by inflation, then by deflation, the banks will deprive the people of all property until their children wake up homeless on the continent their fathers occupied." Is this what's happened with the mortgage crisis that occurred in the fall of 2008? Have the banks ended up with all the money and millions of people are going to end up homeless—foreclosed on? The mortgage crisis is definitely related to the Federal Reserve System, isn't it?

Yes. Of course. There wouldn't be a mortgage crisis if it weren't for the Federal Reserve artificially adjusting interest rates to lure people into mortgage contracts that they shouldn't have gone into.

Anybody who believes that bankers wouldn't deliberately take actions to enrich themselves knowing that their actions will lead to severe problems for millions of people can just look at the mortgage crisis. The mortgage crisis didn't just happen by chance, right? Banking officials did things to make themselves rich and they knew that their actions would or could very well lead to the current crisis, right?

Yes. They did know that. They knew it was going in that direction. But meanwhile they were up to the trough, they were making a lot of money on it and nobody wanted to do anything about it.

CBS's **Sixty Minutes** *reported that something like $60 trillion dollars disappeared into the mortgage banks.*

Uh huh. Well, it never existed in the first place, that's the other part of that story. It was all just numbers.

You ended **The Creature from Jekyll Island** *by postulating that eventually there could be a banking crisis in America that leads to an economic and civil breakdown, then Washington's politicians would announce that they passed new laws and America is going to start using an international currency from the International Monetary Fund and that would lead to America slowly but surely merging into a United Nations*

world government. Could the type of mortgage crisis that happened in 2008 be the sort of banking breakdown that leads to this?
I'm sorry to say that I think that it's part of that very process. I wrote that chapter in my book back in 1993 and it was published in 1994 and I went back and read it recently.

It seemed very prophetic.
It was prophetic. It wasn't clairvoyance, or anything. Anybody who understands the economic forces at work could do the same thing. But it was kind of startling how many things have actually happened exactly as I wrote they would.

This could be the breakdown that leads to what you wrote about.
It's happening.

To try to cure the economic crisis, President Barack Obama poured $800 billion dollars of fiat money into the economy by borrowing if from the Federal Reserve. That's just going to cause more debt and inflation, isn't it?
Obama did what he was told to do. Obama didn't have a background in economics, or banking. He surrounded himself by all these Council on Foreign Relations people, or similar people, and he said, "Okay, tell me what to do." And they told him what to do. And then he got on television and says, "This is what we're going to do!" And everybody thought Obama came up with this. No, no. He was just a puppet like all the other presidents.

He was surrounded by CFR people?
Well, yes, some CFR, and the rest, who weren't CFR, they thought like CFR. Trilateral Commission people. They all have the same political viewpoints. They all believe in collectivism. Large government. They all believe in

internationalism. They believe in merging into a world government. You'll see very soon they'll be talking about creating a new international monetary system and a new currency. And all of that means no more US dollar, no more American independence and sovereignty, and so forth. You'll see it all come out.

The nations of Europe are now, of course, all using the same currency—the Euro—and many people believe this is leading to the European nations losing their independence and sovereignty to a European Superstate— the European Union. That was manipulated into being by the New World Order think tanks? That's a movement towards world government?
Absolutely. It's one of the most obvious components of it, actually. Yes, they—the CFR, and the Bilderberg Group, and the internationalist think tanks—they have been talking about that for decades. And, so, they finally pulled it off at the European level. The Euro dollar. And now they're working on the Amero for here, of course.

The Amero is the plan for North America? There's a plan to have America, Canada, and Mexico start using the same money and become a part of a North American Union?
Oh, absolutely. It's much further advanced than most people realize. Everybody in Washington knows about it. They're tooling up for it. They may leapfrog over that and go directly for an international currency, but I still think that they're going to go through the Amero.

In early 2009, a top banking official from China suggested that the world economic crisis could be cured by all nations using the same currency from the International Monetary Fund. Tim Geithner is the former head of the Federal Reserve Bank of New York and was Obama's secretary of the treasury. When Geithner was asked about that, he surprised everybody by replying that it might not be a bad idea. Geithner basically said that abolishing the American dollar and having all nations use an IMF currency might be a good idea.

Yes. So, you see where Geithner's coming from.

Then when President Obama made his Middle East speech in Cairo he used the phrase "war of necessity, war of choice" to explain America's policy in the Middle East. That phrase is the title of a book that had been recently written by the president of the Council of Foreign Relations. After Obama's speech, the president of the CFR was being interviewed on all the networks and the newsmen were telling him "it looks like President Obama has taken his cue from you."

Yes. You see?

President Obama is a great admirer of Abraham Lincoln. Maybe someone should remind Obama what Lincoln did. When the Civil War broke out, Lincoln didn't want to send America into debt by borrowing money from the banks, so Lincoln had the government print up a debt-free currency—greenbacks. To cure the crisis, perhaps someone should have suggested to President Obama that he do what his hero, President Lincoln, did and just have the government issue its own money? Instead of going deeper into a debt that future generations will have to pay?

Well, I could never endorse that. The greenbacks that Lincoln created were totally, totally unconstitutional. The greenbacks were fiat money not backed up by gold.

But Lincoln didn't want to go into debt and pay interest to the bankers, so maybe that was sort of a good thing.

That was part of it. There were two elements. Not paying interest to the bankers was good. But creating money out of thin air, contrary to the Constitution, was bad. . . . If Obama wanted to be an agent of change then he should have put us on gold and just let the free market be. Our economic problems are all a result of the manipulation of the forces of supply and demand. If the government would just back off and set the rules that everybody has to be honest and keep your contracts and then get out of the marketplace and just stand back and enforce honesty then the economy would take off and you'd have no problems whatsoever. But the politicians and government figure they're so wise that they have to manipulate this and control that, and control everything. And, of course, they make a little money on the side.

In your most idealistic vision, America could be like the Byzantine Empire where the monetary unit was kept on the gold standard and for eight hundred years there was no debt or inflation, the economy was healthy and prosperous, and there was political stability, and the populace was employed and content.

I do believe America could be like that. I look forward to the day. . . . Obviously, the most important thing for the welfare of a nation is the economy. You can't have political and social stability if too many people don't have money for the basic necessities of life, and don't have a job. History shows that whenever politicians manipulate the money supply—when there's too much fiat money being printed—that will lead to economic and political disaster. In the rare times when a society has refrained from manipulating the money supply and has allowed it to be determined by the free market and the gold standard, there has been prosperity and tranquility. America could be like the Byzantine Empire was for eight hundred years. We could have a strong dollar, a healthy, flourishing economy, political stability, and a content populace.

CHAPTER 6

Researcher Claims AIDS Epidemic Came from Contaminated Vaccines Administered by the United States Government and United Nations World Health Organization

An interview with author and AIDS researcher Dr. Alan C. Cantwell

In 1932, during the infamous Tuskegee Experiments, scientists working under the auspices of the US government's Public Health Service recruited four hundred poor African American sharecroppers from Tuskegee, Alabama, to participate in a clinical study.

All of the black men were diagnosed with syphilis, but were not told that they had the disease. The purpose of the study was to observe how syphilis spreads and progresses. The subjects were told that they had "bad blood," and in return for participating in the study they would receive free medical treatment, rides to the clinic, meals, and burial insurance in case of death.

By 1947, when penicillin had become the effective, standard treatment for syphilis, the Tuskegee scientists were withholding penicillin from their subjects. By the end of the study, only seventy-four of the participants were alive. Wives were infected, and children were born with congenital syphilis. Later, when the ethics of the study were being questioned, Dr. John R.

Heller, who had headed the program for many years, stated: "The men's status did not warrant ethical debate. They were subjects, not patients; clinical material, not sick people."

The Tuskegee Experiments ended in the early 1970s when a whistleblower working for the Public Health Service brought the story of what was happening to the press. As a result of a class action lawsuit, the surviving participants were eventually awarded nine million dollars. In May 1997, five of the eight remaining survivors of the study were invited to the White House where President Bill Clinton made a formal apology on behalf of the United States Government.

Beginning in November 1978, the government health agency that evolved from the Public Health Service, the Centers for Disease Control, was involved with administering a hepatitis B vaccine to thousands of young healthy gay men in cities across America. Shortly after the inoculation, the AIDS virus broke out in America's gay urban communities.

To some researchers it is time for the government to make another apology, and to admit that the hepatitis B vaccine was contaminated with AIDS and was the cause of America's AIDS epidemic.

At around the same time that the hepatitis B vaccine was being given to gay men in American cities, the World Health Organization (WHO) was inoculating approximately one hundred million Africans with a smallpox vaccine. After the inoculation, AIDS broke out in Africa in the areas where the smallpox vaccine had been administered. Today, twenty-three million Africans are infected with HIV; some scientists are projecting that AIDS will eventually kill a quarter or more of Africa's population.[3] On May 11, 1987, *The London Times*, one of the world's most respected newspapers, printed a story suggesting that the WHO's smallpox vaccine program was responsible for Africa's AIDS pandemic. A WHO employee, interviewed for the story, was quoted saying, "Now I believe the smallpox vaccine theory is an explanation for the explosion of African AIDS." Dr. Robert Gallo, the American scientist credited with discovering the AIDS virus, the scientist whom the medical establishment considers to be the world's foremost expert on AIDS, has said, "The link between the WHO program and the epidemic is an interesting and important hypothesis. I cannot say that it actually happened, but I have been saying for some years that the use of live vaccines such as that used for smallpox can activate a dormant infection such as the AIDS virus."

It is known that vaccines can sometimes be risky and cause health problems, and to AIDS researchers such as Dr. Alan Cantwell, Dr. Robert Strecker, Dr. Len Horowitz, and others the theory that AIDS came from the vaccines is more plausible and logical than the official, widely accepted theory on the origin of AIDS. The official, widely accepted theory on the origin of AIDS is that somewhere on the continent of Africa one green monkey bit one human being on the posterior and this caused AIDS to spread to millions of people around the globe.

To Dr. Robert Strecker, the first American doctor to claim that AIDS was made by scientists in a lab and spread through vaccines, this official theory on the origin of AIDS doesn't hold water for a number of reasons. Dr. Strecker has claimed that it is clear that the genetic structure of the AIDS virus does not exist in primates, and, so, the AIDS virus couldn't have come from monkeys. Strecker has also pointed out that if AIDS began in the jungle with monkeys than the disease would have spread from the Pygmy populations in the rural areas of Africa into the urban communities. Instead, AIDS in Africa began in the urban areas—where the smallpox vaccines were given—and spread to the rural areas. And, according to Dr. Strecker, if the disease had originated from one monkey biting someone—or a handful of monkeys biting a few people—AIDS could not have possibly spread as quickly and as widely as it has.

In July 1969, the Department of Defense asked the United States Congress for ten million dollars to develop an "infective microorganism"—a virus—that "might be refractory to the immunological . . . processes." (A copy of the declassified document that shows that the Defense Department asked the Congress for money to create a virus that destroys the immune system can be viewed in Dr. Leonard Horowitz's book *Emerging Viruses*.) Prior to that, the Pentagon had decided that the most inexpensive way to kill an enemy in warfare would be to inflict a virus on them, and, so, the Department of Defense asked for—and received—ten million dollars to develop an immunosuppressive virus. It has never been satisfactorily shown by any scientist or health official where the AIDS virus was before it broke out in Manhattan and Africa in the early '80s. The most that any official has been able to claim is that there might have been one or two isolated cases of AIDS here or there, but researchers say that even those claims can be easily refuted. What can be documented is that in the 1970s drug companies working on contract from the US government were developing viruses that destroy the immune system because at that time the US military was contemplating using such viruses for warfare. The same companies that were creating immunosuppressive viruses—AIDS—were also in the business of making hepatitis B and other vaccines and were the companies that supplied the American blood banks and the World Health Organization the vaccines for their vaccination programs. To Cantwell, Strecker, and Horowitz, the most logical and obvious explanation as to the origin of AIDS is that these vaccines were contaminated with AIDS because the vaccines and the immune destroying viruses were being manufactured in the same labs.

The only question in the minds of these researchers is if the contamination was accidental or intentional. Some of the world's top scientists meeting at a biohazard conference at Asilomar in northern California in 1973 agreed that it was possible that the immune destroying viruses that were then being manufactured in scientific labs could accidentally escape the labs and infect the public. At that conference, the virologists and epidemiologists even planned how they could track and monitor such a deadly virus if it was mistakenly released into the population. But could AIDS have been intentionally released? Could AIDS be a depopulation program?

Harvard graduate Dr. Leonard Horowitz has written that in the 1960s and '70s top US government, United Nations, and WHO officials considered the problems of global overpopulation to be a dire emergency. Overpopulation meant too much famine, and, according to a 1970s State Department report, was "an underlying factor in certain international conflicts and major internal disorders." *National Security Study Memorandum 200, The Kissinger Report*, released in late 1974, was an extensive, detailed paper showing the adverse implications of global overpopulation, and called for depopulation programs to be immediately initiated in many Third World countries. After *The Kissinger Report* came out, Thomas Ferguson, a government employee in the *Office of Population Affairs*, said—shockingly— "The quickest way to reduce population is through famine like in Africa, or through disease like in the Black Death. . . . Population reduction is now our primary policy objective." Henry Kissinger, himself, had been covertly manipulating the politics of Africa, had an intense geopolitical interest in the resources and nations of Africa, and felt strongly that Africa had to be depopulated. Could AIDS be an official depopulation program, a genocide aimed at two segments of society that have been traditionally ostracized and hated: homosexuals and blacks?

Dr. Alan C. Cantwell is a retired dermatologist who has written numerous scientific papers. Dr. Cantwell has also written two books claiming AIDS is a man-made disease that was spread through vaccines.

Cirignano: To you, what is the strongest evidence that AIDS came from the hepatitis B vaccine in the US and from the smallpox vaccine in Africa?
Cantwell: Well, I think in any kind of investigation as to when an epidemic starts you have to go back and see where the earliest cases are, where they came from. And I think it's pretty much accepted that AIDS came from Africa. But when you trace the first cases, AIDS doesn't come from Africa at all. The first cases came out of Manhattan. The first cases started being

reported to the CDC in 1979. My research traces it very clearly back to the hepatitis B vaccine experiment which started in 1978.

AIDS broke out in New York City shortly after the hepatitis B vaccine was given to promiscuous gays in Manhattan. Did the AIDS virus break out at the same time in other major cities across America?

Well, no. The hepatitis B vaccine experiment took place in New York City beginning in November 1978, and the first AIDS cases began being reported in New York in January 1979. But the hepatitis B vaccine wasn't administered to gays in Western American cities until March 1980, and AIDS didn't start breaking out in those cities until a few months after that. So AIDS broke out in different cities corresponding to when the hepatitis B vaccine was being administered in those particular cities.

Dr. David Sencer approved the continuation of the Tuskegee study in 1969 when he was the Director of the Centers for Disease Control. In the early 1980s, Dr. Sencer became the NYC Health Commissioner. So, Dr. Sencer was then in charge of disseminating all information about this new disease, AIDS, that had broken out in New York City. Do you think that government health officials and the CDC used their influence to put Sencer in charge of the health department in New York because he was a CDC insider who had covered up the Tuskegee study and would facilitate covering up the true origin of AIDS?

The CDC could not possibly *not* be aware of evidence pointing to AIDS as a man-made disease. The CDC is run like the military. And in the military there is only one way to think—and that is to think as you are told. The US government always wanted AIDS to be a disease "out of Africa." Therefore, every scientist, doctor, and researcher has to accept that explanation, otherwise you cease to get your government paycheck or grant.

The statistics of what happened to the 1,100 men who received the hepatitis B vaccine in Manhattan are pretty alarming, aren't they?
By 1982, over twenty percent of those men had HIV. By 1984, forty percent tested positive for HIV. Projecting those statistics, AIDS experts believe that the majority or all of those men who received the hepatitis B vaccine would eventually die from AIDS or AIDS-related diseases.

The data of what ultimately happened to those men who volunteered for the hepatitis B vaccine trials are now being kept secret and classified by the CDC?
Yes. Conveniently so. Also, the great majority of those men did develop antibodies for hepatitis B. That would have been impossible if they had HIV before they took the vaccine because an immunosuppressed body can't develop antibodies.

Those men gave blood samples before they received the hepatitis B vaccine and after AIDS broke out those stored samples were tested by scientists and none of them were positive for HIV?
Yes. Which indicates that those men got HIV from the vaccine. There were also thousands and thousands of blood samples that were stored in blood banks that were donated by gay men before 1978–1979 and those were tested in the 1980s and none of those samples were positive for HIV. HIV began showing up only after 1978 after the hepatitis B vaccine had been administered.

You've written that government scientists studying the nature of AIDS used the men who received the hepatitis B vaccine as their epidemiological models?
Yes. After the AIDS epidemic broke out government epidemiologists began taking blood samples every few months from the gay men who received the hepatitis B vaccine. These men—it seems—were used by government epidemiologists to study AIDS.

So do you think that the hepatitis B vaccine was like another Tuskegee Experiment—that people in the government intentionally put AIDS in the vaccine so that it could study how the disease progresses and spreads?
Well, yes. I believe the vaccine was contaminated.

Do you believe the contamination was accidental or intentional?
I believe it was intentional. And the reason I say that is because if it was unintentional then why can't we discuss the evidence? The government knows that immunosuppressive viruses were being experimented with in scientific laboratories in the 1960s and '70s. They also know that these laboratories had connections to the blood banks that gave out the hepatitis B vaccines. So to not even acknowledge or consider the possibility that that's where AIDS could have come from is, to me, unconscionable.

And you believe the AIDS virus was connected to the military's bio-warfare program?
Yes. But also to the National Cancer Institute. You see, ever since the early to mid 1960s, the NCI had a program called the Special Virus Cancer Program. Since then, scientists working for the SVCP were developing viruses that destroy the immune system because the NCI wanted to know if these viruses could cause cancer. Then in 1969, the Department of Defense asked the Congress for ten million dollars to create an immunesuppressive virus for use in warfare. And in 1971, President Nixon moved part of the National Cancer Institute to Fort Detrick in Maryland. Fort Detrick had long been the facility where the army had manufactured chemical and biological weapons for the biowarfare program. So it seems certain that the biowarfare program to create an immune-destroying virus was being operated at Fort Detrick under the guise of cancer research. I and others feel that it's entirely possible that AIDS came from Fort Detrick and the SVCP.

It's accepted that the scientists at the Tuskegee Study diagnosed four hundred black men with syphilis. But don't some people believe that those men were actually injected with syphilis by the Tuskegee scientists? Do you think that's a possibility?

I don't know. But if you look at the history of secret human medical experimentation then you have to realize that that's a possibility. Scientists and government scientists have done that sort of thing in the past.

We don't know that AIDS was intentionally put into the hepatitis B vaccine. That's the theory and speculation.

I don't know that it was. It could have been an accident. In my personal opinion, it was intentional. But whether it was accidental or intentional, it's clearly obvious to me that AIDS in America did come from that hepatitis B vaccine.

If this did come from the government, that doesn't mean that the president met with the vice president, and the Cabinet, and the Joint Chiefs of Staff and said, "Okay. We're going to put this virus into a vaccine to test it for the biowarfare program." Or, "We're going to put this virus into a vaccine to try to solve the problems of overpopulation." It could have come from just a few bad guys in the Pentagon and CIA.

Yes.

Dr. Robert Strecker was the first medical doctor to claim that AIDS was a man-made disease. Anyone who downloads the Strecker Memorandum can see that Dr. Strecker is a very knowledgeable doctor and scientist who makes a convincing case that AIDS was made in a laboratory and was in all likelihood spread by the contaminated vaccines. You know Strecker well, don't you?

Strecker was the first one to clue me in to the evidence that AIDS is manmade. I've been associated with him since the very beginning of the AIDS epidemic.

Strecker and his brother, Theodore Strecker, were pushing hard to make the government realize that AIDS was a biological attack that was man-made. But, then in August 1988, Theodore Strecker was found dead of a gunshot wound. It was ruled a suicide. Robert Strecker doesn't believe that his brother committed suicide, does he?
Well, I don't know. I think you would have to ask Strecker.

Strecker has said that his brother's death is suspicious.
Yes. But my feeling is if the government was going to kill somebody they would have killed Bob Strecker.

But Theodore Strecker was just as active as Robert Strecker, making Freedom of Information requests, getting all these documents and evidence that suggested AIDS came from the the government's biowarfare program.
Well, yes, that is true.

Illinois State Representative Douglas Huff of Chicago was perhaps the only politician in America who supported Strecker, and was doing everything he could to make people aware of Dr. Strecker's work. Huff was found dead of a drug overdose in September 1988.
Yes, and as I understand it some of Huff's associates feel the death is suspicious and wasn't an accident.

In the 1980s, Strecker and his brother were sending solid scientific data to all the government health agencies trying to make the government see that AIDS was man-made. At that time, Theodore Strecker claimed that he obtained a document that showed that the CIA was telling everyone in the government that Robert Strecker should be ignored. Eventually, Dr. Strecker's offices were burglarized and he claims that that document and all his research on the AIDS virus was stolen. Dr. Strecker believes that it was the government that burglarized his office?

Strecker did say to Len Horowitz that he believes the CIA burglarized his office.

Strecker is no longer out front and vocal and energetic about trying to make people realize that AIDS is a man-made virus. Did the suspicious deaths of his brother and Representative Huff, and the burglary of his office, intimidate Strecker into silence?

I don't think so. I think he kind of felt that he was beating his head against the wall. And I can see why, because I've gotten that feeling for years, you know, that I keep beating my head against the wall and hardly impressing anyone with the idea that there could be some substance to this evidence that AIDS is man-made. But Strecker and I feel strongly that this is not a crackpot theory.

Dr. Strecker has said that's it clear that the genetic structure of the AIDS virus does not exist in primates—in man or apes—and so the AIDS virus couldn't have come from monkeys.

I have the highest regard and respect for anything Strecker says. And I know he says that. But I'm not a virologist, so I don't think it's appropriate for me to comment on that.

Strecker and others have said that it is very clear and obvious that the genetic structure of the AIDS virus is actually a cow virus mixed with a sheep virus. He said that it's so unusual that it couldn't have come from nature that it had to have been made by scientists in a lab.

I know that he's said that. It could be.

Horowitz and Strecker have reasoned that the way the NCI was creating a virus that destroys the immune system for the SVCP was by mixing bovine and sheep viruses and then growing it in human tissue cultures. Hasn't Len Horowitz said that the scientific literature from the NCI's

SVCP shows that the NCI was creating an immunosuppressive virus in that way?

He may have. I know that both Strecker and Horowitz believe that the AIDS virus is the bovine and sheep virus mixed. So it certainly could be. But, again, I'm not a virologist and that's not my area of expertise.

The World Health Organization's (WHO) own literature proves that the WHO was working with viruses that destroy the immune system. In a 1972 issue of the **Bulletin of the World Health Organization,** *it was written that "An attempt should be made to see if viruses can in fact exert selective effects on immune function. The possibility should be looked into that the immune response to the virus itself may be impaired. . . ." That shows that the WHO was working on developing and studying viruses that destroy the T-cell system of man. That's exactly what AIDS is, right?*

Yes, it's clear they were working with an immunosuppressive virus. An AIDS–type virus. They are connections between the WHO and the CDC. And between the WHO and the pharmaceutical and vaccine industries, the moneyed industries.

Why was the WHO developing and studying viruses that can destroy the immune system?

My research didn't concentrate so much on the WHO. I know more about the Special Virus Cancer Program. The SVCP was seeking viruses that would negatively influence the immune system. They thought if they could create cancer in animals with these viruses that they could better understand cancer and the forces that would lead to cancer in humans. Of course, some of this is utter craziness. To intentionally create a deadly virus. But it is what animal researchers and virologists do.

In another 1972 issue of the Bulletin of the World Health Organization, WHO officials are talking about how to study how immune-destroying viruses would affect human beings. It's written that one way "would be to study the relationship . . . of the immune response . . . to bacterial and viral antigens during preventative vaccinations." WHO officials emphasize that "human controls should be carefully chosen." So the WHO was talking about studying how immune-destroying viruses would affect humans by putting the virus into vaccines?

Yes, I honestly think this was the plan.

How could the WHO get away with writing that? How could the WHO say that it wants to study immune-destroying viruses by putting them into a vaccine?

How many people read the bulletins of the WHO? Hardly anybody. I am sure that ninety-nine percent of the doctors who treat AIDS patients don't read them. And certainly not in the 1970s when these papers were published. So those doctors would have no idea that that's where AIDS could have come from. I'm sure that that bulletin is an "insider" thing. Basically, government sponsored scientists can do exactly what they want to do. Who is going to question them? There are no controls on crazy science. Are there any controls on biowarfare research? I think not.

Robert Strecker said that the WHO eventually published a map of Africa showing the places where the WHO was going to administer its smallpox vaccine, and after the inoculations AIDS broke out in those places in Africa.

Strecker and his late brother Ted brought these WHO documents to my attention in the mid 1980s. So, yes, there's strong evidence of a correlation between the smallpox vaccine and the outbreak of African AIDS.

On May 11, 1987, **The London Times** *printed an article—*Smallpox Vaccine Triggered AIDS Virus—*suggesting that the WHO administered vaccine caused the AIDS epidemic in Africa. Apparently, an employee of the WHO was asked to write a report on where AIDS in Africa had* *come from, and the employee ended up concluding that African AIDS came from the WHO vaccine. The WHO buried the report, never released the report, but the employee ended up bringing the report to the* **London Times?** *He wanted the story to get out?*

Yes. But that story was not picked up by any other major newspaper or media outlet. I believe it was the power and influence of the vaccine makers' industry—the pharmaceutical corporations—that kept the story out of the rest of the media. The WHO employee who brought the story to the *London Times* editor remained anonymous.

After *that* **London Times** *article came out even Dr. Robert Gallo said that AIDS in Africa might have come from the smallpox vaccine, correct?*

Yes, he did.

This Dr. Gallo really seems like a man of questionable ethics and character, doesn't he? By being credited as the scientist who discovered the AIDS virus, Gallo became a world famous scientist and a wealthy scientist. But wasn't there a big controversy as to whether or not Gallo was really the first man to discover the virus?

Yes. Ultimately, Gallo had to share credit for discovering HIV with Luc Montagnier, a scientist from France. Gallo and his staff were accused of all sorts of violations and improprieties. The fact that whoever got credited with discovering HIV would begin to receive about $100,000 a year for the patent on how to identify HIV might have had something to do with Gallo wanting so badly to be credited as the discoverer.

When the NCI was creating viruses that destroy the immune system for the Special Virus Cancer Program, wasn't Dr. Robert Gallo the chief scientist in charge of that? Isn't there a real chance that Dr. Gallo is the scientist who created the AIDS virus?

The SCVP was made up of leading scientists working at the leading medical institutions in the USA. Gallo was one of the heads. His position was at the National Cancer Institute.

Other investigators believe that Gallo was the chief scientist in charge of creating immune destroying viruses. . . . According to Len Horowitz, Dr. Gallo has made some blatantly false, misleading statements regarding AIDS. Gallo has said AIDS can't be man-made because virologists like himself didn't have the technology to create such viruses in the '60s and the '70s. But his own published scientific literature shows that Gallo was creating and working with such viruses as early as the early 1960s. Gallo also said that the DNA in the AIDS virus is different from the viruses he was working with, but other experts say that is not true. These misleading statements really make Gallo look bad, don't they? Is Gallo trying to hide something?

The last thing Gallo would ever seriously speculate is that HIV/AIDS came from a government lab. Although he did admit such an explanation in his book *Virus,* but called it "far-fetched" and "baroque."

Gallo made the official announcement that he had "discovered" the AIDS virus in 1984, but the specific biological aspects of the AIDS virus that he "revealed" in 1984 were data that he was working with and knew about as far back as 1970 when he was creating viruses that destroy the immune system, right?

Yes. So to say that Gallo "discovered" the AIDS virus is really a dubious statement.

In your opinion, was Dr. Robert Gallo the scientist who created the AIDS virus?

I think it had to be a team effort, and was conducted under the strictest secrecy. Top secret. And everyone involved was told that if they spilled the beans they would be under penalty of prison. Or *worse.* There is no way to investigate secret science. That's why such science should be banned. But, obviously, the US biowarfare program was heavily funded and totally secret.

Gallo has had connections to and has worked for the highest levels of the government and the big drug companies. Do you think it could be said that Dr. Gallo is the government's and the drug companies' chief dispenser of disinformation and propaganda regarding the AIDS virus?
Gallo is considered the most influential AIDS researcher due to his "discovery" of HIV. So when he pronounced that AIDS came from the green monkey that was basically accepted as fact. I, certainly, though, don't consider it a fact.

But do you think that Robert Gallo has consciously and deliberately made false statements about AIDS?
I believe his insistence that HIV/AIDS jumped species from a green monkey is meant to totally discourage any attention paid to the man-made theory.

Right before Bill Clinton left the White House, he gave Robert Gallo a pardon for something, didn't he? What did President Clinton pardon Gallo for?
I am not aware of any pardon from Clinton. Gallo was, as I recall, exonerated from accusations of "scientific misconduct." Many aspects of AIDS "science" are sleazy. And, Gallo, I believe is *not* well respected by many colleagues. Consider that he never won the Nobel Prize—although he has been given many other prizes.

Do you believe AIDS may be a population control project? During the 1960s and 1970s top US government, United Nations, and WHO officials considered the problem of global overpopulation to be a dire emergency. Overpopulation would mean too many starving people, and the unruly masses causing too many economic and social problems for the ruling governments. A State Department report released during President

Carter's administration said, "Overpopulation has been an underlying factor in certain international conflicts and major internal disorders. This danger continues and may intensify as populations burgeon. . . ." **National Security Study Memorandum 200, The Kissinger Report,** *released in December 1974 was an extensive, detailed paper showing the adverse implications of global population, and called for depopulation programs to be immediately implemented in many Third World countries. Henry Kissinger, himself, had been covertly manipulating the politics of Africa, had an intense geopolitical interest in the resources and nations of Africa, and felt strongly that Africa had to be depopulated. Do you believe that AIDS could be an official depopulation program?*

That evidence certainly suggests that. And I also think that the fact that the government really had no interest in the spread of this disease in the first few years is suspicious. The government didn't even mention the word AIDS until about three years after it broke out. Nor did anyone of note bring out the possibility that this could be some biological warfare agent that might have escaped into the community. Not one person in science, or the government. And of course that was—for the decade or so before HIV broke out—that was one of the big fears of the scientific community.

They talked about that at the conference at Asilomar.

Yes. That's very, very important. Top scientists, government scientists knew—and had even prepared for the possibility—that one of these government-made viruses could escape into the population. Yet, not one government health official mentioned that possibility.

In his **Vanity Fair** *articles, writer Christopher Hitchens makes a strong case that Henry Kissinger was a war criminal and if Kissinger felt that some global area had to be controlled for some corporate interests then Kissinger wouldn't hesitate to initiate a war or bombings that he knew would end up killing thousands of civilians.*

Apparently, some mainstream publications have questioned Kissinger's actions and character. That's something Horowitz wrote about, also. I know Len Horowitz wrote about how the CIA and Kissinger were involved in Africa's politics, and how they felt that Africa had to be depopulated. Those are interesting theories. My books are more about the overwhelming evidence that AIDS in America came from the hepatitis B vaccine, and how that evidence is being ignored by the government, media, and medical establishment.

In his book, **Emerging Viruses,** *Horowitz makes it clear that in the 1960s, Henry Kissinger was in charge of the military's biowarfare program and Horowitz feels certain that it was Kissinger who prompted the Defense Department to ask the Congress for ten million dollars to develop a virus that destroys the immune system. It's well known that Kissinger belongs to these elitist, very influential think tanks that want to manipulate the nations of the world into a world government, a New World Order. Individuals belonging to these New World Order think tanks have written that the strongest impediment to forming a world government is overpopulation. What's your opinion of the theory that there's a small fraternity of super-influential, wealthy men that wants to use its influence to set up and control—from behind the scenes—a one-world government and that these influences decided to start the AIDS virus to decrease the world's population because it would be easier to force the people of the world into a world government if there were fewer people?*
It makes sense to me. I also feel that AIDS is just one of these man-made viruses. And the reason that I feel that's it so important to get this information out is because if people do not recognize AIDS as—to me—such an obviously man-made disease, then the government is going to pull the wool over our eyes with all these other emerging viruses, some of which I personally think are experimental. Like SARS. And like the Hantavirus on the Indian reservations.

You think those are man-made diseases, too?
Well, I think they're experimental stuff. That scientists or doctors—or the government—were experimenting with certain vaccines and drugs, and that's where SARS and the Hantavirus came from.

Len Horowitz feels strongly that the New World Order influences are intent on using vaccines for depopulation and that the Ebola and West Nile viruses are also man-made.
It certainly could be. If you look at the evidence, you could believe it.

The WHO would be considered a New World Order organization involved with globalization. You've written that it's no secret that since the 1970s the WHO has been testing and funding antifertility vaccines. The WHO has been—apparently—trying to retard population growth by giving out vaccines that cause sterility in young women?
That's true. A few years ago, the WHO and the CDC were involved with sponsoring a polio vaccine that was going to be given to seventy-five million Africans. But officials in Africa are now suspicious of government- and WHO-administered vaccines. A Nigerian health official got samples of the vaccine, tested them, and found that they were contaminated with estrogen and other female sex hormones that could cause sterility in young women. The official commented that those who imported the fake drug in the name of a polio vaccine should be prosecuted like any other criminal.

The WHO also gave out a vaccine to millions of female Mexicans, Nicaraguans, and Filipinos that caused sterilization?
That's true, also. In the '90s, millions of these women were duped into taking tetanus vaccines. Later, it was discovered that the tetanus vaccine was laced with the pregnancy hormone HCG, a hormone that can cause miscarriage and sterilization. The WHO had recommended the vaccines only to women of childbearing age. Afterwards, many of the women

experienced vaginal bleeding and miscarriages. They had developed antibodies to tetanus, but also to HCG. Without HCG, growth of the fetus is impaired. The Philippines Medical Association found that twenty percent of the WHO tetanus vaccines were contaminated with the hormone. The WHO, of course, denied it.

So it would seem the WHO is trying to retard population growth by giving out these antifertility vaccines?
Yes. About twenty years ago the WHO sponsored a symposium on antifertility vaccines and contraceptive vaccines. These vaccines can make a woman's immune system attack and destroy her own baby in the womb.

If some clique of power deliberately and intentionally inflicted AIDS on us, then something like that wouldn't be unprecedented, would it? The US government has a history of using its own citizens as guinea pigs for scientific tests.
The Army's department of biological warfare and the CIA have a well-documented tradition of experimentation on human beings. Anyone who thinks otherwise would be naïve. Some of these incidences were investigated by the Congress back in the '70s. A good book that talks about that is *A Higher Form of Killing*. In the '70s, the CIA admitted that it had engaged in about two hundred experiments using dangerous drugs, or electric shock, or hypnosis to see how people reacted. There must be hundreds of horror stories of US military personnel and civilians who have been damaged or even killed by such experiments. The army certainly damaged some of their soldiers when they tested LSD on them. One of the most infamous military biowarfare tests occurred in 1950 when the army tested a harmful bacteria by spraying it over the city of San Francisco. People developed pneumonia, and one elderly man died. These tests also take place on soldiers on military bases. Back in the late '50s, the army did a test with mosquitoes that may have had yellow fever, releasing the mosquitoes into some

poor black communities in the south. Some of the people there died, others developed strange fevers. There are other examples. And, of course, there was Tuskegee. And anyone who thinks that government scientists haven't tested risky vaccines and treatments, or used citizens as guinea pigs for other scientific tests, can google "secret human medical experimentation" and read what comes up.

If you investigate that, you can see that there have been a lot of scientists who have had the mentality of the "mad scientist." There have many times when government scientists or other scientists have intentionally put a disease into people so they can study the disease. Or intentionally used a risky, dangerous vaccine on people to test the vaccine. The people that the scientists are using are usually either minorities, or prisoners, or gays, or the mentally retarded.

Some of these doctors have been as diabolical as the worst hardened criminals and murderers.

In 1972, after the Tuskegee Experiments were exposed, a journalist wrote that the CDC "sees the poor, the black, the illiterate, and the defenseless in American society as a vast experimental resource for the government." That sums it up pretty well.

You've pointed out that if AIDS is eventually proven to be an intentional mass murder, that wouldn't be something new for mankind. That genocides are a part of the human race's history.

Mankind has always found ways to justify murder of large groups of people who were disliked for various religious, cultural, and political reasons. Hitler tried to exterminate the Jews. In the early 1900s, the Turks killed off four and a half million Armenians. Joseph Stalin killed millions of Russians. In the 1970s, the government of Cambodia executed millions of its own citizens. Mao Tse Tung eliminated fifty million reactionaries in

China. Recently, in the 1990s, about a million Rwandan citizens were killed in a three month genocide. Gays have been hated. Blacks have been hated. So if the powers that be felt that the world needed to be depopulated, and they decided to do that by killing off gays and blacks, something like that wouldn't be a new experience for our planet.

In 2001, some of the leading scientists in the world met at a conference on the origin of AIDS at the Royal Society of London. Some of those scientists concluded that AIDS could very well be man-made and could have come from vaccines, correct?

Perhaps, but the main conclusion of the conference was that AIDS is not man-made. The purpose of that conference was to consider the theory that AIDS could have come from the polio vaccines given out in the '50s and '60s. But the conference ended up concluding that AIDS didn't come from the polio vaccine. That AIDS is zoonotic—that the virus probably jumped species from a monkey. The Strecker-Cantwell-Horowitz theory that AIDS came from the hepatitis B vaccine wasn't even considered. Our theory wasn't even on the table.

Some scientists and writers attending the conference, though, did write independent papers saying they believed that AIDS could very well be man-made. Dr. Gerald Meyers, the US government's chief DNA sequence analyst, and a highly respected AIDS origin theorist, has expressed that he believes AIDS had to be man-made.

Then Myers is one scientist who is talking sense.

Myers has pointed out that there are so many different types of HIV that they couldn't have possibly occurred from one single isolated cross species transmission—from a monkey bite. He wrote that the most likely explanation as to the origin of AIDS is that is man-made and that the contaminated vaccine hypothesis is a likely, strong possibility.

But I'm sure the AIDS establishment and the media haven't paid any attention to Myers's opinions. The theory that AIDS is man-made has always been completely ignored by the AIDS establishment and the media.

Dr. Julian Cribb is another scientist from the Royal Society of London conference who believes AIDS could very well be man-made. Dr. Cribb has said that he believes that the reason why the important medical journals don't publish any papers theorizing that AIDS came from vaccines is because it's the vaccine makers that finance the medical journals.

Yes. It is the pharmaceutical corporations—the vaccine makers—that are the financial backers of the most influential medical journals. So, naturally, if it's the vaccine makers that are funding the medical journals there probably won't be any papers there that are questioning or criticizing vaccines, will there?

You've also pointed out that AIDS research in America is controlled by the Pentagon.

It's the Pentagon that controls and grants the big money for AIDS research. So if you're not toeing the government-Pentagon line—that AIDS came from one green monkey—then you're not going to get any money for AIDS research, or any recognition as an important AIDS researcher.

So, basically, there hasn't been a free inquiry into the origin of AIDS in America. The inquiry is controlled by the Pentagon and the vaccine makers?

Yes.

AIDS is not a homosexual disease, is it?

No, it's not. About ninety percent of the people in the world who have AIDS are heterosexual. In Africa, more than ninety-five percent of the time AIDS is transmitted from one person to the next through heterosexual sex. AIDS became known and is still considered by many to be a homosexual disease because, I contend, AIDS in America came from the hepatitis B vaccine given exclusively to gay men in 1978 and 1979. So, after that, people had a convenient scapegoat—homosexuals—to blame the AIDS epidemic on. Pronouncements were made that it was the promiscuous, immoral lifestyle of homosexuals that was the cause of AIDS.

You've written that you believe that there's evidence that the AIDS virus in Africa has a strain in it that makes it more transmittable through vaginal—heterosexual—sex, while the AIDS virus in America has a different strain that makes it more easily transmittable through anal—homosexual—sex? If that's true, does that give more credence to the theory that AIDS is man-made?
I think so. It would seem to me that if American AIDS came from Africa—which it did not—then the strains would be similar, not different. Max Essex, an AIDS researcher from Harvard, has talked about the different strains in HIV.

There's a growing movement of more and more people who are concerned that vaccines are dangerous and are causing serious health problems. Barbara Fisher, president of the National Vaccine Information Center, claims vaccines are responsible for the increasing number of children and adults who suffer from immune system and neurological disorders, and many other ailments. Vaccine investigator Neil Z. Miller insists that before mass vaccination programs began fifty years ago we didn't have cancer in epidemic numbers, that autoimmune ailments were barely known, and childhood autism did not exist. You've written that vaccines can be dangerous and might cause more problems than they solve. Why do you say that?
Well, because they can be contaminated. And, certainly, it's not rare to have vaccines contaminated. A couple of years ago, as I recall, the flu vaccines that came from England—half the country's supply was contaminated.

Recently—I believe it was in France—some people were suing the makers of a hepatitis B vaccine because they felt that vaccine had injured their health. There are many other examples. Vaccines can also be the perfect way, I mean if you're diabolic and you want to seed something into a population, and you want to seed it in large numbers, the best way to do it is through vaccines.

So there have been instances in the past when the WHO and other health agencies have knowingly used unproven and dangerous vaccines on people and this has led to deaths and illnesses?
Well, you could certainly find evidence for that. Yes. A few years ago, they were using a vaccine on some minorities in the inner cities that caused problems. Certainly, the polio vaccines of the 1950s are a prime example of how an inoculation can be contaminated. There's a book called *The Virus and the Vaccine,* and the gist of that was that with the polio vaccine half the American population was injected with a cancer-causing monkey virus. The manufacturers didn't have a clue that it was in the vaccine. People think that vaccines are sterile. But, of course, vaccines can't be sterilized because then they don't work. And people think, well, a vaccine must be tested for viruses, but vaccines are not tested directly for viruses.

It's been well documented that there was—as you just said—a cancer-causing monkey virus in the polio vaccine. The government—the National Cancer Institute—has admitted and acknowledged that. There have been a number of investigations and studies to determine if that virus led to many people getting cancer. The investigations sponsored by the government concluded that the polio vaccine virus didn't lead to any outbreak of cancer. The investigations done by reporters and scientists who had no connection to the government concluded that that virus could have led to millions of people getting cancer.
Yes.

So the polio vaccine has probably caused cancer in some people?
Yes. Maybe in a lot of people.

Even Jonas Salk admitted that something in his polio vaccine could have caused cancer?
Yes. He was talking about that monkey virus. He said that and admitted that at a scientific convention.

*In a book called **Vaccine A**, journalist Gary Matsumoto has made a convincing case that the Gulf War Syndrome from the first Gulf War came from an anthrax vaccine. The US military knew that the vaccine was dangerous, and they gave it to soldiers anyway. Now all these soldiers are ailing, and the government is ignoring the problem and denying any possibility that Gulf War Syndrome came from the vaccine, which, in all likelihood, it did.*
Yes, there's certainly some strong evidence pointing to that. But, of course, the government denies it. I think whenever the government says that something can't be, we have to realize that that is a cliché and not a satisfactory explanation.

There's evidence and many people feel strongly that autism comes from vaccines, don't they?
Well, absolutely. My feeling is that the only way that you can really test the validity of the hypothesis that autism came from vaccines is to take a group of people—kids—and don't vaccinate them. Of course, the government does not want to do that, but that is the only way. I thought maybe this Mormon group down in Texas—I thought they would be a great group to check for autism. I don't know if they get vaccines, but I have a feeling that they don't get the large number that is required for kids in America now. I thought, wouldn't that be a perfect group to see how many of those kids are autistic.

Some people say that parents who are leery of vaccinating their children because they're afraid vaccines might be dangerous are wrong and putting the community at risk. But the fact is that since the late 1980s judges have ruled in more than three thousand court cases that a child or adult's health was injured by a vaccine. And the pharmaceutical industry has had to pay out about three billion dollars in compensation.

Yes. The pharmaceutical companies have paid out billions of dollars to people who have been injured by vaccines. So how could it not be logical to be concerned about the health effects of shots?

The FDA states that a certain amount of mercury and aluminum is very dangerous and toxic to our bodies. But the amounts of mercury and aluminum put into certain everyday vaccines is more than the amount that the FDA itself says is safe.

It sounds crazy, yes. So, again, why shouldn't we be concerned about the safety of vaccines? Why there would be unhealthy, toxic amounts of mercury, of aluminum, in vaccines is really a mystery. . . . It doesn't seem to make a bit of sense.

Is there any other way to protect ourselves from diseases besides being inoculated with vaccines? Do you think we'd be better off without vaccines?

Well, you know, when I grew up I had mumps, I had measles, I had chicken pox, and I'm still *here*. I mean I realize that those diseases can be serious. But my point is, you know, are those diseases as bad as an epidemic of AIDS? I don't think so. When the government decided to use gay people and to save gay people from hepatitis B, in the process—as far as I'm concerned—they gave the gay community a plague. So, you know, to do an experiment and say we're going to save the gay community and improve their health and then kill off half of them, to me, is not much of an advantage.

*Vaccines are very profitable, big business for the manufacturers of vac-
cines and doctors, aren't they?*
Vaccines are extremely profitable. When you start casting doubt on vaccines, that is like taboo. They're one of the best ways for the medical profes-
sions—one way or another—to make money. Patients have to keep coming
back to the office for their shots. When I was a kid I got maybe a couple of
shots. Now, what is it, you get like two dozen vaccines by the time you're
four or five years old. And we don't know what is in the vaccines, so, you
know, it's scary how they make them.

*There may be a couple of smoking guns that prove that AIDS is a man-
made disease created by scientists. Dr. Maurice Hilleman was considered
the world's leading vaccine developer. In the 1970s, Hilleman was working as the chief vaccinologist for the pharmaceutical corporation Merck,
which was connected to the Litton corporation. Merck and Litton had
long been two of the companies that made biological weapons for the
US government's biowarfare program. A medical historian interviewed
Hilleman in 1986, and in that interview Hilleman stated that back in
the '70s Litton sent a bunch of green monkeys from their labs in Africa
to Merck in America. Merck was the company that made the hepatitis
B vaccine given to gay men in 1979 and it was these green monkeys that
Hilleman used to create that vaccine. In the interview, Hilleman then
said, "I didn't know we were importing AIDS virus at the time." . . .
The way that vaccinologists make vaccines is they deliberately put a
virus or disease into lab monkeys, the monkeys develop the antibodies
to destroy the virus or disease, and then the vaccinologists create the
vaccine from that blood. Apparently, though, according to Hilleman's
own words, Litton had also deliberately put the AIDS virus into these
monkeys because Litton was one of the companies developing immune-
destroying viruses for the US military. So, right there, Hilleman was
admitting that AIDS came from the hepatitis B vaccine?*

Yes. And we have Len Horowitz to thank for that. Horowitz found that during his research. The first time I heard that I found it to be mind blowing. That's more strong evidence that AIDS came from scientists.

How could Hilleman get away with saying something like that? Was it a slip of the tongue? Or do scientists working for powerful corporations on contract from the US government know that they can say anything they want and get away with whatever they want?
Anyone who has carefully studied the history of US involvement in biological warfare should understand that scientists can get away with anything. Including murder. All that is needed is government support.

Is it possible that Hilleman was saying that these monkeys had developed the AIDS virus naturally in the jungle?
These were lab monkeys. These were monkeys that Litton and Merck were injecting with all sorts of immunosuppressive viruses because Litton and Merck were connected to and worked with the Special Virus Cancer Program and the military's biowarfare program. Merck was the company that made the hepatitis B vaccine that was given to thousands of gay men.

In that interview, Hilleman also mentioned that he believes the polio vaccine caused cancer and another vaccine that Merck manufactured for Russian health officials was going to give some Russian athletes cancer.
Yes, he did. Something, huh? What a world.

Anyone who watches that interview on YouTube can see that Hilleman sort of laughs and chuckles when he says Merck imported AIDS. Robert Gallo called Hilleman the most successful vaccinologist in history. Hilleman developed more than three dozen vaccines, and of the fourteen vaccines currently recommended for children, Hilleman created eight of them. And yet Hilleman has casually remarked that vaccinologists brought the AIDS virus into America, and that some vaccines have caused cancer. That clearly shows that we have to be careful and mindful about what vaccines public health officials and doctors are leading us to take, doesn't it?

Undoubtedly. It absolutely does. Author Neil Z. Miller has written a good book about the potential dangers of vaccines.

Another smoking gun might be this government document that a researcher named Boyd Graves has discovered. Graves obtained from government archives documents on the National Cancer Institutute's Special Virus Cancer Program. Specifically, Graves obtained a flow-chart that details the plan and the agenda of the SVCP. Graves claims this flowchart proves that AIDS came from the government. Does the flowchart specifically mention that the NCI was working with a virus that destroys the immune system?

I have the documents of that program. There's no question that the scientists wanted to create an immunosuppressive virus. And the rationale for that, of course, is if we could produce cancer in animals then we could study it better. So there's no question that they did that. And there was no question that this program had ties to the biological warfare people. And ties to the most prestigious medical institutions in the country.

Does it say—anywhere in the flowchart—that the special virus has to be tested on humans?

It says that we can't test this on humans. That would be unethical. But I believe they did. Because doctors know that no matter how many experiments you do with a germ on animals, it's not going to cut it if you haven't proven that it can do the same things in humans. What you can know from reading the history of biological warfare—not only in this country but in other countries—is you always have to test humans. They always test it on humans.

Do you believe this document, this flowchart, proves that AIDS came from the government, from the NCI's SVCP?

Yes, I do. If you read between the lines. And I think that it's very important; I don't think that the flowchart proves anything if you don't read between the lines. But if you read between the lines—like I said, all doctors know you have to test things in humans. So when somebody says "You know, it would be great if we could test this in humans but we can't," you know somebody is going to say "Oh, yes we can. And so why not use fags because if we use fags nobody will suspect anything because we all know fags do things that nobody else does. They're immoral and loaded with all kinds of diseases, and all that." And so actually it proved true. I mean, you know, if you ask a lot of people where AIDS came from and if they're bigoted they'll say, "Oh, you know, those fags started it."

You've been a doctor for a long time and you've written that you believe that the medical establishment doesn't want to find a cure for cancer, or AIDS. Why do you say that?

Well, cancer is big, big business. AIDS is big business, too. And, also, my main claim to fame certainly is not conspiracy theory. I've written other books books; some other researchers and I have discovered that there's a germ in cancer and a germ in AIDS. It's a bacteria. And that's very important. And we feel the fact that the AIDS establishment and the cancer establishment apparently don't have a clue to this research and/or don't consider it to have any validity is a big, big scientific mistake. Even Luc Montagnier himself—the co-founder of HIV—early on Montagnier was saying there was a microplasma—a bacteria—that strengthens AIDS. That caused a sensation at first, but then the AIDS establishment turned off to that. That work pretty much, again, got shoved under the carpet. I think the virologists wanted to make AIDS their disease and they wanted to make the money off it.

Do you also believe that the medical establishment suppresses or ignores evidence that alternative or holistic methods might be effective in treating cancer and AIDS?

Well, yes, I think that alternative and holistic methods are suppressed by the medical establishment. At this point, though, I think that the protease inhibitors have been very good in terms of keeping AIDS patients alive. It's not ideal because most people can't afford it and the Third World people can't afford it. But I do think you have to give the medical establishment credit for having come up with that because prior to this cocktail gay men and other people were dying like flies.

If it was revealed, or admitted, or hypothesized that AIDS came from the hepatitis B vaccine in America and the smallpox vaccine in Africa, then scientists might be able to look at the records of what was in those vaccines and might have a better chance at finding a cure? If we knew what caused AIDS would it be easier or more likely that scientists could find the cure?

Well, yes, I think so. I think as long as we continue to believe that this is one monkey who sodomized one African and that's why forty million people are facing death—as long as we believe in what I call these scientific fairy tales, then we're never going to get anywhere. I think it's obvious that we're not stopping AIDS. You know "use a condom" or "stay celibate" and all of that is not working very well. Personally, I think if the public was aware that this was a man-made disease then, first of all, the public would assure that this would never happen again, and the people who were giving the public all this bullshit surrounding the monkeys in the jungle as the cause of AIDS would be severely reprimanded or put of business. I think the ties in to biological warfare would mean that these laboratories would have to be shut down or they would have to fess up to the public about the kind of monsters that these biowarfare makers were or are producing. Also, I think that if it were shown that the government was behind this as a man-made disease that the people who were the victims of this agent should be given free medication. Of the very, very best kind.

As it is now, AIDS is big business?
AIDS is a billion dollar business. AIDS scientists profit, and some drug companies have become very rich. Merck, in particular, makes exorbitant amounts of money manufacturing drugs for AIDS patients.

After the Royal Society of London conference in 2001 when some of the world's leading scientists concluded that AIDS very well could have been man-made and come from vaccines, Dr. Julian Cribb wrote that the medical establishment has ignored any scientist who has suggested that AIDS came from contaminated vaccines and that there has never been a serious scientific investigation on how AIDS entered our species. He then gave a number of reasons why it is important to know the origin of AIDS: because the source of no great human catastrophe should go uninvestigated, and it is essential we understand how to avoid such calamities in the future; because understanding an origin sometimes reveals ways to solve the problem; because other dangerous viruses undoubtedly exist, and acknowledging the possibility that AIDS is man-made will compel a far more cautious approach to using primates to make vaccines and other trans-species experiments; and, for the sake of the integrity of science, and for the preservation of trust in science in the eyes of the community.
I would agree and concur with all of that. Personally, I think the evidence pointing to AIDS as a man-made disease is the most important story of the twentieth century. AIDS has killed thirty million people. Forty million people are now infected with HIV. And this is still the beginning.

CHAPTER 7

Is the Cancer Establishment Ignoring and Suppressing Effective, Natural, and Inexpensive Treatments and Cures for Cancer?

An interview with author and cancer researcher Dr. Ralph Moss

D r. Linus Pauling was the only person ever to win two unshared Nobel prizes. In 1954, Dr. Pauling was awarded the Nobel Prize for chemistry, and in 1962, for his political activism, Pauling was given the Nobel Peace Prize. He was one of America's greatest chemists and an outstanding, eminent scientist of the twentieth century. In the 1960s, Pauling began looking into cancer and his theory that high doses of vitamin C could help and even cure cancer patients. Pauling believed that vitamin C wasn't "a special anticancer wonder drug" but could "bolster up the body's natural protective mechanisms." In 1971, a hospital in Scotland, under the guidance of Dr. Linus Pauling, began treating cancer patients with intravenous high doses of vitamin C.

The results were positive and the Scottish hospital has the records of the many patients who were helped, who were given significantly more years of life, and some who were even cured by megadoses of vitamin C. Since then other doctors have treated cancer patients with intravenous vitamin C and have had similar results.[4]

Try as he may, though, Dr, Pauling couldn't get the FDA and National Cancer Institute to recognize and publicize his work. For something to become a mainstream treatment for cancer in America, it, of course, has to be approved by the FDA. Even though Dr. Pauling was one of the most respected scientists in the world, the FDA and NCI continually ignored Dr. Pauling, and, ultimately, never properly tested, accepted, or publicized the positive effects that vitamin C can have on cancer patients.

The theory of those who advocate alternative treatments for cancer is that the overwhelming majority of the personnel at the FDA and NCI who are involved with cancer research are people who have been educated and trained to promote chemotherapy. Many FDA officials have already worked for the pharmaceutical-chemotherapy corporations or get a job with Big Pharma after their careers at the FDA. Advocates of alternative cancer treatments also claim that FDA officials won't give serious consideration to any treatment for cancer that can't be patented. Anything like vitamin C, or any vitamin, or any herb or plant can't be patented by a drug company because it comes from nature. If FDA officials—agents of the chemotherapy companies—announced that vitamin C was a better treatment for cancer than chemotherapy, then hundreds of companies could start extracting vitamin C from nature and selling it as the new medicine for cancer. The small handful of pharmaceutical corporations that have a monopoly on providing the medicine for cancer—patented chemotherapy drugs—would lose their corner on the cancer industry. These companies would be out billions of dollars. Hundreds of hospitals that are financially dependent on the revenue from chemotherapy would also go out of business, and so would thousands of oncologists who sell and treat cancer with chemo. The fortunes, lives, and careers of a few major pharmaceutical corporations, hundreds of hospitals, and thousands of health officials in the cancer industry are dependent on the sales of patented chemotherapy drugs and so—the theory goes—no admission that some nonpatentable, natural treatment can help cancer patients is going to come from the cancer industry. Dr. Pauling himself must have come to this conclusion, because during his futile efforts to work with the FDA and NCI he wrote that one of the reasons that the cancer industry wouldn't recognize high doses of vitamin C as a viable treatment for cancer "has probably been the lack of interest of the drug companies in a natural substance that is available at a low price and cannot be patented." After his unsuccessful attempts to get the FDA and NCI to recognize and publicize his work, Dr. Linus Pauling, the only person ever to win two Nobel Prizes, also said, "Everyone should know that the 'war on cancer' is largely a fraud."

Since the early 1900s, Memorial Sloan Kettering Hospital in New York City has been the most influential cancer hospital in America. To the cancer establishment, the scientists and doctors at Sloan Kettering are the most revered in the industry and it is the decisions made at Sloan Kettering that have a determining influence on what is done about cancer in America and even throughout much of the rest of the world. One of Sloan Kettering's most distinguished scientists was Dr. Kanematsu Sugiura. From 1917 until the early '80s, Dr. Sugiura researched cancer treatments at Sloan. During this sixty-five year career, Sugiura wrote many papers and his opinions were highly respected throughout the national and global cancer establishment. If Katematsu Sugiura said something, it was accepted as true. In 1972, Dr. Sugiura's research began showing that laetrile—which is the same thing as vitamin B-17—was stopping the growth of cancerous tumors in lab mice, and was preventing mice from getting cancer. If something works in laboratory animals, it indicates it could behave the same way in humans. Dr. Sugiura's tests and experiments continually showed that laetrile/vitamin B-17 had strong anticancer properties, and Sugiura felt that it "might be the most promising cancer treatment I have ever come across."

It wasn't Dr. Sugiura's job, though, to publicize this information. That was up to the leadership of Sloan Kettering. But on June 15, 1977, the leadership of Sloan Kettering—men who were trained and educated to promote chemotherapy—organized a press conference and announced that Sloan

Kettering's tests had proven that "laetrile shows no anticancer properties and has no positive effects on cancer" and that Sloan Kettering "would no longer be taking the time or effort to test laetrile as a possible cancer treatment." Towards the end of the conference, when a reporter asked Dr. Sugiura, who was sitting off to the side of the meeting, if he still stuck to his belief that laetrile stops the spread of cancer, the eighty-six year old Japanese American defiantly shouted, "I stick!"

At the time of this incident, Dr. Ralph Moss worked as a science writer and assistant director of public affairs for Sloan Kettering. Part of Moss's job was to write press releases for the hospital. Dr. Moss knew that Dr. Sugiura was Sloan Kettering's most distinguished scientist and when Moss met with Sugiura, the scientist showed him all his notes and data that proved that laetrile was a strong anticancer agent. When Dr. Moss asked Sugiura why Sloan Kettering, the NCI, and the American Cancer Society weren't admitting this, Dr. Sugiura repled, "I don't know. Maybe the medical profession doesn't like it because they are making too much money." Three months later, Dr. Moss and other insider employees of Sloan Kettering formed a group called *Second Opinion* and released a report that expressed that the leadership of Sloan had not been truthful. The *Second Opinion* group announced that the research at Sloan Kettering clearly showed that laetrile could stop the spread of cancer and not only did Dr. Sugiura know this, but so did many Sloan Kettering officials. When the leadership of Sloan Kettering realized that Ralph Moss had helped to write this report they demanded that he retract his statements and go along with the Sloan Kettering party line that laetrile was ineffective against cancer. Moss knew this wasn't true, couldn't do that, and, so, in November 1977, Sloan Kettering fired Ralph Moss "for failing to carry out his basic job responsibility"—i.e., to lie to the public about what goes on in cancer research. Today, Ralph Moss is one of the most well known critics of the cancer establishment, and is considered by some to be the world's leading expert on alternative treatments for cancer.

Along with Sloan Kettering, it is the American Cancer Society that is the most influential cancer institution in America. The ACS has a powerful public relations department, has connections throughout the media and government, and much of what the media and government says about cancer comes from the ACS. The Society has always been able to raise millions of dollars, and much of cancer research in America is controlled by what the ACS wants and by the funds that the ACS grants. From their beginnings, both Sloan Kettering and the ACS were financed and controlled by a name very familiar to America and American business: the Rockefeller family. Beginning in the 1920s, the Rockefellers began financial contributions to Memorial Hospital and then donated the land on which the new Memorial Sloan Kettering Hospital was built in the 1930s, giving the Rockefellers a controlling influence over the hospital. The American Cancer Society was originally founded at the New York Harvard Club in 1913 with funding from John D. Rockefeller Jr. and other wealthy New York patrons close to the Rockefeller financial group. In the late 1920s, Rockefeller's Standard Oil of New Jersey merged with the largest pharmaceutical corporation in the world, Germany's IG Farben, and by the 1930s IG Farben had come to dominate the pharmaceutical industry in America. A few of the many drug companies that IG Farben came to own or control were Bayer, Hoffman-Laroche, and Bristol Meyers. From their starts, the boards of Sloan Kettering and the ACS have always been dominated by Rockefeller, other Wall Street bankers invested in pharmaceutical corporations, and other pharmaceutical representatives and CEOs. Cancer research and what is done about cancer in America isn't controlled and guided by doctors and scientists—uninfluenced—looking into ways to cure cancer. Cancer research in America is controlled by the board members of Sloan Kettering and the ACS who are Wall Street bankers and pharmaceutical representatives who have a clear interest in wanting to sell chemotherapy. Much if not all of the funding for medical education and cancer research can also be traced back to the pharmaceutical companies.

To those who believe that alternative treatments could help many cancer patients, the feeling is that no alternative treatment for cancer is ever going to be approved by the cancer establishment because the boards of Sloan Kettering and the ACS are controlled by pharmaceutical representatives, and all the money for medical education and cancer research is coming from the pharmaceutical-chemotherapy industry. Everything is tainted and influenced by the enormous, unparalleled financial resources of Big Pharma. When asked why there has been virtually no progress in the war on cancer in the last fifty years, Ralph Moss said, "Everything points back to the pharmaceutical industry." And former FDA Commissioner himself, Dr. David Kessler, once remarked, "Everything is tainted. Almost every doctor in academia has something going on the side, and I don't know what it is. I don't have the authority to find out. I don't know what they are getting legally as far as financial return, stock, money, whatever. I certainly don't know what they are getting under the table."

There has been a clear history in America of the cancer establishment—Sloan Kettering, the ACS, the FDA, the NCI—ignoring, suppressing, and outlawing promising natural, alternative treatments for cancer. The American Medical Association was originally organized by pharmaceutical representatives to counter the opinions of naturopathic scientists and doctors, and the AMA, also, has never promoted any natural, nonpatentable cancer treatment. Along with Dr. Pauling's vitamin C protocol, and laetrile, there has been:

Burton Method. During the 1950s and '60s, Dr. Lawrence Burton worked in cancer research at St. Vincent's Hospital in New York City where he managed to extract a factor from mouse blood that caused long-term remission of cancer in mice. In the late 1960s, in a demonstration at an annual American Cancer Society meeting, Burton injected cancerous mice with his serum, and science writers watched in amazement as the tumors disappeared within hours. Dr. Burton couldn't get the FDA and

NCI to recognize and test his serum, though, and in 1974, Burton moved to Freeport, Bahamas—where the FDA has no jurisdiction—and began treating cancer patients there. In 1980, CBS's "60 Minutes" did a segment on Dr. Burton when many doctors and patients testified that Dr. Burton had a viable treatment for cancer and had cured cancer patients. The "60 Minutes" show caused members of the US Congress to try to legalize Burton's treatment in America. Since then, Dr. Burton has passed away, but his clinic in the Bahamas still operates and claims to have the medical records of many terminal cancer patients who have been cured.

Coley's toxins. In 1891, a Harvard-educated New York City surgeon, William Coley, discovered that if cancer patients were injected with sterilized toxins from streptococcus—a skin infection—then the patient's immune system would be activated to fight off the toxins and would also kill the cancer cells. In the early 1900s, Coley's toxins cured a number of terminal cancer patients at Memorial Hospital (Sloan Kettering). In the early- and mid-twentieth century, other scientists and doctors used Coley's toxins to help cancer patients, with some of the doctors reporting that Coley's toxins resulted in a much better rate of remissions and cures than chemotherapy and radiation. But at whatever hospital Coley's toxins were used, the treatment was quickly stopped by medical directors who were trained to support and promote radiation and chemotherapy. Coley's toxins are extremely inexpensive, can't be patented, and today it is nearly impossible for a patient to opt for this extraordinary, proven therapy.

The Gerson Method. Dr. Max Gerson was a German-born physician who was educated at a prominent German medical school. Dr. Gerson contended that by detoxing the body, giving the body enzyme supplements, and switching to a specific, all natural, healthy diet, cancer could be cured. In 1946, a United States Senate committee was impressed by Dr. Gerson, who brought with him five patients who he said had been cured by the

Gerson Method, and the Xray photos and medical records of many others who Gerson claimed had been helped. Any cancer doctor, though, who dares to suggest that a healthy diet can be effective in helping cancer patients, has always been looked upon as a quack by the Sloan Kettering/ American Cancer Society-led American cancer establishment. Ultimately, Gerson was ostracized and treated as a pariah within the medical community. Many patients, though, have claimed to be cured by the Gerson Method, and after Gerson's death, Albert Schweitzer, the Nobel Prize-winning physician and missionary, and a patient of Gerson's, said, "I see in Gerson one of the most eminent medical geniuses in the history of medicine. . . . He leaves a legacy that demands attention. . . . Those whom he cured will now attest to the truth of his ideas."

Dr. Burzynski and antineoplastons. In the 1970s, Dr. Stanislaw Burzynski was working at Baylor College of Medicine in Houston, Texas, when his research revealed to him that peptides—the building blocks of protein—might have anticancer properties. Burzynski found that the peptides—or antineoplastons—can be extracted from urine and then be injected into cancer patients. This process immediately started helping and curing cancer patients. Dr. Burzynski published the data from these tests showing that antineoplastons can cure cancer in a number of prestigious scientific journals. When Dr. Burzynski decided to open an independent cancer treatment facility, this began a long, fierce battle with an uncooperative FDA. At one point, when it looked like the FDA was finally going to successfully stop Dr. Burzynski from treating cancer patients, dozens of Burzynski's patients traveled to Washington and testified to the Congress that the antineoplastons had cured their family members of cancer and if they were taken away then their loved ones would die. This enormous outpouring of public support caused the Congress to influence the FDA to allow Dr. Burzynski to continue treating cancer patients. Today, finally, Dr. Burzynski is working in FDA-approved clinical trials to test the antineoplastons on cancer patients. One journalist reported that Dr. Burzynski's treatment is curing brain cancer twenty-five to thirty percent of the time. Chemotherapy cures brain cancer less than one percent of the time. The FDA, of course, has this information, but isn't publicizing it, and neither is the corporate mainstream media.

The Definitive Guide to Cancer. Burton Goldberg is a researcher and writer whose book *Alternative Medicine: The Definitive Guide* is considered the bible to people and doctors who use and are interested in alternative medicine. Goldberg has also written *The Definitive Guide to Cancer*, which lists thirty-seven physicians who are successfully using alternative, natural, nontoxic treatments for cancer. Many of the physicians have been harassed by the FDA. A main theory of these physicians is that by detoxing the body, and using vitamins, healthy diet, and other natural health supplements, the body's own immune system can be boosted and destroy cancer. With each of the doctors' profiles, Goldberg gives the case histories of two or three patients who have been cured by their alternative methods.

There are many more cases of doctors who were using promising, effective alternative treatments for cancer who were harassed and shut down by the FDA. The suspicion of those who feel that the cancer establishment isn't paying enough attention to viable, valid alternative treatments is that too many of the most important FDA officials are being promised well-paying jobs in the pharmaceutical industry and so are protecting the financial interests of the chemotherapy companies. To those who advocate alternative health theories, the evidence is that the FDA doesn't operate so much as a watchdog for the public but as a "protection racket" for the pharmaceutical industry. As a result of this cozy relationship with the FDA, Big Pharma gets the FDA to use the police powers of the government to harass and destroy their competitors—the producers of nonpatentable, natural treatments for cancer. Perhaps this is what former FDA Commissioner Dr. Robert Ley was alluding to when he said,

"The thing that bugs me is that the people think the FDA is protecting them. It isn't. What the FDA is doing and what the public *thinks* it's doing are as different as night and day."

The FDA will harass and prevent a doctor from using an obviously safe treatment like vitamin C or laetrile/vitamin B-17, but will quickly approve the use of a drug whose safety is unknown if the drug is being manufactured by one of the giant "insider" pharmaceutical corporations. Dangerous drugs that ultimately prove harmful or even fatal quickly pass through the regulatory system, but nontoxic treatments for cancer that show no signs of being hurtful are not allowed to be used. In 1970, FDA Commissioner Charles C. Edwards was called before a Congressional committee to explain why the FDA approved within one week a drug from Searle Pharmaceutical Company when it was known that the drug wasn't proven to be safe. While being grilled by Congressman Lawrence Fountain, Commissioner Edwards blurted out that is "not our policy to jeopardize the financial interests of the pharmaceutical companies."

Unlike other advocates of alternative medicine, Ralph Moss believes that chemotherapy is the best treatment for some types of cancers. According to Moss and other researchers, though, evidence for the life-prolonging effect of chemotherapy on other cancers is weak, and proof that chemotherapy significantly prolongs or saves lives doesn't exist for the majority of cancers. A low percentage of cancer patients who begin taking chemotherapy will be alive after five years. For all these other cancers, Moss and other advocates feel that patients should know that there are other viable, good treatments for cancer. Dr. Moss has written pieces for the the *New York Times*, the *Journal of the American Medical Association*, *Encyclopaedia Britannica*, and other publications. His books include *The Cancer Industry*, *Questioning Chemotherapy*, *Antioxidants Against Cancer*, and *Customized Cancer Treatment*. Ralph Moss was a founding advisor to the National Institute of Health's Office of Alternative Medicine, and has been a member of an Advisory Editorial Board of the National Cancer Institute.

Cirignano: You know as much about cancer as anyone, don't you?

Moss: Well, I study cancer. I study the phenomenon of cancer. I'm sure people who treat cancer know about it from one angle which is the most important angle—which is how you treat it. I study the statements these people make about cancer and I think I know a lot about it, sure.

After Sloan Kettering fired you, you talked with some of the scientists and doctors at Sloan and they told you they knew laetrile could be a good cancer treatment, but they couldn't say that and admit that because if they did they would lose their careers and salaries at Sloan Kettering and within the cancer establishment?

Well, nobody actually said that to me, no. But the same people who fired me—the powerful leadership of Sloan Kettering—they knew laetrile had promise as a cancer treatment. And if they had talked about that then, yes, that would have probably been the end of their careers. . . . The animal testing that was done with laetrile at Sloan Kettering was essentially positive. The laetrile was working on the lab mice. But that was not what the statement that we gave out indicated. So, it was really a cover-up on positive animal experiments.

There have been many doctors and scientists all over the world who have said that their practices and tests show that laetrile can be effective in fighting cancer, haven't there?

There are people who claim that. But there never was a rigorous study that was done that showed that that was the case. . . . I've been looking into alternative treatments for cancer for a long time, you know. And one thing that concerns me is that laypeople who advocate natural treatments sometimes tend to exaggerate. I'm not saying alternative treatments can't help people, or aren't worth looking into. But just because a treatment has helped some patients doesn't mean it's a cure-all. Laetrile may work for some people, but that certainly doesn't mean it's going to work for everybody. What we need—and I'm probably going to repeat this a few times in this interview—is clinical trials. We need clinical trials to show us exactly what the alternative treatments can and cannot do.

But it's not only laypeople who are advocating laetrile. There are some very qualified doctors and scientists who have advocated laetrile. Dr. Dean Burk, for instance, was one of the founders of the National Cancer Institute, and was one of the most respected biochemists in the world. He felt strongly that laetrile could be a good cancer treatment.
I knew Dean Burk. He was a great scientist. And, of course, yes, he was a strong advocate for laetrile.

And have you heard of Dr. John Richardson? Back in the 1970s, Dr. Richardson testified before Congress about laetrile. Dr. Richardson wrote a book about that called **Laetrile Case Histories** *in which he lists the first and last names of many people who were told in the 1970s by their chemotherapy oncologists that they only had weeks or months to live but who are today alive and well because Richardson treated them with laetrile.*
Yes. Most of those cases, if I remember correctly, also had other treatments at the same time that they had laetrile. So, it'd be very hard to say that those people were cured by laetrile. . . . This is another thing I find—when you try to track down if a specific alternative treatment cured someone of cancer, it often happens that the patient took the alternative treatment but they also took a little bit of another vitamin, let's say. Or they also took some herbs. Or maybe they had some chemo. So, it's very difficult to determine exactly what provoked the positive response.

Well, the doctors around the world who advocate laetrile seem to be saying that the laetrile itself can't cure cancer. They're saying that laetrile used along with other treatments and supplements can destroy cancer. Dr. Ernesto Contreras has been running the Oasis of Hope cancer hospital in Mexico since 1963. You've visited that clinic, right? Dr. Contreras says laetrile helps to alleviate tumors and then he uses other treatments along with the laetrile. And there are a number of people who say they were diagnosed with terminal cancer but were treated at the Oasis of Hope clinic and now no longer have cancer.

Yes. How are you going to know if laetrile did it or—I'm not saying people weren't benefited by laetrile—but this is often the case when you try to track down a treatment: it's very hard to establish what it was that actually had the benefit.

Dr. Linus Pauling, the only person to ever win two unshared Nobel Prizes, believed that vitamin C could provide much better cure rates than chemotherapy. Dr Pauling said that he believed that if cancer patients were treated with megadoses of intravenous vitamin C, that would cut cancer deaths by seventy-five percent.

Dr. Pauling was a great man. A brilliant man. An honest man . . . unfortunately, we don't have the clinical data to prove that statement.

A few years ago, though, the **Canadian Medical Association** *reported that a number of cancer patients had their tumors destroyed by intravenous vitamin C. And, recently, Dr. Mark Levine of the National Institutes of Health did a lab study and reported that high doses of vitamin C clearly eliminate cancerous tumors in laboratory animals. Dr. Levine feels vitamin C could do the same for humans and feels strongly that there should be clinical tests on humans.*

That's true. Yes. And that's what should be done. . . . Dr. Pauling was a great man. But in medical science, one person's say-so just doesn't carry very much weight. What carries weight are rigorous clinical trials, and that actually still needs to be done. The clinical trial that was done at the Mayo Clinic wasn't good. It was done to replicate Dr. Pauling's protocol with the vitamin C treatment but it didn't follow the protocol that Pauling had used.

The positive effects that vitamin C can have on cancer patients have been reported by a number of news stations. There was a television newscast by the NBC affiliate in Philadelphia, NBC10, which did an interview with a Pennsylvania doctor, Dr. Scott Greenberg, who works with a Dr. Magaziner.
I know Dr. Magaziner.

Dr. Magaziner and Dr. Greenberg are using vitamin C on their cancer patients. Dr. Greenberg said the treatment won't work for all cancer patients, but he had a number of patients who no longer have fatal cancerous tumors, thanks to intravenous vitamin C. The NBC newscast confirmed this by interviewing people who were diagnosed with terminal cancer but who are now cancer-free.
Well, good. Very good. I'm happy they did that . . . but it doesn't settle the issue. I mean if you try to go before a medical audience—and sometimes I do go before medical audiences—and you try to argue that case, people would very understandably say that's one doctor's impression. Until you've reproduced something in a clinical trial, you can't really say that something works or doesn't work. Clinical proof is something different than one doctor's impression. Because as we just established, people can be taking a lot of other treatments and sometimes people who report on this forget that they were also getting some other treatment.

But there certainly seems to be some good evidence that high doses of intravenous vitamin C can help cancer patients. . . . Do you believe that, in general, chemotherapy is a failed cancer treatment?
In general. But there are certain cancers that chemotherapy is clearly effective for.

Unlike other advocates of alternative medicine, you believe chemotherapy is the best treatment for some cancers. Many advocates of alternative medicine say: "Don't ever take the chemotherapy."

I disagree with that. Chemotherapy is highly effective for a small percentage of cancers. It's somewhat effective for another group. But then for many, many of the other cancers, there's really no evidence that it cures or significantly prolongs life.

Does chemotherapy work for stage IV cancer patients?
Unfortunately, chemotherapy is not very effective in stage IV cancer—in other words, when cancer has already metastasized, spread elsewhere in the body. Unfortunately, it's a very minimal benefit in that situation and so in that situation, in most kinds of cancer—not all, but most—it would make as good sense to try natural treatments as it would to do the chemo because there's very, very little basis for thinking chemo does any more—in clinical trials—than extend survival by a few months, sometimes a few weeks or even days. And yet you do take a lot of punishment from the side effects of the treatment.

Many times when the FDA approves a new chemotherapy drug, the only thing the drug has been shown to be able to do in trials is to temporarily shrink a tumor for a few weeks or months. Shrinking a tumor for a few weeks or months isn't really going to help, is it?
Of course not. But if in trials the drug temporarily shrinks a tumor, then the FDA declares that that's an effective treatment for cancer. Then all it will do is increase a cancer patient's life by four or five months. Or four or five weeks. Or days. With brutal chemotherapy. . . . They will give you three months extra survival with vicious chemotherapy and call that a cure.

You've written that chemotherapy works for a small percentage of cancers but the proof of its efficacy for the majority of cancers is non-existent. In 1993, the **Journal of the National Cancer Institute** *published the results of a study that showed that chemotherapy cures cancer only three percent of the time, and produced a somewhat longer survival* *period another four percent of the time. So, according to that study, chemotherapy is worth taking only seven percent of the time. And the* **Journal of Clinical Oncology** *has reported that only two percent of cancer patients who start taking chemotherapy will be alive after five years.* The conventional drugs being used on cancer patients are generally very toxic and ineffective.

In medicine, five years is the yardstick to determine if something's a cure, right? If the patient's without the disease and alive after five years, then they're cured. So it seems that it can be said that chemotherapy fails ninety-eight percent of the time.
I know that there are better treatments than chemotherapy . . . but, you know, chemotherapy does work well for some cancers. We have to acknowledge that. And there's some wiggle room with chemo. Each cancer patient is an individual case. With some patients and some kinds of specific cancers, the statistics show that if they take the chemo, that might give them a chance of a longer survival time. So it's up to the patient. And with integrative oncology they use low doses of chemo with natural treatments which, apparently, can be good.

Every cancer patient who's about to be given chemotherapy can get the statistics of how often chemotherapy works for the type of cancer they have, right? You can ask for the statistics, the scientific papers. And the statistics are clear, right? Every patient can know which cancers the chemo is or is not going to work for.
Absolutely. And that's exactly what every cancer patient should do. Ask questions and get the facts. Know how the chemo is going to affect your particular type of cancer. Then make an informed decision.

So if you have a type of cancer that chemotherapy can't do anything for, then you should certainly have the right to look into and try all these other

viable alternative treatments for cancer. . . . Lawrence Burton's treatment—the cancer clinic that operates out of Freeport, Bahamas—is a very viable cancer treatment, isn't it? You knew Burton, didn't you? Dr. Burton's treatment has put many cancer patients into remission, hasn't it?
I did know Burton. . . . They can't prove, though, how many people he put into remission. Their case files are in rather poor shape. There was, though, an investigation by a branch of the US government some years ago that showed that patients treated there were in remission and it was, you know, impossible to say that anything else but Burton's treatment had caused the remission. So I think that there's good reason to think that he did have successes.

Dr. Burton made it clear that his treatment won't cure everyone. But could you estimate what percentage of cancer patients who get the ITA treatment in Freeport, Dr. Burton's treatment, are cured of cancer?
There is no way to analyze their own data to see what percentage of patients actually benefit there. Their records are just not in a sufficiently well organized form in order to do that. And they don't have the staff or the money to be able to do that.

There's a website that's been set up by some of Dr. Burton's patients. It's inspiring and exciting to see the videos of all these patients who testify that they had these horrendous, fatal cancerous tumors and were told they only had a few weeks or a few months to live but now it's ten or twenty years later and they're healthy and cancer free, thanks to Dr. Burton's treatment. These people certainly don't seem to be lying.
No. And I'm not saying that they're lying. I believe that there are cases of people who had remissions of cancer after taking the ITA treatment. I do believe that. And I base that not just on my own examination of the records but also by an examination that was done for the US government a few years ago. I think that's very compelling. But it's impossible to say

what percentage of people had that positive effect. How do we quantify that?. . . So at the end of the day the only thing that would satisfy scientific curiosity would be a randomized trial, and this never was able to be arranged. When Burton was alive there were so many personality conflicts between Burton and people at the National Cancer Institute that it repeatedly fell apart. The level of mistrust on both sides was very high, so they couldn't ever arrange the clinical trials. Now Burton's treatment has kind of gotten off the radar.

If anybody has a conflict of interest and can't be trusted, it seems like it's the politicians and FDA officials. Burton seemed like a doctor who just wanted to help his patients. Politicians are taking donations from pharmaceutical lobbyists and FDA officials are being promised well-paying jobs in the pharmaceutical industry.

The FDA is very, very closely aligned with the pharmaceutical industry. How it all happens, who gets what from whom, I don't know. And it doesn't matter. It's just quite clear and easy to see that the FDA is the loyal enforcer for Big Pharma.

You believe strongly that Coley's toxins could be a very good treatment for cancer, don't you?

It's an extremely promising treatment.

You have said that Sloan Kettering certainly knows about Coley's toxins. In a previous interview, you said that "Sloan Kettering was able to cure cancer one hundred years ago and this has been kept from the public. This is an outrageous crime and fraud being perpetuated on the people."

Well, after William Coley died, a researcher gathered a thousand cases of cures or remissions attributable to Coley's toxins. But Coley's toxins can't be patented. So who is going to pay the millions and millions of dollars to put Coley's toxins through the clinical trials to get Coley's toxins approved as a cancer treatment if they're not going to be rewarded with a patent on that investment?

You were interviewed by the actress and writer Suzanne Somers for her book **Knockout: Doctors Who Are Curing Cancer.** *Suzanne Somers played a blonde bimbo on a TV sitcom, but she writes serious books about health and her books become* **New York Times** *bestsellers. One of the doctors Somers profiles in her book is Dr. James Forsythe, who practices in Reno, Nevada. Dr. Forsythe is a board-certified oncologist, but also a board-certified homeopath. He uses low doses of chemotherapy, but also a mixture of vitamins and other natural and homeopathic treatments. Dr. Forsythe claims that if cancer patients—even terminal patients—follow his protocol strictly, he feels that could heal eighty-five percent of cancer, patients who come to see him. There are a number of patients on Dr. Forsythe's website who testify that they were diagnosed with terminal cancer, but who are now healthy after following Dr. Forsythe's protocol. Again, these people don't appear to be lying.*
No, they're not lying . . . if he's using conventional treatments with alternatives then that's very good. In general, I think that's the best way to go now. Integrative oncology.

Another doctor who Suzanne Somers profiles is Dr. Nicholas Gonzalez, who practices in New York City. Dr. Gonzalez uses healthy diet, enzyme supplements, and natural health supplements to help cancer patients. Somers says that Gonzalez's office was immediately able to give her the names of twenty stage IV cancer patients who were told by chemotherapy oncologists that nothing could be done for them, but who are now alive and well after doing Dr. Gonzalez's treatment. Is Gonzalez's treatment a good treatment for cancer?
I know of Dr. Gonzalez. And Burzynski. Suzanne also interviewed Dr.

Stanislaw Burzynski in Houston. They're both doing interesting and inspiring work. I've looked into some of their cases. Burzynski and Gonzalez have had successes. But their successes haven't been one hundred percent. We don't know what percentage of people who go to them are helped. And, again, maybe some of the patients who had positive responses there were also taking other treatments. . . . I agree that some of the alternative doctors have had success and they are not being given fair credit and recognition. . . . Burzynski and Gonzalez are innovative doctors and they have made progress with cancer, and they have helped many people.

Have you seen the television commercials for the Cancer Treatment Centers of America? The cancer patients in these commercials say they were told by their chemotherapy oncologists that nothing could be done about their cancer and they should go home and get their wills in order. But then these people went to the Cancer Treatment Centers of America and now they no longer have any cancer. That's because the CTCA uses more than just radiation and chemotherapy to treat cancer, correct? The CTCA uses radiation and chemotherapy but they also use other complementary, alternative treatments.
I think they're very good. I think they're very, very good.

The Cancer Treatment Centers of America list the results of their treatments on their website. According to their website, they have a better rate of remissions and cures than patients who use only chemotherapy and radiation. Their cancer patients live longer and are cured more often. Again, that's because the CTCA use chemotherapy and radiation, but also use other complementary, alternative treatments.
Correct. Again, I think that actually, at this moment, that's probably the best way to go. In general. I think the integrative oncology is a superior form of treatment over straight-up conventional therapy.

What do you mean by integrative oncology?
By integrative I mean the combined, judicious use of conventional with alternative treatments. And that's what they do there. So, that's very good.

Why doesn't the mainstream media do more reporting on the effectiveness of alternative or integrative treatments for cancer? It seems that if somebody's been cured of cancer then that should be the first story on the nightly news. Dr. Burzynski has cured cancer. High doses of vitamin C have cured cancer. The Cancer Centers of America have cured cancer. And many other people say they've been cured of cancer. But the mainstream media doesn't inform the public of this.
Well, because I think there aren't any official trials to see what the alternatives can do and so when you look at the level of documentation offered for the alternatives it very often turns out to be inadequate. And some people will exaggerate, claiming some alternative treatment is a cure all for cancer. So I think that alternative medicine has gotten a very bad name with the mainstream science reporters. But, unfortunately, what has happened is that even the treatments that are actually very promising get tarred with the same brush because of the exaggerated claims that are made by some people for an alternative treatment.

So there's a stigma attached to alternative medicine?
Correct. Exactly. Also, the reporters—you know, there's a certain way that things are done. In other words, they're going to report on the stories that appear in the biggest, most important medical journals like *New England Journal*. If the study appears in a lower impact journal they're very unlikely to even hear about it.

All the biggest, most well-known medical journals are financed by the pharmaceutical companies, right? The largest, most influential medical journals are dependent on advertising revenues from Big Pharma.

So there could be a conflict of interest there, right? . . . But then if you're engaged as a full-time reporter, a medical writer, you have to keep up with the stories that other people are reporting on. In other words, if the *New York Times* reports on a new drug and you don't report on it, your editor's going to say, "What's going on? I see all the other papers are running a story about this new drug, and you're not reporting on that. Instead, you're reporting on some unknown doctor using some 'eccentric' treatment."

But could it be that the same people on the boards of the Big Media companies are also on the boards Big Pharma? Back when the laetrile incident was happening at Sloan Kettering, you pointed out that the chairman of the board of Bristol Meyers—the main company producing chemotherapy drugs—also happened to be on the board of Sloan Kettering, and also was on the board of the **New York Times.** *Other reporters and journalists claim that the same corporate people who run the media are also running the pharmaceutical industry.*

The Bristol Meyers chairman was also on those boards. That's true . . . there could be something to what you're saying.

Isn't it true that many times when Sloan Kettering, or the Mayo Clinic, or any cancer center connected to the FDA or NCI is testing an alternative, nonpatentable, natural treatment for cancer, they intentionally flub and mess up the tests so that the alternative treatment will look like it doesn't work?

Yeah, there are certainly instances of that. I don't think it happens all the time. But, look, it happened with laetrile, so, I certainly will be the last person on earth to say that it never happens.

This happened when the NCI was going to test antineoplastons for Dr. Stanislaw Burzynski. They weren't following Dr. Burzynski's

instructions and protocol. It also happened when the Mayo Clinic was testing vitamin C for Dr. Linus Pauling. The Mayo Clinic was apparently ignoring Dr. Pauling's instructions and there were errors made during the trials. Dr. Pauling thought the errors were deliberate.
Well, he did. He did. And that was a shocking thing. And he had never made a charge like that before in his life, to my knowledge. I spoke to Dr. Pauling at the time this happened. And he was truly shocked by it. . . . I don't know . . . I was not inside Charles Mortell's head—he was the scientist running the trials—when he did this, the trial. But I know Martell was a true, devoted enemy of alternative treatments.

Like most all people in the FDA, it seems.
Well, he was not at the FDA. He was at the Mayo Clinic. And when they went to do the trials for vitamin C, he made one very big error. Pauling and his medical collaborator, Dr. Cameron, had given both intravenous and oral forms of vitamin C. And this had worked well on their cancer patients in the Scotland hospital. And Mortell only gave the oral form of vitamin C, which is about one fiftieth of the effectiveness. Whether this was done deliberately or not, it was certainly set up to fail. And it did fail. The clinical trial is a very powerful weapon, but it can be used for good or for evil like all weapons. And the danger with the clinical trial is that every scientist knows how to set up a clinical trial so that you tip the results in the direction that you want them to go.

And people in the cancer establishment always seem to tip the results so they make the alternative treatments look ineffective and worthless.
There haven't been that many clinical trials of alternatives. Unfortunately, there aren't too many cancer establishment people who are favorable towards alternative medicine. They don't control too many oncology departments. If there were, I'm sure we'd have more testing of alternatives, and more honest tests. So it's tough.

In an interview that you did a few years back, you talked about a well-known case when the data on a breast cancer study at the National Cancer Institute was faked. The one run out of the University of Pittsburgh.

That was widely known. The data was fudged. The question of whether lumpectomy was as good as mastectomy was somewhat in doubt because of that fake data that was submitted out of Pittsburgh. . . . People who pay for cancer research can come up with any results they want to come up with. You can pay hired hands to attack any natural, non-toxic treatment you want. Publish inaccurate results. It happens.

Dr. Marcia Angell, the former editor of **The New England Journal of Medicine,** *the most prestigious medical journal in the world, once said: "Trials can be rigged in a dozen ways, and it happens all the time." And in that interview on the breast cancer test, you said, "This kind of corruption and fakery and abuse of the public has been going on as long as the war on cancer has been going on. The fact is that all of the studies that have been supervised by the National Cancer Institute should now be reexamined by congressional committees to see whether or not there is real corruption in all of them."*

Well . . . I probably did say that.

Even though all this goes on, you, yourself, don't believe that powerful people running the cancer industry are consciously and deliberately engaged in a conspiracy to suppress less expensive, natural treatments and cures for cancer? You don't believe there's a conspiracy? You wrote that the "evidence points to the fact that it is the system itself, rather than any particular clique of individuals, which is really to blame for failure to make progress against the cancer problem." What do you mean by that?

I don't think there's any evidence for an overarching conspiracy. I think that what happened at Sloan Kettering around the laetrile situation—certainly there was collusion on the part of some individuals to make statements that they each knew were incorrect. And there is corruption at times. But I don't think there's an overarching conspiracy that controls the cancer establishment and suppresses natural medicine.

You've written that one doesn't have to propose a conspiracy theory to answer the question of why there hasn't been any progress in the war on cancer and why the cancer establishment never approves a natural treatment for cancer. It's just a matter of that it all revolves around money. To get a new treatment for cancer approved you have to spend $200 to $300 million dollars for the trials. And the only ones who can afford to do that are the large pharmaceutical companies, and the only thing they're going to do that for is a drug that they can have the patent on.

Yes! Why do you have to bring a conspiracy theory into it? The conspiracy is the conspiracy to make money. To make the most possible money. But I don't think there's a central organization that's suppressing natural treatments. I know some people believe that. . . . A long time ago, unfortunately, we kind of turned this over to the marketplace. This has been a process in science as a whole and in medicine as a whole that cancer became a profit opportunity for entrepreneurs and corporations. The government stepped out of the business of drug development and turned it over and basically yielded that space to industry. Now industry has to return a big profit to even get involved. Inevitably, what happened is that all the mainstream cancer treatments became of the patented, profitable variety. And the natural treatments like vitamin C, and melatonin, and so forth kind of fell by the wayside.

It seems we miss out on a lot of good treatments because of this system.
I believe so. I believe there should be a mechanism by which the government or a very wealthy foundation funds inexpensive treatments that are not otherwise commercially viable.

You've also written that chemotherapy is an industry. And in the past, leaders of certain industries have always tried to prevent a new way of doing things from destroying the financial advantages of their industry.
There are many examples of that. Western Union telegram fought the development and use of the telephone. Automobiles put trolley cars out of business, and passenger trains lost business to buses and planes. When television started becoming popular, Hollywood moguls didn't support that because they didn't want people to stop going to the movies. . . . The cancer establishment is like a very, very large ship—the ship is headed towards and is powered by the sales of chemotherapeutic drugs—and it's going to be extremely difficult to turn that ship around, and to turn it even one inch from its true north—which is the profits and power of Wall Street, really. And that's what it is. And that's what most doctors don't even understand.

They probably did that because they've received so much criticism for having so much to do with a failing cancer establishment—and to make it appear that they're really looking for a natural treatment for cancer. The office of alternative and complementary medicine at Sloan Kettering doesn't accomplish anything, does it?
That's true. It doesn't accomplish anything. That's very true. . . . I got to know Lucy Rockefeller—Laurence Rockefeller's daughter, David Rockefeller's niece—about ten years ago when we were on a couple of boards together. And I would say based on my knowledge of her and familiarity with her I couldn't imagine that she was involved in anything intending to suppress alternative medicine.

When people say "the Rockefellers control the cancer industry," they're not referring to all the sons and daughters and cousins of the Rockefeller family. They're referring to the institutions that arose from the Rockefellers' enormous wealth. JP Morgan Chase. Citibank. IG Farben. Pharmaceutical companies. The inner circle of the Council on Foreign

Relations and Trilateral Commission. And, yes, some patriarchs of the Rockefeller family and the executives that work for them, but not Lucy Rockefeller and all her brothers and sisters and nieces and nephews. . . . The point is that the American Cancer Society and Sloan Kettering only advocate and approve patented drugs for cancer, and never advocate and promote natural treatments.

That's for sure.

And that's because Rockefeller and other pharmaceutical representatives control the boards of the ACS and Sloan Kettering.

I don't know if the board is any longer controlled by the Rockefellers. But I think there is a very strong pharmaceutical bias within medicine as a whole. . . . You may want to introduce some conspirators into the picture, but what I'm saying is let's reduce it to its essence. In essence, the system does not want, or encourage, or even particularly allow for the development of these nontoxic, inexpensive treatments. As we've said, it costs about a quarter billion dollars to get a cancer treatment approved. And, yes, the only ones who can afford that are the giant pharmaceutical companies, and they're only going to do it for a drug they can patent. And in cancer, if you get a strongly patented agent you can make—your investment can return manyfold—you could make a billion dollars a year off a pretty mediocre drug. If you think how we are going to create a system that maximizes profit, this is the system we have. It's already there. And since we accept the idea of the unbridled marketplace, pretty much, with a few exceptions, then what we've got is the perfect example of the profit-driven medical system.

But some writers and historians claim that it's clear that along with controlling the boards of Sloan Kettering and the American Cancer Society, the Rockefellers and their partners took control of the medical profession and cancer industry in America by controlling a very influential American Medical Association paper called the Flexner Report.

In 1910, the AMA wanted to reform the medical profession and medical schools. The Carnegie Foundation convinced the AMA to let a man named Abraham Flexner write the report for that.

Yes, I know about Abraham Flexner.

The Carnegie Foundation was closely allied and was almost synonymous with the Rockefeller Foundation. The AMA publicized the Flexner Report extensively, and the way things are done in our present-day American medical profession comes from the Flexner Report. One thing Abraham Flexner wrote and stressed is that all naturopathic medical schools should be closed down. Flexner believed—probably because Rockefeller told him to and paid him to—that the only true medical science was allopathic medicine—the medicine that uses patented drugs. After the Flexner Report came out, all naturopathic and natural medicine clinics were shut down and all colleges and universities that taught naturopathic and holistic medicine were closed. People say this is because Flexner was working for Rockefeller and the pharmaceutical industry.

Well, that's what they say . . . I think the reason he closed them was because he thought they were inferior and he had high standards relating to sort of how the American medical schools imitated or were in the model of the German medical schools.

The German medical schools? Where IG Farben was? The German medical schools were all allopathic, right?

Yes, but, I think Flexner and those people had a high standard, you know, that the American medical schools be very scientific.

Well, advocates of natural medicine would argue that an allopathic treatment like chemotherapy isn't very scientific. Because chemotherapy fails so often. And the idea of cutting the cancer out through chemo, or radiation, or surgery isn't the best science because that isn't getting to the root

of the problem of cancer and the cancer will just grow back. . . . You, your-self, once wrote, "It is my personal opinion that the best of these alterna-tive, nutritional, non-toxic treatments are based on more plausible theo-ries and offer more compelling evidence than most chemotherapy."
Yes.

Advocates of natural medicine would say that it's more scientific to get to root of the problem of cancer. They claim that we get cancer because our immune systems are weakened, or we don't have the proper vita-mins and nutrients in our bodies, or we're toxic, or don't have enough oxygen in our cells. And the best, most effective, most scientific way to treat cancer is to naturally boost the immune system, or get the right vitamins and nutrients, or detox the body, and get more oxygen flowing.
Yes, I know, I know.

So was Flexner really being more scientific? Or was he being manipu-lated by Rockefeller so the pharmaceutical industry could sell a lot of drugs? The Rockefellers had a clear interest in pharmaceuticals because their Standard Oil company had merged with IG Farben, the largest drug company in the world. And the pharmaceutical industry is now the most lucrative, richest, most powerful industry in America. And the world. Richer than the oil industry now, right? And people would say that's because Flexner turned us away from natural medicine, and turned us into an allopathic, drug-taking nation.
There's that aspect to it. But again I'm not going to believe that Flexner's aim was that he was going to put out of business a treatment that he thought was actually effective just because it wasn't allopathic. I think he and Morris Fishbein—the editor of the AMA journal—and all those peo-ple really believed that all the herbalism and everything was quackery.

But herbalism isn't quackery.

Well, we now know it isn't. But they may not have known that. They thought that, you know, that this was going to be a higher, much superior form of medicine. Now we see that they went to an extreme because they put all those naturopathic schools out of business. But the essence of it was that there is value in naturopathy.

Many people would probably argue that Flexner and those people weren't concentrating on being more scientific. And that they were concentrating on cashing the checks they were receiving under the table from IG Farben. . . . After the Flexner Report came out, the Carnegie and Rockefeller Foundations began funding and pouring millions into the medical schools of American colleges and universities. Carnegie and Rockefeller had more money than the US government to control the health field. Whatever colleges accepted and agreed to live by the Flexner Report received money and funding, and whatever colleges didn't accept the Flexner Report didn't receive money. At the beginning of this process, there were about one hundred eighty medical schools. By the end there were only about eighty. All of those eighty medical schools supported drug research and taught allopathic medicine—the medicine based on the use of patented drugs. Any college or university that taught naturopathic or holistic medicine was closed down. So it seems that Rockefeller had taken over the medical profession and turned America into an allopathic nation and had taken over the medical schools in America through his manipulation and control of the Flexner Report and through his funding of American universities.

Yes. I know. I'm very familiar with that history. I think you give them too much credit. Too much foresight. You're sort of connecting the dots after the fact. I don't think that they had that much foresight.

It didn't seem like foresight. It seemed like an ironclad grip on the medical establishment. They knew if they controlled the AMA and this Flexner

*Report and funded the medical schools that they had the medical estab-
lishment under control. . . . This is the problem, isn't it? If you're a young
person now and you want to become a cancer doctor then all the medical
schools are going to train you that chemotherapy is the only way to go.
And chemotherapy fails the great majority of the time.*

Well, that's generally true. Although there's been quite a bit of infiltra-
tion of the medical schools over the past twenty years. And many medical
schools have programs now in natural medicine.

But, still, the medical schools are mostly allopathic.

Yes, of course, the allopathic paradigm is still the dominant one.

*Researchers claim that another way that the Rockefellers and their
partners monopolize the cancer business is their control and influence in the major insurance companies. In the early '70s, a researcher
reported that the Rockefeller interests included vast stock holdings in
the first and third largest insurance companies in the US, **Metropolitan**
and **Equitable**. The Rockefellers also maintained a powerful presence
through board of directors memberships in **Traveler's** and several other
major insurers. You'd have to think it's still that way today. Large health
insurance companies don't support alternative treatments for cancer,
and so if a cancer patient wants to try a natural treatment for cancer
their insurance won't help pay for it. But the insurance companies will,
of course, pay for the chemotherapy. So, if the same business interests
that own the pharmaceutical corporations also control the insurance
industry, then this is another way that Big Business, and Rockefeller,
and Big Pharma, and Wall Street can force chemotherapy on us.*

Right. But again the insurance companies will follow the lead of the medical profession, ultimately. You still have to convince the medical profession
and the only way you can do that is through clinical trials, which are very
difficult to arrange.

But you don't believe there's a blatant conspiracy to suppress natural treatments for cancer. You believe it's just "the system." But wouldn't you at least say that perhaps a "culture of corruption" exists in the cancer industry? It's well known and well accepted that a "culture of corruption" exists on Wall Street. The financial crisis of 2008—the mortgage crisis—didn't happen accidently and haphazardly. The banksters on Wall Street knew the things they did were going to cause severe financial problems for millions of people, but they did them anyway because they were making millions of dollars. Perhaps this same "culture of corruption" exists in the cancer industry? Somewhere in the cancer industry there have to be powerful people who know that there are good treatments for cancer that the public should be made aware of, but these people are keeping these treatments from the public because the cancer industry—the pharmaceutical corporations, the hospitals, the doctors, the ACS—are making billions of dollars.

You have to consider and look back at when and why the FDA was created. Back then there was this rampant patent medicine advertising going on—quackery—and the FDA came into being to stop the quackery, and to advocate more scientific drug development. So the basic mindset of the FDA is very much disposed against the individual or small company—even if the individual or small company has a good idea for cancer. If you're a small company—especially a naturopathic company—or if you're one lone, unknown doctor, then the FDA is automatically going to assume you're a quack and your idea isn't worth looking at. The attitude of the FDA is that if something is coming from a small developer whose idea is not mainstream, and if they don't have two or three hundred million dollars to get their idea tested and passed, and can't do things the FDA, multimillion dollar way, then that company's idea isn't worth looking into or supporting.

So it's the mindset of the FDA that's the problem.
I've known people who worked in the FDA. They seemed okay to me. I

didn't get the feeling that they were corrupt or taking money from the pharmaceutical companies. But it's a mindset—adamantly against alternative medicine. And adamantly pro Big Business, and pro Big Pharma. . . . I don't think pharmaceutical representatives are getting together with the FDA and saying, "Isn't it wonderful to fool and make billions off the public?" At least, I hope they're not doing that.

Did you hear of Daniel Haley's well-reviewed book, **Politics in Healing?** *Haley was a New York State Assemblyman. His well-researched book talks about ten effective, good alternative treatments for cancer that were stopped by the FDA and AMA. This is going back to, like, 1900. All these doctors and scientists had non-toxic, safe treatments for cancer and they were helping and apparently even curing cancer patients. In each case, the FDA and AMA swooped down on the doctor like the Gestapo, harassed them, arrested them, and ultimately stopped them from using their treatments. If you read that book you don't get the feeling that the FDA is a bunch of naïve health officials who innocently believe they're doing the right thing because they were trained by medical schools that promote chemotherapy. Instead, you get the feeling that the FDA is a bad agency controlled by bad people who are being guided by a "culture of corruption" and who are deliberately suppressing effective treatments for cancer to protect the financial interests of the pharmaceutical corporations.*

I remember that book from about ten years ago. I haven't looked at it recently. . . . Again, I actually don't see any need to introduce the concept of a conspiracy theory. You're going to spend your life chasing after a punitive conspiracy, when you have no way of ever being able to isolate who might be doing this, where are they located, where is the headquarters. I mean you talk about the Rockefellers, but Laurence Rockefeller's been dead for ten years, or five years now, but the problem continues.

Laurence Rockefeller was running Sloan Kettering right up to the 1980s and 1990s, right?

He was there, yes.

It just seems that the cancer establishment is as corrupt as Wall Street. It just seems so suspicious. There have been so many instances when a qualified doctor starts using a safe, non-toxic, natural treatment on his cancer patients and then the FDA and AMA swoop down on the doctor like the Gestapo, raid his office, arrest him, treat him like a criminal, and stop him from using the non-toxic treatment. . . . Dr. Robert Atkins was best known as the founder of the famous Atkins diet, the low-carbohydrate diet. Dr. Atkins was very critical of the medical establishment and believed that there was too much emphasis on drugs and that diseases would be better treated with vitamins and other natural health supplements. This is how Atkins treated cancer, which he considered "a controllable chronic illness." Dr. Atkins once stated, "There is not one, but many cures for cancer available. But they are all being systematically suppressed by the ACS, the NCI, and the major oncology centers. They have too much of an interest in the status quo." And regarding the cancer industry, and the medical establishment in general, Atkins once said, "If it isn't a conspiracy, it sure seems like one."

That's probably true. It *isn't* a conspiracy. And it *does* seem like one. That's probably a true statement. He's right.

If there's a "culture of corruption" in the cancer establishment, maybe it comes from the fact that the German pharmaceutical corporation, IG Farben, that Rockefeller's Standard Oil merged with in 1927, was the corporation that funded Adolf Hitler and the Nazis. It's historical fact that a number of the top IG Farben executives were convicted for being Nazis at the Nuremberg Trials. IG Farben manufactured and had the patent on the poisonous gas—the Zyklon B gas—that the Nazis used on the Jews in the concentration camps. Chemotherapy came from Nazi science. Chemotherapy was just like and very similar to the poisonous gas, the mustard gas, that the German military developed during World War II. That gas was also tested on some cancer patients back then.

Well, that is true. It is historical fact that the pharmaceutical-chemical company that Standard Oil of New Jersey merged with in the '20s, IG Farben, was the company that financed the Nazi movement.

Whether it's a small clique of powerful men who are deliberately suppressing natural treatments for cancer or it's just a faulty system that's preventing good natural treatments for cancer from being used, it seems certain that something has to change about what's done about cancer in America. Because the chemotherapy-radiation cancer establishment isn't finding a cure for cancer—after billions has been spent—and the rates of cancer deaths haven't decreased in the last fifty years. . . . Your main point seems to be that anybody who has cancer has a right to know how effective the chemotherapy drugs they're going to be given are. If you get cancer and they're getting ready to give you chemo, you should get the facts and data—"How often do these chemotherapy drugs cure the type of cancer I have?" If you have one of the cancers that chemotherapy can cure, then you should take the chemo. But researchers claim that literally about 90 percent of the time the chemo isn't going to do much to save or prolong your life. And if the facts and data are clear that the type of cancer you have isn't cured by chemotherapy, then you have a right to refuse the treatment and opt for an alternative method.

Patients and their families should question their doctor. Get the proof. Ask to see the scientific papers. The data is available—how often does this chemotherapy for this particular cancer actually work? You should be suspicious of any hospitals or physicians who say, "Our treatment is so novel that we haven't fully judged it yet." Some doctors will talk. Others won't. If a doctor gets impatient, or condescending, then maybe it's time to look for a different doctor. If a treatment has not been shown to cure, significantly prolong survival—if it only temporarily shrinks tumors—then it is still experimental and unproven. People need—and have a right—to know this.

Maybe it is useless to speculate or wonder if some sort of conspiracy controls the cancer establishment. Maybe it's enough to know that the statistics show that in so many cases the chemotherapy isn't going to work, and that there are many other viable, good treatments that could help cancer patients. . . . If you look into alternative treatments for cancer you get the feeling that there's real hope for any cancer patient.

That is enough. The alternative guys have made advances and had successes and they are not being given fair credit and recognition. To just say that is a very daring position. So, yes, to me it's enough to acknowledge that these treatments exist, and to expose the realities of the drugs being administered in conventional medicine.

But we have to have the right to refuse any treatment we don't want, and to opt for any treatment we do want, right? Because in some cases, if a cancer patient decides they don't want the chemotherapy, the cancer doctor becomes offended and angered and reports the patient to the police and medical authorities and tries to force them to take the chemotherapy. And isn't it true that there are some states that are now trying to make it illegal to treat cancer with anything but chemotherapy and radiation?

The issue of an individual's right to medical freedom goes back to the Founding Fathers. Benjamin Rush, a Founding Father who signed the Declaration of Independence, felt strongly that America and democracy meant that the Constitution should include medical freedom and rights.

That Founding Father, Benjamin Rush, said if we don't have medical freedom and rights then "an undercover dictatorship will organize to restrict the art of healing to one school of thought and deny privileges to others."

I think that's it. Right. And many of America's most well-known judges have come to the same conclusion—that individuals are sovereign over their own bodies and have a right to do with them whatever they desire. Louis Brandeis wrote about that at Harvard back in the late 1800s. He wrote about it again in the 1920s when he was a Supreme Court judge. And then another Supreme Court judge came to the same conclusion—that every human being has a right to determine what shall be done with his or her own body. Now, that includes, of course, going outside currently approved medical methods in search of an unconventional treatment—if that's what you choose to do. . . . Over and over, judges have concluded that when it comes to health, it is our bodies and our lives. In America, we have the right to refuse any treatment we don't want. And we have the right to opt for any treatment that we do want.

NB: *It was in 1992 that the Journal of Clinical Oncology reported that only 2 percent of cancer patients who take chemotherapy will be alive after five years. The survival rate may be higher now, and may be as high as 20 percent.*

Many of the alternative approaches to treating cancer require that the patient stick to a healthy, pure diet. It seems that if one has the desire, discipline, and ability to stay on a healthy, pure diet that that can go a long way in preventing cancer or in even eliminating an existing cancer. There are many good, fine, caring "establishment" doctors, though, who do use surgery, radiation, and chemotherapy to help and heal their patients. What an individual patient chooses to do about his or her particular cancer is up to that individual.

CHAPTER 8

Did George Bush and Republicans Steal the 2000 and 2004 Presidential Elections? Can Computer Voting Machines Be Trusted?

An interview with election reform activist and Black Box Voting *author Bev Harris*

M any would accept it as historical fact that John F. Kennedy's camp stole the 1960 presidential election. Although it's never been conclusively shown, there is evidence that there was election tampering in Illinois and Texas, and this gave JFK the electoral college votes of those states and the presidency.

Considering this, some might wonder why our leaders and media don't admit or at least talk about the strong evidence that could lead any reasonable person to conclude that George Bush and Republican operatives stole the 2000 and 2004 presidential elections.

If the elections were rigged, they were rigged in Florida in 2000 and Ohio in 2004. These were the decisive swing states. At those times, the elections in both those states were being run by two ardently partisan Republican secretaries of state—Katherine Harris in Florida and Kenneth Blackwell in Ohio. To many election researchers, vote fraud and election tampering were allowed to occur because these two partisans were in charge.

There were numerous dirty tricks used. The strongest evidence for election tampering in Florida in 2000 has come from a report by BBC reporter Greg Palast. Palast was able to obtain a copy of a contract that Katherine Harris's office had with a company called Choice Point. The contract called for Choice Point to come up with a list of thousands of Florida citizens who had committed felonies in other states. Harris's office then—on orders from Florida Governor Jeb Bush—sent this list to election officials in all the counties of Florida, instructing the officials that those on the list were not allowed to vote. About ninety percent of the names on the list were Democrats. It could be easy to suspect that Harris and Jeb Bush were intentionally preventing thousands of legitimate, registered Democrats from voting, because later it was revealed that ninety percent of the citizens on the list had not committed felonies in other states. The list was bogus. More than fifty percent of the names on the list were African American, so, it would also seem that Harris and Bush were, in the spirit of Jim Crow, intentionally preventing African Americans from voting. Ninety percent of African Americans will vote for the Democrat.

Eventually, *Salon.com*, *The Washington Post*, and even the United States Civil Rights Commission confirmed that the Choice Point list was erroneous and prevented thousands of legitimate, eligible Democrats from voting. After the Civil Rights Commission made this finding, Katherine Harris wrote a letter to *Harper's* magazine and admitted that she had forced Florida election officials to use the Choice Point list, and that the list was wrong and had unjustly barred thousands of registered Democrats from voting. But, Harris claimed, the whole thing was an accident. She didn't mean to do it. Those who have looked at the matter closely, though, can't imagine how Harris and Jeb Bush didn't know exactly what was happening. After Harris sent the list to election officials, a Florida judge ruled that even if a Florida citizen had committed a felony in another state, he or she was still eligible to vote in Florida. Jeb Bush's office then drafted a letter to Florida election officials telling them to—in effect—ignore the judge's ruling, continue to use the Choice Point list, and bar those on the list from voting. When Greg Palast called up Jeb Bush's office and asked for an explanation of this, an employee in Bush's office told Palast, "The courts tell us to do one thing, but we do something else." Ultimately, Harris's and Bush's purge list prevented approximately eighty thousand legitimate, registered Democrats from voting. By the official vote count, George Bush ended up defeating Al Gore in Florida by 537 votes. If Katherine Harris and Jeb Bush hadn't forced election officials to use their erroneous, bogus, illegal purge list, then Gore would have easily defeated Bush in Florida by thousands of votes and would have been elected president.

Besides the Harris/Bush purge list there were other dirty, sometimes illegal tactics that the Harris/Blackwell-led Republican forces utilized to tamper with the elections and take the White House. Many of these dirty tactics were Jim Crow-like actions to prevent African Americans from voting. This was reported by the *Washington Post* and other newspapers, The United States Civil Rights Commission, and the *Conyers Report*, the investigation that Congressman John Conyers's committee did of the 2004 election in Ohio. In both Florida and Ohio, not enough voting machines were put in the African American precincts; blacks had to wait sometimes for hours to vote, causing many African Americans to lose patience and go home without casting a vote. Republican interests engaged in an illegal tactic known as caging. Caging occurs when members of one party send registered letters to members of the opposite party; if the letters aren't answered, it is assumed that the addressees have moved and their names are taken off the voting rolls. Blackwell and Harris also unjustly forbade the use of provisional ballots, a type of ballot used by citizens who are moving, or who don't have a permanent address. Provisional ballots are used much more often by African Americans and other inner city, Democratic minorities.

There were still more dirty tactics. But the most stunning evidence for vote fraud in Ohio in 2004 has come from author Richard Hayes Phillips's book *Witness to a Crime*. Phillips, a college professor, claims to know more about the 2004 election in Ohio than anyone. He and a team of investigators took months to examine thousands of ballots, poll books, and election records. Phillips agrees that there were many dirty tactics that Republicans utilized in Ohio, and that if there hadn't been these tactics then John Kerry would have won Ohio and the presidency. To Phillips, though, the clearest evidence of fraud in Ohio is that the ballots themselves were rigged. Phillips and his investigators took the time to pull and photograph thousands of the ballots that were used in the 2004 Ohio presidential election, and the photographs clearly show that thousands of ballots were altered to change a vote for Kerry to a vote for Bush or were pre-punched for a candidate other than Kerry. Congressman Conyers's committee also found that ballots had been altered, and reported this to the FBI. To anyone who might doubt such a seemingly outrageous claim, Phillips includes a CD in his book and anyone can see for themselves the photographs of the thousands of altered, rigged ballots. When asked how Republican interests thought they could have gotten away with such a thing, Phillips answered, "Because they didn't think anyone would take the time to look." Phillips and his investigators took hours and hours to tediously pull and photograph thirty thousand ballot books. Researcher and writer Robert F. Kennedy Jr. called *Witness to a Crime* "incontrovertible evidence of how the Republicans stole the election in Ohio."

Beyond the specific dirty tactics that were used in the 2000 and 2004 presidential elections is the issue of the reliability and corruptibility of computer voting machines. This issue is at the heart of election reform activist Bev Harris's work. As Ms. Harris's book *Black Box Voting* points out, if computer voting machines are counting the votes in an election, then the persons who control the electronic-computer ballots are the computer technicians working for the private computer voting machine company. In most cases, election officials can't look into the computers and see and check that the ballots are being counted correctly. The public can't see and check the ballots, either. If the computer voting machine company has a partisan prejudice, or has received a multimillion dollar voting machine contract from officials from one of the political parties, or if one of the computer technicians is corrupt, then the real, actual vote count can be easily altered and changed. Any outside hacker with even the slightest knowledge of hacking computers could also get into the system and change votes around. Computer voting machines also tend to malfunction.

To Harris and other election reform activists, such a system in which private companies control the ballots and citizens can't check to see if their ballots are being counted accurately is so plainly unreliable and corruptible that it should be outlawed. *Vanity Fair* magazine has called *Black Box Voting* "the Bible of the election reform movement." Bev Harris's investigative work has been featured by the *New York Times*, the *Washington Post*, and *Time*, and has been on CNN and other major networks. In 2006, HBO did an award-winning documentary, *Hacking Democracy*, based on Harris and her activism. In August 2004, Ms. Harris appeared on CNBC with former Vermont Governor Howard Dean. Governor Dean was alarmed and impressed as Bev took just a few minutes to tamper with an in-studio voting machine and rig a simulated election.

To Bev Harris and other activists like her, their concern isn't that the computer voting machines might someday malfunction or be rigged or tampered with. Their concern is that it has already happened dozens of times and probably happens on a regular basis. In *Black Box Voting*, Ms. Harris lists a hundred cases when the computer voting machines made grievous, egregious mistakes, giving thousands of votes to the wrong candidate, and in some cases declaring the wrong candidate the winner. All of these cases were reported by local and national newspapers:

- In 2002 in Clay County, Kansas, computer voting machines reported that a candidate for county commissioner lost the race, garnering forty-eight percent of the vote. But a hand recount revealed that the candidate had actually won by a landslide, receiving seventy-six percent of the vote.

- In 2003 in Boone County, Indiana, computer machines counted one hundred forty-four thousand votes when only five thousand people had voted.
- The *Wall Street Journal* reported that in the 2000 general election an optical-scan machine in Allamakee County, Iowa was fed three hundred ballots and reported 4 million votes.

Either the computer voting machines are being rigged and tampered with, or they are malfunctioning. Bev Harris feels that the one hundred cases she lists in her book are just the tip of the iceberg, and that there are many more times when the computers got an election wrong that were never noticed at all.

This can, of course, happen during a presidential election. During the 2004 presidential election, hundreds of voters in Ohio and other states reported that they pushed a vote for John Kerry but the light on the computer lit up as a vote for George Bush. At a certain point on the evening of the 2000 presidential election, it was known exactly how much of a lead George Bush needed to have in the state of Florida to declare Bush the president-elect. At that time, the precise lead Bush needed came up on a Volusia County, Florida, voting machine. But the vote count came up because the Volusia County machine had registered that Al Gore had minus 16,022 votes. Citizens don't cast negatives votes and a voting machine shouldn't be able to report a negative vote total. Either the computer malfunctioned or somebody tampered with the computer and gave Al Gore a negative 16,022 vote count—which was the exact amount George Bush needed to win. The miscount was eventually found and the votes were given back to Gore, but this incident caused all the TV networks to call the election for Bush. It also nearly caused presidential candidate Al Gore to concede the election.

The question at the core of Bev Harris's activism is: Why do we use a system where private companies control the ballots and citizens aren't allowed to see and check their own ballots?

And why do we use these computers if they can't be trusted?

Cirignano: In your opinion, how did that minus-16,022 vote total appear for Al Gore on the Volusia County, Florida, voting machine during the 2000 presidential election?

Harris: Fraud. In my opinion. I mean it's so very, very, *very* easy. It's not even hacking. It's actually just editing. Whoever has access to the computer can just put a different number in.

It was **Fox News** *that immediately called the election for Bush after the Volusia County machine reported those numbers. All the other networks then followed* **Fox's** *lead and declared Bush the winner. The* **Fox News** *analyst who called the election for Bush was a man named John Ellis. John Ellis is George Bush's cousin, correct?*

It was Bush's cousin. Uh huh.

The information is that this John Ellis had been talking on the telephone with Jeb Bush on the night of the election. That negative-16,000 vote total came up, so Jeb Bush told him, "We won." John Ellis got off the phone and started saying, "Jebby says we won!" Then Ellis called the election for his cousin and then all the other networks immediately followed his lead and called it for Bush.

What happened with Gore was that the 16,000 was exactly the amount that was needed to call the race. So, you know, it wasn't a random number that just popped out of anywhere. And it actually happened on two machines in two counties in Florida. It also happened in Broward County to the tune of four thousand votes. So, there was a total of twenty thousand votes that got bogusly dumped in there. And the networks knew for a number of hours that those numbers were bogus because they had been alerted by the *60 Minutes* journalist Ed Bradley. And, so, they ended up, you know, just continuing it—they just kept calling the election for Bush—until they could not anymore. . . . We were literally within minutes of having the concession of the presidential candidate.

Based on bogus numbers.
Based on bogus numbers.

The explanation that the voting machine company, Diebold—a company that supports the Republican Party—gave for this minus-16,022 vote total report was that the computer card used to program the machine was faulty and caused the error. But the card changed only one number in one election—the minus-16,022 total for Gore. If you have a faulty memory card programming a computer that's counting a dozen or more elections, it wouldn't just change one number in one election, would it? I don't think it would. A memory card is like a floppy disk. What will a bad disk do? It will give you an error message, or it will fail to read the file at all, or it will make weird humming and whirring noises while your computer attempts to read the disk. I don't think it would just change one number in one file. It's fishy.

So is the most sensible and logical explanation for the negative-16,022 vote total that somebody working for Diebold inserted a second memory card and changed the numbers and tried to take votes away from Al Gore and steal the election for George Bush? No, it probably wouldn't have been Diebold. Well, it could have been Diebold. But it's probably just somebody who was inside. . . . By the way, it wasn't Diebold then—it was the same company, same guys, but Diebold bought it in 2002.

Only one memory card is allowed to be put into a computer that's count-ing the votes of an election, correct? Election officials check the memory card, certify it, and then only that card is to be used on election day.

Of course. Any computer's software program that's going to be counting an election has to be checked and certified by election officials. Then, of course, no other software program can go into that computer.

But Talbot Iredale, a vice president of Diebold, admitted that a second memory card was uploaded on the Volusia County machine. Iredale said he didn't know where the second card came from or who uploaded it. Trying to explain the negative-16,022 vote total, Iredale wrote, "There is always the possibility that the second memory card or second upload came from an unauthorized source."

Iredale said that and wrote that in an internal Diebold memo. So right there he was saying   that somebody could have been tampering with the machine and trying to rig the election.

Do you know if there were any instances in Florida or anywhere in 2000 when the computer voting machines changed a vote for Gore to a vote for Bush? Because during the 2004 election there were hundreds of voters in Ohio and other states who reported that they pushed a vote for Kerry but the light on the computer lit up as a vote for Bush.

Probably. It happened in 2004, certainly. But . . . You know, in Volusia County in 2000 actually they flipped votes from Bush to Gore. And the Democrats badly wanted that to be shut up. I don't see the problem with elections as being a Republican or Democratic conspiracy. I think both par-ties partake. Absolutely. I live in a state, Washington, that's controlled by Democratic forces and they are amazing with the stuff they do.

In Washington, there's corruption?

Yeah. Oh, yeah. I think it serves no purpose to look at one or two elections and say "the Republicans stole it," or "the Democrats stole it." One of the things that I think is actually hurting election reform and harming the effort to restore public control is the fact that so many people refuse to look at it as anything other than partisan. And they want it to be "just the Republicans," or "just the Democrats," and it isn't. I can tell you. I've been out on the front lines for ten years and it is both parties.

This interviewer is an independent and doesn't trust Democrats or Republicans. But the most glaring examples of major election fraud in recent years—the biggest elephants in the room at this point in history—seem to be the apparently stolen presidential elections of 2000 and 2004. So, this interviewer would like to talk about that. If, in 2000 and 2004, the Democrats stole the White House from the Republicans, then this interviewer would be emphasizing that.

Okay. Bush had his brother and Katherine Harris in Florida in 2000, and he had his man, Kenneth Blackwell, in Ohio in 2004. The Republicans engaged in major tampering, and took the presidency. But with other elections . . . I know from being on the front lines that it's definitely both parties. So I think there is no purpose when talking about election reform in taking any type of partisan view. I interviewed quite heavily with Bobby Kennedy Jr. for his *Rolling Stone* articles. And I told him and gave him the facts and the sources that show that Democrats engage in tampering as much as Republicans. But Kennedy left that out of his articles.

Okay. Election reform isn't a partisan issue. Democrats engage in tampering, Republicans engage in tampering. But if we could talk just a little more about 2000 and 2004. Because besides malfunctioning and potentially rigged voting machines, there were other dirty tricks that partisan Republicans used in Florida in 2000 and Ohio in 2004. The purpose and effect of these dirty tricks were to prevent Democrats—especially African Americans—from voting. For instance, blacks had to wait much longer and in much longer lines to cast their votes. Not enough voting machines were put in the black urban precincts?

There was vote suppression. There were a number of dirty tricks they used to prevent Democrats from voting. But, you see . . . essentially, you got the two sides. You got Republican and Democrat. The Republicans—their *modus operandi* is to knock people off the roles. But the Democrats like to stuff people onto the rolls. And that's the truth—the Democrats do stuff the voter rolls and the Republicans do suppress the rolls.

There were more, many dirty tricks aimed at decreasing the Democratic vote. The Republicans were able to get away with these tactics because Blackwell was in charge in Ohio and Harris in Florida? Whichever party the secretary of state belongs to can have a monopoly over the election and how the election is run?

In a way, yes, because the secretary of state can really put their thumb on the scale. However, if you get a county who wants to play ball for the other party, the county can also put their thumb on the scale. The thing is there's like eighty-eight counties in Ohio and something like sixty-five in Florida. And so you have the state official who can do stuff and then you have each individual county also can do stuff.

But the secretary of state has the most and wields the most power over what's going to happen during an election.

True.

Some writers like Mark Miller and others have claimed that Blackwell and Harris and the other Republicans who tampered with the election did it because they were fanatical theocrats—they felt that their party is the party "of God," and so they had a right to steal the election from the "godless, pagan liberals" who might do things like let a woman retain her right to choose an abortion, or give gay people their civil rights.

Because it wasn't only Blackwell and Harris rigging things—there were plenty of fanatical Republicans in the field who were doing things like putting less voting machines in the black districts, and altering ballots, and calling up minorities to intimidate them into not voting. And there was a strong, theocratic, "holier than thou" tone to the Republican rhetoric then. So if you're fanatically religious it could even lead you to believe that you have a right to steal an election?

Whenever people do something that is later deemed to be corrupt, they often try to come up with a justification for it. They try to justify it in their own minds. So it could be.

Maybe the strongest evidence for election tampering in Florida in 2000 is the BBC reporter Greg Palast's report. As Palast's report showed, Katherine Harris's office hired Choice Point to come up with a purge list of mostly Democrats, and this led to probably about eighty thousand legal, eligible, registered Democrats being unjustly denied their right to vote. Do you believe Katherine Harris's statement that all this was some sort of an unintentional error? Or do you think it's more sensible and logical to assume that Harris and Jeb Bush deliberately did this, knowing that it would prevent thousands of eligible Democrats from voting, and knowing that this would steal the election for Jeb Bush's brother?

What happened with Bush in Florida with his brother being the governor was over the top. Just ridiculous tampering. With that purge list—it ended being about ninety thousand purged after it was all said and done. I think she totally knew what was going on, yeah. Somebody did it on purpose. . . . Now whoever it is that actually planned that purge list . . . I will say this—the secretary of state's office in Florida—not just under Katherine Harris—like the last five of them have been unbelievably dirty. It's not just that. The Florida legislature just keeps changing laws to make these—what I call—corruption protection laws. They make laws that say that citizens can't see and check their own ballots. What reason could there possibly be for that other than to cover up corruption?

There seems to be a lot of evidence that Florida is a corrupt state.
Yes. And the current secretary of state in Florida, Kurt Browning, he's a piece of work, too. The lady after Katherine Harris, she got run out. And then the legislature puts these things through that are just unconscionable. It's certainly a system where the good old boys are running the game. And in Florida, the good old boys are Republicans.

Way back in the 1970s, two election reform advocates, Jim and Ken Collier, found clear, strong evidence of election fraud in Florida. The Colliers were even able to videotape election workers forging ballots. They wrote a well-known book about that called **VoteScam**. *If Richard Daley ran a corrupt, election-tampering political machine in Chicago for years, it seems that Florida has been the same way.*
The Sunshine State has corruption. And it's probably been that way for years.

After the election, Palast tried to interview on camera an official from Katherine Harris's office who was in charge of getting the purge list from Choice Point. At one point, Palast took out a copy of the contract that Harris's office had with Choice Point. When the official saw Palast was taking out a copy of the contract, he tore the microphone off his lapel, yelled "Turn off the cameras!" and ran away.
Well, that's not very becoming behavior for a public official, is it?

Professional political people consider exit polls to be very reliable. Some experts conclude that the exit polls data from the 2004 presidential election prove that the election was stolen. At around 8:00 p.m. EST on the evening of the election, exit pollsters were telling the TV networks that

Kerry had an insurmountable lead and would win in a rout. Statisticians say that, according to the figures that the exit pollsters were giving then, George Bush had only a 1 in 450,000 chance to win the election. But when the computer voting machines started printing the official count, the tallies were far off from what the exit polls said, favored Bush, and gave Bush the election. Experts say that it's virtually impossible that the exit polls could have been that far off, and that there had to be vote fraud.

Exit polls can be formative. Informative. But you can't *prove* fraud with statistics. As an election reform activist, you have to get in there and get access to the ballots and see if the ballots were counted correctly. That's proof.

But professional political people take exit polls to be very accurate. There have been foreign elections where the exit polls were so off that citizen groups—and even the US government—called for a recount and the recount proved that the winner of the election won through fraud and the election was reversed. Dick Morris, for instance, is one of the people who ran Bill Clinton's successful presidential campaigns. Since then, Morris has also worked for Republicans. Regarding the 2004 presidential election, Morris said, "The exit polls were way, way off. Exit polls are usually never wrong. I suspect fraud."

They can be formative. Exit polls still poll a very tiny number of people, though. They're based on a lot of assumptions and so forth. I don't think exit polls prove things. I want the proof.

But, again, professional political people take them to be accurate. Lou Harris, the father of modern political polling, a man who probably knows more about elections that anybody, has said, "Ohio (in 2004) was as dirty an election as America has ever seen." And the election polls data would seem to show that. A team of mathematicians from the National

Election Data Archive, a nonpartisan watchdog group, compared the state's exit polls against the certified vote count in forty-nine precincts in Ohio. The team found that in twenty-two precincts the exit polls differed widely—unexplainably—from the official, certified tallies. All the discrepancies favored Bush. Ron Baiman, the vice president of the archive, and a professor at Loyola University, said the study provides "virtual irrefutable evidence of vote fraud" and the final results are "completely consistent with election fraud—specifically vote shifting."
The exit polls can provide good indications and information. But, to me—to repeat myself again—they are not proof of fraud. We can get the proof of fraud when the public has access to the ballots.

*Well, then, is Richard Hayes Phillips's book **Witness to a Crime** proof of fraud in Ohio? Phillips and his investigators photographed thousands of ballots, poll books, and election records. The photographs showed that thousands of ballots were altered to change a vote for Kerry to a vote for Bush, and thousands were pre-punched for a candidate other than Kerry.*
He and Paddy Schaffer, who is an Ohio citizen—yes—they actually went and pulled all the ballots and looked at the ballots. The ballots were altered. And destroyed. They destroyed so many ballots. But then what happened there—this new secretary of state came in, Jennifer Brunner, and Brunner was a Democrat. They were destroying ballots left and right in Ohio. Richard and Paddy—they wanted to take a look at the rest of the ballots and Brunner would not enforce their right to see them. Brunner let them destroy the ballots with no consequences. And Brunner was a Democrat so it seems there was something going on there.

You're saying that Brunner was covering something up for the Democrats? Richard Hayes Phillips's book doesn't present evidence that the Democrats engaged in tampering in Ohio. It presents evidence

of overwhelming, massive, election-turning tampering on the part of Republican interests. That's the conclusion of the book.
Okay. But Brunner was a Democrat. And she wouldn't let them look at the rest of the ballots. The ones that they did look at proved tampering.

And those ballots were altered to favor Bush.
Fifty-five counties in Ohio destroyed evidence. Brunner wouldn't let them look at the rest of the ballots. I think that in 2000 and 2004 both parties did stuff. The Democrats were pretty ineffective. I see no purpose in looking at election reform in any kind of partisan way.

Was Kerry trying to cheat? Was Gore trying to cheat?
I don't know that Gore was. He had a couple of operatives that were pretty. . . . Bill Daley was on his team. I wouldn't trust Bill Daley any further than I could throw him. The Democrats certainly weren't as ruthless, or weren't as effective. Or weren't as over the top. As I said, what happened in Florida with Jeb Bush as governor was just over the top, ridiculous tampering.

Just a few more questions about 2004. According to election attorney Cliff Arnebeck, John Kerry himself seems to have known that the election was rigged. New Mexico is another suspicious state because the exit polls indicated that Kerry would win New Mexico, but later the computer-counted vote tallies gave Bush a victory in New Mexico. Cliff Arnebeck says that on the evening of the election he, other attorneys, and the Reverend Jesse Jackson had a conference call with John Kerry. Arnebeck claims that during the conference call Kerry said that in New Mexico, whether the area was Democratic or Republican—even if the area was heavily Democratic—if the votes were being counted by computers, Bush was getting the majority of the votes. Arnebeck says that this proves that Kerry knew that the computers were rigging the election.

Kerry said that in a private conversation. Of course, Kerry never made any public comment like that, any comment like that to the press.

Why do you think John Kerry didn't challenge the election? He had amassed a team of lawyers and had promised to fight if there were any suspicious anomalies like there were in 2000. But twelve hours after the election, Kerry made his concession speech.

In the circle of politics, they consider it rude. But what they're not understanding is that the American public is the client, not the candidate. A candidate, if he sees something wrong, I feel like, in a way, it's not really his choice to make. Because the people voted, and it's their choice. And, if he says, "Well I'd just rather not do it," well, okay, you just threw away a whole bunch of people's rights. . . . Kerry had collected all the money and lawyers to do it.

He did. He said he was going to challenge if there were any anomalies, and there certainly were anomalies. And he didn't do anything. . . . This issue of computer voting machines corrupting elections doesn't just pertain to presidential elections. This could happen during runs for judgeships, senator, state legislatures, or any office. Whether this is the machines malfunctioning or somebody rigging them, we already know that the machines have gotten elections wrong. In your book you list more than a hundred cases in which the machines have miscounted, or made egregious errors.

That's right. And all those cases were reported by local or national newspapers. There were some quite horrendous mistakes. I'd think it'd be safe to say that in some cases the mistakes or fraud in the computers put the wrong candidate into office. The one hundred examples I listed in my book are probably just the tip of the iceberg. There are probably many more instances of machines malfunctioning or being tampered with that were never noticed at all.

If one candidate is way ahead in the polls before an election, but then there is a dramatic shift and the other candidate ends up winning the election, then in some cases it's probably perfectly reasonable and logical to suspect that the winning candidate might have won because of computer hacking and fraud, wouldn't you say?

Well, the bottom line is if you set up a system that the public can never see then obviously they're going to use that system for fraud sometimes. Human nature is not going to change. They did use systems for fraud before there were computer voting machines. There's quite a healthy history of fraud in the United States—or unhealthy, however you want to put it—and so the idea that, "oh, well, they're no longer going to commit fraud because there's a computer" is ridiculous. Because what the computer does is conceal from the public the mechanism. It conceals the ballots and how the ballots are counted.

There have been certain elections—even major elections—when election reform people believe that the winning candidate might have stolen the election through the computers. For instance, Senator Chuck Hagel in 1996. Hagel was way behind in the primary polls and behind in the general election against the Democratic candidate for senator of Nebraska. Hagel won, and his win there was considered a major, or even stunning, come-from-behind upset. Later, it was revealed that Hagel was an owner and the CEO of the voting machine company, AIS, that had counted the votes in his election. Hagel had hidden these facts in his personal disclosure documents. Do you think that election was rigged?

You see, I don't actually want to try to speculate. What I know Hagel did do was he was in a position to control the outcome and he didn't disclose that he was in a position to control the outcome. Hagel had been the CEO of AIS. And he did hide that in his personal disclosure documents.

Hagel resigned from AIS a few months before he ran for senator. But the machines that counted his election were manufactured while he was CEO of AIS. It's never been proven that computer hacking won him the election. Maybe it did, maybe it didn't. But it was a stunning comeback, and it seems suspicious. If he wasn't guilty of anything, then why did Hagel feel that he had to hide and lie about his relationship with AIS?

I think anybody could look at all these facts and consider it all suspicious. Bottom line, it's obviously not right if a candidate has such intimate ties to the company that's going to count the votes in his own election.

There have been other suspicious elections. For instance, Georgia in 2002. In August 2002, Diebold employees traveled to Georgia and made a number of secretive, uncertified changes to the computer voting machines. An employee of Diebold, a whistleblower, Chris Hood, told Robert F. Kennedy Jr., "The curious thing is the very swift, covert way this was done." Three months later, on election day, Senator Max Cleland, who had been leading his opponent by five points, lost by seven points. Democratic governor Roy Barnes, who had been leading Republican Sonny Perdue by eleven points, lost by five. There were four other upsets in Georgia. Some people would consider these loses inexplicable. Unless there was computer fraud.

These are other elections that people believe may have been rigged. It's easy to understand why they'd think that. The bottom line with this one is that no uncertified changes can be made on computers or software programs that are going to count an election. That's a crime. All computers and software programs are checked and certified before an election and it's illegal to make any uncertified changes before the election.

There are other elections and other computer blunders that are very suspicious. In many cases, it seems that it was the voting machine company Diebold that was behind these suspicious political victories. Diebold has a shady past, doesn't it? Diebold was fully formed when it acquired a company called Global Elections Systems in 2002. GES was founded by three men—Charles Lee, Norton Cooper, and Michael Graye—who were convicted felons and did time for tax fraud, money laundering, and other crimes?

It's a very, very tawdry story. It is really troubling. Those were the guys who founded Global Elections which was merged with Diebold. Then those three felons hired two men named Talbot Iredale and Guy Lancaster. Iredale and Lancaster developed the optical-scan voting system for Diebold that was eventually used for elections in thirty-seven states. So, the election system used by thirty-seven states was created by two men who were hired by convicted felons.

Lee, Cooper, and Graye also hired a man named Jeffrey Dean.

Jeffrey Dean was a convicted embezzler—he was convicted of twenty-three felonies—who specialized in computer hacking and had helped a client steal money through computer fraud. Dean became head of research and development at Global Election Systems, and then worked for Diebold when Diebold merged with GES. Dean helped Diebold develop its voting machines. At times, he was in charge of programming the voter-registration system for entire areas of the country. Dean also had access to every voting machine Diebold had up and running in thirty-seven states.

While in prison, Dean met a man named John Elder, who did five years for cocaine trafficking. Elder was hired by Diebold and managed a division that oversees the printing of ballots and punch cards for several states. Whoever is in charge of printing ballots can easily engage in election tampering and fraud by manipulating how the ballots are printed, correct?

Uh huh. So we had an embezzler who specialized in computer hacking programming our voting system and a cocaine trafficker printing our ballots. Wonderful.

What do you make of the statement that Diebold CEO Wally O'Dell made back in 2003? O'Dell had raised more than a half a million dollars for Bush/Cheney and had just attended a gathering for fundraisers that George W. Bush had appeared at. Right after that, O'Dell wrote a letter to a hundred of his wealthy and politically inclined friends which said, "I am committed to helping Ohio deliver its electoral votes to the president next year." Diebold, of course, was the company that counted the votes in Ohio in 2004.

You know, a lot has been written and said about that. Some people could easily suspect that O'Dell was letting the cat out of the bag there. The bottom line is that the votes can't be concealed because then a blatantly partisan official like O'Dell can have too much influence in how the votes are counted.

In your opinion, was Diebold a criminal organization?

I wouldn't say that Diebold is the main story. No. I think the organization that started as Global Election Systems and went through a number of permutations. There's no doubt that they designed it so that it would be open for business. Now that doesn't mean that you pre-program in it a rig. It means that you design places for people to do it and make it easy.

The two other companies—besides Diebold—that have dominated the business of providing voting machines for elections are Election Systems & Software and Sequoia Voting Systems. ES&S and Sequoia also have shady pasts.

The principal owners of ES&S were Peter Kiewit Sons' Inc. The Kiewit company had been charged and tied to bid rigging cases in eleven states and two countries. Kiewit has broken the law numerous times, is involved with many businesses, and could certainly have a vested interest in what politicians get into office. ES&S machines have been accused of flipping votes, miscounting elections, and were the machines that counted the votes when Hagel won in 1996—it was called AIS back then. And with Sequoia—an employee of Sequoia was once investigated because he gave a $40,000 payoff to an election official in Louisiana whose job it was to give out voting machine contracts. And the company that bought Sequoia in May 2002, De La Rue plc, has been investigated for an illegal price fixing scheme.

Do Diebold and ES&S and Sequoia still dominate the voting machine business?
Diebold's out of it. But not really. Diebold sold itself to ES&S. My organization, *BlackBoxVoting*, did a formal, very well-documented complaint about Diebold to the Department of Justice, and the DOJ finally rolled it back on grounds of it being a monopoly. But they really didn't. What they did—all the Diebold installations then currently in use, which was about thirty percent of the United States—they were bought by ES&S. And new equipment being sold to new jurisdictions were controlled by another company called Dominion. Both ES&S and Dominion come out of Canada. And the interesting thing is no one now knows who really owns either ES&S or Dominion. They could even have the same owner. Who knows?

So, now ES&S has a monopoly on counting elections in America?
ES&S has a monopoly. They're running about seventy percent of the elections.

ES&S has a shady past, too.
Yes.

Do you think all this could be a major conspiracy? Is it possible that some very rich businessmen somewhere, some corporate interests, want to control the elections and politics of America? And they decided they'd fund and develop relations with the voting machine companies, make sure that these companies are run by unethical and even criminal people, so that these business interests could get them to fix and rig elections when they want them to?

Simple answers aren't going to really work because the nature of power is that a lot of people want it. Yes, corporations want it. But also I think it's plausible that some people who are at high levels of government may think they're doing the right thing by making sure a system is in place so that "if needed" they could put their thumb on the scale. You know, like if some rowdy person, like a Ron Paul or something—some politician who's really going to go against the political establishment, somebody who "it just wouldn't be safe" to have in office—I can actually conceive of that being a motive for some types to rig an election through the computers. Maybe they'd justify it on the basis of international matters, saying, you know, "it's for the good of the peace of the world that if we have to, we can control it."

You believe people in government are behaving this way?

I'm thinking people at high levels of the government. Chuck Hagel, you know, went right to intelligence. He was on the foreign policy committees, and all that. Another person who is really into these electronics is Hillary Clinton.

Clinton advocates the use of computer voting machines?

I would call her a proselytizer for them. Even as secretary of state, she was inserting herself into India's election systems. I'm in touch with them there and there are a lot of computer scientists and citizens in India who are incensed at what's going on in India. But Hillary Clinton came out and said, "I want to commend India for having its own electronic voting system and going to entirely electronic touchscreens."

So you're saying people in government even want other countries to use computer voting machines because they want to be able to control international politics and elections.

Look at it from that perspective. It could be plausible, right? We have the issue of terrorism. Their thinking may be that it may be safer for the world if a really undesirable dictator was heading in there it could be controlled by elections rather than war. Here's where that breaks down though. The same kind of thing that would hide it from the public and allow that will allow you to hide the local sheriff's race and hide the local commissioner's race. How do you say, "That's okay for international politics, but it's not okay for local. We can use the computers overseas, but we can't use them in America."

So, you're saying that people in power could be doing this for beneficent reasons. But maybe they're doing it for devious reasons. Maybe they want to control the elections so they can get their "man" in there who will start the war for the military-industrial complex, or give contracts to and control politics for Big Business.

The problem is power. The nature of people is when they do something that is eventually deemed to be corrupt they often justify it to themselves that there's a higher purpose in what they're doing.

This happened in Venezuela. The US government had recommended to Hugo Chavez that Venezuela use ES&S voting machines. But then in May 2000, Venezuela's highest court suspended the elections because the ES&S machines were miscounting ballots. Chavez accused ES&S of trying to rig Venezuela's elections. Some people think Hugo Chavez is a good human being and leader, some people think he's not. But at that time there were plenty of people in the US government who wanted Chavez out of office.

Well, yes. This is what I'm saying. I believe they could be doing things like that.

The testimony of a man named Clint Curtis, a former Republican, seems like strong evidence that there is a conspiracy to rig elections in America. Curtis was the head computer programmer at Yang Enterprises in Oviedo, Florida, when he was asked to develop a software program that "could alter the vote tabulation in an election and be undetectable." Curtis said he was asked to do this by Yang's general counsel, Tom Feeney, who was a Republican state senator, and who became a Florida Congressman in 2002. According to Curtis, Feeney told Curtis he wanted the program because he felt Democrats were going to steal elections and he wanted to know how it was done. But later Curtis realized Feeney was lying because the CEO of Yang told Curtis, "In order to get the (voting machine) contract we have to hide the manipulation in the source code. This program is needed to control the vote in South Florida."

I'd accept what Curtis says as credible. I think that's just more evidence of what goes on in Florida. And I think it's reasonable to presume that that goes on in other states, also.

Curtis resigned from Yang, but before he did he says he attended meetings with the Yang CEO and Senator Feeney where Feeney bragged about other ways that the Florida Republican party was going to steal votes. Curtis has testified before Congress, has passed a lie detector test, and his claims are deemed to be truthful by some journalists who have investigated them.

I think he's telling the truth. I believe him. . . . I've had people admit to me elsewhere that people were stealing elections. One election that was particularly troubling was the presidential primary in 2008 in New Hampshire.

When Hillary Clinton beat Barack Obama, Obama had won Iowa and the polls were indicating and the experts were saying he was going to win New Hampshire. But then Hillary won. And the exit polls also clearly indicated that Obama should have won.

Wherever the ballots were counted by hand in New Hampshire, Obama won. Wherever the ballots were counted by the computer machines in New Hampshire, Clinton won. When there was a recount, that's when it really started to stink. I kind of knew it was going to go that way. On election day, before the polls closed, they were announcing to the press "Oh, gee, we had to deliver more ballots to places." But the secretrary of state's office denied that they were delivering more ballots. What that means is somebody witnessed them running a bunch more blank ballots into places. Why would you do that? So you could substitute them. So I went out there and I led a monitoring of a recount that was called for by Dennis Kucinich and a Republican candidate there. Hillary said she needed to win Manchester County and she did. Manchester has fourteen wards—fourteen precincts. Their procedure was they had a metal ballot box and at the polling place when they're done voting the ballots go in the box, the box is locked, and the poll workers sign a seal on it. All of those ballot boxes were brought to the Manchester City Clerk. From there they were brought to the recount location in Concord. Now here's the thing—when they got to the recount location, the ballots for ward five were in the ward six box and vice versa. Now how does that happen? And we have that on videotape.

That's evidence of tampering. Somebody broke the chain of custody. Somebody was fiddling with the ballots.
Yes.

If it's Washington insider-power brokers who are rigging elections, then maybe they wanted Hillary in office more than Obama? Because Hillary seemed to be more the establishment candidate—the candidate more connected to the special, corporate interests that run Washington. And at that time, Obama was coming off like a populist or a maverick. The whole thing seems moot, now, because Obama didn't become any kind of populist or maverick. He was a puppet like all the other presidents.

I don't know. But, you know, New Hampshire is the first primary in the nation. It's not about who wins New Hampshire, it's about who does better than expected and who does worse than expected. If Clinton had lost New Hampshire, she would have lost her donation base. She would have been out of the race. She had to win because Obama had just won Iowa and if he had won Iowa and New Hampshire that would have put her out of the race, just about. So it was a must-win for her.

If there was election tampering, would Hillary Clinton, herself, have known about it?
I don't think it's even necessary to go to that level. There's always someone in the campaign, the campaign manager, or someone at a lower level who interfaces with the people who do the unseemly thing. I certainly think they wouldn't want her to know because if an election is rigged and the candidate didn't know it was being rigged and the candidate is elected, they cannot roll back the election. The only way they can roll back the election is if the candidate knew. So, they would certainly not tell the candidate and the candidate certainly would not say, "By the way, I would like you to rig my election." It would be so not necessary. All you'd need to do would be pick people who you know are aggressive and not ask too many questions.

Have you heard of Stephen Spoonamore and Mike Connell? Spoonamore is a conservative Republican who is also a computer security expert who has set up safe computer systems for large banks and corporations, and for some government departments. Spoonamore claims that computerized elections are set up in America in a way that allows any election to be easily hacked and rigged. He believes that the only reason that elections are set up this way is so that corrupt influences can rig them. Spoonamore was friends with a man named Mike Connell. Mike Connell was Karl Rove's computer expert. Connell set up the computerized election systems for Florida in 2000, for Kenneth Blackwell in Ohio in 2004, and for other elections that some people think may have been rigged. Spoonamore has basically said Mike Connell confessed to him that he had been rigging elections for powerful Republicans.

Spoonamore is a fraud. But the Mike Connell story is very disturbing. But he's dead so . . .

You think Spoonamore is a fraud?

Yes.

But Spoonamore is basically saying the same things that you're saying. He's saying that computer voting machines can easily lead to hacking and fraud.

He basically took my chapters out of my book and resaid them in his own words using the files that I put on my website. Which I don't think he actually looked at because he got that wrong too.

Election attorney Cliff Arnebeck takes Spoonamore to be reliable. But you think what? You think Spoonamore's trying to become some sort of famous whistleblower for election reform or something but he's exaggerating about some things?

I think that he's . . . I don't know. I don't even want to say. To me, he's not reliable.

Author and NYU professor Mark Miller takes Spoonamore to be credible. Investigative reporter Dick Russell believes he's credible. But what about Mike Connell? You think that story's intriguing?

The Connell story is very disturbing.

Connell was Karl Rove's computer expert. Congressman Conyers's committee was going to take testimony from Mike Connell. And, then, in October 2008, Cliff Arnebeck brought a lawsuit against Kenneth Blackwell and other officials in Ohio charging them with election fraud. Mike Connell testified at that trial. Connell didn't spill the beans or anything, but some people say that he was getting ready to confess that he'd helped to rig elections. He was scheduled to testify again in Ohio, but in December 2008 he was killed in a single passenger plane crash near Akron, Ohio. Arnebeck and others believe Mike Connell was murdered.

I have no idea. How would I know? It's obviously not closed if a witness in something highly political goes down in a small plane crash. If you look at the statistical chance of that happening it's pretty remote.

Was Connell getting ready to confess?
I don't know. I have no idea.

But maybe?
Maybe. I don't know.

Author Mark Miller and others claim that Mike Connell told and confessed to Stephen Spoonamore and others that he had helped to rig elections. Spoonamore says that Connell was a very religious man and in a way he may have justified what he was doing because he was helping to take elections from the political party that allows "babies to be killed." He was helping to steal elections from the Democrats who want to keep abortion legal. And Spoonamore and others say that the Republicans that Connell was working for were also fanatically religious theocrats. . . . To you, the whole story is, at least, intriguing?
Anytime someone dies in a small plane crash. . . . There was another guy who also died in a small plane crash in Ohio who was also in a key position. He was the troubleshooter guy for Diebold. And he was, by all accounts, a straight arrow. And he was getting reports of what was going on in 2003. And he up and died in a small plane crash as well. If you look at the total

number of small plane crashes that are fatalities every year and divide it by the total number of flights, the chances that it would happen at an opportune time to a person are kind of remote.

As you've said, America has a long history of election fraud. Over the years, there have been many corrupt political machines and many suspicious elections. Maybe what we're talking about here is the problem with the culture of politics? For years, in major league baseball, it was accepted that if a pitcher could get away with throwing a spitball, then the pitcher would throw a spitball. Perhaps the culture of politics is that if a politician can get away with stealing an election, then the politician will steal the election?

This is what I told Robert Kennedy Jr. And I know this to be true because I've been out there. It started local, and that's where people honed their skills. I look at it as a patchwork in the United States. The first positions to go bad are the sheriff and the county commissioner or county supervisor because the county commissioners and county supervisors are in charge of purchasing certain items that are the gravy train for major kickbacks. And the sheriff is in charge of contraband, drugs, and guns, and so forth, and that's another susceptible position that's a target for corruption. Many, if not most of these guys, are honest. But if they're going to go bad in a certain location it's going to start with that. And then they're going to start perpetuating themselves and they're going to start putting in little local infrastructures where they've got a few good old boys that know how to gain and work the system. But what happens is that in any state—say you've got eighty-eight counties—you're going to have a certain number of counties that have gone bad. And those counties—believe me—the operatives know where they are. I call them the counties that are open for business. For example, in Florida—which is known to be a pretty corrupt state—they don't touch Ion Sancho in Leon County, Florida, because Ion Sancho is a bastion of integrity.

They're not going in there. But, yeah, they'll go to Volusia, and they'll go to Hillsborough, and they'll go to Broward, and Palm Beach. They will set up camp and live in Palm Beach. They know where to go and where it's going to happen.

As you wrote about in your book, there have always been different types of voting machines and methods. But whether it's been lever machines, or punch cards, or whatever, there's always been a way to rig and tamper with each method.

The methodology differs. It's so interesting, because it actually evolves into the electronic and you can sometimes see how. Like I saw in Tennessee— they used to have this old school electronic machine called the shoop. And the method of tampering with that was a certain method. And they actually sort of adapted that method to the new Diebold machine. It's like you go to different places and they have their specialties.

It's the culture of politics.

But I don't think you can just say politics is dirty and they're going to do it. It's just that there're going to be bad apples in the barrel and the guys who are in charge of the state politics and the guys at the national level are going to know—it's their job to know—where the bad apples are.

Whether it's Republicans stealing elections from Democrats or Democrats stealing elections from Republicans doesn't seem to matter because there's not much difference between Republicans and Democrats these days. But if somebody gets into office by fraud, he's going to be a more unscrupulous, corrupt person. If we have honest elections, we have a better chance of bringing upstanding leaders into office.

Of course. It'd be nice, you know, if we could have honest candidates winning honest elections.

Election reform isn't a partisan issue. Both Democrats and Republicans engage in election tampering and fraud. But the most glaring examples of major vote fraud in recent times—the biggest elephants in the room now—are the presidential elections of 2000 and 2004. Because there seems to be enough evidence to conclude that the Bush machine and Republican operatives did steal the 2000 and 2004 presidential elections. But our media and our Congress have said and done nothing about this. So if we have a media and Congress that sit back and do nothing while a president gets elected under extremely suspicious circumstances, then what kind of leaders and presidents could we get in the future? Maybe someone who has an almost Adolf Hitler-type of personality could steal the election and become president?

The problem at its core is the removal of democracy. So when you have those pieces in place—when the public can't see the ballots—sooner or later, someone will certainly take it and probably anybody from either party who is inclined that way will do so. We know from Tammany Hall, my goodness, back in the day, you know, that it wasn't limited to Republicans who did things like this. When you give people a mechanism, when you put a mechanism in place that lets them install themselves at will, then some people will.

Maybe a politician who's a part of the New World Order groups—if you believe that stuff—steals the election, then the Wall Street masters do things that bankrupt America, and lead us into a severe depression. Then there's a shortage of food, rioting in the streets, and the president suspends the Constitution, declares martial law, and turns America into some sort of police state. If we have a media and a Congress that lets politicians steal our offices and our presidency then something like that could happen, couldn't it? Are you one who takes these New World Order theories to be credible?

I don't know about that . . . I don't think it's a matter of new creepy guys who want to take over the world. There have always been creepy guys who want to take over the world.

There are ways to have elections that prevent fraud, aren't there? In your book, you list a number of incorruptible voting methods that can be used on election day. For instance, the way they vote in France.

In France, everybody votes on a paper ballot. Then when the votes are counted, as many citizens as can fit in the room watch the vote count. Sworn officials from both parties count and announce each ballot one at a time while dozens of citizens watch. By having many election precincts throughout the country, all of France can be counted in a matter of hours, in front of thousands of eyes.

We could do that here in America, couldn't we?

Yes, but our country is massive and our election officials have lost the skill set to hand-count. The lobbyists and the vendors of the computer voting machines certainly don't want that because there's no money in hand counts. What would happen if we mandated that the whole country went to hand counting overnight is that you could be a hundred percent certain that it would be a big mess. It would not work if we just forced it down everyone's throats instantly. It would have to be prepared with training programs and so forth.

But it could be done, right?

It could be done.

After 2000 and 2004, dozens of election reform groups became active, protesting and calling for a safer, non-corruptible way of having elections. The mainstream media really didn't cover that. But are we making any progress, any improvements in America? Are we moving away from the non-auditable, paperless, computer voting machines and towards a safer way to vote?

Yes, there's been some definite improvements happening. Let me give a specific example. Humboldt County, California. They have 170,000 voters. They didn't have the ability to go immediately to public hand counting. But what they did was say, "Let's let the public have a way to compare what went into the machine with the results that came out of it." They bought a scanning machine from Office Depot that would high-speed scan their ballots. They scanned the ballots before they were put into the voting machines. They put them on the web. They let anybody have a copy of all the ballots. The very first year they did that, the public looked at the ballots and found that the Diebold machines had miscounted the ballots. So it was very effective. So that's one thing that was a very interesting, meaningful change. The issue is not the security of the machines—the issue is the public right to know what votes went in and out of the machines. Let's use technology like that, in a way that lets the public know. Cheaply. All it cost them was a scanner. There are other methods like that that other places are using. These are the kinds of things I'm interested in. Something that doesn't have a lot of money involved, that's easy, and that restores the public's rights in a meaningful way.

Do you still think that we should immediately stop using computer voting machines, that there should be a moratorium on counting votes by machine?

It'd be a good idea. Because you see a real battle going on in this right now where some states have successfully banned the right of the public to look at and check the ballots ever under any circumstances. That's what I refer to as a corruption protection law. New Hampshire is one of those states. They passed a specific law that prevents citizens from looking at the ballots. It's also that way in my state, Washington. And in Arizona—a law crept in under the cover of darkness that says citizens don't have a right to check the ballots.

Who's behind that? Is there a conspiracy somewhere to force us to use computers and take away our right to see our own ballots? Why would any democratic official or citizen want that? What reason could there be for that?

There isn't a good reason for it. Period. It's nothing more than corruption protection. It's ridiculous.

So what is the ultimate solution to having safe elections in America? We all vote on paper ballots and then officials from both parties and citizen groups count the ballots one at a time?

Hand counting would be good. But there are other ways besides hand counting. You can use machines. The crux of it is not hand counting—the crux of it is the public has to be able to see and authenticate. Like they did in Humboldt County—some way that the public can authenticate what went in and out of the machine. There are actually four things that the public has to be able to see and authenticate: 1, who can vote; 2, who did vote; 3, chain of custody—who handled the ballots; and, 4, the count. The public has to have access to and be able to see that there is no fraud regarding those four things. The public. Not the government.

If you have somebody in the government responsible for telling us those four things, then that government person could easily be corrupted and give a false count.

Of course. People mistake that and they go, "Well if you could just get ES&S and Diebold out of it." No, no. If you have some guy in the government able to control it then that's just the same thing. . . . But something recently happened in Germany that was very important. And that's what we need to be talking about now. Election reform people there took the issue of electronic and computer voting machines to the Supreme Court—Germany's equivalent of the Supreme Court. And they won. Germany ruled that electronic voting, or any method that conceals the ballots and the four essential steps from the public, is a human rights violation. And they banned it. The very next election, six months later, the whole nation of Germany hand counted the ballots in public. That's significant. Very significant. So the guys in Germany who are the plaintiffs in that suit told me—they put it very well—they said the difference between a real democracy and a false democracy is whether the elections are public. It's not whether there are elections, because Saddam Hussein had elections. The Soviet Union had elections. It's whether the elections are truly public. The public has to be able to see and authenticate—without need for special expertise—who can vote, who did vote, change of custody, and the count. If there's anywhere where election officials aren't allowing the public to see and authenticate any one of those four things, then you know there's something wrong. If we are voting under a system in which the public can't authenticate those four things, then we are no longer living in a democracy. We are living in a system much more like totalitarianism.

NB: The election returns in the state of Ohio from the 2012 presidential election would seem to support Bev Harris's contention that election tampering isn't a Republican or Democratic conspiracy but is perpetuated by those who own and control the voting machines companies. In 2012, in fifty voting districts in Ohio, the voting totals were unusually similar—530 votes for Barack Obama, 5 votes for Mitt Romney. Researchers claim that the likelihood of such a similar vote showing up in fifty different districts is highly improbable, atypical, an anomaly, and indicative of election tampering and voter fraud.

CHAPTER 9

Oklahoma Bombing Investigation Committee Claims Startling Evidence Proves Government Cover-Up

An interview with former Oklahoma State Legislature Republican whip Charles Key

S am Cohen is an explosives expert, who is retired after a forty-year career in nuclear weaponry. During World War II Cohen was assigned to the Manhattan Project at Los Alamos, New Mexico. In 1958, he was one of the principal designers of the neutron bomb. Cohen is one of the many people who have criticized the federal government's contention that Timothy McVeigh's forty-eight hundred pound ammonium-nitrate (fertilizer-fuel oil) truck bomb was the sole cause of the destruction of the Murrah Federal Building in Oklahoma City on April 19, 1995. Cohen has said: "I believe that demolition charges were placed in the building at certain key concrete columns and this did the primary damage to the Murrah Federal Building. It would have been absolutely impossible and against the laws of nature for a truck full of fertilizer and fuel oil—no matter how much was used—to bring the building down."

Before the 9/11 attacks on the World Trade Center and Pentagon buildings, the Oklahoma City bombing was the worst act of domestic terrorism in the history of the United States.

On June 11, 2001, Timothy McVeigh was executed for the crime. To some, that brought closure to this horrific chapter of American history.

To others, it did not. Some of the family members of those who were killed in Oklahoma City have stated that they believe that one man couldn't have done the bombing, and that there is too much evidence that McVeigh had accomplices. These bereaved families feel the whole story behind the bombing hasn't been revealed, and they want anybody else who may have been behind the murders of their loved ones brought to justice. Federal Judge Richard Matsch, who presided over McVeigh's trial, has said, "There are many unanswered questions. It would be very disappointing to me if the law enforcement agencies of the United States Government have quit looking for answers in this Oklahoma bombing tragedy."

For the most part, the media has accepted and promoted the government's version of the bombing: that McVeigh—with minor assistance from Terry Nichols—acted alone. The one-man, one-bomb scenario.

Some writers, though, have questioned these conclusions. Reporter James Ridgeway, writing in the *Village Voice* about a week before McVeigh was scheduled to be executed, brought up many unanswered questions. These included: Who was the dark-skinned John Doe #1 who people testified seeing McVeigh with on the morning of the bombing? How could McVeigh and Nichols have built a forty-eight hundred pound ANFO bomb on the evening before the bombing—as the government claims—if bomb experts claim that much more time would have been needed to do that? Could the anti-government militia groups that McVeigh had connections to have collaborated in the atrocity? Gore Vidal's article in the September 2001 *Vanity Fair* was entitled "The McVeigh Conspiracy." In the article, Vidal is extremely critical of the FBI, who, he shows, failed to investigate many promising leads that could have led to the identity of McVeigh accomplices. The famous journalist-novelist feels that the McVeigh-Nichols scenario is unlikely and makes no sense. Vidal suggests and shows evidence that McVeigh could have been working with Arab terrorists, or anti-government groups, or even government agents. He suggests that even the "grandest conspiracy theory of all" is a possibility—that McVeigh neither built nor detonated a bomb, and is a patsy. Vidal had been exchanging letters with McVeigh, and was one of the few people that McVeigh invited to witness his execution. Vidal is convinced that McVeigh confessed to something he didn't do alone—or didn't do at all—because McVeigh felt that his lawyer had "blown" the case, and he wanted to be executed as a martyr, a pro-tester of government abuse, rather than face the prospect of living in a prison cell for fifty years with the threat of rape an everyday fear.

Charles Key was a Oklahoma state representative from 1986 to 1998, during which time he served on the Banking and Finance, Criminal Justice, and other committees. Mr. Key served as Republican whip during part of his tenure. Soon after the Oklahoma City bombing, survivors and relatives of the victims of the bombing began contacting Key to complain about the manner in which the federal government was conducting the investigation. Within hours and days of the bombing, many suspicious facts were coming to light. So many brokenhearted families affected directly by the bombing had unanswered questions and implored Key, in his capacity as an elected official, to pursue further investigation into the case. This resulted in the formation of the Oklahoma Bombing Investigation Committee (OBIC). The OBIC—which consists of Key and three other prominent Oklahoma citizens—was established in April 1997 to investigate matters that govern-ment agencies had refused to consider, and to submit information to the Oklahoma County grand jury which was impaneled in June 1997.

In the winter of 2001 the OBIC released its *Final Report on the Bombing of the Alfred P. Murrah Building, April 19, 1995.* The report is extremely crit-ical of the government and FBI. Citing government documents and the findings of their own investigators, the OBIC claims the government has engaged in a massive cover-up.

Some of the most intriguing information in the *Final Report*—and one of the main reasons that Key founded the OBIC—is that within a few weeks of the bombing, the most preeminent experts on explosives were saying that the destruction of the Murrah Building could not possibly have come from an ANFO truck bomb, and that the bomb—or bombs—had to be *inside* the building. As one of these experts, Brigadier General (USAF, ret.) Benton Partin, said, "It's an entirely different story if you had a bunch of demolition charges in the building in contradistinction to an ammonium-nitrate truck placed out in front of the building. . . . It probably would have taken several people to do this. And it would have taken people with access. You have to remember that these federal buildings have guards on the gate and they have magnetometers and everything else. So it's not only how many people, but who had access. . . . You just don't walk in off the street through security with explosives like this."

Somewhere between ten and fifteen explosives experts and professional engineers have written strongly worded opinions that the Murrah building had to have been destroyed by interior bombs and that the ANFO truck could not have done the damage. These experts included a NASA scientist and demolition experts who have worked in the field for thirty years. What is most eye-opening is that even a government report concluded that the ANFO truck bomb couldn't have possibly destroyed the Murrah building. In early 1997, Wright Laboratory at Elgin Air Force Base in Florida constructed a concrete, steel-reinforced structure that was similar to the Murrah Building, and then did a series of explosions to test bomb effects. The Air Force structure was not nearly as structurally sound as the Murrah Building, and the bombs used against it were more powerful than a forty-eight hundred pound ANFO bomb. Minimal damage was done to the structure. Afterwards, the Air Force released a fifty-six page report that was entitled *Case Study Relating Blast Effects to the Events of April 19, 1995, Oklahoma City, Oklahoma*. The report, which included an extensive technical analysis that the Air Force commissioned from construction and demolition expert John Culberston, concluded that ". . . it is impossible to ascribe the damage that occurred on April 19, 1995, to a single truck bomb containing forty-eight hundred pounds of ANFO. . . . It must be concluded that the damage at the Murrah Building is not the result of the truck bomb itself, but rather due to other factors such as locally placed charges within the building itself. . . . The procedures used to cause the damage to the Murrah Building are therefore more involved and complex than simply parking a truck and leaving . . ." Six explosives experts strongly agreed with the report's findings.

Apparently, Elgin Air Force Base isn't the only government group that came to these conclusions. In his *Vanity Fair* article, Gore Vidal pointed out that the March 20, 1996, issue of *Strategic Investment* newsletter wrote: "A classified report prepared by two independent Pentagon experts has concluded that the destruction of the Federal building in Oklahoma City last April was caused by five separate bombs. . . . Sources close to the study say Timothy McVeigh did play a role in the bombing but 'peripherally, as a 'useful idiot.'"

Brigadier General (ret.) Partin has been the most vocal of the critics of the government's one-bomb, one-man scenario. During his thirty-one-year Air Force career, General Partin's expertise was explosives. During that time, he designed warheads, "had a lot of experience in combat damage evaluation," was trained in all the pertinent military laboratories, and was one of the government's foremost—if not *the* foremost—experts on explosives. "When I first looked at the reports coming out of Oklahoma, I knew that the truth was not coming out. The media was pretty much confused, or passing out disinformation, and I think some of the officials down there were passing out disinformation, and what was going on down there was totally at odds with what I had twenty-five years experience of knowing," General Partin has said. To Partin, the contention that the ANFO truck bomb did the damage to the Murrah Building is "absurd." Within a month of April 19, 1995, the general had prepared a technical analysis of the bombing. In the report, Partin made it clear that by the time the blast wave from the ANFO truck bomb had hit the building, it would not have had anywhere near enough PSI (pounds of pressure per square inch) to collapse the steel-reinforced concrete columns. (By the time the ANFO blast wave hit the columns it would have been yielding 25–375 PSI; the yield strength of concrete is 3,500–5,000 PSI.) The report also made it clear that larger, thicker columns further away from the truck bomb came down, while smaller columns much closer to the truck were undamaged. "You don't have to go any further than that to know that you had demolition charges on those larger columns. There's no other explanation for it . . . unless you believe in magic," Partin said. General Partin examined hundreds of photos of the destroyed building, and his in-depth report listed the many other reasons why he can see "clearly, clearly . . . with a very high probability . . . with a high level of confidence" exactly where interior bombs were placed. Partin eventually delivered his analysis to all 535 senators and congressmen. In his cover letter to the politicians, he pleaded that the "Congress take steps to assure that evidence in Oklahoma City be evaluated by a collection of demolition experts from the private sector before the building is demolished." If experts had been able to examine the building closely, they could have reported definitively on how the building was bombed. On May 23, 1995, though, just thirty-four days after the bombing, the Murrah Building was destroyed, and the rubble was buried in a landfill that is surrounded by a chain link fence and guarded by security personnel. "This is a classic cover-up of immense proportions," the general said.

Five professional engineers and demolition experts firmly concurred with Partin's analysis. The testimony of these explosives experts is one of the main reasons that the Oklahoma Bombing Investigation Committee feels that the Congress should impanel a committee to reinvestigate the bombing. (Currently, Congressman Dan Burton, chairman of the House Government Reform Committee, is strongly considering reinvestigating the bombing.) It is by no means, however, the only reason. The OBIC's Final Report is 550 meticulously documented pages. It was an analysis Key and I would discuss.

Cirignano: Why was the Oklahoma Bombing Investigation Committee formed?

Key: We formed the committee to look into the inconsistencies and problems with the federal government's investigation into the Oklahoma City bombing that were observed beginning with the date of the bombing.

How many hours of work went into investigating the bombing before you published your final report?

The only way I can try to answer that is in terms of years. From 1995 through 2001. A good six years.

You've said that you have sufficient proof that the federal government did have prior knowledge the bombing of the Murrah building could very well take place. What's the strongest evidence that indicates prior knowledge?

Well, I don't know if I would pick one, because there's a number of them— facts that indicate prior knowledge. There's several. And it includes the informant Carol Howe, and the work she did for the Bureau of Alcohol, Tobacco, and Firearms (ATF). ATF field reports that show the information that she gathered and imparted to her handlers, ATF agents. She told them anti-government groups were planning to bomb a federal building. Also, the information that Cary Gagan, another informant, gave to the Justice Department office in Denver about five or six months before the Oklahoma City bombing. Gagan said he was approached by Arab-looking individuals who offered him money to help in a bombing plot. In March 1995, Gagan had a meeting with these people where they examined drawings of the Murrah Building. Three times Gagan was sent by the group to Oklahoma City to case the building. He said he reported this to Justice Department officials in Denver.

This informant Carol Howe, who had infiltrated the anti-government groups, she specified the Murrah Building, too, right?

Yes, that they had actually cased it out, and gone to Oklahoma City and cased that specific building out.

The fact that people saw bomb squads at the Murrah Building a few hours before the bombing would seem to indicate that somebody knew something was going on.
Yes, that's another good proof. Then you have, I mean, there is this long list. The Oklahoma City Fire Department was alerted by the FBI ahead of time to be in a special state of alert. Harvey Weathers, the assistant chief, told that to *USA Today* on the day of the bombing. You also have this judge, federal judge Wayne Alley, who still sits here in Oklahoma City, who gave an interview to his hometown newspaper, the *Portland Oregonian*.

In that interview Judge Alley said, "I was warned (of the bombing) by people who ought to know."
Yes. And there's other reasons to believe the FBI and other government officials had prior knowledge. Some of this information, Stephen Jones, McVeigh's lawyer, tried to get introduced into the trial, and he couldn't. Judge Matsch wouldn't allow it, like he disallowed so much important information. . . . But, you know, after the bombing the ATF Director admitted that the ATF was "very concerned and tried to be more observant" about the specific date of April 19. If the anti-government groups were going to do something, it was feared they would do it on April 19 because that was the anniversary of Waco. And the ATF agents weren't in the building when it was bombed. We have people who told us that ATF agents said they were told the morning of the bombing to not go in that day. Now if someone told the ATF to stay out that day because—as it might seem—they feared something would happen, then why weren't the rest of the people in the building told to stay away?

Many survivors of the bombing stated that they felt the building shaking—for a good long time—before another explosion ripped out the front

windows. That would certainly support the theory that more than one bomb caused the destruction.

Yes, many people feel that's very important information. All of the reports of people that were survivors of the bombing—people who were in the building—they talked about having enough time to discuss the shaking and the trembling of the building. Then having enough time to get under their desks. A lot of the survivors feel if they hadn't gotten under their desks then they would have been killed. Then once they were under their desks another explosion ripped out the windows, ripped out the front of the building. So these people are convinced that one bomb caused the building to start shaking, and then another bomb ripped off the front of the building. At least two bombs.

Seismographic equipment in two locations in and near Oklahoma City recorded the explosions. Dr. Raymond Brown, a highly respected geophysicist from the Oklahoma Geophysical Society, has stated that the most logical explanation of this seismographic information is that there was more than one bomb. Other experts have agreed with him.

Yes. Absolutely. We include all that information in our report. The seismographic graphs indicated at least two events, two explosions.

After the bombing, while the rescue attempts were going on, the Oklahoma TV News stations were reporting that the police and ATF officials were saying that there were more undetonated bombs found in the building. The TV newsmen kept reporting this for hours. Police logs confirmed undetonated bombs were found, and so did FEMA reports. Even Oklahoma Governor Frank Keating, on the morning of the bombing, said, "The report I have is that one device was deactivated, and apparently, there's another device . . ." But since then the government has claimed that all these reports and sightings of other bombs were wrong. That there was only the one McVeigh truck bomb. Does that make sense? Do you believe that?

Yes, the information is just very strong, and to me it's too strong to be able to try to discount it. We have affidavits in our report from paramedics and other rescuers at the scene who say they heard law enforcement people stating there were other bombs found in the building. And then you had bomb experts who had time to drive to a TV station, and sit there, and talk about the undetonated bombs they had, bombs that were found in the building. You know, it's just too much competent information that can't be reasoned away as mistakes.

In that same TV interview, Governor Keating, who is an ex-FBI agent, said, ". . . obviously, whatever did the damage to the Murrah Building was a tremendous, very sophisticated explosive device." But explosives experts have made it clear that an ANFO bomb is an extremely rudimentary bomb. If someone blew up the building by placing charges on different columns inside the buildings, then that would take a sophisticated knowledge of explosives, right?
Yes. Authorities have said that an ANFO bomb is a very simple, crude bomb.

What might be the most intriguing information you put out in your Final Report is that the most preeminent experts on explosives—people like Sam Cohen and General Partin—have said an ANFO truck bomb could not have possibly done the damage to the Murrah Building. You've said that the Oklahoma Bombing Investigation Committee tried very hard to find an expert or authority who would say that an ANFO bomb could have done the damage, but you weren't able to, right?
That's true. Yes. We couldn't find anybody who would put their name, put their opinion in writing, that an ANFO truck bomb could have done this. If somebody wants to claim that it could have been done, then they need to put in writing, show how it could work, and give examples of that. And nobody I know of has been able to do that. Not even the witnesses the government used in the trial could do it. They didn't do it.

These experts have even entertained the notion that a larger bomb could have been in the truck, but they discount that. General Partin said, "I don't care what kind of bomb, or what size bomb you had in the truck. You wouldn't have gotten the type of damage you had there."

Yes.

Another thing explosives experts say is that if a truck bomb did this vast damage to the Murrah Building, then a gigantic, enormous crater would have been left where the truck was parked. But there was no enormous crater left there.

Right. As a matter of fact the FBI—this is a real important point—the FBI intentionally inflated the size of the crater to about twice the size of what it actually was.

The government kept changing its story regarding the dimensions of the crater?

Yes. They started off saying it was thirty-two feet and then about a month later when FEMA put together this crew, American Society of Civil Engineers—they brought this crew to Oklahoma City, but the FBI wouldn't let them come to the site. They came to do this official report for FEMA and they wouldn't let them come too near the site, wouldn't let them look at the crater, or measure it. And then the FBI fed them the information, and the information they fed them at that time was—they said the crater was between twenty-eight and thirty-two feet. Those were the figures they used at that time. But the real size of it was between sixteen and eighteen feet, maximum, depending at what angle you're measuring it from.

Weren't photographs taken the morning of the bombing, and the photos showed that there wasn't a large crater in front of the building?

Yes. We really researched that for a long time. We've looked at this very extensively and there was a crater, but it just was not anywhere near the size that the FBI claimed it was. And the pictures prove that beyond any doubt.

If it's so obvious that the truck bomb couldn't have done the damage in Oklahoma City, then why didn't Timothy McVeigh's lawyer bring this up? Or did he?

Well, that's a good question. You know, there's been a lot of speculation about that. Stephen Jones has done so much to try to bring out the truth about this case, so I think it's real hard for anybody to say that he had complicity in some way in trying to cover it up. . . . One of the reasons might be that—simply—that they just missed this one. The lawyers just blew it.

It seems that if they brought in General Partin—he makes you see that there's no way the truck bomb could have done it—if McVeigh's lawyer had brought Partin in to testify, then it seems he could have gotten his client off.

They actually had him on the witness list. Why they didn't bring him in to actually use him is the question. But they actually had him on the witness list.

What do you make of Timothy McVeigh's confession? He supposedly said he bombed the building and he acted alone.

You're talking about that book that came out right before McVeigh was executed, written by those two reporters from New York. . . . Well, first of all, it's questionable what he really did say in those alleged interviews. One of those writers called General Partin and told him that he didn't participate in the interviews. Publicly, they've said that they both did the interviews . . . we can know some facts about the case, many facts about the case, without what McVeigh had to say. We know some things that he allegedly said in that book are not true. For instance, he said he was alone on the morning of the bombing, but we know that's false, because many people have testified to seeing McVeigh with a John Doe on the morning of the bombing.

And there are other things there that we absolutely know are not true. So therefore that would bring in some other questions about the other things he said. The supposed confession, and everything else.

Do you think McVeigh was maybe taking blame for something he didn't do, or didn't do alone? Or maybe he never really confessed? Or maybe it was coerced, or something?

Yeah, that's kind of where I would go. Maybe he was protecting some of the other participants, or maybe family members. Maybe he felt if he told who the other bombing participants were then he knew his family would be at threat from those other perpetrators.

You feel strongly that early on the government and FBI decided that McVeigh and Nichols acted alone, and after that the FBI refused to investigate any evidence that might suggest that there were more accomplices. But, in fact, many, many people saw McVeigh with many different John Does. There's a mountain of evidence that clearly suggests that McVeigh certainly could have had more accomplices, right?

There's no question about it. Absolutely. Possibly Middle Eastern terrorists. And/or the anti-government militia groups. It's all in our report.

Due to your efforts, a grand jury was impaneled in June 1997 to investigate the bombing. But you feel that the grand jury ended up being rigged. You feel the grand jury was manipulated by the courts in Oklahoma so that the jurors would hear evidence that would implicate only McVeigh and Nichols.

There was a lot of information they refused to call. The prosecutors worked the grand jury to get the result they wanted. Before the grand jury was impaneled, the judge, Judge Burkett, said that he had no intention of allowing the grand jury to reach any conclusions that would conflict with those reached by the federal government—that McVeigh and Nichols acted alone. We submitted all this pertinent information to them, but it was ignored. We gave a list of 149 witnesses who had pertinent information, but a hundred of them weren't called. From its beginning, the grand jury was manipulated by the prosecutors, the District Attorney, the Attorney General, and even the presiding judge. Justice was not served.

Your **Final Report** *is very critical of the FBI. According to your report, the FBI—among other things—intimidated and harassed witnesses, falsified reports, lied to the court, and failed to investigate dozens of solid leads. Of course, right before McVeigh was scheduled to be executed, it was revealed that the FBI had withheld from the defense team three thousand pages of documents related to the bombing. You make no bones about it that in your opinion the FBI is the culprit in a massive cover-up.* Absolutely. In our *Final Report* we list forty-two instances of government improprieties. Forty-two examples of when we feel the government engaged in misconduct. And something like twenty of those instances are related to FBI misconduct.

There were a couple of surveillance cameras right outside the Murrah Building that would have caught everything on tape that morning—they would have shown who pulled the Ryder truck up to the building, and how the building came down. The FBI confiscated the film from those cameras and they're not releasing it. If the FBI would just release those tapes, then we could see exactly what happened, couldn't we? The film would show who drove the Ryder truck up to the building.
Yes, they could prove real easily with those tapes, and with some others across the street that they also will not release, whether or not people like me are a bunch of conspiracy theorists or not, you know. They could prove finally whether or not McVeigh really was alone, and whether there really was another car, or other vehicles across the street, that were working in conjunction with his activities.

They won't release those?

They will not release them. Recently, we had a Freedom of Information Act trial here in an attempt to get the government to release the tapes. They stonewalled it. They won't release them.

How do most of the people down in Oklahoma City feel? Do they feel McVeigh acted alone? Or do they feel the whole story hasn't been told?

No, most people know that McVeigh did not act alone. They know the whole story's not been told. There's been some scientific surveys that show that at about sixty-five percent. That was several years ago. I'm sure that it's higher now, after all the stuff that's happened in the last year, or so. But, also, there's been a number of polls that radio stations have done, unscientific though they are, that asked even more extensive questions, and they came out real lopsided, people saying McVeigh didn't do it alone.

Do you have any personal opinions about who was behind the bombing?

Well, in my mind I feel it was cooked up, it was thought up and financed by Iraq and other Middle Eastern terrorists. Strong evidence indicates that. But one of the big questions is how did they get McVeigh and Nichols, how is it that a couple of Americans, or more than one, would join in in an effort with some Middle Eastern terrorists to do something like this. That's the big question, because we've never had that happen before.

So you don't believe that this was the government. Because some people have claimed—falsely—that the Oklahoma Bombing Investigation Committee is saying that some people in the government had something to do with it.

Well, after I've seen the way the government's operated, and everything I've learned in this case, I wouldn't exclude other possible scenarios offhand. I *would not* exclude them offhand. And the reason I say that is because

I've seen people do that in this case. They couldn't somehow conceptualize multiple bombs so they wanted to just exclude all the information about multiple explosions. Some people in the early days, they just couldn't understand how Middle Eastern terrorists could be a part of this, and work with white Americans to do something like this. They excluded all the information about Middle Eastern terrorism.

And you've learned that you shouldn't exclude other possible scenarios?
Right, and that's where I'm coming from with this . . . could there be somebody in the government that . . . for example, I'll tell you this . . . I've been told by a source that the genesis of the Oklahoma City bombing began right after Waco, and that some ATF officials and that other government officials—these were the words that were used by the source—began to put together a publicity sting operation to make the ATF look good, because the ATF looked so bad because of Waco. So they started planning a publicity sting operation. And this source told me that "after that I don't know what happened, how it further developed, but I know it started off as a publicity sting operation."

Yes, some people in Oklahoma believe that the bombing was all about a failed sting operation. That ATF and other government agents knew McVeigh and accomplices were planning to bomb a building. And the government agents were following McVeigh, or undercover agents were working with him, and the plan was to catch him at the last moment, and arrest as many co-conspirators as possible. And your source is saying that this was also a publicity thing for the ATF. . . . But then what happened? The sting operation went a little too far and 168 people were killed?
Well, this person made it very clear that he had that information that that's the way it began. This would be in 1993, after Waco. Late '93, early '94. What he was trying to say to me was that, "what else happened, how this

developed further, I don't know. But I know there were officials that were starting to come up with ideas about how could we do a publicity sting operation."

You said that you feel that the bombing started in Iraq with Middle Eastern terrorists. A lot of information about that has come out recently. But if it began in the ATF as a publicity sting operation then it couldn't have started in Iraq. Or could it have? Could those two plans have become intertwined?

Either theory, or set of facts/information, would not cancel out the other. Project Bojinka—the Middle Eastern terrorists' code name for the bombing plot—was in play as early as 1993—or earlier—the same year as Waco. If my source is correct and that government officials planned a publicity sting operation immediately after Waco then the time frame would work. . . . What we don't know is what *all* did the plan include? Who *all* had knowledge about it? Did the plan include getting or using someone like McVeigh or Nichols—knowingly or unknowingly? Did McVeigh discover he was under surveillance and decide to turn the tables on the government by eluding or eliminating the Fed's tracking of him? By changing the time he was going to show up at the building? There are at least several realistic possibilities.

Some conspiracy theorists claim there is government complicity here. Some people believe that elements in the US government want our civil rights destroyed and want America to become a part of a New World Order. An undemocratic, globalized world. The conspiracy theorists believe that government agents planted bombs, or let bombs be planted, in the Murrah Building as a way to justify anti-terrorism legislation that would destroy our civil rights, and bring America closer to the condition of a police state. In April 1996, as a result of the bombing, President Clinton signed the Anti-Terrorism Act. A month prior to that

FBI Director Louis Freeh had informed the Congress of his plans for expanded wiretapping. These actions are a real threat to our civil liberties. Do you believe these conspiracy theorists are crazy and irrational? Or could they be onto something?

This is the way I would respond to that, and how I've always tried to respond to that. In the way I just did—that there's indications that this may have been a failed sting operation. And I would further say that whatever the case may be, it has produced a situation where public officials have taken away, or they're trying to take away, our civil liberties. And that's wrong. I'm not going to go as far to say I believe that there's government officials that wanted to do this because I don't know that as a fact. But I know what the results are, and the results are we're losing our civil liberties unnecessarily. Unjustifiably. I don't think it's necessary. It's not necessary at all.

Some people believe that if the bombs were inside the building then that indicates government complicity. Even General Partin said, "You have to think about who had access. . . . You don't just walk through security with explosives like this." But unless we have the absolute proof then we certainly can't assume that agents of the government planted the bombs, or let the bombs be planted. But the problem is—why isn't the government acknowledging that an ANFO bomb couldn't have done this? And why isn't the government acknowledging that McVeigh was seen with a lot of John Does? And that all the people in the building felt two explosions, not one? There seems to be a lot of dishonesty here.

My theory is that there were other government informants or undercover agents that were involved with this and that's the reason the FBI won't go down this path to identify the other "John Does" because it will identify one or more government agents or informants. We've already had some. For example, the guy who stayed in the Dreamland Motel with McVeigh. This is another one of the instances in which the FBI has tried to claim that a person who was there with McVeigh wasn't there with McVeigh. Witnesses tell that he was there. This is the guy, the Chinese food delivery guy, he clearly tells the story that he delivered food to a hotel room that McVeigh was registered under, but the guy there was not McVeigh. And the FBI's tried to—in essence—tried to pressure him to change his story. But he's adamant. He says, "No. There was somebody else there in the room. I saw him." And, so why would the FBI not—you see, they didn't run the fingerprints. The FBI lifted fingerprints from that room. But they didn't run them. Why would you not do that?

Well, it could be your theory. That the government doesn't want to find these John Does because that investigation might lead back to the government—the John Does might end up being government informants or undercover agents. And if that's true, does it legitimize posing the question: Did some element in the government do it?
I try to maintain credibility. I try not to go and take a giant leap of faith and say the government did it. Because I don't have the facts to back that up. But I do have the facts to back up that the government refuses to find out who did it.

Yes, because your Final Report points out that the FBI has more than a thousand fingerprints and about a hundred palm prints and these all came from places where McVeigh was seen with other people.
That's right. The government does not . . . whether it's city, state, or national law enforcement, where there's a capital murder case like this one—and this is the biggest case the FBI ever had—law enforcement people don't sit around and say, "Well, I wonder if we oughta run the fingerprints." They always run the fingerprints. Especially when it's the biggest case the FBI ever had. So when you don't run the fingerprints, there's a reason for it and it's not because it's too expensive, because it wasn't too expensive to run those fingerprints. They already spent eighty plus million dollars.

And they estimated it might cost four hundred thousand dollars to run all those fingerprints through the thirty-five or forty million fingerprint data base it has. . . . They didn't want to.

Shortly before the bombing, former CIA Director William Colby said in an interview that he felt the amounts of people joining the militias were dangerous. Some people would say that the government used this incident to frame somebody connected to the militias, to make the militias look bad, so that legislation would be passed that allowed the FBI to more easily stop the militia movement. . . . Whether or not conspiracy theorists are irrational, or rational, remains to be seen. But your conviction that the whole story of the Oklahoma City bombing hasn't been revealed isn't based on theory, right? It's based on this mountain of evidence that you've documented that clearly shows that there are still many unanswered questions.

We're raising the questions. We've detailed them effectively. There's information in our report that has never been revealed to the public before. We feel mass murderers are still at large. We want the truth to come out. As I understand it, Dan Burton, the chairman of the House Government Reform Committee, is planning to reinvestigate the bombing. That's because there's new, strong evidence of Middle Eastern and Iraqi involvement. This evidence apparently also has relevance to the September 11 attacks. . . . We have never said the government bombed its own building. I don't think we have proof of government complicity. All we have is very clear proof of government complicity in the cover-up, and wanting to cover this thing up and do whatever it takes to cover it up. That says something right there. That says a lot. But if we could ever prove that the government was involved in it that would be . . . something big. But I haven't seen that, yet.

The Oklahoma Bombing Investigation Committee questions the extent to which the power of government law enforcement agencies has been allowed to expand in recent years. You cite a series of articles from the **Pittsburgh Post-Gazette** *written by reporter Bill Moushey that reveals dozens of cases in which the government "lied, hid evidence, distorted facts, engaged in Cover-Ups, paid for perjury, and set up innocent people in a relentless effort to win indictments." You make seventeen recommendations that the Congress could implement to help curb this tide of government abuse and corruption. Ultimately, the OBIC feels it's critical that a panel be established to scrutinize FBI operations and make recommendations that can be implemented immediately. But, also, you feel the panel should be made up of mostly people outside the government, because it's often useless to have the government investigating itself.*

Yes. Absolutely. Congress supposedly has the oversight responsibility for the FBI, but the Congress has failed to censure this out-of-control agency. The FBI answers to no one. A panel to investigate the FBI should be made up of people from the private sector—investigative journalists, political watch organizations, academia, the legal field. If it's a situation where the government is investigating itself, the FBI is investigating itself, then it just becomes another joke.

CHAPTER 10

Are Big Business and Political Interests Engaged in a Conspiracy to Control the Mainstream Media?

An interview with MIT Professor Noam Chomsky

T he nexus between powerful journalists and people in government and corporate power has become far too close," former CBS News anchorman Dan Rather has said. "Some people say that these powerful people use journalists, and they do. And they will use them to the fullest extent possible. What we need in journalism is a spine transplant. The media has definitely become a political and corporate lapdog. I submit to you, the American press's role is to be a watchdog."

The famous newsman's statement would have been an alarm to the Founding Fathers of America who considered a free, diligent press to be perhaps the most important component for a democratic nation. Newspapers and journalists, the Fourth Estate, were to serve as a strong watchdog over those in power, and were to provide citizens with the facts they needed to run a healthy democracy. In 1787, Thomas Jefferson said: "Were it left for me to decide whether we should have a government without newspapers or newspapers without a government, I should not hesitate a moment to prefer the latter."

Just a few years later, Jefferson had already become disenchanted with the way that the businessmen who owned the newspapers were slanting and distorting the news to favor their political and economic viewpoints. In 1799, Jefferson said: "The man who never looks into a newspaper is better informed than he who reads them, inasmuch as he who knows nothing is nearer to the truth than he whose mind is filled with falsehoods and errors." And in 1807: "Nothing can now be believed which is seen in a newspaper."

Such are the very concerns of not only the former anchorman of the CBS News but of the Media Reform Movement, the many people who believe that the corporations that own the media in America are slanting and biasing the news for political and economic interests, and that the news is filled with distortions, Cover-Ups, prejudices, and lies.

What is the principal concern of the Media Reform Movement is that more and more of our media outlets are being controlled by fewer and fewer corporations. Presently, six major media conglomerates own about 95 percent of our television stations, radio stations, newspapers, and magazines. Theoretically, the six CEOs of those companies could be sitting in a room, and those would be the six men who are determining what the news is, and what the public is going to see, hear, and believe. These media conglomerates got their licenses from the government. The media companies don't want to be at odds with the government lest their licenses be taken away by the politicians that gave them to them. The tendency, therefore, of the media conglomerates is to repeat the government claims, to not question or criticize too harshly what the government says, whether what the government says is the truth, or a cover-up or propaganda. These media giants are in it for the buck. They cost millions to acquire, and millions to run. They want sensationalistic, flashy, fast-moving news stories to attract viewers, readers, and advertising dollars. The media conglomerates are dependent on public relations officials throughout all the departments of the government for their news and information. If a media outlet questions or challenges anything a government source claims, then that media outlet will be cut off from that source, and won't have all the news and information that their competitors have. The prevalent tendency of the media giants, therefore, again, is to ape and mimic whatever the government press agent sources say, whether what they're saying is accurate or not.

The corporations that own the media in America are megacorporations and own companies in other fields and industries. The media conglomerates might, therefore, have a conflict of interest in doing stories and reports related to these other fields and industries. GE, for instance, the largest media company in America, might have had a conflict of interest in finding out if there were really weapons of mass destruction in Iraq, because GE owns a weapons manufacturer and stood to make millions off a war in Iraq. Many board of directors members of the media conglomerates are also board members of some of America's largest, most powerful corporations. There is a network of corporate people running the media, so little criticism of or anything that might counter the interests of the large corporations is going to be expressed through the media. The media is Big Business and exists to promote and protect the interests of Big Business, whether those interests are good for the public or not.

Another concern of the Media Reform Movement is how much influence over the media the CIA might have. In 1975, the Senate, the Church Committee, investigated the intelligence community and the CIA's connections to the media. In 1977, famed Watergate journalist Carl Bernstein did an extensive investigation of the Church Committee for *Rolling Stone* magazine. Bernstein's article revealed that the CIA owned or financed dozens of newspapers and news organizations and had close relations with some of the most powerful people in the media and with more than four hundred journalists. One insider close to the investigation remarked, "If this stuff gets out, some of the biggest names in journalism would be smeared." How much influence does the CIA have over the media? The Media Reform Movement is also suspicious of the power and influence of the Council on Foreign Relations. The CFR is a New York think tank that was created in 1921 by representatives of J. P. Morgan and the Rockefellers. Morgan and

Rockefeller were Wall Street. Their banks and corporations were and are still today the banking, corporate power that runs America. Since 1921 the most important people in the media have come from the CFR. Even today, the heads of all of America's most important media outlets are members of the CFR. How much influence does the Council on Foreign Relations have in the media? Or is the Council on Foreign Relations running the media?

One of our harshest critics of the mainstream media is the distinguished MIT professor Noam Chomsky. In his book *Manufacturing Consent*, the professor theorizes that there are certain characteristics of the media—what Chomsky refers to as "propaganda filters"—that prevent most all challenging of the government's position or of corporate power. In Chomsky's model, there are five "propaganda filters." First, the major media is owned by megacorporations and, so, the news content of the media has to align with the political persuasions of these corporations; the corporate media has interlocking relationships with the corporations that lobby and determine government policy. Second, the media is financially dependent upon advertisers and the news has to agree with the interests and politics of these advertisers, which is, again, corporate America. Third, the corporations that own the media fund and subsidize think tanks and these think tanks— along with the government press sources—become the "established, connected" sources of opinions throughout the media. Fourth, if anything contrary to the corporate-government position slips through a media outlet, that outlet will be inundated with flak—a barrage of editorials and interviews will attack that outlet's position; it can be extremely costly, inconvenient, and controversial for a media outlet to defend itself against a corporate-funded flak attack. Fifth, in the past, the media always had to agree with the government's anti-communist viewpoints and actions; today, the media always will agree with the government's "war on terror" viewpoints and actions. In Professor Chomsky's view, the propaganda filters are quite efficient at keeping most anything out of the media that would question the government's claims or challenge the corporate interests. So, according to

Chomsky, instead of accomplishing the Founding Fathers' vision of being the defender of democracy and the watchdog of America, the media accomplishes "spectacular achievements of propaganda."

Although he is a professor of linguistics, and considered one of the fathers of modern linguistics, Noam Chomsky is better known for his views and bestselling books on politics. Professor Chomsky is one of the most widely cited scholars of recent history, and is considered one of the great intellectuals of the twentieth and now twenty-first centuries. These are his thoughts on the media landscape today.

Cirignano: Do the same corporate interests that own the media also lobby and control the politicians and government?

Chomsky: Well, they're certainly related. My co-author of *Manufacturing Consent*, Edward Herman, is a specialist on corporations. He wrote one of the standard books on corporate power, corporate control. He put in the book a study of the interlocking of the media—how the media corporations are a part of bigger corporations, megacorporations. They interlock. It's very much an interlocking system of a small number of major megacorporations.

Which are connected to the government.

The relationship between the corporate system and the government is extremely intimate in all sorts of ways. First of all, they pretty much staff the executive. Of course, there's lobbying. The campaign funding alone is a very good predictor of policy. Thomas Ferguson, a very good political scientist, studied this for years. Those who provide the campaign funds basically set the conditions within which policy is made. We've seen it very dramatically in the last couple of years.

You monitored the media—the **New York Times, Los Angeles Times, Washington Post, Time,** *and* **Newsweek**—*closely, and it's alarming and* *revealing how the media always just seems to repeat whatever the government wants. Both Democrats and Republicans are a part of this. For instance, when George Bush Sr. was preparing to attack Iraq in 1992, Bush and the government and the media were claiming Iraq and Saddam Hussein had a tremendous, powerful army that could menace and conquer the world. But, in fact, Iraq's military was a third-world, peasant army. And the first Iraq war ended up being like a heavyweight beating up a flyweight.*

That's true. It is now being conceded that there was a ton of disinformation about the fortifications, the chemical weapons, etc. But has anyone pointed that out? They had to exaggerate Saddam's power to justify the invasion. But then how long did it take us to defeat Iraq? Less than twenty-four hours? There are many other examples of this. For instance, when Bush and the media were saying that Manuel Noriega was a creature larger than life who was going to destroy us. Noriega was really a minor thug. He wasn't a threat to America. But we had to crush Noriega, and then US military officers took control of Panama's political system, reinstated the white oligarchy.

Whenever the US government claims we have to attack a country or get rid of some leader, the government always says it is for the purpose of preventing atrocities and defending democracy and human rights. This may seem like an obvious question, but in many cases that might not be true, right? That's propaganda. And the real reason we're attacking these countries is so the government and the corporations that are controlling the government—what you call the "state-corporate nexus"—can get more economic and political leverage in those areas.

You always have to consider what business interests are influencing the government's actions.

If it really was a matter of America preventing atrocities and defending human rights, then there would be plenty of other places in the world that America would attack. The government and the media only mention the atrocities and human rights being violated in the areas that the state-corporate nexus wants to control.

We looked at that closely. The media will always play up and shine a light on the atrocities being committed in countries that are America's foes, or countries that are out of favor with the current administration. But the torture, the atrocities, being committed in countries that are America's allies won't be reported. At times, these atrocities are worse, more brutal. The media fails to mention that. So we have "worthy" victims and "unworthy" victims. "Accepted" atrocities and "unaccepted" atrocities.

Saddam Hussein wasn't a good guy. He was definitely a bad guy. But the atrocities he committed weren't as bad as some other leaders and countries. The brutalities that Israel has committed in Lebanon are just as bad or worse than Saddam Hussein's. In the 1980s, the government of South Africa killed off about a million and a half people. The Indonesian invasion of East Timor back then was far worse than anything Hussein ever did. But if a nation is an ally of the state-corporate nexus then we don't hear anybody in the government or media complaining about the far worse atrocities and brutalities being committed there.

In the past what has happened is that when an enemy state commits a genocide, the media will print that that nation engaged in a "homicidal genocide." But when an ally of the United States does the same exact thing, the media will say that the nation had to necessarily "repress" the populace. . . . Unfortunately, some of the most brutal regimes are in countries being supported and manipulated by the CIA and US military. And White House.

Perhaps the most notorious and most recent example of the government propagandizing to get us into a war was when Bush Jr. said we had to attack Iraq because Iraq had weapons of mass destruction. Did it surprise you when there were no weapons of mass destruction? Or did you figure that was propaganda all along?

I don't know that Bush and company consciously lied. They may have well talked themselves into believing what they wanted to believe. . . . Take the torture memos. The demand for more and more torture was coming from the executive, from Rumsfeld and Cheney. They apparently wanted to get evidence that there was a connection between Saddam Hussein and Al-Qaeda. Chances were the connection would be pretty slight. But they wanted that evidence. Maybe they convinced themselves that it was true. So they called for more and more harsher measures, meaning torture.

Even the New York Times admitted it dropped the ball on the weapons of mass destruction issue. After the invasion, when it was shown there were no WMD's, the Times wrote that it "failed to deconstruct the WMD issue" and that an "overwhelming majority of government officials were sure that the weapons were there" and so that's what the Times reported. . . . This seems to be the principal way that the media just ends up reporting what the government wants. Newspapers, TV stations, and news organizations get their information from press officials in the government and the news organizations just accept everything that government officials say as being the truth. The reporters and journalists don't do any investigating themselves.

There is a concept of objectivity in journalism. Objectivity in journalism is keeping to the bounds of the debate of what is going on in Washington. They keep to the spectrum of Democrats and Republicans, the major Democrats and Republicans. So they have to say what each of them says. Like, "Here's what the White House says, and here's what the Republicans say."

And the media doesn't go outside of that box.

But if you go outside that box then it's called subjective, or biased, or emotional. Take the invasion of Iraq. There is a dispute inside the beltway—one, "is it a noble cause and we should pursue it?" or, two, "is it what Obama called the strategic blunder and we shouldn't pursue it?" As long as you keep to that spectrum, you're objective. But suppose you say, "Look, its murderous aggression. It's a violation of the UN charter. It's the crime for which people were hanged at Nuremberg." Well, all that happens to be true, but if you say that you're not objective. So nobody has said it.

But what about with concrete, black and white things, and with things that are beyond the Democratic vs. Republican debate? Whether or not there were weapons of mass destruction was a concrete, black and white thing. There either were weapons of mass destruction or there weren't. The government said there were weapons of mass destruction, and instead of investigating that and finding that there weren't weapons of mass destruction, the media just repeated what the government said.

Well, yes, there could be more challenging of these things at times. The media is getting its information from official sources. It'd be naïve to think these official sources have always got it right.

Is it possible that the CIA controls or manipulates the media? In his book, Derailing Democracy, author Dave McGowan quotes former CIA Director William Colby saying: "The CIA owns everyone of any significance in the major media."

That sounds like a bit of an exaggeration. . . . The CIA can undoubtedly influence the media. They provide the information. If you want to be a successful journalist you want to have information from the inside, from anonymous sources. I think that journalists—if they want to be manipulated, they can be manipulated

Back in 1975, the Senate, the Church Committee, investigated the CIA's connections to the media. Famed Watergate journalist Carl Bernstein wrote an article about that for Rolling Stone magazine in 1977. Bernstein's

article revealed that the CIA owned or financed dozens of newspapers and news organizations, had close relations with some of the most powerful people in the media and with four hundred or more journalists. A media analyst who reviewed the hearings said that the Church Committee investigations showed that "the CIA can spread propaganda and disinformation just about anywhere and anytime it wants to."

The Church Committee was a break from the norm. It did some very significant investigations. . . . The CIA has influence to the extent that the media is eager for the experience. When a journalist goes to somebody in intelligence, or somebody in the executive, for that matter, and gets secret information from an anonymous source, they should understand that the person need not be telling them the truth. They're telling them what they want the public to believe and that's the way every anonymous source should be treated. So in that sense, yeah, sure, the CIA will choose information, or disinformation. And the media, eager for the experience, will pick it up and repeat it.

But it seems that the CIA might have arrangements with the media so they can regularly and routinely spread disinformation. Because during the investigation the Senate committee was asking William Colby to talk about the CIA's connections to reporters, and Colby said, "Let's not pick on some reporters, for God's sake. Let's go to the management. They were witting." And, William Bader, a former CIA officer, told the Committee, "There is quite an incredible spread of relationships (in the media). You don't need to manipulate Time magazine, for instance, because there are CIA people at the management level." While the investigation was going on, George Bush replaced William Colby as the Director of the CIA. The Church Committee wanted Bush to give the committee the names of the journalists connected to the CIA and what their functions were. Bush stonewalled the investigation. He said the CIA had a right to secrecy. Bush gave the committee some superficial descriptions of what some anonymous journalists did for the CIA, but the issue of how the CIA manipulates the media basically got swept under the carpet and forgotten about, right?

The Church Committee was a very significant investigation. It uncovered all these intrusive, unconstitutional things that the CIA and FBI were up to. If something like that happened with Bush, it wouldn't be hard to believe.

This corporate-government connection doesn't manipulate and fil-ter news stories just about foreign affairs, correct? Stories related to domestic matters that would make the government or corporations look bad are also filtered.

We feel the propaganda model applies to domestic as well as foreign policy issues.

Take NAFTA, for instance. NAFTA is good for the big corporations because it allows them to move their jobs overseas where they can pay their workers less. NAFTA has led to higher unemployment, and has been bad for the economy. But we don't hear anything about that in the media because the big corporations own and run the media.

NAFTA was designed by the US government in the interests of US corpo-rations. It is a Big Business thing. So we know who it's going to benefit.

Even Barack Obama, before he became president, was saying that NAFTA has been bad for the country. But then when he became president "they"—the state-corporate nexus—must have gotten to him, because Obama actually broadened and strengthened free trade agreements like NAFTA.

In many ways, Obama followed the same policies as his predecessor, George Bush. He treated Iran and the Israeli-Palestinian conflict the same, and he didn't leave Iraq or Afghanistan. No change. Also with the banking crisis—the Obama policy was basically the same as the Bush policy. Preserve the banking institutions, let them take risks, and have the public bail them out. The "We Can Change" slogan—or whatever it was—that slogan was developed by the public relations firms that were paid to get Obama elected.

So it seems the same state-corporate nexus that was controlling Bush was also controlling Obama. A main issue with the media conglomerates is—as you've pointed out—they have interlocking relationships with many of the other large corporations. So one of the main purposes of the media has become to protect the interests of the corporate world. It's natural to expect that people who basically own the media will want the media to protect their interests. What else could be true?

As your book points out, this relates to the chemical industry.
Historically, the chemical industry lobbies and basically controls the Environmental Protection Agency, so that there is no real testing of the potentially dangerous chemicals that are put into innumerable products. But because of the chemical industry's power and the mainstream media's connection and receptivity to the demands of the business-corporate community, the media doesn't challenge any of this. The chemical industry makes millions poisoning us and then—because it controls the EPA—it polices itself. The media stand by mutely.

What the media reform movement probably sees as the principal problem with the media is that fewer and fewer media conglomerates—right now it's down to about six media conglomerates—control about 95 percent of the TV, newspaper and magazine, and radio outlets. So, theoretically, six men—the six CEOs of those media conglomerates—could be sitting in a room and those would be the six men who are determining what the news is and what the public is going to see and hear and believe. It's not only theoretically possible, but I'd be surprised if it didn't happen. They don't sit around in a room. You know, they meet somewhere for dinner. They're friends. They go to conferences together, they discuss and talk, and they probably come up with plans. How could it be otherwise?

And if there wasn't such media consolidation, if six corporations didn't own 95 percent of the media outlets, then the possibility of that happening wouldn't even exist.
Of course not.

These media conglomerates are Big Business. They cost a lot of money to acquire and a lot of money to run. The only real purpose of these conglomerates is to make money. There's no conscience today in journalism that "we are here to watch out for the people's welfare" or "we are here to weed out government and corporate corruption." The true and only purpose of these conglomerates is to get ratings so they can attract advertising dollars and stay in business and make money.
That's the bottom line, yes. The first thing they're thinking about is the quarterly statement. The stockholders. Media is a business. A business has to make money, otherwise it's out. Millions of dollars worth of investment is on the line. And media can be quite profitable. You can make millions being in the business of journalism these days.

The way these conglomerates get ratings is through entertainment and sensationalism. The media conglomerates are all about entertainment. The media conglomerates want ratings, and advertising dollars and the way to get that is through short sensationalistic stories, and images on or about, for instance, celebrities, gossip, and sex and violence.
Just think of all the mindless schlock that comes through the TV. All of that diverts attention from important things we should be talking about. Mindless sitcoms. Endless stories about Laci Peterson's death, or O. J. Simpson, or Tiger Woods's girlfriends. These stories are unimportant and superficial, but they're sensational, and, so, they attract viewers, and

ratings, and, so, more advertising dollars. Investigative reports, though, will cost the stations more money. If you send out a team of investigative reporters to do a report on something of substance, something important, that will cost a lot of money. So the media will shy away from that.

Today's media is really all about the ads and commercials, correct? One top TV executive once said that TV is so dependent on advertising dollars that the advertisers basically control the programming content of television.

Advertisers' control over the media began back in the 1800s. When newspapers began becoming dependent on ads revenue, then the purpose of the newspaper was no longer to serve the needs of the common man, the middle class. Working class and radical, progressive newspapers were out. The purpose of the newspaper became to attract people with money who could afford to buy the products in the ads. That's what the media is today. The media is owned by rich men and directed to people with money who can buy cars, and vacations, and jewelry, and everything else. Stations and newspapers with the most advertising dollars will survive and outlets with not enough advertisers will go out of business. So with this severe dependence on advertising—with this hypercommercialism—there will be less and less time for public affairs content. Ad executives don't want serious pieces that contemplate serious social and political complexities. They don't want any educational documentaries, because people will switch the channels. The ad people want light and fluffy entertainment that will keep the public in the mood to go shopping and buy products.

These advertisers are, again, the big corporations. So, really, there can be no shows or documentaries or news reports that are anti-business, or make the corporate world look bad, because then those advertising dollars would be withdrawn.

Well, just think, for years and years the media never reported on the dangers of smoking. That's because the tobacco companies were one of the biggest advertisers on television and in newspapers. We've never seen an expose on how much these big SUVs contribute to air pollution. Automobile companies provide the media with millions of dollars of advertising. Similarly—this doesn't relate to advertising but to corporate and banking influence over the media—we're probably not going to see a major report on how to cut down on the corruption and crimes of Wall Street. Media executives and media board members are also involved with banking. These big media conglomerates need loans and financing from the big Wall Street banks. So, there's not going to be—in general, you can't predict it absolutely—but, in general, there's not going to be too much reporting on how we might prevent the corruption of Wall Street from hurting America. Wall Street is going to do what it wants.

Could the issue of corporate media have any relevance to possible conspiracies? Let's speculate here about some conspiracy theories. Let's even go back to the Kennedy assassination. Say the Pentagon, the CIA, and some big defense contractors wanted a war in Vietnam, but then found out that JFK was planning to pull out of Vietnam. Say some people in this military-industrial complex then conspired and assassinated JFK. If, as former CIA Director William Colby said, the CIA manipulates the media, could the CIA have then contacted their media connections and told them, "The CIA has determined that Oswald acted alone. For the good of the country, don't promote any conspiracy theories." Or if the FBI said Oswald acted alone, would the media have just repeated that? Or if big defense contractors were a part of Kennedy's assassination, could these corporate heads then have used their connections to the corporations that own the media to block any real investigation into the Kennedy assassination? Any real investigation into who really killed JFK?

To me, the only aspect of the Kennedy assassination of any importance is whether it was a high level conspiracy that had policy implications. I've gone through the documentation, and my conclusion is that it was not a high level conspiracy with policy implications. That leaves open the question of who killed him. But if it wasn't a high level political assassination then that question doesn't seem any more significant than who carried out the last murder in downtown Boston. It could have been the husband of one of Kennedy's liaisons.

But it seems it was the government's contention that Oswald acted alone and the mainstream media just went along with that. The media never even entertained the possibility that there might have been more to the assassination.

There's been a lot of writing about the assassination.

Not from the **New York Times.** *Or CBS. No mainstream media outlet ever did a serious expose on the evidence that points to a conspiracy. . . . Any journalist with half a brain could have gone down to Dallas, Texas, the day after Kennedy was assassinated and could have interviewed the many people who said they were sure they heard and saw shots coming from the grassy knoll. They could have interviewed all the nurses and doctors in the civilian hospital who were certain that Kennedy was shot from the front, and then there could have been a real investigation into JFK's murder. But that never happened. Why didn't that happen?*

As I said, I don't think the major issue is "who killed Kennedy?" The major question is "was it a high level conspiracy with policy implications?" And, to me, it was not. So then the question of "who did it?" isn't significant.

Well, there's evidence that it was a high level government conspiracy, and that it very well could have had policy implications. Many people are convinced Kennedy was going to pull out of Vietnam. Kennedy was preaching peace and peace isn't good for the profits of the state-corporate nexus.

What he was going to do in Vietnam is the issue and the question. My research led me to the conclusion that Kennedy wasn't going to pull out of Vietnam. He was at the hawkish end of his administration. Kennedy's position was "yeah, we should get out if we can, but only after victory."

Many researchers and historians would strongly disagree with that and say he was going to pull out of Vietnam.
I don't see that.

Could the corporate media have any connection to any possible medical Cover-Ups or conspiracies? Some people believe that effective treatments for cancer are being ignored or suppressed. Say a doctor came up with a treatment—many people claim some doctors already have—that is better than chemotherapy and is helping and even curing some people of cancer. Would the mainstream media publicize that or do an investigation or story about that? Or because the pharmaceutical companies that make billions manufacturing chemotherapy are a part of the corporate network that runs the media and provides the media with millions of dollars for advertising, would any stories about effective alternative or potentially effective alternative treatments for cancer be kept out of the media?
Well, we have plenty of evidence where the media wouldn't go against the interests of big corporations. Say, for example—for decades the producers of lead and tobacco knew that lead and tobacco were murderous and they ran huge campaigns to keep it from reaching the public, and, of course, there was media complicity in that. Actually, the *Nation* had a long study on lead. The tobacco story has been carefully investigated. And that continues. These were major scandals. And, in fact, they're still continuing in many ways. So, sure that happens. But you can find cases where there were exposés. I don't think you can predict mechanically what the media are going to do. There are cases when serious investigative reporters have

exposed things. I mean, there have been major exposés of corporate crimes in the *Wall Street Journal*.

It's probably not the norm, though. A lot of major exposés of corporate crimes are probably not going to get past the propaganda filters that you wrote about.
Yes, but these are not mechanical. These are high probability effects. You know, it's a complex system. It's not going to be a hundred percent. It's not Pravda.

Did George Bush or the powers behind George Bush steal the 2000 and 2004 presidential elections? And did the mainstream media ever do a proper investigation into the possibility that these elections were stolen?
I think there were reports of that, yes. Stolen is a funny word. The Supreme Court made a decision which gave them the election and there's been plenty of criticism of that decision. Exactly who was behind the decision, well, that would be hard to figure out.

But there doesn't seem like there was enough reporting of the shenanigans that went on in Florida and Ohio.
That's true. There was some, but not a lot.

A lot of election reform people feel the media is negligent because it hasn't done a major exposé of how easy it is to corrupt the computerized voting systems. . . . Why wasn't there more reporting of what went on in Florida and Ohio? Do you think there should have been more?
Probably. But why stop with that? How about the shenanigans that got Kennedy elected in 1960? This is unfortunately the way American politics is.

Some reporters claim there's clear evidence that Jeb Bush suppressed the Democratic vote in Florida in 2000 and if he hadn't done that then

Al Gore would have easily won the electoral votes of Florida and the presidency. And they feel the reason that the media didn't report that is because the media conglomerates were dependent on the Bush administration for convenient, profitable media licenses.

There could be something to that. Maybe.

One of the main stories that Project Censored—a well-known media watchdog group—does is how much influence members of the Trilateral Commission have in the government. The Trilateral Commission is a think tank that David Rockefeller began in 1973. Members of the Trilateral Commission are ensconced in the most important, influential positions in the White House and government. The suspicion, of course, is that these people are out to do what's good for the corporate banking power—Wall Street—instead of what's good for the public—Main Street. Is the influence that the Trilateral Commission has over the government not being reported to the public by the press?

It certainly isn't a secret. Take, say, the Carter administration. It was entirely staffed from the Trilateral Commission. It was the staff. It's not a matter of influence. That's where they came from.

And also Obama. Obama's administration was dominated by Trilateral Commission people.

Yes. But these things are not surprising. The executive branch of every administration is largely staffed by representatives of Big Business. That's who the secretary of state is, the secretary of treasury, and so forth.

But why isn't the media up in arms about that?

They're not up in arms about it because they take for granted that that's the way it ought to be.

But shouldn't there be people in media saying that maybe that's not so good, and that representatives of Big Business shouldn't have such a hold over the government?

There should be people who say we should have a democracy.

That's not coming from the media, is it?

It's not coming from the media, but it's not coming from the academic scholarship. It's not a part of the intellectual culture. The intellectual culture basically accepts this framework. George Orwell wrote some interesting things about this. Everybody's read *Animal Farm*, but apparently nobody's read the introduction to *Animal Farm*. The introduction wasn't published and was found after Orwell died. In it, Orwell says that people shouldn't be so self-righteous about the atrocities of the totalitarian enemy that he was satirizing because people are a part of that and totalitarianism can be enforced and expressed subtly, without the use of force. And then he goes on to discuss it. And he says the basic reasons for that is that the press is owned by wealthy men. He didn't say wealthy corporations. And these wealthy men, he says, have every reason not to want certain ideas to be expressed. And second, he says that if you have a good education and if you're a part of the general elite intellectual culture, you have instilled into you the understanding that there are certain things that wouldn't do to say. That's true. That's what education is about. You can't blame the media themselves for adopting the set of assumptions and beliefs of the general intellectual culture.

Some people believe George Orwell wrote **1984** *and* **Animal Farm** *because he knew about the prominent people who were planning a Big Brother–world government. Specifically, Orwell had connections to the British Round Table Groups, a group of wealthy, influential Brits who wanted to control a world government through the British Empire. . . . Many people believe that the ultimate purpose of the inner circle* *of the Trilateral Commission and the Council on Foreign Relations is to manipulate America and the nations of the world into a world government. An undemocratic Big Brother–New World Order. Former Arizona senator and 1964 Republican Party presidential nominee Barry Goldwater wrote, "What the Trilateral Commission intends is to create a worldwide economic power superior to the political governments of the nation states involved. As managers and creators of the system, they will rule the future." And about the Council on Foreign Relations, Goldwater wrote, "The Council on Foreign Relations is an American branch of a society which originated in England and believes national boundaries should be obliterated and one-world rule established." Do powerful, influential men and groups have the agenda to set up and control a world government, and is that reality being shielded from the public by the mainstream media?*

I am not one who ascribes to this theory or notion that there is an agenda or conspiracy to have a world government. I don't believe it. In fact, the US is unusual—unique, in fact—in the dedication to protecting its sovereignty from international institutions.

But isn't globalization—organizations like NAFTA and the World Trade Organization—chipping away at the independence and sovereignty of America and the nations of the world? Isn't globalization moving us towards a sort of world system, or world government?

No, it's not. NAFTA was designed by the US government in the interests of US corporations. That's not world government. That's corporate power. And the same is true of the World Trade Organization.

But organizations like NAFTA, the WTO, and GATT are handing some decision-making that affects Americans over to these corporate, global organizations. Isn't the European Union taking away the sovereignty of the individual nations of Europe?

Sure, but they agreed to that. It's conscious. They decided to join the European Union.

Well, many people believe there's a plan to have America, Canada, and Mexico merge into a North American Union and start using a common currency. If that happens, there would be no more US Constitution and no more America. People in the Council on Foreign Relations, and even Vicente Fox, the former president of Mexico, have talked about that and suggested that. There's a group of congressmen—Ron Paul and others—that introduced a congressional bill that would prevent a North American Union because they feel that's where the US government is headed. The media hasn't reported on any of this.

I don't believe that's going to happen. If you look through the record, the commitment of Washington since the Second World War is to protect US sovereignty against any international or global treaties.

A lot of people contend there's going to be a North American Union, and then an Asian Union, and along with the European Union, these three areas will eventually be merged into a United Nations world government. . . . This interviewer once bought a book in the bookstore of the United Nations building in Manhattan that was written by a top UN official. In the book, the UN official started talking about how the only hope for the world is if the nations of the world surrender their independence and become a part of a United Nations world government. It seems clear from that book that that is what UN officials are talking about, and planning, and expecting to happen.

Well, maybe some United Nations officials have talked about that. But that's not the US government.

But the UN was built on land that Rockefeller donated. It was started by members of the Council on Foreign Relations. Members of the CFR

dominate the media and the US government. . . . The journalist Lou
Dobbs has said a North American Union would mean no more America.
Pat Buchanan has said it. Congressman Ron Paul has said there's a
movement toward world government. Glenn Beck. On his CNBC show,
Beck has shown copies of US government documents in which govern-
ment officials are talking about moving away from the Constitution
and towards globalization. You probably don't agree with Beck's the-
ocracy and he's probably way too far to the right for you, but this is a
major US broadcaster claiming that people in the US government have
plans to merge into a world government.

I haven't seen that. If you go case by case—for decades now—the US government has always been mindful of keeping the US exempt from international institutions and treaties.

There are a lot of sincere, genuine people who would disagree and who
are concerned that there is an agenda to have the US Constitution
scrapped and for America to move into a North American Union and
an undemocratic world government. They also claim that there is clear
evidence and documentation of that, but the vast majority of the media
is ignoring that.

That's their opinion. It's a view I, personally, don't agree with.

So maybe all the so-called "conspiracy theories" are actually accurate.
And the only reason the public doesn't realize that is because we have
an inept, negligent, controlled media. . . . In the early 1920s, the **New**
York Times *posthumously quoted former president Theodore Roosevelt*
saying, "These International Bankers and Rockefeller-Standard Oil
interests control the majority of newspapers (in America)." In response
to that, in 1922, John Hylan, the mayor of New York City, said, "The
real menace of our republic is this invisible government. . . . These
International Bankers and Rockefeller-Standard Oil interests control

the majority of newspapers and magazines in this country." Do you think these quotes have relevance to the present time?

Theodore Roosevelt was a very mixed person. But he was a trustbuster. He did want to break up the major trusts. And, sure, it has relevance. It doesn't have to be those corporations, specifically. The kind of material that Herman and I reviewed in *Manufacturing Consent* lays out and just describes the facts about corporate control of media. All the main media outlets are major corporations.

In 1917, Texas Congressman Oscar Callaway reported in the Congressional Record that in 1915 J. P. Morgan—the most powerful man on Wall Street—had gathered twelve of the most experienced news-papermen to talk about how to control the national media. According to Callaway, Morgan and that group decided that the media could be controlled by owning twenty-five well-known newspapers, and, so, Morgan bought those twenty-five newspapers and placed an editor at each one of them. From that point on, according to Callaway, the media was controlled by Morgan for Wall Street's banking, corporate interests. Other writers and historians have claimed that Morgan had a lot of editors on his payroll.

I don't know if it's true. But it would be easy to find out. But whether it's true or not, is it a surprise? Adam Smith described things like this. The wealthy will seize control of the media.

If J. P. Morgan was engaged in a blatant conspiracy to control the media then that would go against your and the Media Reform Movement's belief that corporate control over the media is a "non-conspiracy conspiracy." You and the Media Reform Movement believe that nobody is engaged in a blatant conspiracy to control the media, but that there are certain accepted ways of doing things in journalism that have led to an inept media that covers up government and corporate wrong-doings:

that journalists just accept what government press agents say and don't investigate for themselves; that media outlets don't want any major lawsuits so they turn a blind eye to corporate corruption; that media outlets have to be popular and make money and short superficial stories about gossip and celebrities is the way to do that, etc. But, according to Congressman Callaway, in 1915 J. P. Morgan was engaged in a blatant conspiracy to control the media.

Herman and I don't use any kind of "conspiracy theory" to explain the performance of the mass media. The media exists to serve the corporate interests that own the media. The corporate people who represent those interests are well positioned to shape and conform media policy. They select right-thinking people and those editors and journalists develop an internalization of priorities that conforms to the corporate institutions. They have internalized preconceptions of how to do things. It happens naturally. It's self-censorship. It's deeply instilled. The journalists and media are molded to act in a certain way and they're probably not even aware of how they're being molded and how they're being led to act. So there doesn't need to be any crude intervention, or conspiratorial coercion.

But could there be more of a blatant conspiracy to control the media than you imagine? Maybe there is more "crude intervention"? It's a possibility, isn't it, that, say, the richest guys in the Council on Foreign Relations or Trilateral Commission are meeting and saying, "Ok. We're the six CEO's who control 95 percent of the media outlets. We have to make sure that any other important media outlets are bought up by somebody who belongs to our club. We have to make sure that the boards of the media conglomerates are being run by people working for us. Then us six or seven guys can meet and decide what the news is and how we want the public to be molded." That's a possibility, isn't it?

Look. Rich, powerful people get together. Undoubtedly. They talk to each other. They have plans. They try to implement those plans. But is that a conspiracy? That's the way our social system is organized. I don't use the term "conspiracy" for that. If General Motors—let's say—if the board of directors of General Motors gets together and makes plans as to how to maximize profit, I don't call that a conspiracy. That's just the nature of our system.

But with media CEO's, they would not only be talking about profits, but what propaganda they want to spread and how the public can be molded. And, again, if we didn't have six corporations owning 95 percent of the media outlets, then the possibility of six CEO's talking about that wouldn't even exist.

Okay. Yes. The consolidation of the media puts too much influence into too few hands.

The Bilderberg Group is an extremely influential, secretive club that meets one weekend a year at an unpublicized location. The most well-known and powerful politicians, government officials, businessmen, and journalists attend the Bilderberg meetings. Bill Clinton, Henry Kissinger, David Rockefeller, Baron de Rothschild, Hillary Clinton, John Kerry, Gerald Ford, Tom Brokaw, and Peter Jennings are just a few of the many elites who have attended Bilderberg meetings. Since these guys act so secretively, the suspicion is that they're devious powermongers. Many people contend that the ultimate purpose of the inner circle of the Bilderberg Group is to manipulate the nations of the world into a New World Order, a world government. Yet, never is there a word or mention of the Bilderberg Group meetings from any newspaper, TV station, or mainstream media outlet.

I don't see the Bilderberg Group as secretive or a conspiracy. Rich and powerful and influential people will get together to play golf and go swimming and have parties and talk to each other about their interests and concerns and make plans that will be implemented. That's not a conspiracy. There are real conspiracies. There are real and very important conspiracies. So let me take one that changed the country enormously and may destroy the world. Back in the 1940s, General Motors, Standard Oil of California, and Firestone Rubber got together and they agreed to buy up and destroy the electric rail system and the transportation system in California because they wanted to shift it to the use of fossil fuels, gas and oil, cars, batteries and so on. Well, that was a real conspiracy. In fact, they were brought to court for it. And sentenced. That was a real conspiracy. And one of major consequence. It was part of the system of surburbanizing America, destroying public transportation, creating a major crisis that we're right in the middle of.

Those corporations didn't want the electric railway to become a predominant mode of transportation because they wanted people to use cars. Then General Motors could sell the cars, Standard Oil would sell the gas, and Firestone would make the tires.
Of course.

There's also been a major exposé on how Big Oil bought the patent for the electric car and suppressed and prevented the electric car from becoming popular and widely used. If we all used electric cars, we wouldn't be buying billions of dollars a year of gasoline from the Big Oil companies.
We would not be.

And so the crisis this has led to is that now we have a severe dependence on gas and oil?
Yes, but also global warming. The carbon monoxide from the cars is heating up the world. And might destroy the world.

The media hasn't told the other side of that story, though, because some scientists and a lot of people feel that Al Gore and others like him are wrong. They feel the evidence is that there's global warming but it's not man-made and not nearly as dangerous and threatening as Al Gore says. And that the global warming hysteria is—for whatever reason—propaganda. It could be a money-making thing, because Al Gore and others like him are invested in and could make millions off of companies that sell "green" products and "green" energy sources.

The consensus among many scientists is that there certainly is a problem with global warming.

But it may not be coming from carbon monoxide and it may not be nearly as dangerous as we're being led to believe. . . . But if we could go back to the issue of the Bilderberg Group . . . The Bilderberg guys aren't meeting to go swimming and barbecue. They're meeting to talk about what politicians they need to manipulate so they can control the economy and politics of the world and rule over the masses like fascist mattoids. They're meeting to talk and plan of course. What else would you expect them to do?

But these are the most influential, powerful men in the world. It seems a responsible, diligent media would do an investigation and story about that. . . . If the coaches, the owners, and the captains of every NFL football team met once a year for a three day conference to talk about the future of football and the NFL, do you think sportswriters would cover that? Of course.

But with the Bilderberg Group, the most powerful and influential businessmen, journalists, politicians, and government officials are meeting once a year to talk about world events and the future of the world and not one media outlet mentions that or covers that. What explanation could there be for that other than that the media is being censored and controlled?

I don't think there's anything secretive about Bilderberg. We all know Bilderberg takes place.

You in academia may know about it. But 90 percent of the public has never heard of the Bilderberg Group. Or maybe 95 percent, or 99 percent. First of all, the media can't get in and won't be let into the meeting.

Well, then if Bilderberg won't let the media report on the meeting then they're being very secretive. There's an adage: "Evil is done in the darkness. Good deeds are done in the sunshine." Margaret Thatcher once said, "The Bilderberg are a stuck-up set. They will never have a New World Order." Thatcher was apparently saying that the goal of Bilderberg is to manipulate the peoples of the world into this world government. I don't know that she said that.

She did. . . . In June 2008, when he was on the campaign trail, five months before he was elected president, Barack Obama was—apparently, in all likelihood—secretively hustled off to the Bilderberg meeting which was being held a few miles from an airport in Virginia. The press corps that were following Obama were surreptitiously packed into a plane and flown to Chicago. The press couldn't understand why they weren't allowed to follow the candidate to where he was going, which is always the routine, regular procedure. Obama's handlers wouldn't specify where Obama had gone. If a man who's about to be elected the country's leader goes off to this meeting, then doesn't the public have a right to know about that? The Bilderberg is just a group that prefers to keep their meetings private. They can have a right to privacy.

Even when elected officials are attending the meeting? Government officials—paid employees of the people—always attend the Bilderberg meeting. It seems there should be an investigation of that. What does Bilderberg believe and stand for? Why is the man who's about to be elected the president of the United States attending the meeting? Who has such influence that they can facilitate a total blackout on any media stories about Bilderberg? Is it the Council on Foreign Relations?

I don't see that.

But could Morgan's and Wall Street's control over the media have continued through the formation of the Council on Foreign Relations? One of the founders of the CFR was J. P. Morgan's lawyer and the other founders were representatives of the Rockefellers. Since 1921, members of the Council on Foreign Relations have held the most important positions in the media. Even today, the heads of the New York Times, the Washington Post, NBC, CBS, and ABC, the UP and the AP, and most all the major magazines are members of the CFR. So is the CFR running the media?

The Council on Foreign Relations is almost completely open. It's just that rich, influential people belong to the Council on Foreign Relations.

But why should another think tank that was started by Rockefeller—started by Wall Street—have so much dominant influence over our society? Shouldn't somebody in the media be saying that influence should be coming from other places, too? Why shouldn't a think tank that was started by, say, Ralph Nader—a think tank that believes that the government should work for the people instead of the corporate, banking power—why shouldn't a think tank like that be running the government and media?

Sure, I think we ought to have a democratic society. We don't. And it's perfectly well known that we don't. There's a high concentration of power. People with power stick together. But the CFR is quite open.

Most people in the public don't know about the CFR.

See, that's not the fault of the media, particularly. That's the fault of scholarship, the educational system, and so on.

It seems the CFR is more stealthy than you're saying. For instance, Dick Cheney once made a speech to the Council on Foreign Relations. In the speech, Cheney mentioned that he once had been the director of the CFR. Then Cheney smirked and said "I never mentioned that when I was campaigning for reelection back in Wyoming." Cheney apparently concealed his relationship with the CFR during his congressional career.

I have never heard that.

You can watch it online. It's Cheney talking to the CFR. . . . In 2009, when Hillary Clinton became the Secretary of the State, she made a speech at the office of the CFR and made a statement to the effect that the CFR tells government officials "what to do" and "how we should think." Perhaps that's the case for people in the media, too? Is the state-corporate nexus centered in the CFR?

She was saying that because she wanted to butter up the CFR. First of all, I don't think she said that.

She definitely did. You can read Clinton's speech on the website of the CFR.

If she said nice comments about the CFR when she was there, she was saying, "You're a bunch of nice guys. I really like you."

It seems that statement might have been revealing and indicative that the state-corporate nexus is centered in the CFR.

No it's not. It's just the group of people who are involved in the state-corporate nexus, the powerful, influential ones, happen to be members of the CFR.

But it seems too much influence and power is coming from one place. A lot of people see that and believe that it's a reasonable hypothesis to think that the state-corporate nexus is centered in the CFR. The Republican Party's 1964 presidential nominee and others have written that the purpose of the CFR is to manipulate America into a world government. It seems an investigation should be done on that. . . . Do you think the CFR is being guided by the philosophy of Walter Lippmann?

Yes. Absolutely. Since Lippmann wrote his essays in the 1920s his ideas have been a substantial part of contemporary political science.

You wrote about the philosophy of Walter Lippmann and, also, Harold Lasswell. In the early twentieth century, Lippmann was the dean of American journalists, and Lasswell was the founder of the modern field of communications and a highly regarded political scientist. Lippman and Lasswell believed that government officials—"a specialized class"—had a right to propagandize to the masses—"the bewildered herd"—because the "specialized class" was intellectually superior and the great majority of the "bewildered herd" was intellectually incapable of knowing what was right and good for themselves. You claim that this philosophy of a "specialized class" having a right to propagandize and lie to the "bewildered herd" was widely accepted amongst many twentieth-century political scientists and government officials. Do you think the CFR and our present-day government are being guided by this idea?

That's the general assumption of government, of people in power. It's a widely accepted view. A very general assumption. It's also true of the Council on Foreign Relations. Lippmann wrote the government—the "specialized class"—should manufacture consent. Get the public to think a certain way.

And the way that the government was to get the public to think a certain way was by spreading propaganda and lies?

Propaganda isn't necessarily lies. For instance, with Iraq—when you keep the debate about Iraq within the bounds of blunder or success you're not lying, but you're not telling the truth either. You're constraining the frame to a very narrow spectrum. The public is allowed to think in only a few ways. We call that propaganda when the enemy does it, but we just call it objectivity when we do it.

But it seems that this philosophy and propaganda very easily slips and morphs into outright lies. Because this seems like a very prevalent thing. Politicians and government officials thinking they have a right to lie to and mislead the public. J. Edgar Hoover believed this and would regularly use his media connections to spread disinformation. So did William Donovan, the founder of the OSS, which was the precursor to the CIA. Officials in Lyndon Johnson's administration lied about the Gulf of Tonkin, and officials in Bush's administration lied about weapons of mass destruction. Richard Nixon used to look straight into TV cameras and say he wasn't bombing Cambodia, but the fact was was that he was bombing Cambodia. This seems like a very common, routine thing. Politicians and government officials—the "specialized class"— thinking they have the right to lie to and mislead the public—the "bewildered herd." And the worse thing, of course, is that the media seems to be a part of the "specialized class." We don't have a media that calls the government out on its lies and propaganda.

Well, that could be an interesting way of putting it. It's certainly a prevalent and pervasive thing—the "specialized class" and the "bewildered herd." You could go on and on with examples of this. I once did a talk on this and a publisher based a whole book on it. Examples of this. . . . it's prevalent and pervasive.

The Internet has been a great and even a revolutionary way for people to learn new things, and to exchange ideas, and start political movements because the Internet is a free and open flow of ideas and opinions. There's no corporate filter. This "people's Internet" is probably seen as a threat by and to the state-corporate nexus. But now the corporate media is trying to take over the Internet, correct?

That's right. And this is something very important to the Media Reform movement. Net neutrality. To keep the Internet free. Because right now, the same corporations that own the media are trying to lobby the Congress to pass laws that only those who pay for expensive licenses will control the Internet. In other words, the big corporations will own the connections and the search engines of the Internet. Then when you do a search on the Internet, the corporate media would highlight only the websites that they want you to go to. They would direct you away from any alternative news websites, or alternative, independent news bloggers, or from any political or social movements that they don't want you to see. The Internet would move much slower. It would be much harder to advertise on the net or start up a successful website. Only those who have a lot of money to pay to and who are in favor with the corporate-owned Internet will get their websites quickly and widely displayed.

That really smacks of fascism and totalitarianism, doesn't it? Why shouldn't the Internet be free?

It should be. This is a very important part of the Media Reform movement. To keep the Internet free. Net neutrality. And to support those politicians who are trying to pass laws that would keep the Internet free.

This issue of media conglomerates taking over more and more media outlets extends globally, doesn't it? The media giants don't seem content just controlling the media outlets in America, but are expanding more and more into all areas of the globe. Maybe what we're heading towards is one worldwide Big Brother media company that we are all dependent on and that we're all being molded by?

Well, one might understand if someone was concerned that that's where we're headed. The media consolidation is certainly antithetical to democratic values.

Former Lyndon Johnson White House Press Secretary and well known journalist Bill Moyers has said, "The Founders didn't count on the rise of megamedia. They didn't count on huge private corporations that would own not only the means of journalism but also vast swaths of the territory that journalism should be covering." So, we really can't trust the media, can we?

I read the *New York Times* every day. I think you get a lot of information from them. Do I trust them? Well, you know, I—just like everyone does I'm sure—you evaluate what you read. Try to determine its credibility, ask where it's coming from. But the *Times* can be a marvelous source of information.

If you read your book, **Manufacturing Consent,** *Professor Chomsky, one gets the feeling that the government is constantly propagandizing and lying to get us into unjust conflicts and wars and that the media is complicit in that. One also gets the feeling that the media is constantly turning a blind eye to the malfeasance and corruption of Big Business. But here, in this interview, your criticism seems far less harsh and severe.*

I'm criticizing in exactly the same way. But, in fact, most of my writing is a critical analysis of scholarship and of general intellectual culture. Which is not very different. The media is infused by the general intellectual culture.

Whether it's a "non-conspiracy conspiracy" or a blatant conspiracy, something has to be done about the media. . . . Leaders of Media Reform have said that the Media Reform movement needs to coalesce so it becomes a stronger organization and could be as visible a political movement as, say, Greenpeace, or even the NRA. The Media Reform movement should adopt a specific platform, specific goals that it wants to accomplish. The first goal would have to be to break up the monopolies that certain companies have over the media. To make it illegal for one corporation to own too many newspapers, and too many TV stations and radio stations.

That would be a very good start. There are existing anti-trust and broadcast regulations that activists could use to break up the media monopolies. This could, ideally lead to a media that facilitates a true, wide-ranging democratic dialogue.

It might be an uphill battle, though, because media lobbyists already have the main Republicans and the main Democrats paid off and in their pockets. . . . Might it also be a good idea to require all journalists to reveal what relationships they may have with the CIA and/or Council on Foreign Relations and how those relationships affect how they do their jobs?

If they have relations with the CIA, they should. But relations with the CFR is nothing to reveal. It's public. Connections to the CIA would not be public, and therefore it should be revealed.

But it seems the CFR slyly positions their people throughout the media and government so they can manipulate and control. The Council on Foreign Relations was started by Morgan and Rockefeller, and the suspicion is they're doing what's right for Wall Street instead of Main Street.

But that's going to be true whenever you pick a group—you know, there are some exceptions—but, overwhelmingly, if you randomly select a group of powerful, influential, wealthy people, yeah, they'll be focused on the needs of business power. Automatically.

Yes, but you could pick people from other places. You could pick people who are going to do what's right for the public, that have that conscience, can't you?

Sure, you could believe in democracy.

PBS is supposed to be "the people's" station but even PBS has sold out to corporate sponsors and become pretty commercial, hasn't it?

The major grants that are funding PBS are coming from corporate funded foundations. A few years ago PBS did a story on how a corporation had moved into some Third World country and exploited the population and resources there. Some corporate interest—I believe it might have been GE—threatened to withdraw the funding for PBS and so PBS pulled the story, stopped doing shows like that. It seems PBS is not any great people's watchdog.

Maybe what we need to do—as Media Reform people say—is to establish a real visible group of noncommercial radio and television stations.

That could be a great thing for the country. Noncommercial radio and TV stations could be set up on college campuses, or in local communities. The best journalism is going to come from stations that are not for profit.

What else do you believe needs to be done to fix the media?

I think a lot should be done. We should have a much more diverse, much freer, much more representative, much more participatory system of social and economic institutions. Including the media.

CHAPTER 11

Is There a Conspiracy to Have a Big Brother World Government? A New World Order?

An interview with New York Times *bestselling author Jim Marrs*

In 1776, a German law professor named Adam Weishaupt founded a secret society called the Order of the Illuminati. Weishaupt had been influenced by the French philosopher Jean Rousseau and claimed that society had to be restructured and that religion and national governments were preventing humanity from living in a natural, free state. Weishaupt's aim was to form a group of powerful lawyers, professors, bankers, politicians, writers, and other prominent men who would use their influence to foment a revolution, to topple the religious institutions and national governments of the world, and to create and control a new society. A world government. Weishaupt believed the Order would "rule the world" by obtaining "an influence in all offices which have any effect either in forming, or in managing, or even in directing the mind of man."

By the late 1700s, the Illuminati had become a formidable group, and had amongst its members some of the richest and most powerful men of Europe. Members of the Order helped to form the Jacobin Clubs, the movement behind the French Revolution, and there is good reason to conclude that the French Revolution of 1789 was instigated and organized by the Illuminati.

Weishaupt ran his organization with a pyramid structure; only he and a few others at the top knew the true intentions of the group, and the majority of the Illuminati's members likely believed the purpose of the group was benevolent, a genuine desire to make men more free of oppression. No matter what Weishaupt's outer statements were, though, his private writings indicated that he had more of the mentality of a power hungry dictator than a benevolent revolutionary. Weishaupt was an atheist and believed there was no higher power and no higher purpose, so there was no accounting for one's actions and no morality or karmic justice to life. "The ends justifies the means," he wrote, and, "the wise ought to take all the means to do good which the wicked take to do evil." Some historians claim that when Weishaupt and the Illuminati were overturning the French monarchy, they decided that France's population could be more easily controlled and unemployment could be solved if there were fewer people. The French Revolution's Reign of Terror was initiated and France depopulated as thousands of French citizens were decapitated by the guillotine. In the late 1780s, the government of Bavaria seized some of Weishaupt's writings and concluded that the Illuminati was a dangerous, seditious group and outlawed the Order, sending Weishaupt and other Illuminati fleeing to other countries. After the Bavarian government outlawed the Illuminati, it sent letters to all the nations of Europe, informing them that the Illuminati was a powerful, influential cabal of men who wanted to overthrow the governments of the world and that this conspiracy was potent and a genuine danger to the nations of the world.

During the late 1700s, it was widely known and accepted in America that the Illuminati existed and were a bona fide threat. Preachers preached against it, and politicians talked out against it. In the 1780s, the Illuminati tried to recruit into the Order a highly respected, well-known British historian and Edinburgh University professor, John Robison. Instead of becoming a member, Robison wrote a book, *Proofs of a Conspiracy*, revealing the agenda of the Illuminati, claiming it was "formed for the express purpose of rooting out all the religious establishments and overturning all the existing governments of Europe." *Proofs of a Conspiracy* became a popular book, and in 1798, a Reverend G. W. Snyder sent the book to George Washington, who was living in retirement in Mount Vernon. At that time, Washington and others believed that the Illuminati-Jacobins had infiltrated the Democratic Clubs, an American political group, and might try to overthrow the US government. In 1798, the Congress passed the Alien and Sedition Acts for the purpose of arresting any Jacobin agents who might be operating in America. After reading *Proofs of a Conspiracy*, Washington wrote to Reverend Snyder, "I have heard much of the nefarious, and dangerous plan, and doctrines of the Illuminati, but never saw the book until you were pleased to send it to me. . . . It was not my intentions to doubt that, the Doctrines of the Illuminati, and principles of Jacobinism had not spread in the United States. On the contrary, no one is more truly satisfied of this fact than I am."

At that time, many people also believed that Freemasonry was linked to the Illuminati conspiracy-plan and that the Freemasons were also a group intent on covertly controlling politics and society. In the present day, the public generally assumes that the Freemasons were and are a philanthropic, fraternal organization dedicated to charity and good works. Many researchers and former Freemasons have claimed, though, that the higher degree Freemasons are—like the Illuminati was—a secretive brotherhood intent on penetrating and controlling politics. And many researchers have said that the ultimate purpose of Freemasonry is to have so many Freemasons stationed in the most powerful positions in government and business that the Freemasons are controlling world politics or even a world government. In the letters that the Bavarian government seized, Weishaupt had written, "The great strength of our Order lies in its concealment; let it never appear in any place in its own name, but always covered by another name and another occupation. None is fitter than the three lower degrees of Freemasonry . . . " Illuminati members were recruited from the Freemasons, and when top members of the Illuminati attended the Masonic Convention in Hesse, Germany, in 1782, a formal alliance was forged between the two groups.

In *Proofs of a Conspiracy*, Professor Robison claimed that the Illuminati and Freemasons were virtually the same group, working together to control and revolutionize the world. Many early Americans read *Proofs of a Conspiracy* and other books like it and were convinced that the higher degree Freemasons were a devious group intent on selfishly controlling politics. John Quincy Adams, the sixth president of the United States, wrote: ". . . the Masonic oath, obligations and penalties cannot possibly be reconciled to the laws of morality, of Christianity, or of the land." In 1826, a Masonic brother, William Morgan, was murdered in upstate New York. Morgan had written, "The bane of our civil institutions is to be found in Masonry, already powerful and daily becoming more so. I owe my country an exposure of its dangers." Morgan was planning to write a book about the Freemasons and it was believed that Morgan had been murdered because he was going to reveal the political secrets of Freemasonry. After Morgan's murder, Masonry got such a bad reputation that thousands of Masons quit the Order and dozens of Masonic lodges were closed down. In 1829, the New York state legislature launched an investigation of Masonry and concluded that it was composed of powerful and wealthy men whose members held office in almost "every place where power is of any importance." In 1834, an investigation by the Massachusetts legislature found that Freemasonry was "a distinct independent government within our own government, and beyond the controls of the laws of the land by means of its secrecy." Because of such widespread suspicion that Freemasons were controlling our national and state governments, in 1828, in upstate New York, the Anti-Masonic Party was formed. The Anti-Masons became an influential party whose principal political platform was to prevent any Freemasons from gaining political office.

Although it is probably not as accepted and well known in today's world that groups like the Illuminati and the Freemasons are out to covertly control politics and move nations to a world government, there are many people who believe that the idea of world government and the New World Order is still with us today. In fact, many researchers strongly insist the Illuminati–Freemason idea of a powerful secretive elite controlling the world and manipulating the world to a world government was passed down to future generations, and in fact the most powerful, wealthiest, and most influential men and groups in today's world have adopted this idea.

One group that researchers feel embraced this idea of a powerful elite controlling politics and setting up a world government is the international bankers, and, specifically, the patriarchs of the Rothschild banking family. In 1782, the Illuminati set up one of their main headquarters in Frankfurt, Germany, and Adam Weishaupt and top Illuminati members became part of the Frankfurt Masonic Lodge. Frankfurt, Germany was the hub of the Rothschild banking dynasty. The Rothschilds were Jews, and when the Illuminati came to Frankfurt, the Freemasons began accepting Jews into their Order and the Rothschilds and their employees joined the Frankfurt lodge. In the 18th and 19th centuries, the Rothschilds owned Europe's largest banks and were lending money to and had relations with Europe's most important monarchs and political leaders; a well-known quote from the time was: "There is only one power in Europe and that is Rothschild." The bankers preferred to work from behind the scenes, but, as one historian put it ". . . all the while they were helping to shape the major events of the day: by granting or withholding funds; by influencing appointments to high office; and by an almost daily intercourse with the great decision makers."

The *Niles Weekly Register*, a Baltimore newspaper published from 1810 to 1826, was one of the most widely circulated and respected publications of its day; modern day historians still consider the archives of the *Niles Weekly Register* to be a reliable and accurate source for early American history. In 1835, it was written in the *Niles Register*: "The Rothschilds are the wonders of modern banking. . . . The Rothschilds govern a Christian world. Not a cabinet moves without their advice. They stretch their hands with equal ease from Petersburg to Vienna, from Vienna to Paris, from Paris to London, from London to Washington. . . . Baron Rothschild, the head of the house . . . holds the keys to peace or war, blessing or cursing. They are the bankers and counselors of the Kings of Europe and of the republican chiefs of America." In the mid 1800s, Karl Ferdinand Graf, an Austrian diplomat and the Foreign Minister of Austria from 1852–1859, wrote: "This Rothschild House, through its enormous financial transactions and its banking credit connections actually achieved the position of real Power; it has to such an extent acquired control of the general money market that it is in a position either to hinder or promote, as it feels inclined, the movements and operations of potentates, and even of the greatest European powers." The Rothschilds were said to be the wealthiest family in the world, and one historian claimed that at one time they controlled half the world's wealth. It seems if anybody could have gotten behind politics and controlled the world it would have been the Rothschilds.

The Rothschilds' influence was especially strong in Britain, where they were the principal stockholders of the Bank of England, the bank which was the model for our modern central banks. In 1838, Amschel Rothschild said, "I care not what puppet is placed upon the throne of England to rule the Empire on which the sun never sets. The man who controls Britain's money supply controls the British Empire and I control the British money supply." This Rothschild influence over Britain apparently continued for decades: seventy years later in 1909 British Prime Minister David Lloyd George stated that "Nathan Rothschild is the most powerful man in England." Since the late 1500s, the British Empire reigned as the world's foremost global power. The Empire was most powerful during the 19th and early 20th centuries when ten million square miles of territory and almost four hundred million people were conquered. It could be argued that the British Empire of the 19th and 20th centuries was the Rothschild Empire— that it was the financial backing of the Rothschilds that was enabling Britain to take over so much of the world.

In 1871, Cecil Rhodes, a British businessman, moved to South Africa and developed a monopoly over the diamond fields there, and then a monopoly over the global diamond trade. In the present day, on their own website, the Rothschild family confirms that they were the financial backers of Cecil Rhodes; in his will, Rhodes left a large portion of his enormous wealth to a Rothschild. In the late 1880s, Rhodes set up the Round Table Groups. The Round Table Groups were groups of British businessmen who were sent out to the countries of the world to train business leaders loyal to Britain in ways to maintain control over that country's economy, and politics. In his personal writings, in his own words, Cecil Rhodes said: "I contend that we English are the finest race in the world, and that the more of the world we inhabit the better it is for the human race because we are the supreme masters of the human race. What scheme could we think of to forward this object? . . . In the present day, I became a member of the Masonic Order. I see the vast power and wealth they possess. The influence they hold . . . Why should we not form a secret society with but one object: the further-ance of the British Empire and the bringing of the whole uncivilized world under British rule." The Round Table Groups were run with the same pyra-mid structure as the Illuminati: only Rhodes and others at the top knew that the true purpose was to have Britain take over the world. Many people and researchers look at all this and feel that the Illuminati-Freemason plan to conquer the world had morphed into the Round Table Groups and had been taken over by the power of the Rothschilds and the British Empire.

The British Empire dissolved in the early 20th century and, so, of course, could no longer be the viable channel through which the Rothschild-international banking network and Round Table Groups could control a world government. President Woodrow Wilson, and others from the Paris Peace Treaty, though, had close ties to Wall Street and the banking indus-try, and it was these men who were behind the creation of the League of Nations. To those who contend that there is an agenda or conspiracy to have a world government, the belief and the evidence is that the League of

Nations and then the United Nations were never created with the sincere purpose of developing more diplomacy between nations. To those who believe there is a world government conspiracy, the League of Nations and then United Nations were created by the influence of the Rothschild international banking network for the purpose of influencing the nations of the world into losing their independence and sovereignty to a League of Nations or United Nations world government and then finding themselves living in a world government that isn't a democracy, that has no bill of rights, and is being controlled and manipulated by the international banking network for their purposes, aims, and profits. This would be the world government that Adam Weishaupt envisioned.

In 1920, according to Jim Marrs, the League of Nations sounded too much like world government to the United States Senate; the United States Senate didn't want America to be part of any organization that smacked of world government, and, so, the Senate voted that America would not join the League of Nations. So, twenty-five years later , in 1945, the Rockefellers, international bankers who had become associates and partners with the Rothschilds, in an apparent attempt to appease the US Senate, donated the land and money and built the new attempt at world government, the United Nations, on American soil. It is United Nations documents themselves, and the statements of United Nations officials themselves, that cause many people to believe that the true purpose of the United Nations is to fool and dupe the nations of the world into losing their independence and sovereignty to a United Nations world government. The belief is that the big international banks and their multi-national corporations want some organization they're running to be in control of global politics so that they can move around the world and do what they want and profit how they want without the interference of pesky things like the policies of national democracies and governments. From 1948–1952, Brock Chisolm was the UN's World Health Organization's first Director-General, when he was quoted saying: "To achieve world government, it is necessary to remove from the minds of men their individualism, loyalty to family traditions, national patriotism, and religious dogmas." Robert Mueller, former Attorney General of the UN, once wrote: "We must move as quickly as possible to a one-world government, one-world religion, under a one-world leader."

One historian who claimed to have an intimate knowledge of the Round Table Groups and the world government plan was Dr. Carroll Quigley. Quigley was a professor at Georgetown University and also lectured at and was a consultant to the Naval College, the Smithsonian Institute, the State Department, and other institutions. Dr. Quigley was one of Bill Clinton's professors, a mentor to Clinton, and during his second nomination acceptance speech, President Clinton thanked Dr. Quigley for being, along with John F. Kennedy, one of the inspirations for his life. In a book published in 1975, *Tragedy & Hope*, Professor Quigley wrote, "There does exist and has existed for a generation, an international anglophile network, that operates, to some extent, in the way the Radical right believes the communists act. . . . This network . . . we may identify as the Round Table Groups. . . . I know of the operations of this group because I have studied it for twenty years and was permitted for two years in the early 1960s to examine its papers and secret records." Quigley claimed the Round Table Groups "acted in secret" and their purpose was "nothing less than to create a world system of financial control in private hands able to dominate the political system of each country and the economy of the world as a whole. The system was to be controlled in a feudalist fashion by the central banks of the world, acting in concert, by secret arrangements arrived at in frequent private meetings and conferences.

"The apex of the systems was to be the Bank of International Settlements in Basel, Switzerland, a private bank owned and controlled by the world's central banks which were themselves private corporations." Mentioning Cecil Rhodes, Quigley wrote, "What is not so widely known is that Rhodes in his will left his fortune to form a secret society which was to devote itself to the preservation and expansion of the British Empire. And what does not seem to be known to anyone is that this secret society continues to exist to this day. . . . It holds secret meetings. This group is, as I shall show, one of the most important historical facts of the twentieth century." Quigley was saying that the Round Table Groups that Rhodes founded in the 1800s still existed in the 1970s and were still trying to move the world to a world system or world government. Quigley claimed the main Round Table Group in England was called the Royal Institute of International Affairs and had round table groups around the world that answered to it: " . . . the Royal Institute of International Affairs had as its nucleus in each area the existing submerged round table group. In New York it was known as the Council on Foreign Relations and was a front for J. P. Morgan & Co."

Since its inception, many people have accused the Council on Foreign Relations, the nation's most influential think tank, of having too much influence over American politics and being the "shadow government" that controls America. Since the 1920s, CFR members have always held the most important positions in the US government and many of the policies that America adopts comes from the CFR. Fourteen secretaries of state, fourteen treasury secretaries, eleven defense secretaries, and scores of other federal department heads have been CFR members. CFR members also hold the most important positions in the media, in the corporate world, and in "all offices which may have any effect in either forming, or in managing, or even in directing the mind of man." The firm conviction of many researchers is that the true purpose of the CFR is to move America to a world government.

Recently, in 2003, the CFR was behind a movement to get the United States, Mexico, and Canada to merge into one political union, the North American Union. New World Order theorists claim that the New World Order groups were behind the formation of the European Union, and now want a North American Union, and then have the Asian nations form an Asian Union, and, then, in something out of an Orwellian novel, have all three areas merge into a world government. In 2003, the CFR formed the

Independent Task Force on North America to look into ways to form a stronger, deeper, economic and security alliance between the North American countries; prior to that, in 2001, Dr. Robert Pastor, a member of the CFR, who became the Vice chairman of the Independent Task Force on North America, wrote a book calling for the formation of a North American Community. Critics of Pastor claimed the North American Community he was calling for would be the same thing as the European Common Market, the organization that eventually led the nations of Europe into surrendering their independence and sovereignty to the European Union. In Europe, there is, of course, only one currency now, the euro, and in his book, Dr. Pastor wrote that it would be a good idea if the United States, Mexico, and Canada formed a closer union and then all used the same currency, the *amero*.

Congressman Ron Paul and other legislators in Washington criticized the CFR's Independent Task Force, claiming it was an attempt by the CFR and the corporations and banks behind the CFR to destroy national sovereignty for a North American Union. Congressman Ron Paul has also said that the United States's political establishment is trying to move America to world government. In 2007, Virginia Congressman Virgil Goode introduced a resolution, supported by Ron Paul and forty-two other congressmen, proposing that America should have nothing to do with a North American Union because it was a direct threat and attack to national sovereignty. Little of this was reported by the corporate mainstream media, but it is believed that Congressman Goode's resolution successfully thwarted, for the time being, the CFR's desire to have a North American Union. It is the publications of the CFR itself or the statements of former CFR members that convince many people that the CFR wants to move America to a New World Order. *Foreign Affairs* is the official publication of the CFR and since the 1920s has been the most influential journal of America's political establishment. The second edition of *Foreign Affairs,* published in September 1922, stated, "Obviously, there is going to be no steady progress in civilization . . . until some kind of international system is created that will put an end to the diplomatic struggles incident to the attempt of every nation to make itself secure. . . . The real problem today is that of world government."

Barry Goldwater was the distinguished senator who represented Arizona for twenty-five years and was the Republican Party's 1964 presidential nominee. In his book, *With No Apologies*, Goldwater wrote, "The Council on Foreign Relations is an American branch of a society that originated in England and believes national boundaries should be obliterated and one-world rule established." The Judge Advocate General of the US Navy is the Navy's most powerful attorney, and from 1956 to 1960 Admiral Chester Ward held that position. Ward was also a member of the CFR, and in the 1970s, Ward wrote a book criticizing the CFR, claiming that, "One common objective of CFR members is to bring about the surrender of the sovereignty and the national independence of the United States. . . . Primarily, they want the world banking monopoly from whatever power to end up in control of global government."

By the 1960s and '70s there was so much criticism of the CFR, writers and reporters claiming that its members had so much influence that the CFR was basically running the US government, that David Rockefeller, to divert attention from the CFR, created the Trilateral Commission. Trilateral Commission members, like CFR members, are globalists and internationalists, who, since 1974, have held the most important positions in the government. Trilateralists have been behind the creation of organizations like the North America Free Trade Agreement, the General Agreement on Tariffs and Trade, the Trans-Pacific Partnership, and other free trade agreements that are moving America and the world to globalism and a New World Order. Zbigniew Brzezinski, President Jimmy Carter's National Security Advisor, was, along with Rockefeller, one of the founders of the Trilateral Commission. Brzezinski has authored a number of books, in one book stating that "in the future the State will be able to monitor and watch the movements and activities of all citizens." When writing things like this, Brzezinski comes off sounding like the CEO of Big Brother. In a book written at the time of the founding of the Trilateral Commission, in 1974, Brzezinski wrote:

National sovereignty is no longer a viable concept . . . (what is needed is a) movement toward a larger community by the developing nations . . . through a variety of indirect ties and already developing limitations on national sovereignty." In *With No Apologies*, Senator Goldwater wrote,

> The Trilateral Commission is international. It is intended to be the vehicle for multinational consolidation of the commercial and banking interests by seizing control of the political government of the United States . . . What the Trilateral Commission intends is to create a worldwide economic power superior to the political governments of the nation states involved. As managers and creators of the system, they will rule the future.

Some people would say that the New World Order is just about the big international banks and multinational corporations wanting more control and power. The bankers and corporate owners want an organization that they're running to be in control of global politics so they can move around the world how they want and profit how they want without the interference of pesky things like the policies of national democracies and national governments. Other people, though, would say that the New World Order is more a conspiracy—that the New World Order is what the Illuminati was, a group of powerful, wealthy men like the patriarchs of the Rothschild family, the patriarchs of the Rockefeller family, and others—who form secretive clubs, and meet in back rooms and believe that they're the elites and masters of the world who will eventually be controlling a worldwide Big Brother government. These people would say that the New World Order is the one percent of the population that owns ninety-nine percent of the world's wealth and eventually want to live like royalty behind guarded gates in splendor and luxury while the ninety-nine percent live like Third World peasants and serfs in state-controlled work camps and villages.

To many people the United Nations Agenda 21 Plan is the proof and confirmation that there is a conspiracy-plan to have a world government. The United Nations Agenda 21 Plan isn't a conspiracy theory but is a specific program of the United Nations that can be read about on the UN's own website. The Agenda 21 Plan was initiated in June 1992 at *The United Nations Earth Summit* in Rio de Janeiro, Brazil, when the leaders of 178 countries—including President George H. W. Bush—signed on and made Agenda 21 the official policy of their nations. According to the Agenda 21 Plan, global warming is eventually going to get so bad that all world citizens are going to have to undergo a radical change in their lifestyles. The ultimate goal of the Agenda 21 Plan is to have all Americans and all world citizens move into United Nations living facilities where their action and lives will be strictly monitored and controlled by a UN police force; no cars, certain household appliances, or anything else that could lead to more global warming will be allowed to be used. The Agenda 21 Plan sounds like a science fiction novel or a futuristic dystopian movie but isn't. It is the official policy of the US government. In 1995, President Bill Clinton signed Executive Order #12858 to create the President's Council on Sustainable Development in order to align the US government's policies with the Agenda 21 Plan. Currently, many United Nations living facilities—groups of tall buildings in urban areas where each citizen will have a bunk and sparse living quarters—are being planned and built all over America and the world.

There are many scientists who claim that global warming is a serious danger, but there are also scientists who say that global warming will not destroy our environment. To New World Order conspiracy theorists, the global warming scare is propaganda spread by New World Order paid scientists and think tanks so that the Agenda 21 Plan will be implemented and the United Nations can have its Big Brother-world government.

Many people would look at the Agenda 21 Plan and wonder how the US government and United Nations are ever going to get millions of people to accept and move into the tenement-like UN living facilities. Other people believe that it is inevitable that eventually there will have to be a financial breakdown—another Great Depression—that will cause millions of people to become impoverished, unemployed, and homeless, and, so, have no choice but to move into the Agenda 21 living facilities. Republicans in Washington take the Agenda 21 Plan seriously enough that in 2012 it became an official plank of the Republican Party platform that America should disengage from the Agenda 21 Plan because not doing so will destroy America and American sovereignty and independence. But whether the New World Order is just the banks and corporations wanting more control or whether the New World Order influences will ever get the Agenda 21 Plan up and running, there seems to be little about globalization and the New World Order that is beneficial to or aimed towards helping the common man. The New World Order has all the earmarks of the corruption and greed of Big Business and Wall Street. It is the super-wealthy and super-powerful wanting more wealth and more power with no regard for democracy, the public welfare, or natural rights.

Writer Jim Marrs was the world's best known "conspiracy theory" author. Far from being an over-imaginative conspiracy theorist, though, Mr. Marrs was a professionally trained journalist and reporter who never failed to provide footnotes and resources for his claims. Marrs began his career in the 1960s working for the *Fort Worth Star-Telegram*, and then went on to work for several other Texas newspapers. By 1980, he had become an author, freelance writer, and speaker. It was Jim Marrs' *New York Times* bestselling book *Crossfire* that was the basis for director Oliver Stone's iconic Hollywood movie *JFK*. For thirty years, Marrs taught a course on the Kennedy assassination at the University of Texas. Before passing away in 2017, Jim Marrs' other *New York Times* bestselling books included *Rule by Secrecy*, *The Trillion Dollar Conspiracy*, and *The Rise of the Fourth Reich*.

Cirignano: To you, what is the proof or strongest evidence that this agenda or conspiracy to have a world government, a New World Order, is for real?
Marrs: The strongest evidence is—number one—the activities of certain organizations and the flow of recent world events. Everybody from leading luminaries of the Council on Foreign Relations to the Trilateral Commission to the Bilderberg Group—they all talk about a New World Order. And we see these questionable trade agreements like NAFTA, and Bush and the former president of Mexico, Vicente Fox, signing up to this Security and Prosperity Partnership between Mexico and the United States. And now the controversial Trans-Pacific Partnership. Obviously, this is what they're working towards.

They're working towards globalism. They're creating free trade agreements and political agreements that supersede the power of national governments.
Yes, globalism. In fact, they call themselves globalists. And on the one hand I am not philosophically opposed to the idea of globalism. After all, we all share this planet called Earth. The problem is do we go in that direction with our eyes opened knowing what we're doing and working towards the betterment of everyone, or are we pushed and shoved by these globalists into a New World Order in which they rule as if over a fiefdom.

Many people believe that it's international bankers and, specifically, the patriarchs of the Rothschild banking family that have been and are behind the movement for world government. Do you believe that's true— that the Rothschilds and their international banking partners and the think tanks and organizations that they create and finance, for a couple of centuries now, have been the ringleaders for world government and the New World Order?
I think it's not as pat as a lot people would think. But, in general, I think that is true. Because if you go back you'll find that old man Rothschild put his five sons in charge of the central banks of France, Italy, Austria,

Germany, and England and they've been working for this. Now people would say, "yeah, well what about North America?" Well, North America has been done by their surrogates. The Rockefellers.

And Morgans.

And the Morgans. The reason I can say that is because in my research I found that John D. Rockefeller, who, of course, by the late 1800s had a complete lock on the petroleum industry of the world—the money he got to start in the oil business came from the Bank of Cleveland, which was a registered Rothschild bank.

Many people would probably say that this idea that the Rothschilds and international bankers are out "to control the world" is an irrational, crazy, stupid conspiracy theory. But in his private writings Cecil Rhodes said that the purpose of the Round Table Groups was for England to conquer the world. And the Rothschilds were the financial backers of Cecil Rhodes.

Exactly. And Rhodes made no bones about it. He called it a conspiracy. He called them a secret society. That's because they have the idea that they have the god-ordained right to rule and everybody else is just, you know, serfs.

Why do they think they're god-ordained?

Well, some of the Rothschilds claim that they're the direct descendants of Nimrod. Nimrod was the first king of Sumeria, and Sumeria was, of course, the first human civilization—in the area of what's now Iraq. About 5000 BC. Back then, the Sumerians considered their king a 'god' or a 'god-king'. So, these Rothschilds believe they're the descendants of the first 'god-king' of the first civilization, and, so, they're destined and have a right to control and rule.

The Freemasons also believe something like that, don't they? The top level Freemasons believe they have some sort of esoteric knowledge that nobody else has. And they see that many of the most important and influential men of history—prime ministers, presidents—have been Freemasons, and, so, they feel it's their destiny or right to rule and control.

Yes. And many of these New World Order people are Freemasons, or are, in some way, connected to Freemasonry.

Professor Dr. Carroll Quigley wrote that the purpose of the groups that evolved out of the Round Table Groups was to create a "world system" of financial control run in a feudalist fashion by the central banks of the world and that the Bank of International Settlements—the largest central bank in the world—was to be the apex of that system. The Bank of International Settlements was started and is owned by private banks that are owned by the Rothschilds and their associates, correct?

Well, yes, it's the central banks of the world that own the BIS and these banks are certainly Rothschild banks, and banks of the other international bankers. The Bank of England was very involved with the BIS and the Bank of England was always a big Rothschild bank.

Then there's the Bilderberg Group. The Bilderberg Group is a secretive meeting held once a year where the wealthiest, most powerful business-men in the world cozy up with the most important government offi-cials. Researchers claim that the ultimate aim of Bilderberg is to move nations to world government. The Bilderberg Group was created in 1952 by a man named Prince Bernard of the Netherlands. Prince Bernard was an employee of the Rothschilds, wasn't he?

Exactly. Prince Bernard ran Royal Dutch Shell. Shell Oil. One of the richest oil companies in the world. The Rothschilds were the principal stockholders.

In the present day, on the Rothschild family's own website, it's written, "We have been at the center of the world's money markets for more than two hundred years." If you're the richest guys in the world, it seems your influence is going to be seen all over politics. . . . In one of your books you wrote that the Rothschild influence "can be found behind the scene of many major world events."

Yes. . . . If you want another example, go back to the American Civil War and you find that that was greatly agitated by a secret society called the Knights of the Golden Circle which was set up by Dr. George Bickley of England who was connected to the Rothschilds.

So. it really doesn't seem to be a crazy, irrational conspiracy theory to say that the Rothschilds have a lot of control over world politics or are globalists who want to control a world government. There's seems to be good evidence for that. . . . The Rothschilds were, and are, of course, Jews. This interviewer is not anti-Semitic, and doesn't think you are, either. It isn't a Jewish conspiracy, is it?

No. It's not. It's not Jewish. I'm the first one to say it is not right or proper to discriminate against somebody because of their religion or because of their race.

Not all the people at the United Nations who are working to set up the Agenda 21 Plan are Jews. Not all the people who attend the Council on Foreign Relations and Bilderberg meetings are Jews. Not everybody who works in international banking is a Jew.

It's not a Jewish conspiracy.

It has been reported, though, that the Rothschilds were deeply involved with political Zionism—the movement to give Jews their own home-land—Israel—in the Middle East.

Well, when you look into it you can see that Israel is essentially a creation of the Rothschilds. Everybody knows about the Balfour Declaration—when, in 1917, Alfred Balfour, the Prime Minister of England, wrote a letter that said "Yes, we have no problem with a Jewish state in the Middle East." What most people don't understand is that letter was originally a response to Lord Rothschild who had said, "You don't mind if we set up a state in the Middle East?" The Balfour declaration is basically where Israel came from. And then, also, it was the Rothschilds who created the first pipeline and the first central bank in Israel, and, in fact, the Rothschilds have been called the grandfather of Israel.

This is another example of the enormous power and influence of this family of bankers.
Yes.

But anybody has a right to disagree with political Zionism and not be labeled an anti-Semite. A bigot or an anti-Semite is a closed-minded, ignorant, moronic person who is prejudiced against people simply on the basis of their religion, or race, or ethnicity. Anybody, though, has a right to disagree with Zionism. Or the ways of international banking.
Yes. They're two different things. And not all Jews are Zionists. And not all Zionists are Jews. It's two different things.

If you make the statement "Italians dominate the Mafia," you're not making an anti-Italian statement. Any sensible person knows that the great overwhelming majority of Italians have nothing to do with the Mafia. If you make the statement "International banking is corrupt and the Rothschilds dominate international banking," you're not making an anti-Semitic statement. The great overwhelming majority of Jews have nothing to do with the Rothschilds.
Yes, I agree.

So, so-called conspiracy theorists say that it's a group of interna-tional bankers—the Rothschilds and their associates, along with the organizations that they create—the Round Table Groups, the Council on Foreign Relations, the United Nations—that want to control a world government. Critics of that say that's nonsense, that's not true. But former Arizona senator Barry Goldwater, the Republican Party's 1964 presidential nominee, once wrote, "Most Americans have no real understanding of the operation of the international money lenders. The bankers want it that way. We recognize in a hazy sort of way that the Rothschilds and the Warburgs of Europe, and the houses of J. P. Morgan, Kuhn, Loeb and Company, Schiff, Lehman, and Rockefeller possess and control vast wealth. How they acquire this vast financial power and employ it is a mystery to most of us. . . . International bankers make money by extending credit to governments. The greater the debt of the political state, the larger the interest returned to the lenders. The national banks of Europe are actually owned and controlled by private interests." . . . So Barry Goldwater, himself, was saying that these international bankers manipulate the world economy and politics from behind the scenes and the public isn't really aware of that.

Well, most people don't even understand how modern money works. They think money represents something real and it does not, anymore. It's not on the gold standard. For example, if you want a mortgage on your house, you tell the bank, "I want a mortgage on my house," and, so, they create an account for you and debit it for the $200,000 or whatever the house is going to cost. They just type $200,000 into a computer and say, "Now you have this money and you have to pay it back plus interest."

Yes, they create money out of nothing.

They say this is what you owe, and then you pay and you pay and you pay and yet they just created this money out of thin air.

That's fractional reserve banking. Throughout the years the banking industry has lobbied governments and politicians to make fractional reserve banking legal. Through fractional reserve banking, a bank is allowed to lend out more money than it has in its reserves. If a bank has, say, 10 billion dollars it's allowed to lend out ten times as much—100 billion dollars. The bank is allowed to create 90 billion dollars out of thin air and lend that out and charge interest on it. . . . The bank just types a number into a computer or writes a number on a check and that becomes money.

Yes. The theory is that all the depositors aren't going to withdraw their $10 billion all at once so the banks will always have enough to repay the depositors. And, so, they create more money than they actually have.

So the banks are constantly making billions and billions and billions of dollars, creating money out of nothing that will eventually be paid back to them—plus the interest. Money just becomes numbers typed into a bank computer. But the middle class and lower classes of society will be destroyed because when you have billions of dollars of cheap money— money created out of nothing, money off the gold standard—circulating in society that will inevitably cause prices to rise. Inflation. And the middle class and the lower classes—the ninety-nine percent—will be wiped out by inflation. Destroyed economically.

Exactly.

But the banks—the 1 percent—will come to own 99 percent of the wealth of a society because they're being paid back billions of dollars that they created out of nothing. . . . Most people probably don't know about fractional reserve banking but anybody can research this and see that this is what banks do.

Yes.

And this is the legalized scam that we believe is destroying the American and world economy. And we also believe that the guys who are behind this scam—the international bankers—are the ones who want to have a world government.

Exactly. And, if you go back in US history, you find that early on one of the biggest fights between the colonists and the early Founding Fathers was whether or not to have a central bank. And Jefferson and all his liberal, freedom-loving people said, "No, a central bank always creates problems." But Alexander Hamilton, a rich guy, said "No, the rich guys should own a bank. The rich guys need to run this thing."

Alexander Hamilton was a big advocate for the First Bank of the United States which was chartered in 1791.

Yes. So, every time we had a central bank—they tried it about three times— people lost their homes, people were in debt, it was a problem. So, finally in the 1830s Andrew Jackson—who called the Second Bank of America a "den of thieves"—shut down the bank and from that point on—from about 1830 all the way up until 1913—that was the period that the United States economy just boomed. And then, of course, in 1913 they rammed through the Federal Reserve System. And we were back to a debt-producing, central bank situation.

And the evidence is that, over the years, the Rothschilds and their associates have created groups and think tanks and if you became a member of one of these "prestigious" groups you were groomed in and worked for the philosophy of world government. Sometimes members of these internationalist think tanks have slipped and made statements that clearly show that there is an agenda or conspiracy to do away with national governments and have a world government. Right?

Absolutely.

For instance, well-known British historian Arnold Toynbee was a professor at the London School of Economics, and was a member of Cecil

Rhodes's main Round Table Group in London. Toynbee once wrote, "I will hereby repeat that we are at present working discreetly but with all of our might to wrest this mysterious political force called sovereignty out of the clutches of the local national states of our world. And all the time we are denying with our lips what we are doing with our hands."
Yes. And that's a good quote to cite. Because they're doing it secretively; they're doing it behind closed doors. They're not openly saying, "We want a worldwide socialist system, a one-world currency. We want world government." They're trying to get there on the sly, surreptitiously.

How much influence does the Council on Foreign Relations have on our government and society?
It's been said and I agree that the Council on Foreign Relations *is* the State Department in the United States. They have determined foreign policy since prior to World War II.

Do you believe there's an agenda to have a North American Union—to have the United States, Canada, and Mexico merge into one union—and the Council on Foreign Relations is behind that?
Oh, absolutely. Again they talk about this openly—about creating a North American Union. The problem for them is that they were moving right along with that plan until—with the advent of the Internet—more and more people became aware of this plan and so there's been more and more foot dragging and it's caused them a problem.

Yes.
But, hey, if you want to see what the ultimate game plan is, go back and read a book that was written in 1948 by a British Fabian socialist by the name of Eric Arthur Blair. He didn't use that name, though. He used a pen name. George Orwell.

George Orwell.

Go back and read *1984* and you'll find what the plan is, which is to divide the world into three socialist blocks and then pit them off against each other alternately for maximum profit and control. And this is what they're working on.

Orwell was from England. Did Orwell write about that because he knew about the Round Table Groups? He had some inside information about what the men of the Round Table Groups were thinking and planning?

Yes, I think so. He was not part of the British aristocracy but he had very close contacts. He was a member of the Fabian socialists. And I think, yeah, I think he knew what the game plan was.

So when Orwell was writing 1984, *he wasn't just imagining a fictional story. He was writing about what he knew the most powerful men in the world—the men of England's Round Table Groups—were planning.*

Exactly. And when you look and see what's happening—Winston Smith, the protagonist of *1984,* you know, he said you couldn't even talk above a whisper without Big Brother listening in. And think about the surveillance that's going on today. The NSA being able to monitor our emails and phone calls. The ubiquitous video cameras surveilling everybody. And we now have appliances—TV sets—I believe it was Sony—they even warned, "Don't say anything you don't want out because it's two way and they're broadcasting back whatever's said in your living room."

That's happening with Google now, too. Google recently put a software program into Google Chrome so that whenever somebody's using Google Chrome it's listening in to whatever's being said around your computer and broadcasting it back to Google.

Yes. So, you know, *1984* was very prophetic. . . . In *1984* there were three main blocks. There was Oceania, Euroasia, and Eastasia. And now they have a European Union, and they want the North American Union and Asian Union.

It was in 2005 that President Bush, and President Fox of Mexico, and the Prime Minister of Canada, Paul Martin, created that Security and Prosperity Partnership of North America for the supposed purpose of creating greater cooperation between the countries. At that time, even CNN anchorman Lou Dobbs claimed that the real purpose of this agreement was to merge the US, Canada, and Mexico into the North American Union. So did the journalist Pat Buchanan, and Congressman Ron Paul, and some other legislators.

Right. There have been a number of well-known journalists and politicians who have spoken out against the movement to the North American Union.

So, they have a European Union and if they now want a North American Union and then an Asian Union then it seems the New World Order groups are trying to take away sovereignty and independence gradually, piece by piece. Maybe this is what Richard Gardner, a member of the Council on Foreign Relations, meant when he wrote in **Foreign Affairs** *in 1974, "The New World Order will have to be built from the bottom up rather than from the top down . . . but in the end run around national sovereignty, eroding it piece by piece will accomplish much more than the old-fashioned frontal assault."*

That certainly seems to be what he's talking about there. That came directly from the CFR's main publication. These guys are always alluding to a New World Order.

So researchers and many people believe that this New World Order agenda and philosophy came from the Illuminati, which merged with the Freemasons then went to the Rothschilds and international bankers, then to the Round Table Groups and then to the CFR and United Nations and

Trilateral Commission. There is also clear evidence that the Rothschild and Rockefeller banks funded Communism and that Communism was an apparent attempt of the New World Order groups to create a world government. Critics of this would say that all that is nonsense. All that is conspiracy theory rubbish. But in 1920, Winston Churchill himself wrote, "From the days of Adam Weishaupt, Karl Marx, Trotsky . . . this world conspiracy has been steadily growing. This conspiracy played a definite recognizable role in the tragedy of the French Revolution. It has been the mainspring of every subversive movement during the 19th century. And now at last this band of extraordinary personalities from the underworld of the great cities of Europe and America have gripped the Russian people by the hair of their head and have become the undisputed masters of that enormous empire." So Churchill himself said there was a conspiracy to have a world government that started with the Illuminati and was eventually adopted by the Communists and was behind the Russian Revolution.

Yes. And other people have talked about it. . . . The Bavarian Illuminati was very real. But today when people say the Illuminati they are not talking about any organized group. What they are talking about is a philosophy. So, today you have people like, oh, Dick Cheney, say. He certainly doesn't have a card in his pocket that says "Illuminati member." But he obviously subscribes to Illuminati philosophy, which is "the end justifies the means." Lie, cheat, steal, deceive people as to your real goals, you know, promise one thing, give them something else. Control from the top.

Globalism.

Globalism. So you can say that globalism itself is an adherent to Illuminati philosophy. So in that regard you could say, yeah, they're all Illuminati. But, you know this is where it throws a lot of people off. You try to say "well, the Illuminati's doing this" and the naysayers will say "well, there is no Illuminati anymore." And, technically, they're correct.

It's the philosophy.

Yes. The philosophy lives on.

A lot of people would agree with that—that there is no actual Illuminati organization anymore, but the philosophy is still very prevalent. But there are also a lot of people who believe that very powerful, influential, wealthy men meet in secret groups and they talk about controlling and manipulating the world and they still call themselves the Illuminati. . . . The international bankers Barry Goldwater talked about—the Rothschild-Warburg-Rockefeller international banking network— they were behind the funding of Communism and financed the Russian Revolution, correct?

Exactly. The money that financed all that can easily be traced back to them.

Most people probably haven't heard this, but you've written about this and other authors have written about this—when Leon Trotsky—a Communist leader—left New York to go to Russia right before the Revolution, it was with five million dollars given to him by the Wall Street banker Jacob Schiff, whose family had been close with the Rothschilds in Frankfurt, Germany. When Vladimir Lenin left Germany for Russia it was with five million dollars on a train trip arranged by Max Warburg, the Rothschilds' close associate. . . . All this has been documented, right? It's true.

It is true. It's verifiable, historical fact. The Rockefellers, Morgans, and other bankers associated with the Rothschilds were also involved with financing Communism.

Was Communism an attempt by the Rothschilds and their international banking partners to create a world government? They were trying to get to the New World Order and Big Brother through a Communist takeover of the world?

Yes, that was the whole idea. Even Jacob Schiff's grandson, John Schiff, said his grandfather had ultimately donated twenty million dollars to insure that the Bolshevik Revolution succeeded. And, in fact, Woodrow Wilson wrote that the bulk of money that went from the United States to Russia at the time of the Revolution in 1917 went to the Bolsheviks, not to the Kerensky government—not to the White Russians—who were trying to set up kind of a democratic system. It went to the Communists—to the regimes of Lenin and then Joseph Stalin who turned Russia into a totalitarian state bent on world domination, and who killed off twenty-five million of his own people.

The bankers who financed Communism—the movement that was supposed to wipe out Capitalism—were the richest capitalists in the world. But they apparently knew that if they financed and controlled Communism then they didn't have to fear it.
Yes, they were very much in control. They set up the Russian state.

It's been written that the globalist international bankers didn't care if a nation was Communist or capitalist as long as they were the ones who were lending money to the governments and controlling their leaders.
Yes, you know, Communist countries need money, too. And these are typical tactics for the New World Order. They buy out both sides of an argument—if there's a revolution they support both sides, if there's a war they support both sides. And, you see, that way it doesn't matter who wins—they don't care because they control both sides.

Karl Marx's idea of a World Communist Government was just the continuation of the vision of the Illuminatti, right? When Marx wrote **The Communist Manifesto** *in 1848 he belonged to a group—the Communist League—that was dominated by Freemasons. There were also a lot of exiled members of the Illuminati in that group.*

The evidence is that Marx was being manipulated by the secret societies—by the New World Order influences. He went on to write the Communist Manifesto and the ten planks of the Communist Manifesto—the ten ways to set up a perfect Communist state—were just about almost identical to the ten planks of the Illuminati Manifesto.

Yes, in the late 1700s, Adam Weishaupt had written the Illuminati Manifesto and had included ten ways—ten planks—to form the perfect world government. One of the planks, for instance, was to have a privately owned central bank, and another was to have a graduated income tax. And then the ten planks of **The Communist Manifesto** *that Karl Marx wrote were—as you said—almost the same exact thing that Weishaupt had written. It's obvious that Marx was being manipulated by the Illuminati and was just continuing the plan of the Illuminati.* That's right.

So, Communism arose from secretive groups like the Freemasons and Illuminati and was funded by the Rothschilds and their partners for the purpose of establishing and setting up and running their Totalitarian world government. Communism didn't arise and come from the downtrodden masses wanting to create a better world for the workers of the world. Well, that was the guise.

It was the secret societies trying to get to Big Brother and global fascism. Yeah, exactly, it was all totalitarianism. Again, read *1984*—you know, the Big Brother government was supposed to be the worker's paradise.

Winston Churchill made that statement—that there has been a conspiracy to have a world government that came from the Illuminati and given over to Marx and Trotsky and the Communists and was behind the Russian Revolution—Churchill made that statement in 1920. Do you think this idea that certain elite groups have that there should be a world government went away in 1920? Or is it still with us today?

Oh, no, no, it's advanced. What happened was at the end of World War I they tried to create the League of Nations. And the problem was everybody signed on to that except the United States. And that was because the Senate at that time apparently didn't feel like giving up our national sovereignty. So that led to World War II and then during the war the Allies suddenly became the United Nations and then after the war they actually set up the United Nations and that's been a controversial thing going on ever since. But if you go study Agenda 21 you'll find that the United Nations is now behind all kinds of movements to take over the property, to take over the land of the world.

It seems the conspiracy to have a world government is in the United Nations Agenda 21 Plan now. That's where it is.

Exactly, and, of course, again, this comes back to Illuminati philosophy. You never tell people what your real agenda is.

Yes, they're telling us that the purpose of the Agenda 21 Plan is to save the world from global warming. We're all going to have to stop using cars, certain household appliances, and move into the Agenda 21 living facilities and be monitored by the UN police so humanity will not be destroyed by global warming. . . . But the real agenda is, simply, that these guys are New World Order totalitarians who want to get us to globalism, Big Brother, and the New World Order.

That's it. And what's happening now is that the federal government is trying to take over all the property. In Nevada—eighty-five percent of the land in Nevada is owned by the federal government. Forty-four percent in California. And fifty percent in some of those other states. Now, nowhere in the Constitution does it say that the government's supposed to own all the property.

In 1995, President Bill Clinton signed an order to align the US government with the Agenda 21 Plan. Around that time, an organization called ICLEI, International Council for Local Environmental Initiatives, was formed. ICLEI representatives are now going around America to get local governments to accept the Agenda 21 Plan. Maybe the government is buying up all the land so that it can eventually hand the land over to the United Nations and the Agenda 21 organization? Under the Agenda 21 Plan there's to be no private property. All property will be owned by the State.

Yes. And who knows if this will pan out. Maybe they'll never get Agenda 21 up and running. But they're trying.

Most people probably haven't heard of this either but the international banking globalists—the Rothschild-Warburg-Rockefeller network—also funded Adolf Hitler and the Nazis, correct?

That's right. A number of non-German American and European banks and corporations were involved with financing the Nazis.

Recently released records from the National Archives and also Treasury Department records show that American and European companies and banks helped finance the Nazis. A number of mainstream media outlets have also reported this.

Yes, it's true. It's been documented.

Why did the globalist bankers finance Hitler? Were they trying to get to world domination in any way they could? Was their reasoning that if a Communist takeover of the world didn't work out then maybe they could get to world government and Fascism through a Nazi takeover?

I'd say yes. And again this goes back to their modus operandi—to always control both sides of a conflict, both sides of any war.

And selling arms for a war can be the most profitable business in the world, can't it? It's been written that the Rothschild formula is to sell arms to both sides of a war because that's enormously profitable.

Yes, of course. . . . Two of the largest banks involved with sending money to Hitler and the Nazis—one was the Schroder Bank. The Schroder Bank was represented in the United States by the law firm of Sullivan and Cromwell, and the people in charge of it were John Foster Dulles and Allen Dulles. John Foster, of course, became secretary of state after the war and Allen Dulles was the longest-serving CIA director. The other bank was Union Banking Corporation and its director who was in charge with funding Hitler was Prescott Bush. And he was actually prosecuted in late 1942, halfway through World War II, as being nothing but a front man for Hitler and the Nazis.

A lot of people would be shocked and wouldn't want to accept that—that a father and grandfather of two US presidents helped finance Hitler. But even the **Washington Times** *recently reported that newly released government documents show that the Union Banking Corporation helped finance the Nazis.*

Yes.

The main point of your book **The Rise of the Fourth Reich** *is the desire that the Nazis had for world domination—what they called the Third Reich—is the same desire that the globalist have today for a New World Order because the same banks and corporations that financed the Nazis are behind the movement for the New World Order today.*

Yes, that's right. For instance, the Rockefellers. In the 1920s, the Rockefellers' Standard Oil company became partners with IG Farben, a German company that was the largest chemical company in the world. In 1930, IG Farben provided the majority of the money for Hitler's reelection campaign. IG Farben became the German war machine's key component, the principal financial backer of Nazi Germany. They produced the Zyklon B gas which was used on the Jews in the concentration camps. After the war, thirteen of IG Farben's Nazi executives were convicted of war crimes at the Nuremberg trails. After they got out of prison, they became the heads of some of the world's biggest and most influential banks and corporations.

The fact that the Rockefellers were part owners of IG Farben and IG Farben was a financial backer of Nazi Germany has been written about by a number of authors, correct? There are numerous resources that verify that.
Absolutely. It's historical fact.

Other so-called respectable banks and corporations did business with IG Farben as well, right?
Yes, DuPont and others . . . The Bank of International Settlements funneled money to the Nazis . . . Ford owned Volkswagen . . . General Motors and General Electric were there . . . J. P. Morgan banks and companies were involved with Nazi Germany.

Chase Manhattan Bank too, right? Chase is the Rockefellers' main bank.
And other big New York banks. It's recently been revealed that Chase Manhattan, J. P. Morgan, and a couple other big banks seized the bank assets of some Jews in Paris during the war and actually handed all that over to the Nazi occupiers.

Chase Bank apparently had a lot to do with Nazi Germany. Newsweek has reported that during the war the chief of the Chase branch in Paris wrote to his Chase superior in Manhattan that the bank enjoyed "very special esteem" with top German officials and "a rapid expansion of profits."
Exactly.

So many so-called respectable men and corporations can be connected to the Nazis.
Yes.

Prince Bernhard of the Netherlands, the guy who was the head of Shell Oil—the guy who started the Bilderberg Group—Prince Bernhard was a Nazi officer, wasn't he?

Yes, he was . . . When Prince Bernhard was once asked about his time as a Nazi officer, he said, "Yes. We had a good time."

A man named John J. McCloy, who was once the chairman of Chase Bank and the director of the Council on Foreign Relations—a man whom the media called "the chairman of the American establishment"—sat next to Adolf Hitler at the 1936 Summer Olympics in Berlin.

Right.

And then after the war, the US government brought over 1,500 Nazi intelligence officials and scientists to help set up some government departments and the CIA.

Yes, that was called Project Paperclip. The government apparently felt that the Nazis had a very sophisticated, advanced intelligence operation. So about 1500 Nazis were very instrumental in helping to form the CIA.

A lot of people, though, would probably say it sounds illogical and incongruous to say that the Rothschilds and other Jewish bankers would help finance the anti-Semitic monster Adolf Hitler.

Well, the answer to that, you see, would be that the Rothschilds and the other globalists don't have an allegiance to anything but globalism and world domination and internationalism. They don't have any allegiance to any nation, or even to their own people, the Jews. Yes, they were behind Zionism and the creation of Israel but their ultimate allegiance is to globalism. Their first identification is internationalism. World power.

But it seems they wanted another war so they could form the United Nations.

I'd say so. After World War I, their attempt at world government—the League of Nations—had failed. So they needed to create another conflict—World War II—and then offer another solution of globalism—the United Nations. Then right after the war a lot of so-called "prestigious" well-financed groups sprang up calling for world government through the UN. . . . James Warburg—the son of Paul Warburg, one of the founders of the CFR—began a group called the United World Federalists and actually had a number of senators and congressmen on the verge of agreeing that the United Nations should be the world government. In a hearing before the United States Senate, in like 1950, Warburg said, "We shall have world government whether or not we like it. The only question is whether world government will be achieved by conquest or consent."

And, as you said, one of the main banks that financed the Nazis was the Bank of International Settlements.

Exactly, yes. Money from the Bank of England—a Rothschild bank—and other European and American banks were funneled through the BIS to the Nazis. And the directors of the Bank of International Settlements weren't connected to the Nazis. They *were* Nazis. Walther Funk and Hermann Schmitz were some of the directors of the BIS in the '30s and '40s who were also Nazi officials. Some of them were convicted at the Nuremburg trials and went to prison after the war. . . . The BIS was a Nazi bank. This is historical fact that has been verified.

And the Bank of International Settlements is, of course, the bank that Professor Carroll Quigley said the secret societies, the globalist bankers, want to control the world through.

It's the central bank of the central banks. It still is. Quigley said it was being manipulated by the secret societies, yes.

So, the BIS is the central bank, the most powerful bank, in the world today . . . and the BIS acts with total secrecy, doesn't it? The BIS has been set up so that its offices are on international land and so it's not a part of any country and doesn't have to answer to any nation or police force. It's independent and sovereign to itself. The BIS pays no taxes and doesn't have to show its books to anyone. It's private bankers running the world in any way they want without oversight from anyone.
That's right. That's the way it operates.

The BIS sets interest rates and banking policies that all the rest of the central banks of the world follow. . . . And in 2009 the BIS created a committee called the Financial Stability Board. When President Obama signed an agreement that America would be part of the Financial Stability Board, that gave even more power to the BIS to control America and the American economy. . . . Obama was just a puppet of the banks and Wall Street like every other president.
Exactly. When Obama made us a part of the Financial Stability Board, he was essentially turning over financial control of America to a handful of central bankers. Now all the most important financial institutions of America and all the G20 nations answer to the Financial Stability Board.

These are private bankers—unelected officials—working behind the scenes to control America and the world economy in any way they want. . . . It's the actions of the Bank of International Settlements that determine the economic conditions of the world. Their decisions shape our lives. Just by the interest rates they set, the BIS will make or break an economy. They control foreign exchange currencies, and the price of gold. They decide if they want austerity or growth in the economy. It's the actions of the BIS that determine if there's going to be unemployment or employment. A healthy economy or an unhealthy economy.

Yes. Their actions basically determine the economic conditions of every man, woman, and child on the face of the earth.

This is the New World Order. This is what Carroll Quigley said the secret societies wanted. Unelected officials—private bankers—working in secret to control the world.

You might say The New World Order has already arrived.

When the central bankers of the world meet at BIS meetings, the main thing they're talking about is how to put more money in their pockets. These are privately owned banks. Their principal aim is to make the banks more profitable. All these bankers are constantly changing jobs within the banking industry—sometimes they're working at the BIS, sometimes they're at the smaller central banks, sometimes they're at the big commercial banks. These bankers want higher salaries. The actions that the BIS is taking are so the banks profit more and the bankers get higher salaries, and if those actions happen to be bad for the public and the economy, then that's not really their concern.

I would say that it is human nature that if people are allowed so much unchecked power and influence then they are going to use that power and influence for their own gains.

America isn't supposed to borrow money from a central bank, or be controlled by a central bank, correct? The Constitution states that "only Congress shall coin and regulate the currency." According to the Constitution, the government is supposed to raise money through import and excise taxes, and that's the money that's supposed to circulate in the country. America isn't supposed to borrow more and more from the Federal Reserve—with interest rates set by the BIS—and go trillions of dollars into debt.

Right. We're under a debt-producing money system. We shouldn't have to borrow from a central bank, or be controlled by a central bank—let alone a central bank in a foreign country.

If the government supplies the currency through import and excise taxes, then there would be no debt because we're not borrowing money. If the money is issued on the gold standard or in proper proportion with the expansion of goods and services, then there would be no inflation. Then the government is just supposed to stay out of the way and people get paid for the work they do and people would be fine financially because there's no inflation and no enormous debt to pay off. The economy would be sound. That's the way it's supposed to work.

But as it is now, we're all at the mercy of the Bank of International Settlements. Because we borrow money from a central bank, the Federal Reserve—because all the most important banks of the world are connected to this global banking monopoly—then if the BIS decides to raise interests rates a tiny bit then, can cause millions or billions of dollars to be taken out of circulation. That small act can cause a severe recession and severe unemployment. That's unfortunately how it is.

So if the BIS is controlling our world economy—and that's the bank that financed Hitler—then what kind of world are we living in? Exactly. And that lends tremendous support to the people that claim that it's these international bankers that are trying to run everything.

So if it's true that the international banking globalists financed Hitler, then this is just another reason to conclude that the New World Order can't possibly be a benevolent agenda. If it was benevolent then they should put everything on the table, and everybody should see exactly what they're doing, and they should say,

"This is the way to go, here's what we're doing, everybody get behind us." But, no, it's all done with secrecy.

The Bank of International Settlements acts with complete, utter secrecy . . . and the Bilderberg Group acts that way, too. The press isn't allowed near the meetings, and the people who attend the meetings are sworn to secrecy.
That's right. That's the way they operate.

There's another very influential group—the Bohemian Grove—that acts secretively. Once a year, for a few days, the most powerful government officials in the world—secretaries of state, secretaries of treasury, vice presidents, future presidents—meet in a campground in the woods in California, and the press doesn't report on it and the men who attend the meetings never talk about it.
That's right. Why is there so much secrecy? Is this the way a democracy is supposed to be run?

Some people would say that the New World Order is just about the big banks and corporations wanting more power. Others would say that the New World Order is more of a conspiracy—that elite men form secret groups and believe they're the Masters and Elites of the world who will someday be in control of a Big Brother Government. What do you think—is the New World Order just banks and corporations wanting more political power—or is it Elites secretly conspiring to control a world government? Considering what we've been talking about, it would seem you would say that it's a conspiracy.
Yes, but the answer to that is both. You got people at the very top who really want to try to dominate the world. They're globalists. And then under them are people who are looking to feather their own nest. They just want more and more money. They're greedy.

One of the main points of your books, though, is that secret societies have always been manipulating our world. It very well could be that there are powerful men who meet in secret and they believe they're the Elites and Masters of the world and . . .

Well, there are. They meet at the Bilderbergs under armed guards and nobody knows what they're talking about.

A lot of people would say that the New World Order is going to come as a result of a financial crisis—they believe it's inevitable that there's going to be an economic depression worse than the 1930's and that will cause millions of people to become unemployed and homeless so they'll have no choice but to move into the Agenda 21 camps. Do you think that's how they want to do it—get to the New World Order by destroying the economy?

Well, this seems to be the path that they're on. I mean, they just keep printing money. And as my old dad used to say, "There comes a time when you have to pay the fiddler." And one of these days we're going to have to pay the fiddler and there's not going to be any money and the whole thing is going to be like a house of cards and it's all going to collapse. You cannot simply borrow indefinitely.

Then millions of people might have no choice but to move into the Agenda 21 camps.

Exactly. And that's why these New World Order people—a great many of them—can trace their heritage back into the Freemasons. And the Masons' motto is, of course, *Ordo ab Chao*, which means "order out of chaos." It's the Hegelian dialectic—it comes from the writings of the German philosopher George Hegel. Hegel said if you have some goal in mind then you yourself should cause a conflict and then you offer the solution and the solution is the goal you wanted. Well, these globalists figured out early on "Why wait for a problem? We'll create the problem. And then offer the solution." So, you know, if there's a worldwide economic breakdown, they'll say, "The systems aren't working. We need a world currency. We need a world government."

Yes, because you, and other researchers believe that the international bankers, the elites, and the New World Order groups know that the world's economy is being destroyed and they know that they're the ones causing that. And they wouldn't mind that happening. Because if all the economies and nations are destroyed, then everybody will have to accept a new system.

Well, as I said, you can't borrow indefinitely. And I think they realize that a collapse is inevitable and that's why today they are making decisions that are obviously not in the best interest of this country. What they're doing is they are siphoning every last drop of money out of this system, trying to get it out of there while they still can.

If you look at all these banking scandals, it seems obvious that they couldn't happen unless the bankers and those in charge are intentionally letting them happen.

That's right. In the past few years, you're going to find that there are hundreds of major banking officials in the world who have either died off, or resigned, or stepped down. I think they're fleeing the system. Of course, they're never going to tell people that because they want people to continue to buy stocks and bonds and keep consuming and keep operating the system.

Did you ever read G. Edward Griffin's well known book on the Federal Reserve, The Creature from Jekyll Island? In his book, Griffin presents what he feels is a realistic scenario as to how we might lose our liberties and freedoms and be shepherded into the New World Order. According to Griffin's book, it is not unrealistic to foresee a future when the banks and banking system lead America and the world into an unfixable, catastrophic financial breakdown, similar to but worse than what happened in 2008 with the mortgage crisis. A financial meltdown that destroys the economy and forces millions of people into poverty, unemployment, hunger, and homelessness. In Griffin's scenario, this would lead to social chaos and the government would declare a state of martial law, and then send in the United Nations troops to round up the masses and place them in fenced-off work camps. The State would bail out and come to own all businesses and industries. And we'd find ourselves in the New World Order. . . . Do you think that's realistic?

Well, yes, it could happen that way. Maybe. That's one realistic scenario. Griffin has very keen perceptions about things and is an astute writer. So, yes, I think he is presenting a realistic possibility there.

The principal author of the Agenda 21 Plan was a man named Maurice Strong who was the one time Under-Secretary-General of the United Nations.

Yes.

Maurice Strong—who died in November 2015—had written articles and made statements that the wealthiest nations are destroying the environment and can't go on using cars, air conditioners, electronic household appliances, and living in expansive suburban housing. He, like the rest of the New World Order people, apparently believed the masses had to live like Third World serfs in order that the environment be saved. And this is what the Agenda 21 Plan is—a plan to force humanity to accept a decline in their standard of living and live like serfs in a collectivist, classless society.

Yes, if you read the statements and papers of these globalists, it seems they want the world to be in two classes: the super rich class, themselves; and then the poor, the serfs—all the rest of us. This is a typical totalitarian model, you know. And if you look at what's happening now—the middle class seems to be getting wiped out and what's going to be left is the super rich and the poor.

But Maurice Strong didn't live like a serf, did he? Maurice Strong was a multimillionaire capitalist who made a large fortune in the oil industry and lived a lavish lifestyle. It's also likely that Strong was involved with the UN Oil for Food scandal that led to many UN officials being indicted for corruption and money embezzling.
Yes.

When it looked like Maurice Strong was about to be indicted, he quit the UN and ran away to live in China where he couldn't be arrested. . . . So the main author of the Agenda 21 Plan—the man who believed he knew how the rest of the world should live—was probably a corrupt big businessman who lived on the lam from the law for the last few years of his life.
Probably.

A story that appeared in the Canadian magazine **West** *back in the 1990's might prove that the wealthy elite of the world are planning to bankrupt the world so they can form a new government. . . . Back in 1990, a* **West** *magazine journalist named Daniel Wood spent some time interviewing Maurice Strong. During that interview, Strong told Wood that he was planning to write a novel. In the novel the richest men in the world are meeting at the World Economic Forum in Davos, Switzerland. The men agree that the people of the rich nations of the world are destroying the environment but are not going to accept a decline or loss of their lifestyles, so, the men decide that they have to force the industrialized, wealthy countries to collapse, and they form a secret society to bring about economic collapse. These men have the most powerful positions in the world's commodities and stock markets, and they engineer, using their access to stock exchanges and computers and gold supplies, a* *financial breakdown and panic. And the economies of the wealthiest nations are destroyed. . . . After telling Wood this, Maurice Strong said to him, "I probably shouldn't be saying things like this."*

Well, Maurice Strong is talking about writing a novel there but it's a novel based on reality—on what might actually happen. Maurice Strong attended the World Economic Forum. He knew all the millionaires and billionaires there. He was one of them himself. So Maurice Strong's novel is what these men might actually do. Or what he, himself, heard them talking about.

Maybe this interview should have been just about the Agenda 21 Plan, because the Agenda 21 Plan seems to be the specific way that the New World Order groups want to manipulate society into the world government.

Maybe. A number of countries signed on to the Agenda 21 Plan at that Earth Summit in Rio in the '90's. Then Bill Clinton signed an order to start implementing the Agenda 21 Plan. Whether they ever get this Agenda 21 Plan up and running or not, just the fact that this exists—a plan to hand all land and sovereignty to a United Nations government—the fact that this *just* exists—that tells you a lot right there.

There were actually two principal authors of the Agenda 21 Plan. Maurice Strong was one. And it's been reported that the other principal author of the Agenda 21 Plan was Steven Rockefeller, Nelson Rockefeller's son.

I'm not sure.

Well, even if it's been inaccurately reported that Steven Rockefeller—a college professor—was one of the authors, this Steven Rockefeller is very active in advocating for the Agenda 21 Plan.

Well, that wouldn't be hard to believe.

When the Rockefellers donated the land on the East River in Manhattan where the United Nations building was built in the 1940s, it was because

the Rockefellers are part of the globalist international bankers who want to have a world government.
Exactly.

Do you believe that the Agenda 21 Plan came from **The Report from Iron Mountain?**
Yes. Yes, I actually do.

It's been reported that back in the early 1960s a group of government connected people—probably CFR members—met in secret at a location in upstate New York. The purpose of the meeting was to decide how society can be controlled if it can't be controlled by war. Traditionally, governments have always been able to unite and control a society through war. The government says, "We'll provide your defense and this is the enemy we have to fight" and, so, society comes together for a common cause— a war. But the men of the Iron Mountain report were concerned that if there ever comes a time when there are no national governments—when there's a world government—then how could they then control the public? If there's a one-world government then there would be nobody for the government to declare a war against and, so, no way to keep society unified and compliant. So these men wrote a report—The Report from Iron Mountain—and concluded that society could be controlled by scaring the public with an environmental disaster. For instance, if the people were told, "You all have to live in a certain way otherwise global warming will destroy us all" then government can bring a society under control.
Yes, but if you go on Google or you ask most people they're just going to tell you *"The Report from Iron Mountain* is just a hoax. It didn't happen." But that's not true because I have on my bookshelf a hardbound copy of the original release. And the report there is just too sophisticated to be written by anybody other than knowledgeable government people. I have also talked to people—including some military people—who were working

with Henry Kissinger at the time back in '61, '62, and they told me "Yes, he left quite frequently to go to upstate to work on the program."

Military people told you that Henry Kissinger was one of the authors of **The Report from Iron Mountain?**
Yeah, so, it's very real. The report was brought to a publisher by an anonymous person who had attended the meetings. And, afterwards, the publisher—I think somebody twisted his arm—he said, "Oh, well, this was nonsense. It was just a hoax." But, no, this was very real. Yes, they were concerned with how to control a society if there was no war. But also—this took place in '61, '62, right after John F. Kennedy had just been elected president, and I think they knew that he was truly working to end the Cold War and bring about peace. And, so, this concerned them. They say all this in *The Report from Iron Mountain*—that to provide for the common defense is the basic foundation for government and if peace breaks out then how are they going to control the public.

And their conclusion was that the public could be controlled with an environmental panic. And this is exactly what the Agenda 21 Plan is.
Yes.

When **The Report from Iron Mountain** *was published, it sold a lot of books. When that happened all these government officials and White House officials had to deny it and say it was a hoax, because The Report from Iron Mountain makes the government look like a bunch of Adolf Hitlers. It has such a totalitarian, fascist tone to it. Even President Lyndon Johnson released a few statements saying that* **The Report from Iron Mountain** *had nothing to do with the government or government officials.*
Yes, but it was real.

Maybe at the deepest level the real purpose of the Iron Mountain meeting was to find a way to get to Big Brother. The Agenda 21 Plan is a plan to get to Big Brother.

Maybe that was the whole purpose.

A lot of people still claim—as you said—that the Iron Mountain report was faked. But John Kenneth Galbraith, the world famous Harvard University economics professor, said he knew the report was real because he participated in the meetings.

The meetings were held at a huge underground office at Iron Mountain near Hudson, New York, which is the site of the Hudson Institute, a Council on Foreign Relations think tank. The underground meeting place was actually a nuclear fallout shelter that contained offices for Rockefeller's Standard Oil, one of the Morgan banks, and Shell Oil.

The media always cites the reports of scientists who claim that global warming will destroy the earth. But there are just as many scientists who claim that global warming isn't a danger, aren't there?

Yes, there are. There are plenty of scientists who will tell you that global warming is not going to destroy our planet.

Most Republicans in Washington don't believe in the global warming scare . . . and the scientists who say that global warming isn't a danger are just as qualified as these other scientists, aren't they?

Yes. But these aren't the scientists that the mainstream media lets you hear about.

So do you think that the global warming scare is nonsense? It's just propaganda to get us to accept Agenda 21?

It's obvious there's climate change taking place. But whether this is natural or unnatural is open to question. There are certain places in the world where it's been colder the last few years than anytime else. But here's the main thing—there is climate change but whatever's doing that—I'm sorry Al Gore—it is not us just driving our SUVs. And I say that because something is impacting or changing in our entire solar system. The polar caps on Mars are diminishing, which mean they're melting. We've got ice melting on the moons of Jupiter. We've got outer planets which are becoming more luminescent, which means they're warming up. So something is changing.

But there's no imminent danger or emergency, is there? It's not about to melt our planet, is it?
I wouldn't think so. I wouldn't think we would have to worry about it for a few hundred thousand years. And, plus, we all know the sun goes through cycles. It could be just a cycle. Although, I am keeping a very sharp eye on this idea that there's a huge body, a tenth planet that's coming into our solar system on an elliptical plane. Because this certainly could account for some of these changes and if it is a huge body then the gravitational electromagnetic effect of that would be causing permutations.

In **The Report from Iron Mountain** *it's written a number of times that the environmental scare used to control society doesn't have to be real. They say it can be faked . . . as long as the public believes it.*
Well, then you might consider this more of the legacy of the Illuminati. You know, lie and cheat to get what you want. The whole thing very well might have been a Council on Foreign Relations operation. It might have been commissioned from the highest levels of government—from Defense Secretary Robert McNamara. The founder of the Hudson Institute was a man named Herman Kahn. Both McNamara and Kahn were members of the CFR.

The Agenda 21 Plan is laid out in an official three hundred page document that anyone can order and read. The basic premise behind Agenda 21—as we've already mentioned—is that global warming is eventually going to become so threatening that everyone will have to move into Agenda 21 cities where no cars, air conditioners, or other modern conveniences that add to global warming will be allowed. Everyone will have the same living quarters—a sparse apartment and bunk—and will ride their bike or walk to work. No one will be allowed to leave the Agenda 21 cities which will be surrounded by thousands of acres of wild land. . . . It sounds like a science fiction novel. It sounds crazy.

Yes.

But here's where it gets really crazy. In the Agenda 21 Plan it says that these thousands of acres of wild land surrounding the Agenda 21 villages will be filled with hundreds of large carnivorous animals—bears, wolves, mountain lions, bobcats, etc. . . . Did you hear about that?

I've heard that. That would take some doing. I don't know about that.

It's the craziest thing you ever heard in your life. It's written right into the Agenda 21 Plan.

Yes.

You get the clear feeling that they want to surround the Agenda 21 villages with hundreds of carnivorous animals so that people won't try to leave and escape the Agenda 21 villages. . . . Where did they get such an idea? One of **The Hunger Games** *movies?*

Well, I don't know about that. As I mentioned, I don't know if they'll ever get the Agenda 21 up and running. Maybe. But a lot of the things they talk about sound crazy—and when I say "they" I'm talking about the wealthy ruling elite. The Club of Rome is another internationalist New World Order think tank and if you look at some of their reports they talk about—yes—having everybody, all the serfs, living in cities under constant surveillance and then actually embedding a microchip under the skin of our wrists. And unless you have this microchip you can't buy or sell anything or travel anywhere.

Yes. Even ABC and NBC News and other sources have reported that certain companies are working on developing microchips that can be embedded into people for surveillance, identification, or other purposes.
Yes. Just the fact that these sort of plans exist—that tells you something right there. Who knows how far the New World Order people will get with their plans for totalitarianism? But it's happening. It's certainly a legitimate danger and something we should be aware of.

Do you believe that our mainstream media and our most important journalists can be relied on, or are they being influenced and manipulated by the corporate, New World Order influences?
The media is a tool of the New World Order. So many of the media outlets are being run by Council on Foreign Relations people. They're owned by the corporate people who attend the Bilderberg meetings. They're just out to make money. The media outlets are delivery systems for the advertisers.

It's true that so many of America's most powerful and influential journalists are or have been members of the Council on Foreign Relations and it's believed they're being censored or manipulated—knowingly or unknowingly—in one way or another. Take, for instance, the most iconic journalist in the history of America: Walter Cronkite. Cronkite once accepted an award at the United Nations, and in his acceptance speech, Cronkite said: "It seems to many of us that if we are to avoid the eventual catastrophic world conflict we must strengthen the United Nations as a first step toward a world government patterned after our own government with a legislature, executive, and judiciary, and police to enforce its international laws and keep the peace. To do that, of course, we Americans will have to yield up some of our sovereignty. That would be a bitter pill. It would take a lot of courage, a lot of faith in the new order. Pat Robertson has written that we should have a world government, but only when the messiah arrives. He wrote, literally, any

attempt to achieve world order before that time must be the work of the devil. Well, join me. I'm glad to sit here at the right hand of Satan."
Well, it looks like they got to old Cronkite, right?

Walter Cronkite probably wasn't at the top echelon—the inner circle— of the Council on Foreign Relations. The people at the bottom level of the CFR don't really understand what the people at the top are doing, right? The people at the top level of the CFR are Illuminati-like control freaks who want to rule over the world like elite dictators. But the people on the lower levels of the CFR are probably told "We want a United Nations world government because it will bring peace to the world and make the world a better place." And Walter Cronkite was probably a well-meaning person and believed that. What Cronkite didn't realize is that the real purpose of a United Nations world government is to get us to fascism and totalitarianism.
Yes, and this is something that Cecil Rhodes and Adam Weishaupt said— that the secret society is run by "circles within circles." "Circles within circles" means the guys at the bottom don't know what the guys at the top are really planning. A pyramid structure of control. Cecil Rhodes and Adam Weishaupt said this themselves.

You believe, don't you, that any politician who gets to be the Democratic or Republican presidential nominee—the most important Democrats and Republicans—are being lobbied and controlled by Wall Street, by the CFR, Trilateral Commission and Bilderberg Group?
I'd say so, yes. I think that's obvious. They're controlling both the Democrats and Republicans.

Take Bill and Hillary Clinton. Both Clintons have attended a Bilderberg meeting. Both are members of the CFR. Bill Clinton was a Rhodes Scholar. Do you know if the Rhodes Scholar students are trained in the idea of collectivism and the idea that there should be a world government? Because the Rhodes Scholarship was established in accordance with Cecil Rhodes's will and was first administered by Nathan Rothschild.

Yes, absolutely. That's Cecil Rhodes. Rothschild. That network of influence. They're groomed in the idea of collectivism. Globalism.

One has to wonder if the Rhodes Scholars are groomed in the idea of world government because of a statement made by a man named Strobe Talbott. Strobe Talbott was a fellow Rhodes Scholar and close friend of Bill Clinton's. When Clinton became president, he appointed Talbott his deputy secretary of state. In a 1992 **Time** *magazine interview, Talbott said: "In the next century, nations as we know it will be obsolete; all states will recognize a single global authority and realize national sovereignty wasn't such a great deal after all."*

I've heard that quote, yes. He's making no bones about it. Why doesn't the mainstream media do an investigation of what he's talking about? Strobe Talbott was, obviously, influenced by and is working for the New World Order.

A statement recently made by General James L. Jones, President Obama's national security adviser, could make you believe the theory that the New World Order groups are controlling the government. Henry Kissinger has been a long time member of the CFR, the Trilateral Commission, and Bilderberg, and is considered to be one of the main ringleaders for the New World Order. In a speech made on February 9, 2009, national security adviser General James L. Jones said, "As the most recent national security adviser of the United States, I take my daily orders from Dr. Kissinger, filtered down through General Brent Scowcroft and Sandy Berger, who is also here. We have a chain of command in the National Security Council that exists today." Why is Henry Kissinger running the National Security Council?

That's a good question. Why is he? Kissinger hasn't held an official government position since—what—the Ford administration? But he's running the NSC? This would clearly seem to lend good support to the claim that the globalists, a shadow government—the New World Order think tanks—are running the government.

Two of the most famous novels of the twentieth century were the dystopian novels 1984 *by George Orwell and* **Brave New World** *by Aldous Huxley. Both novels were about a future time when a Totalitarian-Fascist world government is running the world. We've already talked about Orwell. But Aldous Huxley was from England, too, right? And Huxley's family seems to have had very close connections to the British aristocracy and to the men of the Round Table Groups who were planning a New World Order.* Yes, absolutely. And Huxley's thing—in *Brave New World*—all the citizens were on the drug Soma. Which drugged everybody out and made them compliant. Well, all you have to do is look at the statistics and it seems like more than half our population is on some anti-depressant, or some drug that's zonking them out and sedating them. It's like the *Brave New World*.

Huxley seemed very close to the New World Order groups. In one interview, Huxley said, "It is inevitable that in the future an elite class will rule the world." . . . *And Aldous Huxley once wrote this in an essay:*

> "There will be, in the next generation or so, a pharmacological method of making people love their servitude, and producing dictatorship without tears, so to speak, producing a kind of painless concentration camp for entire societies, so that people will in fact have their liberties taken away from them, but will rather enjoy it, because they will be distracted from any desire to rebel by propaganda or brainwashing, or brainwashing enhanced by pharmacological methods. And this seems to be the final revolution."

Yes. Huxley knew what was happening. Both Huxley and Orwell were well connected to the British aristocracy and in their books *Brave New World* and *1984* I think they actually were reflecting what they knew the game plan was.

And Huxley taught Orwell, didn't he? Huxley was some sort of mentor to Orwell, wasn't he?
Huxley was a teacher at one of the English schools that Orwell went to.

The government that would exist if the Agenda 21 Plan is implemented is very much like the governments described in Huxley's and Orwell's novels. So if the New World Order globalists ever successfully get the Agenda 21 Plan up and running, then the **Brave New World** *and* **1984** *will have arrived?*
It will have arrived.

In your books you recommend a number of things we can do to take our country and world back from the influence of the New World Order. Two things seem to really stand out: The first thing is we need a Third Party. We need independent candidates. People need to understand that both the Democrats and Republicans are being controlled by the same special interests, right?
Absolutely.

Is there any purpose in voting for either the Democratic or Republican nominee for president? Both those guys are put there by the Council on Foreign Relations, and the Bilderberg Group, and Wall Street, right? There's not going to be a significant difference if the Democrat or the Republican gets into the White House.
No, I see no purpose. Throughout my whole career, I would always preach to people, "If you don't go vote then you're not participating and you have no right to complain." But I'm changing my tune because of the computer

voting fraud and the lack of paper trails and the money from the corporations that's going into the candidates. And the control over the major news outlets, and media. You know, it is so rigged . . . let me put it this way—I don't watch the World Wrestling Federation because it's fixed. And, likewise, now I don't think voting does you any good because it's fixed.

Unless we get a third party. An honest, third party candidate who understands that we have to eliminate the Federal Reserve. A candidate who doesn't appoint members of the CFR or Trilateral Commission to his administration, who's going to defend the US Constitution and American sovereignty, who is a populist and has the people's welfare in mind, and who isn't controlled by lobbyists and covert groups and secret government.

Yes. Unless somebody comes along who is a third party. Right now, the only person I see who, I think, is trying to be that is Donald Trump. And I've got a lot of reservations about him.

But if Trump is really against the political establishment and the New World Order, then it seems his presidency will be sabotaged in one way or another.

Oh, absolutely. They don't take competition lightly. If you go back through the US presidents, you'll find that starting with Andrew Jackson, who shut down the latest edition of a central bank—the Second Bank of the United States, he called them "a den of vipers'—he was the first US president to suffer an assassination attempt. Now he lived through it, so you don't hear much about that—but they certainly tried it. In fact, the rumors, even at that time, were that this had all been instigated by bankers in Europe. And, then, you go forward, and, of course, you have Abraham Lincoln who tried to issue his own private money—greenbacks—and not pay interest to the international bankers. He was shot in the head. And then you've got John F. Kennedy who in June of 1963 issued $4.2 billion dollars in silver backed treasury notes—real currency that no interest had to be paid on—and he got shot in the head.

It's extremely difficult to go against the establishment. So who knows what will happen with Trump?
Right. And then you've got Ronald Reagan, who, at least, started talking about trying to fight against these people and he got shot.

There might be a few honest, uncorrupted, aware Democrats or Republicans who aren't sold out to special interests, like a Dennis Kucinich or a Ron Paul, but if they ran for president they'd be sabotaged by the corporate media, or their votes would be stolen by the computerized voting machines.
Yes. The computerized voting machines can't be trusted. And, the way I see it, the media is just a tool of the New World Order.

A man named George Green once raised funds for Jimmy Carter. After being a fund raiser for Carter, Green switched parties and became a Republican. When Carter became president, he and some of his people asked Green to become the Democratic Finance chairman, but Green told them he was now a Republican. When Green told them that, Paul Volcker, the former chairman of the Federal Reserve and the then chairman of the Trilateral Commission, said to him, "That's okay, kid. It doesn't matter, we control them both."
Yes, I've heard that story. And that's exactly it. That's exactly the truth.

We shouldn't vote for either one of those guys! None of the above!
Exactly. We should have that on the ballot. See, we're just one step above the old Soviet Union where when they had an election for president they had only guy. You could vote for him or don't vote. We used to laugh about that, but today in America when you vote you've got one candidate from

the Republicans, one candidate from the Democrats, and except for some of the semantics, they're both controlled by the same people and they're both going to do the same thing. Our choices are fiddle dee and fiddle dum. So, it's not any better.

And the other main thing we have to do to get out from under the New World Order is to stop being a part of the banking system. No country has to borrow money from a private bank. All countries can and should issue and raise their own currency. If all countries would raise and issue their own money, then we would no longer be slaves to debt, inflation, and the corrupt banking monopoly that runs our world.

Absolutely. It's the tyranny of interest. The way the tyranny of interest works is they charge you so much interest that pretty soon it's all you can do to just keep up your payments on the interest and then you never get to pay on the principal and you just keep paying for the rest of your life.

In America we borrow our money from the privately owned Federal Reserve, so, in America, the Federal Reserve should be abolished. . . . This is what former Congressman Ron Paul's **New York Times** *bestselling book* **End the Fed** *is about. Congressman Paul writes that the nature of the Federal Reserve Banking System is destroying the economy, so we have to eliminate the Federal Reserve, have America issue and raise its own debt-free money, get on the gold standard, and then we can have a healthy economy and society.*

Yes, and other authors, and writers, and politicians have talked about this issue.

If the international banks are engaged in a conspiracy to put the entire world into debt, buy up all the world's industries and natural resources, foreclose on the planet Earth, and form and control a world government, then the way to stay out of the New World Order is to dismantle the international financial system and stop borrowing money from the big banks.

Exactly. And one way to look at it is the whole international financial system is one big Ponzi scheme.

Yes. A lot of people would say the entire financial system is a Ponzi scheme. . . . Say a country has no money and, so, decides to borrow, say, $500 million dollars from the IMF, or World Bank, or Federal Reserve. The country has to pay that $500 million back—plus the interest. Say, $500.3 million. How is the country going to pay back $500.3 million if it only has $500 million? It's going to have to borrow more money to pay the interest. And then more money to pay the interest on that interest. So the countries will spiral further and further into debt until they no longer can pay their bills, while the banks become astronomically wealthy.

Right, the tyranny of interest. The way the banks always set up the loans they know that the borrowers—the countries—will just go on paying more and more interest forever and never get to pay the principal. Compounding interest . . . and, also—if all money circulating in a society is borrowed money then, in essence, all that money has to be paid back. But if the money was all paid back, then there wouldn't be one cent left to circulate in the society. So the debt can never be paid back—because then there would be no money left. So any society that exists on borrowed money will just have to keep borrowing and borrowing and borrowing to pay back more and more interest and debt.

And as you said before, this is something that the Founding Fathers were very aware of. The Founding Fathers were very aware that a central bank and borrowing money from a central bank is going to cause severe problems. Thomas Jefferson once said, "I sincerely believe that banking institutions are more dangerous to our liberties than standing armies, and that the principle of spending money to be paid by posterity, under the name of funding, is but swindling futurity on a large scale. The issuing power should be taken from the banks and be restored to the people to whom it properly belongs."

Yes. Jefferson knew. That's why he and his cohorts wanted no central bank—which is what the Federal Reserve is. They wanted America issuing its own currency. That's why it's written into the Constitution that "only Congress shall coin and regulate the currency."

Do you know if Jefferson made this statement? A lot of people believe that Jefferson said this: "If the American people ever allow private banks to control the issue of their currency, first by inflation, then by deflation, the banks and corporations that will grow up around them will deprive the people of all property until their children wake up homeless on the continent their Fathers occupied."

Absolutely. I've used that quote in maybe more than one of my books and I went back and doubled-checked to make sure that he actually said that and he did.

That really explains what happens when you have private bankers controlling a society through a central bank and through fractional reserve banking—when private central banks are lending hordes of money off the gold standard, out of proportion with the expansion of goods and services. They're going to keep raising and lowering interest rates, causing inflation and deflation, booms and busts, and ultimately the public will be destroyed by debt and inflation and the banks and their corporations will come to own everything, 99 percent of the wealth.

And that's what's happening today.

*In his book **End the Fed**, Congressman Paul pointed out that every economy in history that was controlled by a central bank issuing and lending worthless fiat money has eventually crashed and gone bankrupt.*

Yes. Jefferson's statement really explains it. Jefferson was warning us. The Constitution says that only the Congress shall have the power to coin and regulate money. But, see, they handed that over to the Federal Reserve System in 1913. And the Federal Reserve System is neither federal nor does it have any reserves. It's a collection of twelve banks owned in turn by other banks which are owned in many instances by people who are not even United States citizens.

Do you think money should be gold—has to be on the gold standard—or can it be a paper currency? If money is on the gold standard then there's only so much gold in the world so there can't be too much money destroying a society through inflation. But if there's a paper currency that's issued in proper proportion with population growth and the expansion of goods and services, then there would be no inflation with that system, either.
Yes, it could be a paper currency. But it's got to be—what you just said—it's got to be in proportion to the amount of goods and services. In fact, we started off that way. People don't know their history, but one of the reasons that the thirteen colonies broke away from Britain in the 1770s—according to Benjamin Franklin—was because they took away our money. The colonies were issuing their own money but then England forced us to use Bank of England money.

Benjamin Franklin said that himself. He said England forced us to use and pay interest on Bank of England money, and this was the real reason for the Revolutionary War. In his autobiography, Franklin wrote, "The colonies would gladly have borne the little tax on tea and other matters had it not been that England took away from the colonies their money, which created unemployment and dissatisfaction. The inability of the colonists to get power to issue their own money permanently out of the hands of George III and the international bankers was the PRIME reason for the Revolutionary War."

Yes. Each colony or state was issuing their own money—it was called the Continental—and it was based on the goods and services of that state and it was solid and people were prospering. But, you see, the Bank of England and the people who ran the Bank of England—the bankers—were not ripping off money from this system. They weren't getting paid interest for creating money out of nothing—they weren't controlling the American economy. So they pressured King George into passing a law that outlawed the Continental and said "the colonies have to use Bank of England notes." And this was one of the major reasons for the Revolutionary War. And then after America won the war, and as they began to put together the Constitution and the Bill of Rights, one of the biggest arguments they had was whether or not to have a central bank. And that's been going on ever since.

So, as you mentioned, in the beginning of America when the colonies were issuing their own currency, the economy was strong and sound because the money was being issued in proper proportion with the expansion of goods and services. But then when the Revolutionary War came, the colonists started printing too much money because they needed to finance the war and this led to bad, terrible inflation.

Yes. That did happen. They printed more and more money to finance the War and that devalued and destroyed the purchasing power of the Continental.

So, the Founders realized that printing too much of a paper currency can destroy an economy through inflation, and, so, when they drafted the Constitution they put in that "only Congress shall coin the currency." "Coin" means gold and silver. There's only so much gold and silver in the world and, so, if we use gold or silver for money there can't be too much money causing inflation. So, according to the Constitution money can't be a paper currency, can it? It has to be gold or silver.

Well . . . it . . . it should be gold. It'd be best . . . if it was gold. But anything would be better than what's happening now—fractional reserve banking, and borrowing billions of paper fiat money from the Federal Reserve.

Fractional reserve banking should be made illegal, shouldn't it? Fractional reserve banking is really the bane of society, isn't it? It's not fair and it's going to lead to severe inflation and devaluation of the monetary unit.
Yes. Because it's been so abused. Fractional banking is, of course,—as we've said—simply the idea that if a bank has a hundred dollars in assets they can loan out a hundred thousand dollars. Because the idea is that everybody who owns that hundred dollars is not going to come in and ask for it all at the same time. . . . Well, that is a path to disaster.

The bankers create money out of nothing, and they're the only ones who are allowed to do it. . . . It's cheap money that's eventually going to destroy society through inflation.
Yes.

But, as you said, when the American colonies first started out they were issuing their own money in proper proportion, and the economy was strong and sound. A diplomat from Europe came over at that time and asked Benjamin Franklin, "How are you doing so well? How do you manage to have such a healthy economy?" Benjamin Franklin said to the diplomat, "This is simple. In the colonies, we issue our own paper money. It is called 'Colonial Scrip.' We issue it in proper proportion to make the goods pass easily from the producers to the consumers. In this manner, creating ourselves our own money, we control its purchasing power and we have no interest to pay to no one."
Yes. And that's the key.

That could be the key—the main factor in making an economy and country healthy. A country issuing its own money—on the gold standard or in proper proportion—and, so, causing no inflation or debt. There are other factors that determine a healthy economy but that could be the key factor. It could be. It's very important.

And if you have a healthy economy, you can have a healthy society. . . . The edict for a happy personal life is "Happy wife. Happy life." Maybe a good edict for a healthy social life would be: "Happy economy. Happy society."
That could be it.

Thomas Jefferson, Benjamin Franklin, and the rest of the Founding Fathers probably weren't perfect guys. But they seemed like pretty decent guys. They were very smart guys. It's been written that never in history has such a collection of knowledge and intellectual capability been gathered in one space and time for the purpose of forming a new government and society. The Founders had a clear understanding of how easily and readily government becomes tyrannical. They believed that all human beings had natural rights, and liberties, and freedoms, and they were determined to form a government whose laws prevented those rights and freedoms from being infringed upon. They also had a clear understanding that there has to be a separation of powers. If you have a government where there's only one president, or one king, or one office of centralized power, then it's much easier for that government to be corrupted because there's only one person or one office to control.
Yes, centralized power—one office of power—is the way to and leads to corruption. Tyrannical forces taking over a government. Centralized power is vulnerable. The Founders knew this.

That's why the Founding Fathers made sure there's a separation of powers in the American system. A system of checks and balances. In America, we have the executive, legislative, and judicial branches. We have one

president, twelve Supreme Court judges, 435 congressmen, and 100 sena-
tors. It's going to be much more difficult for the New World Order to
manipulate all these politicians to change our laws and get to globalism.
But they're still trying. But, yes, the separation of powers in our government is a bulwark against corruption, tyranny, the New World Order. The
Founding Fathers made it that way. How are they going to control and
dupe all these representatives and senators? It has to have the New World
Order worried.

The New World Order influences don't want a separation of powers—
in American or global power. They don't want global power to be sep-
arated into one hundred or two hundred national governments. They
want one United Nations Agenda 21 Plan or one Bank of International
Settlements to be in control of the world. Do you think it would be a
good idea if the Bank of International Settlements and Goldman Sachs
and other banks like that were in control of the world?
That would be an emphatic no. Here are the basics: throughout the history of the world there have only been two methods attempted at government. One is what was attempted in ancient Greece for a little while
and in America for the last two hundred and forty years. A participatory
democracy. A democratic republic—a government where the power rests
with the people who elect representatives. The rest of history is the second
method—which is central authority. Now whether you want to call them
the Pharaoh, or the Caesar, or the King, or the Fuhrer, it's central authority
and the people are under its thumb. Now with the United States—every
revolution in the history of the world has been started by intellectuals—
smart, educated people who say, "The system we're under is not operating correctly. We need to change this." In every other revolution in the
world—particularly the French Revolution, the Russian Revolution—once
the revolution started and there was violence, well, then, the intellectuals
are usually the first ones to be killed off. And then the strong men, the

thugs take over—like Stalin, like Hitler, and then they run the show. Now, the United States is a kind of unique example in world history because at the end of the Revolutionary War the very intellectuals—Madison, Jefferson, Benjamin Franklin, Adams—all these intellectuals who had started the revolution were still alive. They were still in power. So they sat down—these very educated, thoughtful men—and they devised—which while imperfect—probably the best system of government ever devised in the history of the world. And that's the Constitution and the Bill of Rights. . . . And the problems we have today in America are not because of the Constitution. It's because we are not following the Constitution.

Many people would say that it was a perfect alignment of positive forces or Divine Providence that brought the Founding Fathers together and inspired them to form a government that insured the peoples' natural rights and freedoms were protected and where there was a separation of powers. To base a government on the idea that the Creator, or higher power, or nature, or the Universe inherently made all men free and equal to pursue happiness seems like a pretty good idea to base a society on. It'd be a shame if we lost it, wouldn't it?

Oh, absolutely. . . . It'd be more than a shame. It'd be the destruction of the greatest system of government that the world has ever known.

CHAPTER 12

9/11 Truth Movement Claims US government Let 9/11 Happen or Caused 9/11 to Happen. Was 9/11 a New Pearl Harbor?

An interview with author and 9/11 Truth movement leader Professor David Ray Griffin

Major General Albert Stubblebine had a thirty-two year US Army career, and from 1981–1984 was the commanding general of US Army Intelligence and Security Command. During that time, Stubblebine was in charge of every US Army intelligence report throughout the world. General Stubblebine has said: "The airplanes that hit the World Trade Center did not cause the collapse of the buildings. The collapse of the buildings was caused by controlled demolition. All of the air defense systems in that part of the country had been turned off that day. Why? Apparently, because Vice President Dick Cheney had ordered them to be turned off. Strange. The real story to me is: Who was the real enemy? Who planned this attack? Why was it planned? Were the real terrorists people in Arab clothing? Or were the real terrorists the authorities in the White House?"

Mahathir Mohamad, the Prime Minister of Malaysia from 1981–2003, has said: "I can believe that they (the US government) would kill three thousand of their own to have an excuse to kill six hundred fifty thousand

Iraqis. These are the kind of people we are dealing with. Please don't think this is fiction."

William Christison worked for the CIA from 1950 until his retirement in 1979. From the early 1970s, Christison served as National Intelligence officer, a principal advisor to the director of the CIA. Before he retired, Christison was also the director of the CIA's Office of Regional and Political Analysis, a 250-person unit responsible for political analysis of every country and region in the world. William Christison has said:

> David Ray Griffin's *Debunking 9/11 Debunking* is a strong compendium of the strong body of evidence showing the official US government story of what happened on September 11, 2001, to be almost certainly a monstrous series of lies. . . . I now think there is persuasive evidence that the events of September 11 did not unfold as the Bush administration and the 9/11 Commission would have us believe. . . . David Griffin believes this all was totally an inside job. . . . I've got to say I think it was, too. . . . I have since decided that . . . at least some elements in the US government had contributed in some way or other to causing 9/11 to happen or at least allowing it to happen.

Lt. Col. Robert Bowman, PhD, US Air Force (ret.), flew over one hundred combat missions during his twenty-two year Air Force career. After combat duty, Col. Bowman served as director of the Star Wars Program under presidents Ford and Carter. Bowman is also the former head of the Department of Aeronautical Engineering and assistant dean at the US Air Force Institute of Technology. Bowman has said:

> A lot of these pieces of information, taken together, prove that the official story, the official conspiracy theory of 9/11 is a bunch of hogwash. It's impossible. . . . Taken together, these things prove that high levels of our government don't want us to know what happened

and who's responsible. . . . Who gained from 9/11? Who covered up crucial information about 9/11? And who put out the patently false stories about 9/11 in the first place? When you take those three things together, I think the case is pretty clear that it's highly placed individuals in the administration with all roads passing through Dick Cheney. . . . I think the very kindest thing we can say about George W. Bush and all the people in the US government who have been involved in this massive cover-up—the very kindest thing we can say—is that they were aware of impending attacks and let them happen. Now some people will say that's much too kind.

These four men are part of the more and more people who are joining the 9/11 Truth Movement, the many groups that don't believe the government's official version of 9/11. In a September 2006 MSNBC poll, when sixty-eight thousand Americans were asked if they believed "any of the conspiracy theories suggesting the US government was somehow involved in 9/11," 60 percent of the respondents answered "YES." At around that same time, a Scripps Howard/Ohio University poll found 36 percent of the public believing that "federal officials either participated in the attacks on the World Trade Center and Pentagon or took no action to stop them because they wanted the United States to go to war in the Middle East." After the Scripps poll came out, *Time* magazine wrote: "36 percent adds up to a lot of people. This is not a fringe phenomenon. It is a mainstream political reality."

Prior to the 9/11 attacks, it had already been the plan of George W. Bush's White House to attack Afghanistan and Iraq, and remove Saddam Hussein. The Bush White House needed an excuse—a reason to present to the Congress—to do it. In March 2001, Secretary of Defense Donald Rumsfeld's Defense Intelligence Agency had been mapping Iraq's oil fields and had prepared a document entitled "Foreign Suitors for Iraqi Oilfield Contracts." The Bush White House and the Pentagon not only wanted to control the oil fields in the Middle East but, according to many sources, also wanted to establish several military bases in Iraq and throughout the area. Many of George W. Bush's top advisors—Vice President Dick Cheney, Secretary of Defense Donald Rumsfeld, Deputy Secretary of Defense Paul Wolfowitz, and others—belonged to a neoconservative think tank called the *Project for a New American Century (PNAC)*. In the fall of 2000, the *PNAC* published a paper entitled *Rebuilding America's Defenses* in which it was stated that "a substantial American force presence is needed in the Gulf" and "Saddam Hussein and his regime must be removed from power." In this *PNAC* paper, it was also written that taking military control of the Middle East would be difficult and take a long time unless a "new Pearl Harbor" occurred. This paper—stating that a "new Pearl Harbor" could more quickly facilitate a military takeover of the Middle East—was signed by many officials who went on to work in the Bush administration. Now many people believe that the Bush administration let 9/11 happen or caused 9/11 to happen in order to have their "new Pearl Harbor" and a justification to present to the Congress to attack and take military control of Iraq and the surrounding area.

One 9/11 Truth Movement community member has said: "Right after the Kennedy assassination, most people believed that Lee Harvey Oswald killed John Kennedy because that's what the government said. But so many suspicious facts surrounding the Kennedy assassination eventually came out so that now the great majority of Americans believe that there was a conspiracy that killed Kennedy and many people believe elements in our own government were behind it. In the same way, there are so many suspicious facts surrounding 9/11 that eventually it will be the majority opinion in America that the government was complicit in the 9/11 attacks."

These suspicious facts and anomalies surrounding 9/11 have caused many professionals, scholars, and intellectuals to form 9/11 Truth Movement groups to express their dissatisfaction and disbelief in the official, government version and to call for a new investigation into the 9/11 tragedy.

"Architects and Engineers for 9/11 Truth" is a group of 2,600 well-regarded, successful professional architects and engineers who state that it is obvious that the three World Trade Center buildings—WTC 1, WTC 2, and WTC 7, the forty-seven story building next to the Twin Towers that collapsed at 6:00 p.m. on September 11, 2001—were brought down by bombs set *inside* the buildings. In history, no skyscraper has ever collapsed because of a fire—as the government claims happened on 9/11—and the *Architects and Engineers for 9/11 Truth* group aver that it is impossible for a skyscraper to collapse as fast as the WTC buildings collapsed—symmetrically, in free fall—without the columns inside the buildings being compromised by explosives. According to this group, the evidence is so strong that it is "beyond a reasonable doubt" that the WTC buildings were brought down with interior bombs.

"Air Traffic Controllers for 9/11 Truth" is a group of experienced air traffic controllers who claim they "know 9/11 was an inside job because whenever an airplane goes off course in America it is immediately, within minutes, intercepted by military planes." According to these air traffic controllers, in the years prior to 9/11 dozens of planes had gone off course and they were "all, with no exceptions, immediately intercepted by military planes." The hijacked planes on 9/11 were, of course, never intercepted, and according to *Air Traffic Controllers for 9/11 Truth* the only way this could have happened was if "high government officials had issued a stand-down order—an order that the hijacked planes not be intercepted."

"Pilots for 9/11 Truth" is a group of active and retired military and commercial pilots who among them have thousands of hours of flight experience. According to this group, it is highly unlikely that a group of inexperienced pilots who had flown only small planes could hijack a large commercial airliner and have the piloting expertise to crash the planes into buildings. The technology to remotely control airplanes existed in 2001, and these pilots, like many other people, believe it's a realistic possibility that the airplanes were remotely controlled on 9/11. The pilots' most ardent contention, though, is with the government's claims about the plane that allegedly hit the Pentagon. According to the government, the hijacker pilot of this plane did a quick, 360-degree turn over the Pentagon, got low to the ground, and crashed the airliner into the Pentagon. The Pilots for 9/11 Truth group avows that this is a physically impossible maneuver for a commercial airliner to make, couldn't even be done by the most experienced, expert pilot, and, so, therefore, couldn't have happened. This group, like many others, believe that the evidence is strong that a missile—not an airplane—hit the Pentagon building.

"Scientists for 9/11 Truth" is a group of professors and PhDs who contend that many of the claims of the National Institute of Standards and Technology (NIST)—the government organization responsible for giving a scientific explanation as to how the WTC buildings collapsed—are "improbable and impossible," ignore scientific evidence, and "defy the laws of physics." The Scientists for 9/11 Truth group makes it clear that fires being heated by airplane fuel can't possibly burn hot enough to destroy or melt steel columns, and, so, couldn't have caused the WTC buildings to collapse. Like the Architects and Engineers for 9/11 Truth group, *Scientists for 9/11 Truth* declare that the "overwhelming evidence" indicates that the WTC buildings were brought down by explosives set inside the buildings.

Many active and retired military and government officials from America and around the world have stated that Osama Bin Laden couldn't have been behind the 9/11 attacks and that the planning for the attacks had to have come from within the government. These men held or hold high ranking positions in the militaries and governments, and their intimate knowledge and expertise is in how militaries and governments and intelligence agencies operate. Many of these men and women have joined the Military and Government Officials for 9/11 Truth group.

Professor David Ray Griffin is the most well-known and outspoken leader of the 9/11 Truth Movement. Professor Griffin has authored nine books on the subject that have sold more than one hundred thousand copies. Prior to becoming a 9/11 researcher, Griffin had been a professor of

Theology and Religion at Claremont School of Theology where he was the founder of the Center for Process Studies and the author of more than twenty books on philosophy, theology, and natural science. Asked if his role as a 9/11 dissenter departs from his life's work as a scholar and theologian, the professor answered, "At first glance it may seem strange, but the task of a theologian is to look at the world from how we would imagine the divine perspective would care about the good of the whole and would love all the parts. So, 9/11, if it was brought about by forces in our own government for imperial reasons, is antithetical to the general good."

Professor Griffin says he was "rather slow getting on board with the 9/11 Truth Movement" but once he "started reading all these stories drawn from mainstream sources that contradicted the official account, I decided I needed to look into it more carefully, and the more I looked, the worse it got." Griffin now feels that "the evidence that 9/11 was an inside job is overwhelming." Over the years, the exposé that the 9/11 Truth Movement has gathered that shows that the government version of 9/11 is questionable and "demonstrably false" has grown; according to Professor Griffin, "that exposé is now so compelling as to be virtually undeniable to anyone who will take the time to study it."

Cirignano: Will it eventually be the majority opinion in America that the government was complicit in the 9/11 attacks?
Griffin: I can only hope so. . . . I, and many others, feel strongly that the official explanation for 9/11 is a big lie. Unfortunately, this big lie has had many negative—and disastrous—effects on America and the world.

Is it already the majority opinion?
Not yet, I think. But it's hard to say. I don't think there have been any recent polls. There have been polls in the past where thirty to forty percent of the respondents have answered that they believe it was an inside job.

What would you say to people who say that it's immoral or unpatriotic or wrong to believe that the government let 9/11 happen or caused 9/11 to happen?

I would say that is silly. It is now accepted and been proven that there were no weapons of mass destruction, and, so, no real justification for going to war in Iraq. So is it unpatriotic to say that the Bush-Cheney administration was lying about Iraq?

This is one of the main points of your new book **Bush and Cheney: How They Ruined America and the World.** *After 9/11—and because of 9/11—America went to war in a number of places in the Middle East, and all those wars were based on lies and untruths.*

They not only lied about weapons of mass destruction, but they lied and said that Saddam had connections to al-Qaeda. But Saddam had no connections to al-Qaeda. And they knew that. Bush was told that by US intelligence about a week or two after 9/11.

In your book you pointed out that the Bush White House even had the CIA write a fake letter that was supposedly written from the head of Iraqi intelligence to Saddam Hussein talking about Saddam's relations to al-Qaeda.

That was reported by Ron Suskind, the Pulitzer Prize-winning journalist. Yes. The White House had the CIA fake a letter stating that Saddam was linked to al-Qaeda, and news of that went out to the media and was used as a justification to attack Iraq. . . . Another journalist, Charles Lewis, founder of the Pulitzer Prize-winning Center for Public Integrity, has written a book called *935 Lies*. In that book, Lewis details 935 lies the Bush administration told in the weeks and months preceding the invasion of Iraq. *Nine hundred and thirty-five.*

The neocon servative influence continued into the Obama administration. The US-led NATO invasion and takeover of Libya, the removal of

Muammar Gaddafi, a war that was basically led by Secretary of State Hillary Clinton, was also based on lies, wasn't it?

Hillary Clinton was and is, basically, a neocon. Forty members of the neocon Foreign Policy Initiative sent Obama a letter pressuring him to take military action and remove Gaddafi. Gaddafi's army was fighting against an insurrection of Muslim extremists and Clinton and the neocons claimed Gaddafi had planned a bloodbath in Benghazi. It wasn't true. Gaddafi wasn't planning a bloodbath. . . . The Obama administration also claimed that Gaddafi was targeting peaceful citizens, that his air force had bombed and strafed civilians, and that Gaddafi had his soldiers raping civilians. None of that was true. The Defense Intelligence Agency itself reported that there was no evidence that Gaddafi wanted a bloodbath.

So not only the Bush administration, but the Obama administration told plenty of lies.

All these wars Bush and Obama got us involved in after 9/11—Afghanistan, Iraq, Libya, Syria, and all the rest of them—they've all clearly been based on lies and disinformation. Propaganda and false flags, all of them.

When the Bush administration lied and said they knew there were weapons of mass destruction, they knew these lies would lead to a war and thousands would be killed. So your point is if they can tell lies that cause wars that kill hundreds of thousands of people, then why should it be hard to believe that they set up and lied about 9/11? A comparatively low number of people died on 9/11—three thousand.

Exactly. It's clear now that the Bush people were lying about weapons of mass destruction. They weren't mistaken about it. They were lying. So how is lying about the weapons of mass destruction different from lying about 9/11?

You claim that it was the neoconservatives who were behind 9/11 and who are behind all these recent wars in the Middle East and elsewhere. Can you explain who the neocons are?

The neocon movement began with some New York intellectuals in the 1960s. They were originally Democrats. They have beliefs and policies that are not traditionally conservative. One of the main things that the neocons believe is that America should be the world's policeman. They believe that America should use its military power to control the world, and that America should use force and wars to enforce democracy and free markets everywhere.

Some people would question if the neocons really want democracy. What they really want, probably, is political and economic control over the world.

Yes. I'd agree. The neocons became more and more influential and powerful in the '70s, '80s, and '90s, and then with Bush Jr.'s presidency, they basically came to rule the White House and Washington. The neocons believe in power and empire through aggression, and through military takeovers. Before 9/11, the neocons had a plan to change the regimes in—to invade—Afghanistan and Iraq. And probably a few more Middle East countries. 9/11 allowed them to do this.

Many people believe that's the clear, obvious motive for 9/11. The neocons needed an excuse to invade the Middle East. That's what General Wesley Clark said, right?

That's right. General Clark, who was once the supreme commander of NATO in Europe, said that a few weeks after 9/11 a three-star general told him that the White House and Pentagon were going to take out and invade seven countries in five years—Iraq, Syria, Lebanon, Libya, Somalia, Sudan, and Iran.

And 9/11 allowed the White House and Pentagon to do this?

Exactly. The clear motive for 9/11. After 9/11 all the White House neo-cons—Cheney, Rumsfeld, Wolfowitz—they were all saying things like "this will allow us to reorganize the world." They all said that all these invasions in the Middle East couldn't have happened without 9/11.

But this isn't a partisan issue, is it? Because—as we've said—the Obama administration was basically neocon too, wasn't it? What Obama did in the Middle East is just as bad or worse than what Bush did, right? More wars, more bombings, more deaths and chaos.

Yes, that is basically correct. The presidency of Barack Obama has been a blood-soaked disgrace. He expanded on his predecessor George W. Bush's criminal foreign interventions. At least seven countries in the Middle East have been routinely bombed under Obama's watch. In 2016, it's been reported that the US military dropped about twenty-five thousand bombs around the world, killing countless thousands of people. Drone assassinations have increased tenfold, killing thousands of innocent civilians as collateral damage. Not one war has been ended. He started this Cold War with Russia. . . . The Obama presidency has been a tragedy.

It seems clear that the Bush White House was dishonest about the safety of the air at the World Trade Center site after 9/11, doesn't it? The Bush White House knew that the air at the 9/11 site was unhealthy—the dust was full of toxins—but they sent firemen down there anyway to clean up the mess.

That's true. After 9/11, the head of the EPA, Christie Todd Whitman, assured the public and the firemen sent down there that the air was safe. But, in the early 2000s, the Inspector General of the EPA reported that Whitman's statements had not been true. Whitman had been pressured by Bush's White House to say that the air was safe—even though it wasn't.

Aren't there suspicions that George Bush wanted Wall Street to get up and running—whether the air was safe, or not?

That's right. Whitman, herself, told that to a congressional committee. She told them President Bush expected the Financial District to reopen within a few days after 9/11. And further investigations suggested that the Bush administration had Whitman say the air was safe so Wall Street could keep operating. . . . A number of EPA whistleblowers have claimed that the EPA blatantly lied about the safety of the air. And, a few years after 9/11, a judge ruled that Whitman and the EPA had been untruthful.

Thousands of firemen's health was injured by working at the 9/11 site and about three thousand firemen have died as a result of that. So you and others have said that if the Bush White House knew that the air was unhealthy and knew that sending firemen down there would injure their health—and even kill some of them—then that shows the Bush White House could let 9/11 happen, even though that would lead to the deaths of about three thousand people.

Well, it makes sense, doesn't it? It's logical. They knew the air was unhealthy and they sent people down there anyway. And three thousand people died from breathing that bad air. Cancers. Respiratory diseases . . . Three thousand is the same number of people who died on September 11, 2001.

If what you're saying is true—that the government orchestrated 9/11— then this is what's known as a false flag operation. A false flag operation is when a government stages an attack against itself and then blames the attack on another country so as to have a justification to attack and wage war on that country.

Yes, false flags are a traditional military strategy. Most people probably don't know what a false flag operation is but such attacks are far from uncommon.

According to some retired intelligence and military officials, false flags happen much more often then people realize. . . . Operation Gladio was a well-known false flag operation.

Operation Gladio occurred after World War II. Western European countries didn't want their citizens to vote for Communists, so, NATO—which was basically controlled by the US, the CIA—organized terrorist attacks and then planted evidence to implicate Communists. One of the attacks—a bomb detonated in a railway in Bologna, Italy—ended up killing eighty-five people and wounding another two hundred.

That was just one of the violent acts organized by Operation Gladio. There were more.

Yes. Many historians would say that the hostilities that eventually led to WWII began with a false flag operation—the Mukden Incident. In 1931, Japanese military officers planted bombs on a Japanese railway and then blamed Chinese dissidents. Japan then used that as an excuse to invade and take control of Manchuria, China.

The Nazis used false flags.

The Reichstag fire. Shortly after the Nazis took power in 1933, they burned down the Reichstag building—the German Parliament building—and blamed the Communists. The Nazis then used this incident as a pretext to persecute Communists, shut down left-wing newspapers, and do away with civil rights.

The Reichstag fire gave the Nazis more power. It basically led to the establishment of a full-fledged Nazi Germany.

Yes. And then in 1939 when Hitler wanted to invade Poland he had German soldiers dress up as Poles and attack German posts on the German-Polish border. The next day Hitler attacked Poland in "self-defense" and World War II began.

On the website of Paul Craig Roberts, a former editor of the **Wall Street Journal,** *there's a link to an article that list about seventy false flag operations committed by America and other nations that have been admitted to and proven to be true. It is startling how many times government and military officials have committed violent acts—acts that many times have led to the serious injuries and deaths of civilians—and blamed these acts on other countries.*

I think it wouldn't be inaccurate to say that false flags happen all the time. It is a very common practice for militaries and governments.

For instance, it's been established that back in the 1950s the Israeli Mossad—Israel's intelligence agency—exploded bombs in various buildings in Egypt—including the US Embassy—and then planted evidence to blame Arabs. After that, a US Army official said: "The Mossad is ruthless and cunning. It has the capability to target US forces and make it look like a Palestinian/Arab act."

Yes. There are many examples. And there have been a number of false flags used in all these recent wars in the Middle East and nearby areas. False flags and lies and propaganda.

The US government has used lies to start many wars, hasn't it?

Well, the Spanish-American war started on the basis of the false claim that Spain had sunk the US battleship *Maine.* The Mexican-American war was based on President Polk's false claim that Mexico had "shed American blood on American soil." The war in the Philippines was based on the untruth that Filipinos had fired first. And the Vietnam war commenced full-scale after the Gulf of Tonkin hoax.

Have you heard of Operations Northwoods?

Of course. Operation Northwoods was a military plan presented by the Joint Chiefs of Staff to President Kennedy in 1962. These US military generals wanted to invade Cuba, and Operation Northwoods was a plan to stage attacks against America, blame them on Cuba, and use that as an excuse to attack Cuba. The generals wanted to blow up ships, blow up planes, attack anti-Castro Cubans, attack the Guantanamo Naval Base, and blame all that on Castro.

Operation Northwoods was never initiated, but it really shows that high military officials are capable of telling huge, enormous lies to the public and taking actions that they know will lead to the deaths of civilians. Absolutely. Kennedy rejected the plan, but the Chiefs were eager to get it going.

The hijacked planes were not intercepted on 9/11. Is that proof right there that 9/11 was a government conspiracy? Whenever a plane goes off course in America, it's immediately intercepted, isn't it?
It is. It's an extremely routine matter. And it happened dozens of times before 9/11. A plane goes off course, or loses radio contact, or the transponder is turned off—it's intercepted by military planes within ten, fifteen minutes. It's happened dozens—maybe hundreds—of times. But it didn't happen on 9/11. That's extremely unusual. And strong evidence that 9/11 was an inside job.

The military has a very efficient system for intercepting planes that are having problems, doesn't it?
Yes. And it occurs very quickly. If there's any sign that a plane is off course or having problems, then within a minute the FAA controller notifies NORAD and the Pentagon. Then within another minute NORAD will order jets to be scrambled—sent up—from the nearest airport. These jets can fly at about 1800 mph, so given the number of airport bases we have in the country, just about any plane will be intercepted within about ten to fifteen minutes.

But the planes on 9/11 were in the air for thirty–five, forty–five minutes and never intercepted.
Right.

What is the government's story on this? How does the government explain that the planes weren't intercepted?
That's complex. I spent the latter part of my book *The 9/11 Commission Report* dealing with the various flights. The government kept changing its story regarding why the planes were never intercepted. One government office would say one thing, but when it found out what it said contradicted what another government office said, it would then change its story. But then when it was found out that its new story didn't jibe with the facts, it would change its story again. . . . The bottom line is that the government did have enough time to intercept the planes, but the planes were not intercepted.

The government agency in charge of protecting American air space is NORAD—the North America Aerospace Defense Command. Dick Cheney was in charge of NORAD and the White House at the time of the 9/11 attacks, correct?
Yes, he was.

How did Dick Cheney, the Vice President, become in charge of the White House and the government on 9/11?
He was not technically in charge. But because Bush was out of town, Cheney was able to put himself in charge of the White House, and, so, it was Cheney running the government.

What do you make of the statement that Norman Mineta made to the 9/11 Commission? Mineta, the Secretary of Transportation at the time, was in the basement of the White House with Dick Cheney on the morning of 9/11. It was about 9:30 a.m., after the two hijacked planes had already crashed into the World Trade Center, and it was known that another hijacked jet was heading towards Washington. Mineta told the Committee that a young aide of Cheney's kept coming into the room reporting on how far the hijacked plane was from Washington. The aide would come in and say, "The plane is fifty miles out." Then, "The plane is thirty miles out." Then, "The plane is twenty miles out." After the aide reported that the plane was ten miles away, he asked Cheney, "Do the orders still stand?" Cheney whipped his head around to the young man and shouted, "Of course, the orders still stand! Have you heard anything to the contrary?" What was being said there?

It appears Cheney was giving a stand-down order. An order that the plane not be intercepted or shot down.

That certainly seems to be what was being said there, right? They knew another hijacked plane was heading to Washington, Cheney said "The orders still stand!" and that plane was never intercepted or shot down.

Yes. It looks like Cheney was giving a stand-down order.

The 9/11 commission never mentioned this testimony from Norman Mineta in the official 9/11 Commission report, did it?

It did not. That's right.

You've written—and other people have said this—that you believe that Dick Cheney was the real president during the Bush–Cheney years. You and others believe that Cheney was the one who was really running the White House.

Cheney had much more experience in the White House and in Washington than Bush, who was probably the most unqualified man to ever become president. It was Cheney who got the Supreme Court to give the contested presidential election to Bush. The Bush administration's first focus was to coordinate an energy task force and Cheney organized and ran that without Bush. It was Cheney who was in charge on 9/11. It was widely suspected around Washington that Cheney was really running the White House, and there's been a few books written about it. . . . It seems Cheney was running the show.

Ultimately, that plane that was heading towards Washington— American Airlines Flight 77, AA77—probably didn't hit the Pentagon, though, right? It appears a missile, not an airplane, hit the Pentagon.
The overwhelming evidence is that a missile, not a jet plane, hit the Pentagon. . . . Anyone can go online right now and look at the picture of the Pentagon after the jet allegedly hit it. The hole left in the Pentagon clearly isn't big enough for a jet to fit through. The size of the hole is totally consistent with a missile hit. Also, there is no wreckage of a plane there. There's no fuselage. No tail. No wings. No sign of a plane. . . . Many current and retired military officials and employees have stated that a plane never hit the Pentagon.

Weren't there also some Pentagon employees who actually walked through the hole left in the Pentagon and said there was no plane there?
Army officer April Gallop was a Pentagon employee who worked right near where the Pentagon was hit. She was initially injured by the explosion but when she came to, she walked through the hole in the building and says she saw no evidence of a plane crash. No plane. Other Pentagon employees and even some journalists have said the same thing.

Another apparent untruth is that this woman named Barbara Olsen made a call from AA77 to her husband Ted Olsen just before the plane allegedly hit the Pentagon.
Ted Olsen was the solicitor general in Bush's administration. Olsen claimed that his wife Barbara—who was on flight AA77—made two calls to him saying that the plane had been taken over by hijackers who had knives and

box cutters. Originally, Olsen said his wife made the calls from her cell phone, but then it was established that a cell phone call couldn't have possibly been made from the height the plane was at. So then it was assumed that she must have made the calls from an onboard phone but then it was discovered that American Airlines 757s did not have onboard phones. . . . Ultimately, in 2006, the FBI reported that phone records showed that Barbara Olsen had attempted one call, which was not connected, so it lasted "zero" seconds.

So why did Ted Olsen, an official in the Bush administration, claim that his wife called him and told him that the plane was being hijacked by men with knives and box cutters?
Good question. The reported Olsen calls were the only basis for the idea that any of the flights had hijackers with knives and box cutters.

But now that has turned out to be, apparently, a big lie.
A big lie.

The government claims that an al-Qaeda terrorist named Hani Hanjour was the pilot who crashed flight AA77 into the Pentagon. That can't be true, can it? It has to be a lie.
The overwhelming evidence is that a missile—not an airplane—hit the Pentagon. But even if AA77 did crash into the Pentagon . . . every flight instructor who taught Hanjour said he was an "extremely poor pilot." And every professional pilot has said to do the flying required to crash AA77 into the Pentagon the way it allegedly crashed would be "extremely difficult" and "almost impossible." Hani Hanjour couldn't have done it. It's another big lie.

There were a number of surveillance cameras at the Pentagon that would definitely show what crashed into the building on 9/11. But the government won't release the films from those cameras?

That's right. The films haven't been released. The government won't release them.

There were so many firsts on 9/11, weren't there? All these "firsts" are suspicious. In history, a skyscraper has never collapsed from a fire, right? But the government says the WTC collapsed from the fire—not from interior bombs.

That's right. It has never happened. It doesn't happen. In the early 2000s, the Windsor Tower in Madrid, Spain, burned for 24 hours but didn't collapse. Just recently, the Grenfeld Tower in London burned for more than 12 hours and didn't collapse. There are many more examples—buildings that had much worse fires and burned for much longer but didn't collapse. Skyscrapers don't collapse from fires. Skyscrapers collapse from controlled demolition.

But it is true, though, that skyscrapers have never been hit with jets as big as the jets that hit the World Trade Center on 9/11.

Well—first of all—Building 7 was never hit by a plane. A plane never hit Building 7 and it still collapsed in free fall. And regarding WTC 1 and WTC 2—both the architect who designed the buildings and the engineer who built the buildings have said that the buildings were designed and built to survive a plane crash. Both the architect and the engineer have said the planes crashing into the World Trade Center could not have caused the collapse of the buildings.

9/11 was the first time that the black boxes from the pilots' cockpits weren't found. Black boxes can't burn and are indestructible. Never in history has there been a jet plane crash where the black boxes weren't found. But according to the government, the black boxes from the hijacked planes on 9/11 were never found.

That's what they say, yes.

What would the black boxes show? If the government is covering up here—if the government is hiding the black boxes—then why would they be doing that?

They would show if the planes that hit the buildings were the assigned flights. The black boxes might also have shown whether the plane had been put on automatic—if they were being flown and directed by remote control. Obviously, no American pilot would have volunteered to crash into buildings. And the consensus amongst professional pilots is that al-Qaeda hijackers wouldn't have had the piloting ability or expertise to crash the planes into buildings.

If there were hijackers, then the black boxes would have recorded the commotion, the argument, when the hijackers took over. But if the plane was just put on autopilot then there would have been no recording of a hijacking.

Right. But now we can't know for sure because the government claims something happened that has never happened before—that the black boxes weren't found.

There are so many reasons to believe that there were bombs inside the WTC buildings, aren't there? The Architects and Engineers for 9/11 Truth group makes a very convincing case that bombs brought down the building, doesn't it?

They absolutely do. Architects and Engineers for 9/11 Truth is 2,800 of the most successful and respected architects, scientists, engineers, and professors giving all the scientific reasons why the collapse of the World Trade Center buildings had to be a controlled demolition. It's an *extremely* qualified group.

Is there any demolition expert anywhere who would look at the collapse of the WTC buildings—they fell symmetrically, in free fall—and say that it is anything but a controlled demolition?

Only someone who was on the take, or had to lie to keep his or her job…so, you're right. The overwhelming majority of independent, non-governmental professionals who have studied the evidence have regarded the government's official account of 9/11 as false. But if you're part of a study funded or influenced by the government—or if you're a government employee dependent on a government paycheck—anybody like that ends up agreeing with the government's official explanation.

Many people who were at the WTC on 9/11 testified that they heard bombs going off, correct? How many people said that?
A lot of people said they heard explosions. On the day of and the day after 9/11, *Fox News, CNN, MSNBC, NBC, The Los Angeles Times*—they all reported there were explosions in the buildings. Some of the reporters and journalists who were at the site said that they, themselves, heard explosions. The official government story was that there were no bombs, though, and, so, by about September 13, there were no more reports of explosions being reported by the media.

Somebody collected the eyewitness accounts from about four hundred New York City firemen who were the first responders at the WTC. About a hundred of those firemen testified that they heard bombs going off, correct?
That's right. It was actually a little more than a hundred firemen who testified that bombs were going off in the buildings. You can watch some of that on YouTube—there's these videos of firemen running away from the World Trade Center saying, "There were bombs going off," "I heard bombs."

Many workers in the WTC say that they heard bombs going off in the lower floors of the buildings even before the planes hit the upper floors. William Rodriguez was a janitor in the North Tower of the World Trade Center on 9/11 and helped many people evacuate the burning building.

William Rodriguez is now a well-known 9/11 Truth Movement advocate. At about 8:50 a.m., Rodriquez and others heard a loud explosion and then a coworker, a man named Felipe David, came rushing into Rodriquez's office with severe burns shouting, "Explosion! Explosion!"
Yes. That's right. A number of people saw that, and they testify that this happened before the planes hit the building. They also saw an elevator shaft destroyed by an explosion and an entire room in the basement destroyed by bombs. William Rodriguez told this to the 9/11 Commission in a closed doors meeting. He told the Commission that a number of his fellow employees were ready to testify to this under oath. But the Commission ignored Rodriguez's testimony.

Then there's the story of Michael Hess and Barry Jennings, two New York City employees who got caught in Building 7 on the morning of 9/11.
Barry Jennings and Michael Hess were employees in Mayor Rudolph Giuliani's administration. After the north tower was hit, Hess and Jennings were ordered to go the Mayor's Office of Emergency Management which was on the twenty-third floor of Building 7.

Building 7 was the 47-story building next to the World Trade Center towers that collapsed on the evening of September 11.
Yes. But when Jennings and Hess got to the offices they were empty—the OEM employees had evacuated the building. While walking down the stairs trying to get back to the street Hess and Jennings heard a loud explosion that came from below them. The explosion destroyed the stairwell and Jennings and Hess were then stuck in smoke and darkness on the eighth floor of the building for an hour and a half. The explosion happened before the collapse of WTC 1 and WTC 2.

Jennings told this story to a reporter—which was videotaped—on the afternoon of 9/11.

Both Hess and Jennings ended up telling this story to a number of reporters and journalists. . . . When the firemen finally rescued them and were bringing them through the lobby, Jennings saw that the lobby had been destroyed by explosions.

Barry Jennings died two days before the release of the government report, the NIST Final Report on the collapse of WTC7. The report included Jennings' story and some people think reporters might have started barraging Jennings with questions and the apparent fact that bombs went off in Building 7 would have gotten out to the public. How Jennings died seems to have never been made clear.
I've heard that, yes.

You and others believe that if bombs went off in the basement of the buildings before the planes hit that's because the bases of the columns holding up the buildings had to be destroyed so the buildings would later collapse. Then later—when the buildings fell—people heard other bombs in the middle of the building that were apparently destroying the columns there. And the buildings collapsed.
Yes, this is standard controlled demolition procedure for large steel-framed buildings. This is how it's done. The base of the columns are destroyed and blasted first. Then the middle and the top of the columns are blasted.

Jet planes are fueled by kerosene gas. And kerosene gas can't possibly burn hot enough to melt or destroy steel. So, it's your contention—and the contention of 9/11 Truth Movement—that the fires from the planes on 9/11 couldn't have possibly caused the buildings to collapse.
That's right. The highest a fire based on jet-kerosene fuel can rise to is about 1700 degrees Fahrenheit. Steel doesn't even begin to melt until it reaches about 2770 degrees. So a fire from jet fuel can't possibly cause a steel framed building to collapse. It defies the laws of physics.

You compare this to putting a pot of water on a stove. The fire from a stove has never and couldn't ever burn so hot as to make an iron pot melt.

That's a good analogy. It would take a high degree of heat to cause an iron pot to melt and collapse on a stove. But the fires from stoves can't burn nearly hot enough to melt a pot. So has a pot ever melted and collapsed on a stove? Could a pot ever melt and collapse on a stove? No. In the same way, has a fire from jet fuel and the materials in an office building ever caused a skyscraper to collapse? Will a fire like that ever cause a skyscraper to collapse? No. It's scientifically impossible.

Even if the fires did cause the upper floors of the towers to start crumbling—scientifically, they couldn't have, but even if they did—the floors under the upper floors—which weren't damaged—would have slowed the collapse and would have, ultimately, stopped the collapse of the buildings. Isn't that true?

This is what any physicist or engineer—anyone who's not being influenced or paid by the government—will tell you. The upper floors collapsing would not have had enough energy and gravity to collapse the lower floors. The lower floors were hundreds of tons of concrete and steel and would have slowed down and stopped the collapse very quickly.

You wrote that Newton's Law of the Conservation of Momentum proves this.

According to the Law of the Conservation of Momentum an object will fall in free fall only if it meets no resistance. But if you look at the collapse of the WTC, the buildings fall in seconds—in free fall. But there were hundreds of tons of concrete and steel under the upper floors that would have provided plenty of resistance and prevented free fall. Free fall wasn't prevented because those lower floors were obviously compromised by bombs.

A structural engineer named Edward Knesl has written, "It is impossible that heavy steel columns could collapse at the fraction of the second within each story and subsequently at each floor below. The engineering science and the law of physics simply doesn't know such possibility. Only very sophisticated controlled demolition can achieve such result." That explains it exactly.

Many firemen testified to seeing molten steel—melting dripping steel— at the bottom of the rubble of the destroyed WTC buildings. A fire from airplane fuel—as we've said—can't possibly burn hot enough to melt steel. But a fire from the explosive chemicals in bombs can melt steel, right?

Not only firemen, but many other people say they saw melted steel—some described it as "flowing rivers of molten steel"—at the bottom of the rubble. Policemen saw that, scientists who were investigating the wreckage saw that. Dozens of people saw it. A fire from jet fuel along with the materials in an office building can't melt steel. It's impossible. But chemical energetic materials in bombs—such as thermite—will melt steel.

Steven Jones is a physicist and a professor of physics. Jones examined the WTC site after 9/11 and says he discovered and collected traces of thermite in the rubble. Thermite is a chemical composition in bombs.

Professor Jones found that, yes. He took traces of thermite from the rubble. That is, to many people, the nail in the coffin that proves that bombs brought down the World Trade Center buildings. Also, there were a few scientists who got to examine the debris from Building 7. There were a few types of metal they examined there that were melted and these scientists wrote that these metals couldn't have possibly been melted by ordinary fires and had to have been melted by the chemical compositions of bombs.

Jones founded a group called Scholars for 9/11 Truth and Justice. There are about nine hundred physicists, professors, and scientists who are members of Scholars for 9/11 Truth and Justice and agree with Jones that the most rational, scientific explanation—especially considering that thermite was found—as to how the WTC buildings came down is that bombs were set off inside the building.

Yes. This is another very qualified group that—on their website and in their presentations—give the very detailed, precise reasons why the official version of 9/11 can't be true. It's a very impressive list of hundreds of professors and PhDs.

Fires continued to burn in the Ground Zero debris piles for months. Ordinary combustible materials would have been quickly consumed by fire and the fire should have expired within a couple of days. Fires will continue for months only if energetic materials—bomb materials like thermite—are present, correct?

That's right. And that was reported by the *New York Times* and other mainstream publications—that fires continued at the WTC wreckage for months. That can't happen if the ordinary materials found in office buildings are burning. Fires become inextinguishable if the energetic materials in bombs are there.

Dwain Deets, a former director of a research engineering division of NASA, has said, the "massive structural members being hurled horizontally" is one of the factors that "leave no doubt" in his mind that "explosives were involved." Large sections of concrete were being blasted and thrown horizontally from the WTC as it collapsed. Isn't that strong evidence that explosives were going off?

It is. According to the government, the buildings collapsed because of fires and gravity. But if it was only gravity collapsing the buildings then everything would have been pulled straight down into a pile. But if you watch the videos of the buildings collapsing, materials are being thrown with great velocity horizontally from the towers. Large sections of concrete were thrown hundreds of yards from the building. Gravity wouldn't have done that. Bombs would have.

William Rodriguez and other people who worked at the WTC have said there were a number of construction crews working at the WTC in the days and weeks preceding 9/11. It seems easy to suspect that these construction crews could have been planting bombs?
Yes, a number of people—people who worked at the World Trade Center— have said that. They've said there were construction crews working in the middle of the night in the weeks prior to 9/11.

To be able to plant bombs in the WTC you would need access to and connections to the security company that's in charge of protecting the buildings, wouldn't you?
Yes. Al-Qaeda operatives would not have been able to do this.

Some people would say that if you bring up this next fact then you're being an irresponsible conspiracy theorist. Others would say that bringing up this next fact could be significant. The fact is: the CEO of the security firm, Securacom, in charge of the World Trade Center buildings in 2001 was Marvin Walker, George Bush's first cousin. One of the top officers of Securacom was Marvin Bush, George Bush's brother. Do you think by bringing up these facts one is being an irresponsible conspiracy theorist? Or could bringing up these facts be significant, a legitimate concern?
I certainly think bringing up that fact could be significant. . . . Of course, it's a legitimate concern.

All this solid evidence that showed there were bombs in the WTC—all the evidence that the Bush White House wanted a New Pearl Harbor because it was imperialistic and wanted to take military control of the Middle East—all this evidence was never presented to the public because the 9/11 Commission—the group responsible for finding the truth about 9/11—was controlled by a man named Philip Zelikow. Philip Zelikow worked for and basically was a member of the Bush White House. The 9/11 Commission was a cover-up. It wasn't independent.

That's right. When Bush became president, Philip Zelikow was a member of the transition team, and then held several posts in the Bush administration. Zelikow was one of the Bush neocons who believed America should take over the Middle East and have an American empire.

Zelikow also probably believed that a New Pearl Harbor like 9/11 would give the neocons a justification for military intervention in the Middle East.

Right. Thomas Keen and Lee Hamilton were the chairs of the 9/11 Commission and were supposedly in charge but they weren't. Zelikow was the executive director of the Commission and Keen and Hamilton answered to him. The entire investigation was directed by Zelikow. All written reports were reviewed and then re-written by Zelikow. The 9/11 Commission Report was basically the Zelikow report.

Before the 9/11 Commission was formed, Zelikow had written an outline on how 9/11 occurred and according to this outline it was nineteen Arab terrorists being directed by Osama bin Laden that orchestrated 9/11.

Yes, Zelikow had decided even before the Commission was formed how 9/11 happened. And then Zelikow made sure the 9/11 report agreed with this outline—he directed and wrote the 9/11 Commission to agree with this pre-determined conclusion. The conclusion of the 9/11 Commission was pre-determined by the outline that Zelikow had already written.

Zelikow was a Bush neocon. After bombs went off in the basement of the World Trade Center in 1993, Zelikow had written a paper stating that a catastrophic act of terrorism on the United States would be like a "New Pearl Harbor" and would create a new world in which the US government "could scale back civil liberties, allowing wider surveillance of citizens, detention of suspects, and use of deadly force."

And Zelikow had even imagined and specified this act of terrorism occurring at the World Trade Center. It's very strange and suspicious how—in that paper—Zelikow basically predicted 9/11. The neocons have used 9/11 to do exactly what Zelikow said could be done—scale back civil liberties, more surveillance, deadly force—drones. Preemptive strikes. More unchecked presidential power.

The NIST report was also controlled by the Bush White House, wasn't it? NIST was the organization responsible for giving a scientific explanation as to how the WTC buildings collapsed. But the most important investigators of the NIST group were reporting to and being told what to do by Bush White House officials, right?

NIST was not neutral and independent. NIST is an agency of the Department of Commerce, so it was an agency of the Bush administration when it did its report on 9/11. All of NIST's directors were Bush appointees. Many of the staffers of the NIST report said the report was being controlled by higher-ups in the White House. So it was being written and controlled by the Bush White House.

Then after the NIST report came out, didn't a group of thousands of scientists release a paper challenging the NIST report, claiming that its science was wrong and inaccurate?

In 2007, a letter stating that the NIST report was full of fraudulent science, and charging the Bush administration of engaging in "distortion of scientific knowledge for partisan political ends" was signed by twelve thousand scientists, including fifty-two Nobel Laureates and sixty-three recipients of the National Medal of Science.

Fifty-two Nobel Laureates and sixty-three recipients of the National Medal of Science have said that the government's official explanation of how the World Trade Centers collapsed is scientifically invalid and wrong.
Yes.

What more of a conclusive indictment of the government's official explanation of 9/11 could there be?
I agree.

But the media doesn't report that!
It doesn't.

The FBI has said that they have no hard evidence proving that Osama bin Laden was responsible for 9/11. Right before bin Laden died, it was noticed that the FBI's Osama bin Laden page on its "Most Wanted Terrorists" website did not mention 9/11 as one of the terrorist acts for which bin Laden was wanted. A journalist named Ed Haas saw this and when he contacted FBI headquarters for an explanation the FBI told him: "The reason why 9/11 is not mentioned on Osama bin Laden's Most Wanted page is because the FBI has no hard evidence connecting bin Laden to 9/11."
Yes, the FBI said that themselves. They have no hard evidence linking bin Laden to 9/11. . . . Also, you know, the Pentagon and White House have never provided any proof that bin Laden was behind 9/11. Right after 9/11, people like Colin Powell and Condoleezza Rice and others said that they were eventually going to provide the proof that bin Laden orchestrated 9/11. But they never did that. The evidence has never been shown.

But what about the tapes of bin Laden confessing to organizing 9/11?
Right after 9/11, on about four different occasions, bin Laden stated very strongly and clearly stated that he had nothing to do with 9/11. The tapes

of bin Laden supposedly confessing were released by the government in December 2001. Why would bin Laden all of a sudden confess to 9/11 when three months prior he had adamantly stated that he was not guilty? Professor Bruce Lawrence of Duke University, who is America's leading authority on bin Laden, has said about the tapes: "They're bogus." The man in the tape looks different from previous pictures and videos of bin Laden. The "bin Laden" in the video writes something with his right hand, but it's known bin Laden was left-handed. The tape "bin Laden" says things about the 9/11 hijackers that aren't true. Many video experts and political experts assert that the tapes are fake. The Canadian Broadcasting Corporation and the BBC have aired shows suggesting that the bin Laden confession tapes are fake.

Would the Pentagon and CIA do something as deceitful as that—fake a tape?
Well, it's true and it's been reported by a number of reputable news outlets that after 9/11 the Pentagon paid a British PR firm millions of dollars for fake al-Qaeda tapes. The Pentagon bought tapes of actors impersonating al-Qaeda operatives staging violent and terrorist acts and then sent these tapes off to news organizations and TV stations to make al-Qaeda look bad. General David Petraeus himself was involved with this.

Many people would say that anybody who believes that 9/11 was an inside job is being irrational and kooky. But some of the most reputable, distinguished people who held or hold the highest positions in the government and military don't believe the official version of 9/11 and believe 9/11 was an inside job.
If you go to the website *patriotsquestion9/11.com* you can see that there are dozens of former and current high ranking military personnel who don't believe the government's version of 9/11. There are also plenty of former intelligence officials and government officials who believe that 9/11 could have very well been an inside job. Surely, these former military and

government officials are better qualified to tell us what really happened on 9/11 than some snide journalist who hasn't even looked at the evidence and considers anything other than the government version of 9/11 to be an irrational conspiracy theory.

This article has already mentioned Major General Albert Stubblebine, top level CIA official William Christison, and Lt. Col. Robert Bowman, but there are many more current or retired top ranking military and CIA officials who don't believe the government's official version of 9/11. . . . Steve Pieczniak was the deputy assistant secretary of state—the secretary of state's right hand man—under presidents Nixon, Ford, and Bush. Pieczniak has said: "I taught stand-down and false-flag operations at the National War College. I've taught it with all my operatives so I know exactly what was done to the American public. . . . 9/11 was a stand-down, a false-flag operation in order to mobilize the American public under false pretenses . . . it was told to me even by the general on the staff of Deputy Secretary of Defense Paul Wolfowitz. I will go in front of a federal committee and swear on perjury who the name was of the individual so that we can break it wide open."

Yes, this is coming from the former assistant secretary of state. I would say that's very credible testimony. Very credible.

Ray McGovern was a CIA analyst from 1963 to 1990. In the 1980s, McGovern was the chair of the National Intelligence Estimates, the person who is responsible for preparing the President's Daily Brief. During the early 1980s, McGovern met every morning with President Ronald Reagan's top national security advisors to give an intelligence brief. . . . McGovern says 9/11 was an inside job, and says anybody who questions the government should not worry about being called a conspiracy theorist. McGovern has said: "Does it strain credulity for me to believe that Vice President Dick Cheney knew something about 9/11 and caused the stand-down of military planes? Not at all. He's capable of that."

McGovern is certainly somebody who should know, right? The CIA analyst who prepared the daily briefing for the White House. He should have a good idea what the government and government officials are capable of. I'd say his opinion would be worth listening to.

Robert David Steele is a former major in the Marines who was on the faculty of the Marine Corps University and was the developer of the Marine Corps Intelligence Center. From 1979–1986, Steele was also a CIA operations officer. Steele has said that he once ran a false flag for the CIA and that 9/11 was a false flag operation. According to Steele, "False flags are routine in the 'covert' operations world," and, "9/11 was orchestrated by Dick Cheney."

Yes, I believe I've heard that. I've seen some of his articles. Obviously, Steele is a very credible source.

In your latest book, you include a few quotes from Paul Craig Roberts. Roberts was the assistant secretary of the treasury under Ronald Reagan, and a former editor of the **Wall Street Journal.** *Roberts believes that 9/11 was an inside job.*

Roberts is very passionate and sturdy with his beliefs and contentions. On his website he has dozens of articles about why the official version of 9/11 can't be true. I'd recommend his website to anyone. One of Roberts's main points is that because of 9/11 the world has been ruined in so many ways—our Constitution is being shredded, the president now has dictatorial–like powers, the Middle East has been ruined with wars, Islamophobia is exaggerated, etc. And, so, Roberts says the way out of this morass is for the public to realize that the official version of 9/11 is not true. That it's a big lie. I couldn't agree more.

Have you heard of the claims of Susan Lindauer? In the 1980s, Lindauer was a congressional staffer and then the press secretary and speech writer for a senator. Lindauer began socializing with intelligence community members, CIA personnel, and, ultimately, became a CIA asset. Her CIA handler was a man named Richard Fuisz. Lindauer would go on intelligence gathering missions to the Middle East. Lindauer has said that Richard Fuisz and other CIA operatives told her prior to the act that buildings in lower Manhattan were going to be attacked. She claims that her CIA handlers had a foreknowledge of 9/11.

Yes, I've heard that. She might be credible. I haven't looked into her whole story, though.

Lindauer was well known and respected around Washington. Her second cousin, Andrew Card, was George Bush's White House Chief of Staff. A friend of Lindauer's, a professor named Parke Godfrey, testified under oath that Lindauer told him a number of times in August 2001 that buildings in lower Manhattan were going to be attacked.

Yes. So, she could be credible, yes.

As you said, there are dozens more military and government officials who question the official version of 9/11. So if it's irrational and kooky to believe 9/11 was an inside job, then some of the most respected, successful, distinguished men and women in government—men and women who have the ultimate inside knowledge of how governments and government officials behave—are apparently irrational and kooky.

The only thing that's irrational and kooky is to believe the government's official version of 9/11. To look at how the Twin Towers collapsed—symmetrically, in free fall—to know that thermite was found in the rubble, and to know that dozens of people said they heard bombs and to still not admit and realize that a controlled demolition took down the buildings is irrational and kooky. To believe that nineteen thugs using knives and box cutters could penetrate and defeat the world's most powerful, multi–billion dollar defense system is irrational and kooky. To know that hijacked planes were in the air over America for thirty, forty minutes and were not intercepted and to not admit that that's not possible without a stand-down order is irrational and kooky.

You've written that many professionals and other people are slow to question the government's version of 9/11 because then they would be labeled "conspiracy theorists" and in the media the term "conspiracy theorist" is pejorative. And the term "conspiracy theorist" was made pejorative by some efforts of the CIA.
That was written about and clearly delineated in a book called *Conspiracy Theory in America* by an author named Lance deHaven-Smith. Back in 1964, the CIA began using "conspiracy theory" as a derogatory, pejorative term to ridicule the growing belief that President Kennedy was killed by people in the US government, including the CIA itself. The CIA had and has many contacts within the media and they spread the word to their contacts that anyone who questions the Warren Report should be ridiculed and attacked as irrational supporters of "conspiracy theories." Soon afterward, everywhere in the media critics of the Warren Commission were being ridiculed as irrational, crazy "conspiracy theorists." DeHaven-Smith has claimed this was one of the most successful propaganda initiatives of all time because even up to the present day the term "conspiracy theory" does have a pejorative connotation and it is politically incorrect and taboo to question the government's version of any event.

But that shouldn't be, should it? Because it's been shown and proven many times that the government does lie and—especially organizations like the CIA—does engage in covert, secretive actions.
Of course. . . . Anyone who will just take the time to look at the facts on 9/11 can clearly see that the government's version is not true.

It's said if you want to solve a crime then you should look at who benefited from the crime. With 9/11, it seems obvious that who benefited were the neocons.

The neocon agenda was fulfilled as a result of 9/11. They got what they wanted. They got their New Pearl Harbor. They started to "take out" those seven countries. Prior to 9/11, they had wanted to invade Afghanistan so they could put an oil pipe through there. They did that. They wanted to remove Saddam Hussein from Iraq, and they did that. They wanted more military spending so America would clearly be the unmatched military power in the world. They got that.

And the neocons, themselves, have said that they couldn't have done all this without 9/11.

Yes. They said that themselves.

The effects of 9/11 basically enabled the agenda of the neocons to become the policy of the US government.

Exactly. . . . Another thing the neocons really wanted was preemptive strikes. Traditionally, America and other countries can only go to war if another country poses an obvious, imminent threat or if two countries officially declare war. But with a preemptive strike policy, America can go to war if the White House just suspects that another country might be a threat—even without the proof.

Preemptive strikes seem dangerous, don't they? Immoral. A president might think a country is preparing for war but he could be wrong about that and then a preemptive strike would be unjust.

Of course. And this is something that came from Philip Zelikow. In the early 2000s, Condoleezza Rice had Zelikow write National Security Strategy 2002 (NSS 2002) which declared that because of 9/11 the president should be able to engage in preemptive strikes. Never before had a White House set out a strategy that included preemptive strikes.

The neocons want to be able to go take control and rough up any country they want and it seems preemptive strikes allows them to do that.
Yes.

The neocons might have gotten what they wanted from 9/11, but, as your new book points out, the aftermath of 9/11 has ruined America and the world in so many ways. . . . For instance, all these countries America has invaded or helped to invade in the Middle East and nearby have been destroyed. Their infrastructures have been ruined.
It's been a disgrace what's happened. You know, we hear a lot about Muslim terrorism, but not so much about what's happened to these countries. After these wars—Afghanistan, Iraq, Libya, Syria, all the rest of them—all these countries are in terrible condition. Hundreds of thousands killed, millions homeless, millions jobless, millions without doctors.

Even Colin Powell said, "We thought we knew what would happen in Libya. We thought we knew what would happen in Egypt. We thought we knew what would happen in Iraq, and we guessed wrong. In each one of these countries the thing we have to consider is that there is some structure that's holding the society together. And as we learned, especially in Libya, when you remove the top and the whole thing falls apart . . . you get chaos."
Yes. Those countries have been destroyed. . . . And, also, Bush and Cheney, and Obama, have ruined the world by causing this refugee crisis. It's, obviously, a real conflict. Millions of refugees—because of these wars—have had to flee Syria, Libya, Afghanistan, and all these countries. We have millions of refugees looking for a home now.

Not only Europe with this refugee crisis and the Middle East have been destroyed, but you've written that America's been ruined by Bush and Cheney and Obama because after 9/11 our basic rights and Constitution have been altered.

There's been a shredding of the Constitution since 9/11. Some people would say that after 9/11 we no longer have an America because America is the Constitution and since 9/11 the Constitution has been altered and shredded.

You've said that, basically, the First, Fourth, and Fifth Amendments have been destroyed since 9/11.

Because of this exaggerated Islamophobia, since 9/11 the White House has authorized the NSA to monitor and listen to—without search warrants—our phone calls, Internet activities, and text messages. That violates the Fourth Amendment, our right to privacy. The government has used 9/11 as an excuse to turn American into a Big Brother society. And with—also—unwarranted searches of our cars, homes, and bodies, the Fourth Amendment doesn't exist anymore.

And since 9/11, new laws have destroyed and altered the First Amendment, the right to freedom of religion, and assembly, and speech.
If a group of devout Muslims who have absolutely nothing to do with terrorism want to meet to have a prayer session, they could be investigated and arrested, suspected of organizing terrorist plots. If you have an Arab friend and you shake his hand on the sidewalk you could be shaken down and arrested, suspected of terrorism. If a charity wants to send food to starving children in Somalia, they could be arrested, suspected of trying to feed terrorists. These new laws are too broad, unclear, and deprive us of our natural rights.

The use of torture by Cheney and the other neocons would seem to violate the Eighth Amendment that states that "cruel and unusual punishment" is unlawful and unconstitutional.

I agree. But Cheney and the other neocons were never investigated and prosecuted for using torture. And that basically continued with Obama. So, now, in the future whenever a president wants to use torture, he'll do that?

Since 9/11, it seems the president has been given more unchecked, unconstitutional power.
It was the aim of the neocons to give the president more unchecked, dictator–like power. This came from Cheney. In the early 1990s, Cheney wrote a paper saying the president should have inherent powers. Inherent powers means—basically, according to Cheney—that the president should be able to do what he wants, act like a dictator, without the need to get permission from Congress, and without regard to what's Constitutional. This paper of Cheney's became the philosophy of the neocons. Cheney also believed that the president should have the right to immediately declare and go to war. And this is what Obama did with Libya. Obama didn't ask Congress for permission, and attacked Libya on his own. But in America it's the law that a president must first get permission from Congress to go to war. So, now, in the future, when a president has a whim to go to war, he'll do that without first asking Congress?

And the use of drones is an issue.
It is. Now when a president thinks someone might be a dangerous terrorist, he meets with a few advisors in a back room of the White House and decides whether or not to use a drone. If he decides the person might be a terrorist, the president kills him with a drone. This is making the president a dictator who can murder anyone he wants.

That violates the idea of due process, doesn't it?
It does. It violates a person's right of due process—the essence and the clauses of the Fifth Amendment. Anyone accused of any crime has a right

to a trial and to face his accusers in a court of law. He's not supposed to be murdered in the street. . . . The use of drones is probably illegal, and, the way I see it, not a good thing. The government has said that drones aren't accidently killing innocent civilians. That's not true. Hundreds or thousands of innocent bystanders have been killed by drones. All over the world, children and others are traumatized, petrified, because they don't know where the next drone is going to hit. It gives America a bad name. I believe drones will do more harm than good. They'll create more terrorists. Other countries will start using drones, there will be drone warfare everywhere, and just more wars, violence, and chaos.

But chaos is what the neocons want in the Middle East, right? The neocon philosophy is to violently and militarily cause chaos in the Middle East so that new regimes will be installed. Regimes that are puppets of and controlled by America so America can have a global empire, and hegemony. They make no bones about it. They make it clear in their own words and writings that this is what they want to do.

Professor Michael Ledeen is a neocon philosopher who was an advisor in the Reagan administration and worked in the State and Defense departments. In the early 2000s, Ledeen was considered the driving philosophical force behind the neoconservative movement and his ideas were repeated daily by Cheney, Rumsfeld, Wolfowitz, and the rest of them.

Ledeen once said "creative destruction is our middle name." He was basically suggesting that America's manifest destiny is violence in the service of spreading democracy. During the first Iraq war, Ledeen wrote, "We're in a regional war, and we can't opt out of it. We have to bring down these regimes and produce free governments in all these countries. . . . Undermining the governments of other countries? No big deal." Foreign policy through violence. This was his thinking. Ledeen was often critical of the State Department and the United Nations for preferring diplomacy, rather than violence, to solve conflicts. This, of course, reinforced Cheney's own inclinations. . . . And to claim that they were bringing down regimes to install democracies is nonsense. They were changing regimes so the neocons could have control, and economic control.

One journalist wrote that the neocon philosophy and agenda is to create an arc "of instability, chaos, and violence, extending from Lebanon, Palestine, and Syria to Iraq, the Persian Gulf, Iran and the borders of NATO garrisoned Afghanistan. . . . This 'constructive chaos'—which generates conditions of violence and warfare throughout the region— would in turn be used so that the United States, Britain and Israel could redraw the map of the Middle East in accordance with their geo-strategic needs and objectives."
I would say the neocon philosophy is inherently immoral. And evil.

You get the feeling that neocons like Cheney and Rumsfeld would have meetings and say things like, "If we invade this country, five hundred thousand civilians will die and a million civilians will become homeless and hungry. That's acceptable. Let's go." They're crazy.
The first President Bush, himself, used to call these guys crazy. Bush used to refer to the neocons—especially Cheney, Rumsfeld, Wolfowitz, and Perle—as the "basement crazies."

Didn't General Colin Powell say the same thing?
During a phone conversation with the British foreign secretary, Powell once referred to these neocons as the "fucking crazies."

Another neocon philosopher–academic who really influenced the Bush– Cheney White House was Professor Bernard Lewis.
Right. After 9/11, Cheney put together a White House group to decide

what to do about terrorism and Bernard Lewis was the central member, the guiding force, of this group.

Lewis instilled in the White House neocons the idea that "Muslim Rage" existed simply because Muslims were jealous of Western wealth and success and had nothing to do with American and Israeli exploitation and mistreatment of Muslim countries. Lewis urged the neocons to increase political intervention in the Middle East, and in private dinners with Cheney urged Cheney to wage war against Muslims, assuring him that "America was taking on a sick civilization, one that they had to beat into submission."
The only thing that's sick is this neocon philosophy and neocons like Bernard Lewis and Dick Cheney. . . . It makes you wonder how such a biased, ignorant man could gain such a position of power and influence.

This interviewer would like to ask some questions about Israel, but first point out that this interviewer isn't anti-Semitic and doesn't think you are either, right?
Of course not.

Because it often seems that if one makes a statement critical of the Israeli government's actions, then one is immediately considered to be an anti-Semite. And that shouldn't be, should it?
It should not.

So the question is—how much of the neocon's desire to control the Middle East is a result of wanting to protect the area for Israel?
It's certainly a factor. Many of the neocons have dual citizenship with Israel. And the Israeli lobby in Washington is, of course, very strong. But I don't think it's the main reason. The main reason is that the neocons want empire and hegemony. Throughout the world. And protecting Israel is just sort of a by-product of that.

America always supports Israel and agrees with whatever Israel does. But the fact is—sometimes Israel's actions are wrong.
Many scholars would say that the main source of instability and terrorism in the Middle East is Israel's unlawful occupation of Palestinian territory. Beginning in 1947, when the United Nations recommended partitioning a portion of Palestine to the Jewish people, Israel began forcefully taking more and more land, invading surrounding countries, bombing and destroying at will, until the current day when Israel now occupies Lebanese, Syrian, and Palestinian territory against international law.

And America supports all this with economic and military aid.
Yes. Part of the neocon philosophy is to protect Israel, absolutely. Philip Zelikow said this himself. During the Iraq War, when somebody pointed out that Iraq is no real threat to America, Zelikow remarked, "The real threat is the threat to Israel." So Zelikow seemed to be saying that the real reason for the Iraq War was to defend Israel.

You have also written about that WikiLeaks memo that probably came from Hillary Clinton's office.
Right. That came out a few years ago. It was an email that was written by Clinton herself or one of her close aides. The memo made it clear that Hillary Clinton's State Department's support for attacking Syria was for the sake of the defense of Israel. The memo explained in detail that Israel could defend itself from Iran, but not from Syria and Iran both. So, Syria had to be attacked and controlled . . . by America.

In about fifty years there will be about five hundred million Arabs surrounding ten million Jews in the Middle East. If things don't change—if Israel continues to be in violent conflict with its Arab neighbors—then how is Israel going to survive that? The only way Israel will survive

that is if the strongest military in the world—America—maintains con-
trol of the area, right?

Yes. It would be a whole different story if Israel didn't have American support. Israel—probably—wouldn't be Israel.

In your opinion, what do you think is the solution to the problems in the
Middle East? Does Israel have to behave differently?

America—the world's superpower—could do a lot to improve the problems and the conditions in the Middle East. The most important thing
would be for the United States to give up its effort to make its empire
universal. To give up this idea that no countries would go against its
wishes. Accordingly, the United States would quit acting as if it had the
right to all of the world's natural resources that it wants. As a part of this,
the United States would overcome its belief that the needs and desires of
the United States are more important than the needs and desires of other
countries, including, of course, Muslim-majority nations. To put the issue
in terms of a universal moral code: America and other nations would
guide its international relations by the Golden Rule, according to which
we would not do to other nations that which we would not like them to
do to us. Another major solution would be, yes, for Israel to behave differently with respect to Palestinians and Syrians. And, again, America
could do a lot to facilitate that. Eisenhower showed this back in the '50s.
Back then, President Eisenhower threatened to cut off financial and military aid to the Jewish state, and this showed that this could make Israel
behave better.

The fact of the matter is that in the last fifteen or twenty years alone the
United Nations has passed many resolutions criticizing Israel's actions.
But America very rarely supports or agrees with these UN resolutions.

In the last fifteen years there have been about fifteen United Nations resolutions calling for Israel to change its behavior. The overwhelming majority

of the rest of the world supported these resolutions but America didn't. The resolutions condemned killings and attacks in Gaza. They called for the right of self-determination for the Palestinian people, and affirmed the rights that the Palestinians have over the occupied territories and its resources. They called for a halt to the illegal Israeli West Bank settlements. . . . All the United States would need to do to get Israel to behave and to bring more stability to the area would be to quit vetoing these UN Security Council resolutions about Israel.

Let's delve into and indulge in some deep conspiracy theory here. Many people believe that the top level Freemasons have an agenda to control world politics. Many of history's most powerful and important political leaders—men who were behind the most important and iconic events of world history—have been Freemasons. Some ex-Freemason whistleblowers and researchers also say that the ultimate plan of the Freemasons is to someday set up and control—from behind the scenes—a New World Order. A world government. These researchers and former Freemasons claim that the philosophy of the Freemasons is to have three big world wars—that Freemasons were behind the start of WWI, WWII, and want, ultimately, to have a final big war, an Armageddon, a major WWIII between the Muslim and Judeo-Christian nations that will be so devastating—nuclear weapons, genocides, holocausts—that a United Nations Police Force would have to be brought in to take control in a United Nations–New World Order-world government.
Oh, sure, I've heard that. Yeah. I have no idea how much truth there is in that. And I, frankly, haven't looked into it enough to have an opinion.

After 9/11, George Bush Jr. made the statement that 9/11 is an opportunity to bring "Order out of Chaos." "Order out of Chaos" is a well-known Masonic quote and philosophy. According to this Masonic philosophy, powerful Freemasons will take actions that cause chaos and conflict, and then take further actions to establish order out of the chaos. The order from the chaos, though, is just the political end that the Freemasons want. In the case of 9/11, the attack on the World Trade Center is the chaos and the order is the United Nations Big Brother-world government that will come as the result of a devastating World War III Armageddon between the Muslim and Judeo-Christian nations. Why did George Bush invoke this well-known Masonic quote "Order out of Chaos"?

Yeah, I just don't know. I don't know how much of that is involved. And as I said, I haven't looked into it enough to have an opinion.

Your books make a convincing case that 9/11 was an inside job done by elements in the US government. Not by Muslim terrorists. So maybe fear of Muslim terrorism is exaggerated. But what would you say to people who say that fear of Muslim terrorism isn't exaggerated because every month or so a Muslim terrorist acts out and shoots and kill people. Or bombs an airport, or building. We have acts of murder and terrorism every month or so—in the Orlando airport, in Paris, in Manchester, England. All over the world. So shouldn't we be leery of Muslim terrorism?

Answering this question requires some distinctions to be made. First, the talk about "Muslim terrorism" often involves "universalizing," in which all Muslims are blamed for the acts and statements of a tiny majority. There is a type of Islam, known as Salafi-Jihadism, which produces jihadists. There are two other types of the Salafist movement, the members of which are either quietists or non-violent activists. The jihadist group contains only 0.5 percent of the world's Muslims. Also, using violence by some Muslims to show Islam to be a violent religion would only be fair if we use attacks by the Ku Klux Klan, the Aryan Nations, or the Army of God to show Christianity to be a violent religion.

It'd be asinine to blame the acts of the Ku Klux Klan on all Christians.

Exactly. A second distinction involves the question about whether some

Muslims resorted to violence spontaneously, or they were led to engage in violence by Westerners—perhaps to promote violence in order to justify higher spending for the police and military. As for violence that arises spontaneously, one must distinguish between events that happened prior to 9/11 or afterwards. Most of the events referred to as "Muslim terrorism" involve actions that arose in response to the United States-Britain post-9/11 attacks on Afghanistan, Iraq, Libya, and Syria. Prior to 9/11, there was very little concern with "Muslim terrorism."

So, in many ways, because of all these unjust wars we've engaged in, America and the West have brought these terrorist acts upon ourselves?
I'd say so. Yes.

You said Muslims "may have been led to engage in violence by Westerners." Isn't it true that at times the White House and US government have helped to finance and arm ISIS and al-Qaeda?
That's true. Yes. When ISIS and al-Qaeda are at war with a country that Washington wants regime change in, the White House will help arm ISIS and al-Qaeda. For instance, the civil war to remove Assad in Syria was, ultimately, taken over by ISIS. Washington wants Assad out, so the Obama administration then armed and financed ISIS. A leaked tape of Secretary of State John Kerry talking about arming ISIS confirmed this.

A correspondent for the **Toronto Sun,** *Eric Margolis, referred to ISIS as a covert Western asset and called the US war against it a "big charade." And even a former CIA contractor, Steven Kelly, said, "The US has always been the main sponsor and creator of ISIS." In some ways, maybe the neocons want an ISIS and al-Qaeda because that would justify more military spending and justify the neocons invading and taking control of all these Middle East countries where ISIS and al-Qaeda have influence.*
I'd agree with that. Maybe ISIS and al-Qaeda—and even terrorist acts—is

what the neocons want. . . . The neocons want an enemy to justify their aggression.

This will **definitely** *sound like a* **very radical** *question to some people, but some people think that some of these or a lot of these terrorist acts are false flags. You contend that 9/11 was a big false flag, so is it possible that these smaller acts of terrorism are false flags? Maybe these terrorist attacks are orchestrated by the basement crazies in the CIA and military and elsewhere? The neocons want the world to think that Muslims are horrible, violent terrorists so the world will be more willing to accept the neocon-American military invading and taking control of the Middle Eastern Muslim-majority countries. This would also serve to defend and protect Israel. . . . Could these terrorist attacks be false flags?*
There are some scholars who believe that all of these terrorist events, or at least some of them, are false flags. I suspect that this position is largely true.

Some **scholars** *believe that? There are probably a lot of so-called "conspiracy theory" Internet hosts who believe these terrorist acts are false flags, but they don't get much respect. But you're saying there are* **scholars** *who say these terrorist acts are false flags?*
Yes. I suspect it could be true. But I have not done enough study of this issue to say anything about this with much certainty. Charlie Hebdo was one event I studied enough to say that it clearly seemed to be a false flag.

The Charlie Hebdo massacre occurred in Paris, France, in January 2015. Apparently, two Muslim terrorists, two brothers—Said and Cherif Kouachi—barged into the offices of Charlie Hebdo—a magazine that had printed cartoons criticizing Islam—and shot and killed twelve people. What's the evidence that Charlie Hebdo was a false flag?
The killings were done at a time when the French government had voted to

give more support to the idea of a Palestinian state—to give more support to Muslims and Arabs in the Middle East. The neocons, Western intelligence, NATO, CIA, and Mossad want the countries of the world supporting Israel. They want the neocon American military to take control of the Muslim-majority countries in the Middle East.

A well-known, well-respected French politician, Jean-Marie Le Pen, who has been a member of the European Parliament since 2004, has said, "The shootings at Charlie Hebdo have the hallmarks of being a secret service operation. I don't think it was organized by the French authorities but they permitted this crime to be committed. This is only a guess." And so the theory is that the basement crazies used their influence to let the attacks in Paris happen so that the French government would change its policy and turn against the Palestinians and Arabs?

Right. The police pinned the murders on the Kouachi brothers because one of their IDs was supposedly left in the getaway car. These guys would have been so careless that they would have left their ID at the scene of the crime? This is a typical tactic of professional intelligence operatives. Plant an ID. The next day a video of the getaway car was released, and that car clearly looks different from the car where the ID was found.

The police claimed the getaway driver was a man named Hamyd Mourad. But Mourad turned himself into the police, had an ironclad alibi, and, so, was exonerated.

Yes, the police were wrong about the getaway driver. . . . Also—the French police officer in charge of the investigation committed suicide at police headquarters the night after the murders. That seems suspicious. His family said he wasn't depressed and wasn't suicidal. He had just finished his investigation and was about to write a report when he supposedly committed suicide. Was he going to write a report that didn't agree with the official story?

425

There was also a suspicious video of a cop being shot that circulated on the Internet.

Yes, that was supposedly a video of one of the Kouachi brothers going up to a police officer who was lying on the ground and shooting him in the head. But when you zoom in on that the bullet clearly seems to hit the sidewalk and not the police officer. No blood comes from the policeman's head. It clearly looks like a staged, faked video.

But the killings at Charlie Hebdo weren't faked and staged. Twelve people were murdered there.

Well, the thing is . . . you see, with so many of these terrorist acts, the terrorists can be traced back to Western intelligence. So many of these terrorists are known to Western intelligence—the police know these guys are terrorists and the police and NATO and the CIA are tracking and trailing them and they commit these terrorist acts anyway. The theory is—it seems—that at times Western intelligence—CIA, NATO, Mossad—want these attacks to justify more military spending and to justify more military interventions in the Muslim-majority countries in the Middle East. And, so, the suspicion is that with these terrorist acts you have real, horrible acts of violence and murder, but then some aspects of the terrorist acts are being staged and faked. By intelligence operatives.

The Kouachi brothers were considered dangerous terrorists and were being watched and trailed by the French police, Britains's M-16, and the CIA, weren't they?

Yes, they were on the watch lists of those groups. So, it makes you wonder how they could have pulled off these Charlie Hebdo murders.

While they were hiding in a building the day after the murders one of the brothers told a reporter on the telephone that he and his brother had been financed by Anwar al–Awlaki. Al–Awlaki was an American Muslim who was, in all likelihood, an FBI informant and CIA asset.

He was. And, ultimately, al–Awlaki can be connected to many of these terrorist bombings. . . . Al-Awlaki eventually became probably the third most powerful member of al-Qaeda. In 2002, he was on so many Most Wanted lists that as he was getting off a plane at JFK airport in New York the police apprehended him. The FBI stepped in, though, and told the authorities at the airport to let al–Awlaki go. Thanks to the FBI, al–Awlaki wasn't arrested and was let free.

That act right there by might have caused many people to die. Because after 2002, al–Awlaki was apparently involved with a number of terrorist acts that killed a lot of people.

That's right. And after that, *Judicial Watch,* a political watchdog group, was able to obtain the records of dozens of calls that al–Awlaki had made to the FBI. Al–Awlaki was in constant communication with the FBI for a number of years. According to *Judicial Watch* it is clear that al–Awlaki was working with the FBI. He was an FBI informant.

This is something that Army Lt. Col. Anthony Schaffer has talked out about. Schaffer, who was a part of the **Able Danger** *program, the Pentagon group that was set up to find and identify terrorists, has said, "Al–Awalki was actually an asset of the FBI before 9/11. Al–Awalki had a documented relationship with the US government and the FBI preceding 9/11."*

Yes, I've seen that.

Then right after 9/11, al–Awalki was interviewed by the FBI because he had relations with three of the Arabs who were supposed to have hijacked the planes on 9/11. Even though this was so, a few months later, al–Awalki was invited to and had lunch in the Pentagon with some Pentagon officials.

This was the man who rose to be the third most powerful man in al-Qaeda. This is the man whom the FBI already knew had relations with three Muslims who supposedly hijacked the planes on 9/11. And a couple of months after 9/11, he was having lunch in an executive suite in the Pentagon with military officials.

That was reported by FOX News and CBS News. . . . So people who have looked into this feel it's obvious that that al–Awlaki was working for the US government as a double agent. He was with the US government but was also with al-Qaeda. So what was al–Alwaki's purpose? He would be in contact with these terrorists in al-Qaeda and he would report back to the FBI when these guys were planning a terrorist attack? And sometimes US intelligence would stop these attacks but sometimes if the neocon influenced Western intelligence groups wanted more Islamophobia spread in the world then they would let these attacks happen?

It seems so. Or maybe al–Alwaki was organizing the terrorist attacks himself.

And sometimes US intelligence would let them happen? So the world would come to fear Muslims more and support the neocon invasions of the Muslim-majority nations in the Middle East?

It could be. Al-Alwaki was connected to a lot of these terrorists.

Al–Awlaki had relations with the Fort Hood shooter and the Times Square bomber, didn't he?

Yes. And about ten others. Al–Awlaki either inspired with his website or personally egged on about a dozen of these lone, crazed terrorists.

A lot of these other terrorist attacks can't necessarily be tracked back to al–Awlaki but they can be tracked back to other operatives of the CIA and FBI.

They can be. Without getting into the specifics, the Boston Marathon bombers—or patsies—had clear connections back to the CIA. Their mentors were known CIA agents. And Omar Marteen, the shooter who killed people in the gay nightclub in Orlando—he had some very clear connections to CIA.

A lot of people probably wouldn't want to believe that an agency of the US government—the CIA—would take actions that kill civilians, but Operation Gladio proves that it would. Back in 1984, an operative of Operation Gladio, Vincenzo Vinciguerra, was put on trial in Italy and convicted. Afterwards, the Italian judge said that terrorist acts had been committed in many places in Italy by Operation Gladio.

That's right.

An Italian general said the same thing. Then some Turkish officials and even the prime minister of Turkey said that Operation Gladio was responsible for terror acts in Turkey. Vincenzo Vinciguerra and an ex-CIA agent have confessed that violent acts were committed.

Operation Gladio shows that organizations like the CIA can and will take actions that injure and kill civilians. Even the European Parliament issued a paper calling for the termination of Operation Gladio because it had engaged in terrorist acts.

Operation Gladio existed to commit terrorist acts and blame them on Communists because Western countries didn't want Communism to spread in Europe. At that time, apparently, Western governments felt that Communist Russia might try to take over Europe like Nazi Germany had. . . . So, is it possible that there's an Operation Gladio type of program that exists in today's intelligence services and CIA? Could there be a program to commit terrorist acts or let terrorist attacks occur so that the world will accept the neocon American military taking control of the "evil" Muslim countries? With the byproduct being the protection and defense of Israel?

It's a possibility. I think there could be.

Some people also believe that there's an agenda to use these terrorist acts to turn the American government into more of an authoritarian state. Many people believe that there's an agenda to make America a part of a Big Brother-world government, and, historically, when a government wants more authoritarian, unchecked power it scares the public with false flags and a made-up enemy. Some people would say that the government is using these terrorist acts-false flags to take away our natural, civil rights, to try to take away our guns, and to give the president more unchecked, dictatorial powers so America can transition more easily into the New World Order.

Well, anything's possible. It could be. But I definitely do know that the effects of these acts—which very well could be false flags—has been to increase Islamophobia.

Even **The New York Times** *has written about how the government—the FBI—often has ties to terrorists. In April 2012,* **The New York Times** *printed an article—Terrorist Plots, Hatched by the FBI—pointing out that the FBI often has relations with terrorists and often has informants working with terrorists. According to the article, after 9/11—by 2012— there had been twenty-two terrorist plans for attacks on America and fourteen of them had been developed by the FBI for sting operations. In other words, the FBI had undercover agents or informants working with terrorists planning a terrorist attack with the idea that the terrorists would be arrested at the last minute. But if there's an Operation Gladio* *type of program going on in the CIA and FBI, then is it possible that some of these terrorist plots weren't stopped?*

I'd say it's possible.

This is what certainly seemed to happen when the World Trade Center was bombed in 1993. In February 1993, four Muslims set off a bomb in the basement of the North Tower of the WTC that killed six people and injured a thousand others. A New York Times article printed in late 1993—"Tapes Depict Proposal to Thwart Bomb Used in Center Blast"—proved that the FBI had an informant—Emad Salem—working with these Muslims before the bombing. Salem was actually the person building the bomb for these Muslims. The New York Times had obtained tapes of Salem talking to his FBI contacts that proved this. At the last minute, though, the FBI pulled Salem out of the operation, and, so, Salem was no longer working with the Muslim terrorists. But on February 26, 1993, the WTC was bombed anyway. How could the FBI have let this happen? They knew these terrorists were planning to set off a bomb because their own informant was working with them.

Right. It's certainly very suspicious. The FBI knew these terrorists were going to explode a bomb. Why weren't they arrested right away? A lot of people would feel that the only way the bombing could have happened was if the FBI let it happen.

A professor named Dr. Kevin Barrett has put together a book called **Another False Flag? Bloody Tracks from Paris to San Bernardino.** *According to Professor Barrett, many terrorist attacks are false flags. The book includes the commentaries of twenty-six leading public intellectuals—former high-level government officials, professors, and journalists—who all agree that false flags are commonplace. Former Canadian Defense Minister Paul Hellyer has said, "Today's Western*

governments and mainstream media are not trustworthy. If you want the truth, you need to read this book."
He's right. I think people should. That sounds like a very good book.

Robert David Steele, the former Marine and CIA officer, has said, "Most terrorists are false flag terrorists, or are created by our own security services. . . . History is full of false flag operations. . . . Many of the conflicts in the Middle East today have been brought on by false flags." Steele has written a book entitled **False Flag Attacks: A Tool of the Deep State.**
Well, Steele is certainly someone who should know what he's talking about. I think his book would be very much worth looking into.

Ted Gunderson was a top level FBI agent who, before passing away, was the head of the Los Angeles office of the FBI. Gunderson said, "Most of these terrorist acts are false flags."
That's another very credible source.

So, what percentage of Muslims do you think are terrorists?
A very, very tiny amount. Less than one percent. And prior to 9/11, hardly anyone was a terrorist. My family and I lived for several months in Turkey, and we felt safer in Turkey than anywhere. They're very gentle people, the Turkish Muslims. But you push people hard enough, and then they start fighting back. And then we say, "Oh, look. You're terrorists."

Has there always been an element in Islam that wants to convert the non-Muslims? Has that always existed? Or is that something that just developed recently?
It's a very mixed picture. There is an element in the Koran that gives support for using force to convert people. But, of course, Christians have done at least as much of this as Muslims. So, that's a more general point about

these so-called Abrahamic religions. Christianity, Islam, and Judaism. There's an element of that in all of them.

True Islam is a way to strive for and worship peace, brotherhood, and God, right? And that's what most Muslims are striving for and are about.
Yes, and the press, and including—and maybe especially—*The New York Times* gives people a very, very one-sided and even false view of Muslims.

But what about ISIS? Isn't ISIS a horrendous, dangerous organization? Isn't ISIS something we need to be leery of?
ISIS came into being because of America's unjust invasions of Iraq in 1991 and 2001. Hundreds of thousands of Muslims were killed in unjust wars that were based on lies. That's why ISIS and al-Qaeda came into being. And there have been times when the White House and Washington have helped to finance and arm ISIS and al-Qaeda. The way I see it is if America and Israel would stop brutalizing the peoples in the Muslim-Middle East countries then there would be no need for and no ISIS and al-Qaeda. The way I see it is that the overwhelming majority of Muslims are not terrorists, and are good citizens. If America and Israel would stop invading and destabilizing Muslim countries and if America and Israel would offer some apologies and reparations to the Muslim countries they've brutalized then there would be no need for and no ISIS and al-Qaeda.

Some people say, though, that there are passages in the Koran that do call for the forceful defiance of non-Muslims and that Muslim terrorism is a real danger, and that anyone who thinks Islamophobia is unjustified is being naïve and too liberal.
The way I see it is that there is nothing more dangerous than NATO, and the CIA, and the American and Israeli militaries. To hear that a Muslim terrorist—if it's not a false flag—shot and killed a person or people is, obviously, a horrible thing. But the Western military forces have killed hundreds of

thousands of people. In unjust wars based on lies. As I said, the way I see it is that if America and Israel would stop brutalizing and invading—if America and Israel truly wanted and truly endeavored for peace—then there would be little or no ISIS and little or no Muslim terrorism.

The way you see it, the average person or Muslim isn't a terrorist. The average person has common sense. Common decency. Common goodness. The average person doesn't want to send his or her kid off to some useless war to be maimed or killed.
Exactly.

The great, overwhelming majority of Muslims are good, hard working, peace wanting people. The great, overwhelming majority of Jews are good, hard working, peace wanting people. The great, overwhelming majority of Christians are good, hardworking, peace-wanting people. But if it's our governments, and politicians, and government officials who want to mislead us, lie to us, propagandize, get us to hate each other so that they can start wars and gain or shift political and economic power, then that's what we need to beware of.
Exactly. After 9/11, *it is obvious* that the government told lie after lie to conceal what really happened. Then they proceeded to tell lie after lie to get us into all these wars in the Middle East. We have to beware of false flags.

AUTHOR'S NOTES

CHAPTER THREE

It is the opinion of the interviewer that if Edward Clark and/or Lyndon Johnson were involved with the Kennedy assassination, then they weren't the only ones. There is strong evidence that President Kennedy was at severe odds with his military and CIA leadership because of his refusal to take military action during the Bay of Pigs invasion and the Cuban Missile Crisis and because of his inclinations to pull out of Vietnam and ease the tensions of the Cold War. To many serious researchers, it was this leadership that was behind the assassination.

A book that makes a strong case for this is *JFK and the Unspeakable* by James W. Douglass. *JFK and the Unspeakable* presents overwhelming evidence that Lee Harvey Oswald was—even in November 1963—an employee of the CIA. The possibility remains, though, that Lyndon Johnson had a foreknowledge of the assassination, or even participated in an assassination conspiracy. Johnson, himself, said many times that he never believed that Oswald acted alone. This interview has given Barr McClellan an opportunity to express his opinion on the character of LBJ and on his possible role in the assassination.

Roger Stone is a longtime operative of the Republican Party. Stone worked in the Nixon, Reagan, and Bush Sr. White Houses. He was one of

Richard Nixon's closest aides. In 2013, Stone came out with his book, *The Man Who Killed Kennedy*, detailing all the evidence that convinces him that Lyndon Johnson was behind the assassination of John Kennedy. One of the main reasons that Stone wrote his book is, according to Stone, Richard Nixon himself believed that LBJ killed JFK. According to Stone, on one occasion, when Stone asked Nixon, "Who killed Kennedy?" Nixon replied, "Texas!" And on another occasion, Richard Nixon said to Roger Stone, "Both Johnson and I wanted the presidency. The difference is I wouldn't kill somebody to get it."

CHAPTER TWELVE

Since 1947, since the United Nations recommended the creation of Israel, Israel and America have had more political and military power than Muslims, and there has been a mistreatment and brutalization of the Muslim-majority countries.

In previous eras, in previous centuries, though, Muslims had more political, military, and economic power and mistreated and brutalized Jews and Christians.

So, it seems if a true resolution is to come to the Middle East conflict, then a deep, sincere effort has to come from both sides.

1 Paterson, P. The Truth about Tonkin. *Naval History Magazine*. Volume 22, Number 1. February 2008.
2 McClellan, Barr. *Blood, Money &Power*. New York: Hannover House. 2003.
3 Wright, Pearce (11 May 1987). "Smallpox vaccine triggered AIDS virus." *The Times*. London.
4 Moss, Ralph. *The Cancer Industry*. State College, PA: Equinox Press, 1999, 2002.